America's
Generations

D1398620

The Comprehensive Presentation of
Generational Dynamics and Business Strategies

America's
Generations

IN THE WORKPLACE,
MARKETPLACE, AND LIVING ROOM

. . .

Chuck Underwood

ISBN-13: 9781523357871
ISBN-10: 1523357878

Library of Congress Control Number: 2013944940
CreateSpace Independent Publishing Platform
North Charleston, South Carolina

Visit www.amazon.com or www.genimperative.com to purchase additional copies.

Contents

The Generational Disruption Of The Workplace

The Generational Disruption Of The Marketplace

Creating the Right Organizational Culture

Dedication # 1

In the instant when I was born to Bob and Gerry Underwood, I was denied forever the right to complain of bad luck. Mom, Dad, and sister Marcy: thank you for making me feel that I'm tied for first place as the luckiest human on the planet.

Dedication # 2: An Apology to the G.I.s

A message to the G.I. Generation: thank you for earning your label as "The Greatest Generation" by building the most remarkable nation in the history of the planet and then *leading* it for a couple of decades with your vision, humility, integrity, work ethic, sacrifice, and compassion for others.

And on behalf of many younger Americans, I apologize for what we have permitted our nation to become. Like most of you, we are ashamed of the leadership greed, corruption, lack of vision, and ruthless treatment of U. S. workers that followed your own magnificent leadership years...

...which is why this book's final chapter is the script of a special keynote speech that I now present to leadership audiences around the country and hope to soon make the next show in our PBS miniseries *America's*

Generations With Chuck Underwood; a message that will hopefully serve as a Call To Action to the generation that has just begun its leadership era and *should* possess the values that will be necessary to clean up the mess: the Boomers.

Thank you, G. I's. There's never been a generation like yours.

Contact Chuck Underwood

. . .

To discuss training, consulting, research, and speaking on all generational topics...

Or to sling insults, criticisms, and accusations at the author...

Contact Chuck Underwood and The Generational Imperative, Inc. in Ohio:

EM: cu@genimperative.com
WEB: www.genimperative.com

To view short video snippets from Chuck's PBS national-television series *America's Generations With Chuck Underwood*, **please visit:**

www.youtube.com
and type these search words:
"America's Generations With Chuck Underwood"

To purchase this book and the DVDs from the PBS national-television series *America's Generations With Chuck Underwood*, please visit:

http://genimperative.com/17.html

Reviews

. . .

THIS BOOK IS THE 2016 update and expansion of the original 2007 book, entitled *The Generational Imperative*, which generated these reviews posted on Amazon.com:

- "This book should be read by everyone 18 and over and should be used as a textbook in all institutes of higher learning for training prospective business graduates how to mature, learn and grow professionally and personally."

- "Chuck Underwood's 'The Generational Imperative' is at the top of my must-read list. A quick, easy, entertaining read that will open your eyes and feed your mind."

- "After reading this book, I had a greater understanding as to why each generation is so different from the other..."

* "Insightful...well-documented...a terrific mind-opener (and 'explainer of mysterious dynamics') for anyone trying to reach the general public in our culture today."

* "Understanding my Silent partner, my Gen-X children, Boomer self, and our interactions was definitely worth the time. It answered many puzzling questions in my relationships with those closest to me."

* "I have been trying to determine how to deal with and understand the differences between Pre-boomers, Boomers, Gen X[ers] and Millennials. Underwood's book describes the differences in straightforward language and then gives ideas on how to deal with the differences. Though geared to the business community, I found it essential reading as an academic administrator."

* Chuck Underwood's artfully written book about how to talk to, market to, work with and manage anyone from any of the living generations is a Must Read. I coordinate a (Chicago) direct marketing association book club and though we read it a few years ago we STILL reference it! My copy is totally dog-earned. It's well researched, reasoned and the information is laid out

logically so it's easy to absorb. Besides having wonderful business applications, I found I understand myself that much better, too. My personal and professional lives have benefitted.

❦ (And this 2015 email): "I recently came across your book, The Generational Imperative, it's awesome! This is great information that really intrigues me, and [is] very well done. Are there any updates available as my copy was published in 2007? Thank you."

Chuck Camerlin, Vice President
Snowsports Merchandising Corporation–
Springfield, MA

Yes, Mr. Camerlin, here is that update, and this book is twice the size of the first one...

Introduction

This Book Is A "Hybrid":
Meant For Personal And Professional Benefit

· · ·

MY CAREER—WELL, LET'S NOT UNDERSTATE it, my *life*—is devoted to training, consulting, conducting research for, and speaking to business, government, higher education, and religion on generational dynamics and strategies.

But after every business-oriented presentation, individual audience members say the same thing:

Yes, this is terrific business strategy, but I also can't wait to get home to talk to my kids, my spouse, my parents, my grandparents, my best friend. I just learned something about them—and us, and me!—that I never understood before. This changes my PERSONAL life...

And so, this book is meant for:

* the living room, as well as the workplace;
* the bedroom, as well as the boardroom;
* the family reunion, as well as the corporate convention;
* parent and child, as well as boss and subordinate;
* and, classmate, as well as coworker.

So here we go. Grab a drink. Stretch out. And enjoy a memorable stroll through the lives, thus far, of America's Generations...

What Is A Generation?

. . .

CHAPTER 1

What Is A Generation?

The Six Truths

• • •

HERE IS THE ENTIRE FOUNDATION of generational study:

TRUTH # 1: Core Values. Between the time we're born and the time we leave our full-time classroom years and enter adulthood, usually from our late teens to mid-twenties, we are going to mold powerful Core Values that we'll keep for life. Yes, we'll evolve and change, but those Core Values will remain largely intact.

And they will be burned into us by (1) the *times* we witness as we come of age and (2) the *teachings* we absorb from older generations of parents, educators, religious leaders, and others.

The age group that shares the same formative-years' times and teachings will, by and large, share the same Core Values. And by sharing the same Core Values, we become a generation.

And so: a generation is an age cohort that shares similar Core Values as a result of having shared similar times and teachings during their formative years.

And any time in American life when the times or teachings, or both, change in a significant and widespread way, it means that children who come of age during those different times and teachings will mold different Core Values. And they will become our next generation when they reach adulthood.

TRUTH # 2: Two Big Chunks. We get our Core Values in two big chunks. Think back:

In the first ten to twelve years of our lives, we form one set of Core Values that comes primarily from our elders: the teachings and preachings of our parents, educators, religious leaders, and others who pour the foundation by teaching us the values that we'll use to distinguish right from wrong, good from bad, what we should do and shouldn't do.

Then, as all parents know, we kids enter our teenage years and begin to pull away from them a bit, eager to establish our independence.

This is also when our classroom subjects now widen in scope and we begin to understand that there is a bigger world out there beyond our own houses, backyards, neighborhoods, and schools. Our thinking and conversations expand to include the *times* and *current issues* in our communities, nation, and world that shape us for life: economic depression; war; prosperity; bad government, good government; social activism; the strength or breakdown of the family unit; the technology revolution; stable or unstable careers for our parents; and so on.

Key Point: the classroom years are the great incubator of coast-to-coast, generation-wide Core Values. Day after day, year after year, we sit in classrooms shoulder to shoulder with other kids exactly our age, witnessing and absorbing the exact same teachings and times, whether we're in Denver, Dallas, Dayton, or Dubuque. And we *relentlessly* talk—and listen—to each other: in the hallways between classes, the cafeteria at lunch, the walk or bus ride home, the bleachers at the game, strolling the malls, texting, and at the Saturday night party. Everywhere and all the time, we're communicating with our peers.

And although most of us don't recognize it at the time, these conversations with our peers are inching us through the sorting process of youth and answering the questions that will define "our generation" for life:

Who are we? What's important to us? What do we like and dislike? What do we believe? What don't we believe?

And as we absorb and discuss the same times and the same teachings, we tend to mold the same Core Values and become a generation.

We develop, with people our age, coast to coast, a *shared center*. A *common core*.

TRUTH # 3: Five Living Generations. Life in America, in the past century, has changed frequently and sharply. And thanks to modern science and medicine, we are living about thirty years longer, on average, than we did a hundred years ago.

This frequent change and longer life expectancy explain why our nation currently has five living generations, each of whom came of age during different times and teachings from the other four generations and thus developed a different set of Core Values.

And as we live longer and longer, we will someday have six, and then seven, and then more living generations.

TRUTH # 4: Core Values Are Powerful. We now know, from lots of valid research, that generational Core Values exert remarkable influence over Americans' minute-by-minute, month-by-month, life-long decision-making: our consumer choices; career decisions and workplace performance; lifestyle preferences; relationships with other people; and, our own personal behavior. And this means generational Core Values are immensely important in order for us to understand ourselves and each other.

TRUTH # 5: Formative Years. To gain this understanding, we must begin by learning (A) what happened to that generation during its unique formative years and (B) the unique and powerful generational Core Values that emerged from those years.

TRUTH # 6: When It All Begins. We do not become a member of a generation until we leave high school at about age 18.

Key Point: there is no such thing as a 16-year-old, or 9-year-old, or 2-year-old member of ANY generation. The first 18 years of life—and for those fortunate enough to go on and attend college, it extends into our early 20s—are our *Pre-Generation Years.*

Why is this? Because during our classroom/formative years, our Core Values are up for grabs. We're still molding them. We're exploring, experiencing, and trying to figure out life on this planet.

And while we're doing this, we "try on" lots of different Core Values and see which ones do and do not fit, just as we experiment with our looks and fashion. It is one of the privileges of youth. We are permitted to change our values on a whim. And we do.

We are free to be fickle, unpredictable, wacky, wonderful *kids*. But by the time we leave high school or college, and even though we will continue to evolve, other people and institutions can now begin to trust the Core Values they see in each of us, and in our generation.

Generational study is *entirely* about shared Core Values and how those shared Core Values influence each generation's minute-by-minute, lifelong decision-making.

Don't Use This Information To Unfairly Stereotype

Key Point: yes, everyone is an individual, and no one should use this book's content to unfairly stereotype anyone.

There are Gen X'ers who feel more like Boomers. Some Millennials are more like X'ers, Silents like G.I.s, and so on. But when used properly, this content will serve as a trustworthy lighthouse to guide our decision-making and interactions with others.

Everyone is an individual. But generational study works and is trustworthy.

CHAPTER 2

America's 5 Living Generations

Each Is Magnificent. Each Is Imperfect.

• • •

HERE ARE AMERICA'S FIVE LIVING generations:

G.I. GENERATION
Born 1901 through 1926
Formative years: 1900s to mid-1940s

Immortalized by NBC newsman Tom Brokaw's book
The Greatest Generation. They saved the world and then
built the greatest nation in the history of the planet.
Humble. Selfless. Compassionate. Patriotic. *We're
all in this together.* The most revered generation on
the planet. Of those G.I.s who are still with us, the
economic suffering of their childhood was The Great
Depression; their generation's war was The Big One;
their postwar prosperity was the legendary Happy
Days; their Congress passed civil rights legislation; and
their generation's first U. S. president, John Kennedy,

inspired a nation to "ask not what your country can do for you, ask what you can do for your country".

Idealistic, but pragmatic. Assertive and energetic do'ers. Team players. Ethical. Community-minded. When their bold and compassionate Core Values led America during the afterglow of their World War II triumph, our nation ran away from the rest of the world in its quality of life for the masses. They never learned how to "take". All they have ever done is "give". Today in retirement, they are absolutely heartbroken by what they perceive as the mess that corporate and government leadership of their beloved nation has become.

SILENTS
Born 1927 through 1945
Formative years: 1930s to early 1960s

Our country's Last Innocent Generation. Went through their formative years during a time of extreme conformity but also the postwar Happy Days: Peace! Jobs! Suburbs! Television! Rock 'n' Roll! Cars! *Playboy* magazine! The first hopeful drumbeats of civil rights! *America!* Its pre-feminism women were haunted by *what if?* Its Organization Men pledged loyalty to their employers. Silents provided many of the iconic leaders of the 1960s social revolts. Many are working past normal retirement age. More Silent grandparents are involved in the primary care of grandchildren than any prior generation. Excelled in the helping professions but struggled as leaders during the 1990s and 2000s. This generation is overshadowed by, and sandwiched between, two wave-making generations and is under-appreciated.

BABY BOOMERS
Born 1946 through 1964
Formative years: 1950s to early 1980s

America's first Youth-Empowered Generation. An amalgam of two distinct sub-sets: the save-the-world revolutionaries of the '60s, followed by the self-improvement party'ers of the late '70s and early '80s. Came of age during a magical period in America and grew up to be idealistic, patriotic, ethical, and compassionate towards the less fortunate. Career-driven. The Golden Generation in the American workplace. Struggled with divorce and parenting and drugs and indiscriminate sex. America will be led by Boomer Core Values in the 2010s and '20s, and perhaps beyond. And this generation, as it has done throughout its life, will re-define life in America at every future age marker: 80, 90, and yep, 120.

GEN X
Born 1965 through 1981
Formative years: 1970s to early 2000s

America's most misunderstood generation. Overlooked.
Our nation's first Computer Generation, Cable TV Generation, and Latchkey Generation. Grew up street-smart
but isolated, often with divorced or time-starved, dual-career parents. Creative. Entrepreneurial. Independent.
Career "free agents". Ethnically and culturally inclusive
and tolerant. Skeptical: don't give out trust easily. Entered adulthood feeling disempowered and disengaged.
But now starting to find their footing and chalk up major victories in life. Eager to make marriage work and
"be there" for their children. The Family-First Generation is re-strengthening the American family unit. Their
Core Values will lead America in the 2030s and 2040s.

MILLENNIALS
Born: 1982 through 1998 thus far (and still coming)
Formative years: 1980s to ???

America's first full-blown Technology Generation.
Optimistic about their own long-term futures, much less
certain about their nation and its economy (blame The
Great Recession), idealistic, patriotic. Grew up heavily adult-supervised by over-protective *helicopter parents,*

whom they revere. They're also close with their grand-parents. Team players. Group-think. Re-defining life in one's 20s: it's informally labeled "extended adolescence". Not loyal to employers yet. The Tech Revolution is damaging them as much as it's helping them. Delaying marriage and parenting. They will become an excellent career and leadership generation. Mils will lead America during the 2050s and '60s and probably beyond, primarily because their generation will live and work much longer as life expectancy soars.

Born On The Cusp?

And for those of you born on or near the cusp of two generations: yes, you might find that your Core Values are a blend of the older and younger generations on either side of you. It can get a little gray at the edges.

And Cusp'ers seem to enjoy some kind of special "sweet spot". From city to city, following my speeches and training workshops, they tell me the same thing:

I feel lucky. I was born near the end of the _____ generation and at the beginning of the _____ generation, and I feel like I got the best of both generations and none of the bad."

This belief seems to be especially strong among those born near the end of the Boomers and beginning of Gen X. Why? I have no idea.

How About Immigrants?

What about immigrants to our country? Hispanics and Latinos, Asians, Europeans, Middle Easterners, Africans, and the others?

The short and over-simplified answer regarding all immigrants to the United States boils down to this:

How many of an immigrant's formative years did the immigrant spend living in the United States?

Let's say that you were born in 1975 in some other country. Your family immigrated to the U. S. when you were 3 or 4 years old. Assuming your parents encouraged you to embrace American culture and use the English language, today you almost certainly are a card-carrying member of America's Gen X, because you experienced almost all of the same formative years' times and teachings as that generation.

But, if you didn't come to America until you were in your late teens or older, you missed most of the formative years that molded their unique and lifelong Core Values, and thus you will *never* be a full-fledged member of that American generation.

And it's a sliding scale. The more formative years you spend in a country, the more likely it is that you are a member of that country's generation of the same age.

CHAPTER 3

Canada And Other Nations

Brothers And Sisters, Not Merely Neighbors

. . .

DOES THE CONTENT OF THIS book also apply to Canadians, or just Americans?

In 2006, I didn't know the answer but needed to learn it.

I was asked, by a Canadian woman who had attended my presentation at the national conference of the Professional Convention Management Association in Philadelphia, to come to Toronto to present my half-day seminar on Generational Human Resource Strategy to 250 representatives of the Ontario Nurses Association, which represents some 50,000 nurses in that province.

In advance, I hired a professional researcher to help me study the people of Canada before I prepared my seminar content. And then I presented it to them. In the question-and-answer session that followed, I asked the Canadian audience if they felt my content was accurate for their nation. Thankfully, our research and their responses jibed: America's five living generations are very similar in their age brackets, formative years' experiences, and Core Values to English-speaking Canada (less so, it appears, to French-speaking Canadians, who represent about 21% of the population and live mostly in Quebec), but with a few notable differences, which they helped me understand more clearly.

I've since trained Canadian audiences in mass media, finance, travel, and other industries. At each stop, they have shared their thoughts in their formal written evaluations of the training sessions. Among the major similarities between America's and Canada's generations:

* Canada's G.I. Generation experienced The Great Depression and World War II, which American G.I.s also experienced, and this molded similar Core Values in both countries.

* Canadian Silents and American Silents experienced essentially the same childhood, postwar prosperity, and Happy Days.

* Both countries' Boomers experienced similar so-cial activism, the women's and civil rights move-ments (in Canada, they're called the Human Rights Movement), drug and sexual revolutions, and high divorce rates in adulthood.

* Canadian and American X'er kids both caught the computer revolution and the rise of girls' sports in school, but they also felt the sting of their parents' rising divorce rates and permis-sive parenting.

* And, both nations' Millennials have come of age with similar times and teachings, including the Tech Revolution, a resurgence of the strong nuclear family, and a sense of empowerment, engagement, and optimism.

A few of the major differences:

* At times, the generations of these two nations have had different formative years' experienc-es with their respective governments. When Canadians have been pleased with their govern-ment, Americans might have been displeased with theirs, and vice versa.

❧ The States and Canada have sometimes had similar experiences with war (World War II) but sometimes little or no shared experiences (Vietnam).

❧ Another difference is race relations between each nation's majority and its various minorities, with the issues and historical timelines being occasionally different. In the U. S. through the decades, it was primarily a Black-and-White issue. In Canada, it was relations with its various aboriginal peoples or "First Nations", as they're generally called.

❧ And there is another difference, usually discussed humorously, in the *temperament* of Canadians and Americans. Americans tend to live their lives and behave more boisterously and aggressively than Canadians, who spend more time in the emotional Middle, with a more tempered approach to life. If you're an American in the presence of a Canadian, or vice versa, bring up this topic, call in a pizza delivery, kick back, and enjoy the chat.

Since that first presentation, I have gathered additional Canada-specific data and spoken to other national Canadian audiences, constantly refining my content as I listen to, and learn from, their insights.

When I presented a series of workshops in Baltimore to the annual conference of the Jewish Community Centers of North America, Canada sent a number of delegates who agreed with the conclusion I've reached:

Americans and Canadians, especially English-speaking Canadians, are too similar in their generational histories, values, and beliefs to consider each other mere "neighbors". America and Mexico are neighbors, but quite different. America and Canada are more like brothers and sisters.

Translation? Like brothers and sisters, we are free to develop our own unique and distinctive personalities and do things our own way. And we will sometimes disagree with each other. But we share such a sizable "common core" that our two countries' generations pretty much embrace the same Core Values and basic beliefs.

What About Other Nations?

Does the content of this book accurately apply to any other nations?

No.

At least not fully enough that it can be deemed trustworthy for business strategies.

Key Point: generations tend to be very nation-specific.

Yes, age cohorts around the world share some common times and teachings during their formative years. Pop culture—music, movies, fashion, and so on—is often shared globally. And some other nations use America's generational labels: Boomers, X'ers, and Millennials.

But in legitimate generational study, generations tend to be nation-specific because the times and teachings tend to be nation-specific; and so generational Core Values are nation-specific.

When the U. S. Air Force and U. S. Navy sent me on a tour of their European bases to train their personnel in Generational Leadership Strategy and Generational Marketing Strategy, our audiences often included "local nationals": citizens of those European countries hired to work on the U. S. bases. It gave me the opportunity to ask Italians (at Aviano Air Force

Base and Capodachino and Sigonella Naval Bases), Germans (Ramstein and Spangdahlem Air Force bases, and at an all-branches conference at the top of the Alps in Garmisch), Britons (Mildenhall and Lakenheath AFB), and participants who flew in from other countries how their own generations are similar to and different from the ones in America, based upon what they had just heard from me.

Their short and consistent answer? *We are different.* An example:

Italians, with whom I worked during several training sessions in their country, feel their generations are about one generation behind America's. America's Boomers, they say, are Italy's X'ers.

Other countries have not yet developed their own generational study as fully as we've done here. In the early 2010s, a friend of mine, South African-born but working for Accenture Consulting in London, told me England had not yet undertaken the study and creation of its own generational history. Canada is starting. And as our work in the U. S. becomes better known and continues to prove its importance, the discipline will inevitably expand to other nations.

CHAPTER 4

How Generational Strategy Is Used

By Business, Government, Higher Education, And Religion

. . .

EACH OF THE FOLLOWING DIRECT applications of generational knowledge and strategy is introduced in this book, and these are the training programs and consulting that business, government, education, and religion ask me to provide to their organizations:

In the workplace:

1. Generational Workforce Diversity And Culture
2. Generational Workforce Management Strategy
3. Generational Leadership And Governance Strategy
4. Generational Succession Planning And Ownership Transfer

In the marketplace:

5. Generational Market Research And Consumer Research
6. Generational Product Development Strategy
7. Generational Marketing And Advertising Strategy
8. Generational Selling And Customer Service Strategy

Also:

9. The Generational Leadership Of A Nation
10. Generational Manners, Civility, And Courtesy
11. Generational Higher-Education Strategies
12. Generational Patient Care Strategy
13. Generational Behavioral Healthcare Strategy
14. Generational Economic Development Strategy
15. Generational Community-Planning Strategy
16. Generational Campaign/Legislative Strategy
17. Generational Advocacy Strategy
18. Generational Fundraising Strategy
19. Generational Alumni Relations Strategy
20. Generational Faith-Based Strategy
21. Generational Membership/Volunteerism Strategy

22. Generational Media Strategy
23. ...and other applications.

Key Point: Generational influences penetrate just about *everything,* and so Generational *Strategy* should penetrate just about everything.

CHAPTER 5

Beware The Crap

There's Some Very Bad Generational Content

. . .

THIS IS PERHAPS THE BEST place in the book to offer a few "alerts" about generational study and what I consider to be junky information being thrown around these days.

The 2000s will forever be the decade when generational study fully and finally emerged, after that handful of us (including Bill Strauss, Neil Howe, Dan Yankelovich, Walker Smith, Ann Clurman, Ken Dychtwald, Ron Zemke, Claire Raines, Bob Filipczak, and I'm probably forgetting one or two others, with my apologies)—had scratched and clawed for years to push it into daylight.

Our field of study has now become so hot that lots of people have predictably jumped into "generational consulting". This is wonderful, and most are responsible in their treatment of the topic.

But, in order to land a speaking gig, or sell a book, or simply attract attention in this cluttered marketplace in which we all work and live, some are creating generational content that is inaccurate. Some are even trying to create new generations that are not generations at all. And the Internet gives everyone an instant, worldwide platform, without demanding accuracy.

A few examples of the bad information that's out there:

"Millennials are the biggest generation, more than 80 million strong!!" No, they're not, and they probably never will be.

The Millennials have ended, and the next generation has begun! No, they haven't. Not as of January 1, 2016.

Mini-generations that aren't! Some companies use the word "generation" to define, internally only, demographic age brackets that they target with their products and services. This is how the name Generation Y was first used, by the auto industry. This is abuse and misuse of the word. *"Generation" now means something very specific.*

Not only that, but the print media also love to attach the word "generation" to just about any conceivable micro-segment of our population: Generation Next, Generation Y, Generation Z, Generation Net, The Whatever Generation, MySpace Generation, Echo Boom Generation, YouTube Generation, Zoomer Generation, Sandwich Generation, App Generation, and on and on.

Key Point: the word *generation* now has a clear definition and *should* be used accordingly: a generation is an adult age cohort that shares similar lifelong Core Values because they shared similar formative years' times and teaching. As of 2016, there are five legitimate generations of living Americans, and generations begin at about age 18.

But the term will probably continue to be abused. Beware of mini-generations that aren't true generations.

Beware the generational "advocates" and "crusaders". A few are getting into generational consulting more as *advocates* and cheerleaders for their own generations than objective and research-based consultants.

If you want a generational cheerleader to give a seminar or to consult your company, that's your business. But the damage that generational *advocacy*, when masked as consulting or training, can do to your business might be fatal. Beware the crusaders who might feel their own generation is getting some kind of bum rap from the masses and so stand at the lectern and attack the other generations while aggrandizing their own.

Beware generational research that isn't generational research. Statistically valid generational research is growing in importance, but beware of consultants and authors and others who conduct "surveys" that aren't properly controlled.

Oftentimes, they post survey questions online and solicit responses from visitors whose identities and demographics cannot be confirmed. Such surveys might sound impressive: *we surveyed twenty-thousand Millennials before writing our book* or *our report*! But the findings might also put you out of business if you rely upon them.

The Internet enables sloppy, invalid, inaccurate "surveys".

And there's also this: valid, *generationally designed* research studies are notably different from traditional age-designed studies and usually deliver different and richer findings and interpretations. If a researcher conducts a study of one generation's current age group, and does so *without including generational Core Values and formative years' influences in the upfront design and execution of the study,* then she has not conducted generational research; instead, she has conducted age-based research. Big difference.

The Bottom Line

◈ Choose your generational consultant and trainer and speaker wisely and demand legitimacy and objectivity.

◈ Read generational books, including this one, with a critical eye and demand that the author document the content as fact, not mere opinion. Speaking of which...

CHAPTER 6

Where Does Chuck Underwood Get His Information?

Important Question. Happy To Answer.

• • •

1. **Primary research for clients**:   I underwent training by The Burke Institute in qualitative research methodology and focus-group moderating in the late 1990s. This enables me to participate in the design and execution of primary generational research, with clients such as Procter & Gamble, Macy's, Coca Cola, International Association of Exhibitions and Events, and others.

   For some of these clients, I facilitated the focus groups. In others, I consulted/guided the design of the study. And in still others, I managed the entire project and authored the Final Report. And I've partnered with larger research firms, especially when *quantitative* research—in which I am NOT trained—is part of the study. One such firm with which I've collaborated is highly regarded Burke, Inc., one of only five North American research firms to achieve prestigious ISO 20252 certification by the CASRO Institute for Research Quality.

2. **Primary research for my own firm:** I conduct my own proprietary generational research—usually, formal focus groups—to guide my work.

3. **Third-party research:** this is legitimate generational research conducted by other organizations, such as PEW, AARP, universities, industry trade groups, and others. These organizations don't always use the appropriate age brackets with generations, so I take this into account when reading their findings. In the early years when a handful of us were creating this field of study, generationally designed research couldn't be found. Now, it's plentiful. And after all of these years, I've gained a pretty good sense as to which of it is valid and which is not.

4. **Good journalism:** as good luck would have it, I was a journalist in my "first career". From those years, I can now usually distinguish between fact-based and opinion reporting. I make significant use of major daily newspapers, because I strongly believe they remain—to borrow a

phrase from legendary journalist Carl Bernstein of Watergate fame—*The Best Obtainable Version of the Truth.*

Each day, I receive four national newspapers: the *Wall Street Journal, USA Today,* the *New York Times,* and the local *Dayton Daily News.* I also receive weekly and monthly news periodicals such as *TIME* and *Business Week* and *AARP The Magazine,* as well as regular online feeds from such sources as the Wharton School Of Business, Brookings Institution, PEW Research Center, and a couple of others.

In this book, you will see occasional references to *TIME* magazine *covers.* I get some but not a lot of actual content from *TIME,* but I've found that its covers have chronicled the key issues, events, and personalities—*the times*—of weekly American life during the past half-century better than any other single news source. (Until the 1960s, its covers were consistently head-shot portraits of famous people, usually politicians. But in the '60s, *TIME* made a major pivot towards the style we still see today). On my PBS television shows and my PowerPoint slides in my business presentations, those covers have proven to be excellent *visual* aids.

I do not automatically trust these sources. If they fail to identify the sources of their content, or if the research they're quoting in their stories carries too large a margin of error, I ignore them.

I steadfastly avoid: blogs (as the crude saying goes, *blogs are like assholes; everybody has one*); tweets; all of those noisy 30-minute cable-TV-news opinion shows (CNN, Fox News Channel, MSNBC, CNBC); local-TV newscasts; and, other supposed "news" outlets that fail to honor the highest principles of journalism. I cancelled my subscription to the Harvard Business Review when I read an article about generations that was strikingly inaccurate.

5. **My front-line experiences with clients and audiences:** this is the richest source of my generational information. I've worked with more than four-hundred clients over the years, throughout the U. S. and Canada, in every conceivable category of business, government, education, religion, and other disciplines. By working week after week with each client's very talented leaders and employees, and by interacting with audiences of every ethnic and socioeconomic stripe during our "live" events, and by listening rather

than talking, I learn of their experiences with the generations.

And when they tell me—from one client to the next, in city after city, and industry after industry—that they are having the same kind of generational experience, it alerts me that I'm *probably* learning something that is (1) widespread and (2) generationally valid. So I research it more closely, and if it holds up to tighter scrutiny, I add it to my content.

6. **Audience members:** My audiences also alert me when they feel I've said something they feel is inaccurate or insensitive. Thankfully, this hasn't happened too often, but their insights always drive me to put my content—right down to my choice of individual words—under a high-powered microscope.

One quick example: I was speaking to an audience of 150 corporate board directors in Beverly Hills, California, explaining that the Baby Boomers' leadership era, which only recently began, will be the first in U. S. history to be significantly *dual-gender and multi-ethnic.* I finished, walked to the back of the room, and a gentleman in the audience walked up and politely handed me a cocktail napkin, on which he had written

"<u>multi</u>-gender, not dual-gender". *Ahhhh.* I got it at once, thanked him, and permanently updated the wording to include males, females, transgenders, and those who consider themselves to be intersex, queer, or questioning (these terms come from the LGBTQ community, by the way).

My pledge to clients, speech audiences, viewers of our *AMERICA'S GENERATIONS* television series on PBS, and you readers is uncomplicated: I'm a fallible, imperfect human being. But I'm also, in the clinical sense of the word, a perfectionist (thanks, Mom), and so I rather obsessively endeavor to deliver The Best Obtainable Version of the Truth.

Key Principles From Chapters 1 Through 6

1. A generation is an adult-age group that shares similar Core Values that emerged from the formative years' times and teachings they absorbed.

2. Whenever the times or teachings, or both, change in a significant and widespread way, it means children passing through those different formative years will form different Core Values and eventually become our next generation.

3. We do not become a member of a generation until we've finished our high school years, around age 18. There is no such thing as a 16- or 12-year-old member of any generation.

4. Generations tend to be nation-specific. English-speaking Canadians and Americans are fairly close in their generational age brackets and Core Values, but that's it. Do not apply what you're about to read to any other nations.

5. Generational Core Values influence our minute-by-minute, month-by-month, lifelong decision-making. So, in order to successfully "connect" with each generation we encounter each day of our lives, we must understand the formative years that molded that generation's powerful and unique Core Values.

6. For business, government, education, and religion, generational considerations should influence each step of the marketplace, workplace, classroom, and faith-based processes.

7. Beware the crap. There is some very inaccurate generational content floating around out there.

8. Everyone is an individual. We should not use generational study to unfairly stereotype any-one. But used properly, it will prove to be a reli-able and trustworthy lighthouse to guide us.

Well, you've now learned the foundation upon which generational study is built, and you've read a bit about how it is applied.

Now for the fun.

Let's take a stroll down Memory Lane...☺

Their Unforgettable Life Stories

. . .

THE SILENTS

America's Last Innocent Generation

• • •

CHAPTER 7

The Silents

How Can America's First Rock 'n' Roll Generation Be Called "Silent"?

• • •

Birth Years:	**1927 Through 1945**
How Many Born:	**46,582,000**
Formative Years:	**1930s To Early 1960s**
Their Parents:	**G.I. Generation**

IN 2001, JUST AS GENERATIONAL study and business strategy were fully—and finally—emerging, I hosted a local public-television talk show Special, *a la Phil Donahue* with a live studio audience, which was all about the Silent Generation. We taped it at the public-TV station in Dayton, Ohio. This one-hour Special's primary purpose was to serve as a "pilot": a low-budget test to see if generational discussion might make for "good TV". And sure enough, a few years later, this pilot would make possible PBS' nationwide mini-series *America's Generations With Chuck Underwood*.

One of our featured onstage Silent guests was Nick Clooney, the handsome, polished father of celebrated actor George Clooney. During the taping, we talked about all-things-Silent, and when we got to the part about their generation's label as *the most sexually frustrated generation* as they were coming of age a half-century earlier, Nick laughed and shouted, "We still are!"

A quick side-bar: the Clooney family—which includes Silent singer-actress Rosemary Clooney—has, for many years, proudly lived along the Ohio River in Maysville, Kentucky, which is about three hours downstream from Pittsburgh, where another music legend and friend of the Clooneys lived: composer Henry Mancini. Nick and Henry used to jokingly argue that "my stretch of the river is more beautiful than your stretch", until the day came when Nick insisted— once again—that the river is much more beautiful in Maysville than upstream in Pittsburgh. Mancini ended the debate once and for all with, "Yes, but in three days you'll be drinking our bath water."

Their Formative Years And Core Values

The Silent Generation. Overlooked. Under-appreciated. And my goodness, what they have witnessed in their lives!

As *consumers* today, they are financially better off, freer spending, less brand loyal, and more receptive to advertising and new products than the generations that previously occupied their current age bracket. A long list of savvy marketers is pursuing this generation.

As *employees* today, many Silents are working beyond the traditional retirement age, at least part-time, and smart employers are aggressively recruiting and retaining them, because this generation's skills and wisdom and maturity are needed more than ever and can be especially beneficial to younger coworkers.

In their personal lives, there are more Silent grandparents involved in the *primary* care of their grandkids than any prior generation of grandmas and grandpas. As you'll read, some marketers are pitching their products and services to these Silents in order to get to their grandchildren and great-grandchildren.

The Silent Generation is described as the generation born too late to be World War II heroes and too soon (for most but not all of them) to protest in the streets during the social activism of the 1960s.

Silents are *very* small in number—just under 47 million born, according to the U. S. Census Bureau.

Why so small? Because their birth years occur primarily (1) during The Great Depression, when conceiving another mouth to feed is often economically unwise, and then (2) during World War II, when it is kind of *logistically difficult* to conceive a child because 16 million young American men are overseas saving the world.

Great Depression
World War II
The American High

The formative years of the Silents are essentially the 1930s, '40s, '50s, and early '60s.

Three major periods dominate their childhood:

1. the struggle and sacrifice—but also the national cooperation and sense of togetherness—of The Great Depression;

2. followed by the horror, but then the triumph for America, of World War II, in which Silents do NOT fight (with only a handful of patriotic exceptions, who lie about their young age and enlist);

3. followed by the rather odd coexistence of the Cold War threat from the Soviet Union and yet

one of the most joyous and prosperous periods in our country's history for most, but not all, Americans, especially not yet for American minorities: the so-called American High or Happy Days of the postwar period, from 1946 to 1962.

Young Silent kids are coming of age—can you Boomers, X'ers, and Mils even imagine this?—when it is actually *uncool to be young*!

Our nation is not yet worshipping youth.

G.I. Joe And Rosie The Riveter

Instead, the celebrities, the heroes, of American life are twenty-something, thirty-something, and forty-something G.I. Generation men and the millions of G.I. Generation women (I've read estimates that range from 6,000,000 to 18,000,000) who patriotically rush into the labor force during the war and contribute so greatly to our nation's astonishing wartime production, becoming collectively known as *Rosie the Riveter*. And without fully appreciating the historical significance at the time, these women are also setting the stage for the modern feminist movement that will emerge twenty years later.

World War II historian Stephen Ambrose once said Adolf Hitler lost the war, in part, because he badly underestimated how swiftly America could ramp up its production of wartime materiel—from fighter jets to warships to parachutes and combat boots—while it was pulling so many of its men from the factory floor to fight overseas.

Hitler underestimated *G.I. Generation women.*

The Silent kids are not jealous of the older G.I. Generation. They worship them, too. Russell Baker, a Pulitzer Prize–winning journalist and Silent, speaks for most young Silent boys who were too young to fight when he writes this soon after the war ends in August of 1945:

"I hated the war ending. I wanted desperately to become a death-dealing hero. I wanted the war to go on and on."

JAPAN SURRENDERS, END OF WAR!
EMPEROR ACCEPTS ALLIED RULE
(*New York Times* **headline—August 14, 1945**)

But blessedly, it ends, after claiming 406,000 American lives and an unfathomable 50,000,000 to 75,000,000 lives worldwide.

And so the Silents come of age beneath the gigantic, glowing shadow of the older G.I. Generation, whose men are now returning from overseas and pouring back in to domestic life, and whose women are, by and large, relinquishing their wartime jobs to the guys and returning to homemaking.

But during the war, those G.I. women had gotten a taste of financial independence and the satisfaction of working at a job outside the home. And although many of them longed for and welcomed marriage and motherhood and a white picket fence when the boys came home, they had nonetheless tasted "career". And now during the 1950s, a growing restlessness among some of them—and their Silent daughters who are now entering adulthood—sets the stage for *The Feminine Mystique*, the pivotal 1963 book by G.I. member Betty Friedan that pours the concrete for the epochal Feminist Movement of that decade. Friedan famously calls this female frustration "the problem that has no name".

Silent kids' respect for and deference to the older G.I.s are showing up on the job, in the college classroom, down at the corner tavern, everywhere.

The G.I. Generation, from its own unique formative years' experiences, especially including its ultimate triumphs against the Depression and war enemies, is effervescing with confidence, enthusiasm, boldness, vision, humility, patriotism, and leadership.

No challenge is too big to conquer!

Again, historian Stephen Ambrose, speaking on television in 1994, the 50-year anniversary of the famed D-Day invasion, offers this insight into the G.I. Generation:

German troops, he said, were trained to robotically follow orders from senior officers and to never deviate from "the plan". But in military combat, "plans" often get mangled. And when this occurred in World War II—for example, when a German platoon leader got killed—his troops looked around for someone else to tell them what to do, but there was no one. They were lost. In contrast, American troops, said Ambrose, were *free-thinking* men from a free-thinking nation. When their leader went down, the rest of the group rolled up their sleeves, huddled together, and brainstormed, "What are we gonna do?" and then did it. And from this, G.I.s developed their own generational Core Values of leadership and boldness and action and brought those Core Values home when the war ended.

In sharp contrast to G.I.s, the younger Silent kids are now coming of age comparatively...*quiet.*

And in 1949, as the oldest Silents are graduating from college and entering adulthood, historian William Manchester writes this sentence, which is the comment most often credited with giving this generation its eternal name:

"Never had American youth been so withdrawn, cautious, unimaginative, indifferent, unadventurous, and *silent.*"

Cold War Threat
McCarthyism
The American Way!

As young Silents are forming their all-important Core Values, events are taking place that have their parents and educators teaching Silent children to CONFORM.

Remember the word "conform". The formative years of this generation are marked forever by their extreme—and to some Silent youths, *suffocating*—conformity. Why?

- The Cold War is on, so in America this is not a time for dissent or serious protest—especially by *kids*—against our nation's major institutions. Instead, Americans set aside internal disagreements in order to demonstrate absolute national solidarity against the new and significant military threat from the Soviet Union.

❖ McCarthyism, the Cold-War "Communist witch hunt" spearheaded by Wisconsin Senator Joseph McCarthy in the first half of the 1950s, is spreading a fear of speaking out against anything American.

❖ And there's this: an American attitude that we now want—and desperately need, after sixteen years of depression and war—to enjoy and demonstrate to the entire world the freedom, prosperity, and lifestyle that our men and women have just fought so valiantly, and at such staggering human cost, to preserve. We need to smile and laugh and renew our spirit.

❖ So, their parents are *patriotically* displaying their sudden postwar prosperity, Silent kids are happily behaving in *The World's Finest Classrooms*, everyone is exalting in *The American Way*, and no one is seriously rocking the boat.

Well, almost no one.

What I've learned from generational study is this: whenever there is any kind of *extreme* in American life, frequently there is a counter-rebellion to it.

And in this era of extreme conformity, a handful of Silent kids come of age developing a Core Value that will one day *rock the hell out of the boat.* And they do just that in early adulthood, most prominently in the 1960s.

The Nonconforming Silents

Meet just a few of the Silent boat-rockers:

* feminist crusader Gloria Steinem;
* civil rights leader Martin Luther King, Jr.;
* consumer advocate Ralph Nader;
* TV pioneer Phil Donahue (hey, you G.I.s, Silents, and Boomers: want a fun mental exercise? Try to think of any television show ever— other than the networks' daily newscasts—more *important* and influential on American life than Donahue's body of work over 29 years);
* entertainer Elvis Presley;
* business visionary Ted Turner;
* balladeer Bob Dylan;
* and, other Silent mold breakers.

These nonconformists will launch a full frontal assault on the conformity of their own generation's youth and, by doing so, create profound and positive change in American life, especially in the 1960s and '70s when younger Boomers embrace these Silent leaders and add their own passion and masses and idealism to the quest for a better America.

There are two famous Silent comedians whose stand-up acts vividly capture the yin and yang—the opposing sides—of their generation's wrestling match with conformity:

The ultimate conforming, don't-rock-the-boat, *I just want life to be normal and predictable* humorist is Silent Bob Newhart.

The ultimate *rock-the-hell-out-of-the-boat* standup comic is Silent George Carlin.

The American High
1946 to 1962

Try to imagine what Silents—especially their younger half, or "Second Wave", members—are experiencing as they come of age during this wondrous postwar American High:

❧ Peace, after a war in which some 406,000 Americans lost their lives;

❧ Job security for most Dads and middle-class stability and prosperity for many, after sixteen grinding years of Depression and war;

❧ Home ownership for the family, unattainable for many until now;

❧ The invention of this fascinating piece of furniture called the *television set,* which turns American life inside-out (but some Silents are actually disappointed when TV arrives, because the actors they had previously watched only in movies and who appeared to be larger than life when seen on massive theater screens are now little more than fly specs on tiny TV screens);

❧ The discovery of the vaccine that virtually eradicates the most feared disease of the 1950s, polio;

❧ The joyful explosion of national interest in American automobiles, which are suddenly big and flashy and brightly colored and seem to mirror the big and flashy optimism and new hope of the American people in this post-Depression and postwar glow;

* And, with mass-produced cars now priced low enough for the masses, and with another invention, the power tool, making house construction faster and less expensive, America invents...*the suburbs.*

Also because of the automobile revolution, other related industries are created during the American High:

* Roadside motels, instead of just downtown hotels.

* And with motels (and their cheesy—but wonderful—big signs out front) being rapidly constructed alongside the nation's roadways comes the magical era of the *family driving vacation,* which all of those G.I. Generation dads insist must begin with a wake-up call to the wife and kids at 4 a.m.! *Gee whiz, Dad!* And from 1951 to 1956, Americans are encouraged every Saturday night on national TV by singer Dinah Shore to take that driving vacation. She closes her hugely popular variety show with her legendary jingle, "See *the USA in Your Chevrolet,*" which *Ad Age* magazine, a

half-century later, will rate as the fifth-best advertising jingle of the twentieth century. The lyrics:

"Seeeeeeeeeee the USA
In your Chevrolet,
America is asking you to call.
Drive your Chevrolet
Through the USA,
America's the greatest land of all!"

❧ With automobiles suddenly everywhere, drive-in movie theatres are suddenly everywhere. And for many Silent kids coming of age after the war, the drive-in date becomes Saturday Night America. And even though Silent kids, by and large, are trying to "wait until marriage" to have sex, drive-ins instantly earn the nickname *Passion Pits*. Oh, the heat...

❧ During this magical American High, the largest earth-moving project in the history of planet Earth commences: construction of the interstate highway system, championed by U. S. President Dwight D. Eisenhower. Ultimately, this project will create some 48,000 miles of pavement, connecting us Americans coast to coast and pulling us more closely together, both physically and psychologically.

* The Silents can now listen to the radio *while walking down the street* because of the invention, right after the war, of the tiny transistor, and with it, the small handheld and battery-powered transistor radio, immortalized forever by the early-'60s song by Freddy Boom Boom Cannon, entitled "Transistor Sister." Lyrics:

> "If you got it right, you get no static
> The time and weather is automatic
> My transistor sister playing her radio!"

* AM-radio disc jockeys are larger-than-life celebrities as Silent kids come of age. The DJs are upbeat, optimistic, and clean talking. And at midnight, most stations turn off their transmitters and don't broadcast again until about 5 a.m. And most late-night DJs sign off each night very melodramatically, like Gene By-Golly Barry at 1410 WING AM in Dayton, Ohio:

> *Well, cats and kittens, that's all for tonight. Bye bye, buy bonds. I've got to go now; I've got to see a man...* (big theatrical pause)...*about a record.*

* *Playboy* magazine arrives in 1953, and Silent boys suddenly discover additional storage space

in their bedrooms: under the mattress! The Silent Generation is labeled our nation's Last Innocent Generation, and our nation's Most Sexually Frustrated Generation. During their formative years, the birth control pill hasn't yet arrived, and Silent girls are expected to "save" themselves for their wedding night and then, somehow, instantly be *expert* in lovemaking.

Silent girls, in their poodle skirts and saddle shoes, are coming of age watching their mothers around the house, and they see Mom rejoicing in a sudden blizzard of newly invented and affordable household conveniences. Right before their eyes, the American home is evolving from:

* Hand-crank wringer-washer machines, one sock at a time, to *automatic* washers!

* Hanging wet clothes on a backyard line, if the weather permits, to simply tossing them into an *automatic* dryer down in the basement!

* Meals that were always made every day, hours at a time from scratch, to these newfangled pop-'em-in-the-oven *TV dinners* (as the label on Swanson's TV dinner packages read back then, "MMmmm—it's good for you"). But as any

Silent kid will tell you, the food tastes like the aluminum foil it's wrapped in!

✽ Having only the audio of radio as Mom's day-time companion during her homemaking hours to now having real-life moving images on this magical thing called TV! *Arthur Godfrey! Queen For A Day!* All those game shows!

✽ And, from major appliances that used to come only in white to a choice of *three* colors! When I present the Silent story to audiences around the country, I ask the Silent audience members if they remember the other two colors. Instantly, they shout, "Avocado Green!" and "Harvest Gold!" Some add, "Turquoise!" It's more than a half century later and we remember appliance colors! But these were the joyous times of the American High.

Homemaking is suddenly a wondrous experience! And the American housewife is *celebrated* every week in national magazines, which are enormously influential during The American High.

This is a period of raging materialism. "Things" are uncommonly important as Silents come of age, because their parents and grandparents have gone without a lot of things during sixteen years of depression, high unemployment, and the rationing of many products during the war years. And because these are their *formative years*, younger Second-Wave Silents will go through their entire lives placing a special value on their "things," their possessions.

And now today, smart marketers are seizing upon this strong Core Value of the Silent generation.

By the way, Silents: got a few minutes for a trip down Memory Lane?

How many rationed products during World War II can you recall?

Silent Girls

During their formative years, Silent girls are expected to graduate from high school, marry, bear children, and then stay at home to raise them.

If they go to college, even the college administrators assume they're there for one purpose, and these three words are burned forever into the brains of many Silent females: *find a husband.*

On that same television Special mentioned earlier, one onstage Silent female guest was Julia Maxton, now the president of a regional Chamber of Commerce. She described her first day at college back in the early fifties:

"All students filed into the gymnasium. Against one wall of the gym was a row of small desks, where counselors sat. The students lined up single file in front of the desks. Boys in one line, girls in the other. One by one, we sat at the desk and mapped out our entire four-year academic curriculum with the counselor. Each of the boys got about a half-hour, or longer, with the counselor. Each girl got about sixty seconds. My counselor told me, 'Just major in liberal arts and take horseback riding, because *I know you're here to find a man*.'"

Only a couple of professions are widely available to Silent girls coming of age: teaching and nursing; or, perhaps selling this newly invented product line of food-storage containers called Tupperware at neighborhood living room parties, which are great fun during the American High.

In this environment of stable employment for the men and few career options for the women, Silents understandably become the youngest marrying and youngest childbearing generation in modern U. S. history. Silent women marry at the average age of twenty, the men are twenty-three, and together they will bear a whopping 3.3 children per couple.

African-American Silents:
Struggle
Northern Migration
Hopeful Drumbeats

American Negroes—they are not yet referring to themselves as African-Americans and blacks—are still struggling.

Most definitely, these are not the same Happy Days for people of color as for white Americans. Racist hatred and oppression and violence are rampant throughout much of the country.

Many black moms cannot be stay-at-home moms but instead must work—often multiple jobs, as do their husbands—at grossly tiny wages just to survive.

Suburbs? Materialism? Home ownership? Security? Safety?

Not yet.

But during this postwar period, they do see a few rays of sunshine penetrating our nation's racist cloud-cover. They hear distant, but hopeful, drumbeats.

It is during this time that Southern blacks accelerate the largest mass migration in U. S. history, as some 5 million of them move from primarily share-cropping lives in the South to industrial jobs in booming postwar northern cities like Chicago, Detroit, and Cleveland. A portion of them begin a westward migration to cities like Kansas City and, ultimately, on out to the Coast.

The Great Migration is captured in 1945 by African-American and G.I. Generation writer and poet Richard Wright, the grandson of slaves and son of a Mississippi sharecropper:

> "I was leaving the South
> To fling myself into the unknown
> I was taking a part of the South
> To transplant in alien soil,
> To see if it could grow differently,
> If it could drink of new and cool rains,
> Bend in strange winds,
> Respond to the warmth of other suns
> And perhaps, to bloom."

This poem inspires the title, more than sixty years later, of Pulitzer–Prize winning Isabel Wilkerson's acclaimed book about the migration, *The Warmth of Other Suns.*

Because of the miracle of television and its news footage, the whole nation—black and white—now vividly *sees* the true ugliness of racism. And from this come the first hopeful drumbeats of civil rights:

- In 1947, Jackie Robinson breaks baseball's color barrier, and in 1950, Earl Lloyd and several others do the same in pro basketball, and so blacks slowly begin to get their chance in professional sports.

- In 1948, Congress integrates our nation's military forces after blacks—such as the famed Tuskegee Airmen—perform so skillfully and patriotically in the war.

- Also in the '40s, Pepsi Cola acknowledges the importance of the "Negro market" by boldly hiring blacks to sell its soft drink to vendors and to pose as models in its commercial ads.

- In 1954, we get *Brown v. the Board of Education,* the landmark Supreme Court ruling on school desegregation, striking down the doctrine of separate-but-equal that had been in place since *Plessy v. Ferguson* in 1896.

❧ In 1955, a tiny black seamstress decides "enough is enough", refuses to give up her seat on an over-crowded Alabama bus to a white rider as the law and culture mandate she must, gets arrested, and so begins the yearlong, Rosa Parks-inspired Montgomery bus boycott, a seminal event in the modern Civil Rights Movement.

❧ Young black Silents are coming of age reading the increasingly strident writings of black authors like Ralph Ellison, James Baldwin, and Langston Hughes.

❧ They hear the early voice of the Dexter Avenue Baptist Church minister, who was born "Michael" but whose father would change the name of his son, at age five, to Martin Luther King, Junior.

❧ Black entertainers like Nat King Cole, Harry Belafonte, Sidney Poitier, and Sammy Davis, Junior, are starting to show up on TV and in film and become an important source of pride for Americans of color.

❧ And on radio—and this will be noteworthy— *white* teenage Silents are enthusiastically embracing the black recording artists who are singing a new, uninhibited style of music that some older white Americans angrily and hatefully denounce as devil music and demon music and worse (one newspaper headline even proclaims it a "communicable disease") before it gets its permanent name in the early 1950s from white Cleveland radio disc jockey Alan Freed, who christens this new music *rock 'n' roll*. Sometimes against their elders' wishes, white Silent kids dig in their heels, purchase this music, and dance to it at mixed-race nightclubs where black bands are onstage playing it. And so pop music becomes an important bridge between black and white Silent kids. And because these are their formative years, this experience with music influences Silents' lifelong Core Values, which explains why this generation will eventually be labeled by generational authors Bill Strauss and Neil Howe as a *rights-oriented* and inclusive generation.

So, a few rays of sunshine. But the modern Civil Rights Movement, the Glorious Struggle as it will come to be known, is still somewhere over the horizon for Silents coming of age.

But in 1964, one especially powerful song by black Silent Sam Cooke becomes a message of hope for the burgeoning Civil Rights Movement. Part of the lyrics:

"It's been too hard living, but I'm afraid to die
'Cause I don't know what's up there beyond the sky
It's been a long, a long time coming
But I know a change gonna come, oh yes it will."

Sam Cooke dies that same year, at age 33, and never gets to see the change that does indeed come. And he never knows that his song will become an anthem of the Civil Rights Movement.

Speaking of music…

Silents And Their Music

There is a famous advertising campaign by the cotton industry, whose slogan is: "Cotton—the fabric of our lives".

Similarly, it can be said that music is "the soundtrack of our lives".

The formative years of the Silent Generation stretch from The Great Depression through World War II and the prosperity of the '50s and social awakenings of the '60s.

For America's musicians and songwriters, what a period of rich creative opportunity!

The Blues capture the pulverizing hopelessness of the Depression, especially for minorities and the poor.

During World War II, swing music rallies American patriotism and support for our troops.

By the mid-50s, when World War II and the Korean Conflict have ended, America enters a period of joyous peace and prosperity, and this is when uninhibited rock 'n' roll and rockabilly let Silent kids unleash the joy they are feeling. There's also jazz. And oh-so-romantic doo-wop.

And through all of the Silents' formative years, the magnificent Big Band sound—from its emotional ballads to exuberant Swing music—accompanies the nation and this generation through their lowest lows and highest highs.

In one of my very early business presentations with an audience of multiple generations, we took a brief side-trip from biz-talk when I asked each generation's females "Are the men of your generation romantic?", I asked for a show of hands: "yes" or "no".

Millennial men, Gen X men, Boomer men? The women of their generations responded with a half-hearted "Yeah, sorta, I guess."

The Silent women? YES YES YES!!! The many little touches from their men: opening the door for them; pulling out their chair; standing when they excuse themselves, and standing when they return; flowers; candy; "thank-you" and "please" and "may I?"

Credit the manners and courtesies of Silent men towards their women for this romantic era. And credit the music of their youth, whose lyrics revere women and place them on a pedestal.

Silents, here's another enjoyable mental exercise, especially with a few friends: pour an iced tea, take out a notepad, and write down the Top Ten Most Romantic Songs from your youth. I know what you're thinking: the challenge will not be finding ten songs; the challenge will be paring down dozens and dozens to a final ten.

And then do the same with the Top Ten Most Optimistic Songs, the songs that soared with hope and joy and a sense of an unlimited future during a time when America was nine months pregnant with those feelings.

By the way, Boomer men *wanted* to be romantic and often were. But they began their dating years just as the feminist movement was arriving, and everything changed. Suddenly, many of the girls didn't want the boys to open the car doors for them, dinner was Dutch treat, and other traditional courtesies were now considered *sexist*. It was all new, and Boomer males developed a certain hesitation and found they had to re-write the book on "romance" and dating decorum. This life passage for Boomer boys was a 9.5 out of 10 on the *Yikes!* Meter.

War/Prosperity
Suffocating Conformity
Racism/Chauvinism
Pride Of Being An American

So the Silent Generation forms its unique and lifelong Core Values during a time of war but then prosperity, conformity, racism, chauvinism (it isn't yet called sexism), materialism, and the approaching storm clouds of activism.

This is also an era of uncommon community cooperation, low crime rates, job stability for the majority, and the overwhelming joy—after the triumph of World War II and the peace and prosperity that follow—of being an American.

The Core Values Silents have just formed, based upon what they've experienced and been taught by their elders as they've come of age, are now going to influence their consumer decisions, career choices, and lifestyle preferences for a lifetime.

Adulthood For Silents:
The Organization Man

The Silent Generation begins to graduate from high school right at the end of World War II—1945—and does not fight in that war (with perhaps a few exceptions who patriotically lie about their birth dates and enlist under age).

Although the Silents will have "their generation's war"—the Korean Conflict from 1950 to 1953—the timing nonetheless can't be much better for this generation to begin its career passage.

For the white Silent male entering adulthood in this suddenly surging U. S. economy, the company becomes an extension of the man's own personality. He becomes *The Organization Man,* as the 1956 William Whyte book is entitled (subtitle, "The book that defined a generation"), or *The Man in the Grey Flannel Suit,* as the 1956 Sloan Wilson book and, later, the Gregory Peck movie is named.

"The corporation came first."
David Halberstam
The Fifties

Journalist and author David Halberstam, in his highly regarded book *The Fifties,* writes the following words about the corporate culture of General Motors during this era, when GM is *the* yardstick against which most other major American corporations measure their own culture and performance:

"The men who ran the corporation were square and proud of it. Loyalty among employees was more important than individual brilliance. Team players were valued more highly than mavericks. The corporation came first. The individual was always subordinated to the greater good of the company."

And in 1958, also chronicled in *The Fifties,* Ray Kroc, one of the older members of the G.I. Generation (born in 1902) and who was then working with the

McDonald brothers in California to roll out the nation's first fast-food franchises, sent a now famous
memo to the brothers, which said, in part:

"We have found out that we cannot trust some
people who are nonconformists. We will make conformists out of them in a hurry. You cannot give
them an inch. The organization cannot trust the
individual; the individual must trust the organization."

Wow!

So, in this business environment of extreme conformity, the message from the corporation to that
aspiring young white Silent male is very clear: work
hard, be absolutely loyal to the organization, do it our
way, don't rock the boat, pay your dues, and if you do
all of this, *you'll eventually be entitled to reward.*

In other words: *follow, don't lead.*

And after those sixteen wretched years of depression and war, this message sounds absolutely delicious.

So the young white Silent man does all of this. He
pledges that loyalty, conforms to the company's way of
doing business, works diligently, and conducts himself

with a very careful political correctness before *political correctness* is even a buzz phrase.

And because the economy is flourishing as he begins his work years... and because Silent blacks and females are systemically denied the better jobs and promotion paths and the opportunity to compete against that white Silent man...

and because this generation is so tiny in number when demand for workers is so great...

the white Silent male receives the smoothest career ride of any generation of worker in modern American history.

It all *works* for the overwhelming majority of white Silent males. And so they understandably embrace this kind of workplace culture.

However...

Silent Leadership Era: 1990s And 2000s
The Great American Executive Meltdown

These generational Core Values of (1) anything for the company and (2) that strong sense of entitlement—*I will be entitled to reward*—contribute to what the *Wall Street Journal,* decades later in the early 2000s, will describe as the great American corporate meltdown, but which is more accurately labeled *executive* meltdown.

White Silent males begin to dominate corporate America's executive suites in the early 1990s, as the last of the older G.I. Generation leaders retire and pass the baton to the next generation.

And, according to the calculations of Arthur Levitt, then the longest-serving chairman of the Securities and Exchange Commission (1993–2001), this is precisely when the corruptive mindset—the culture of greed and entitlement—begins.

As Mr. Levitt said on CNN just as the infamous Enron and WorldCom and many other executive scandals were surfacing in 2002, the belief that this executive corruption is "merely a few bad apples" is sadly mistaken. Our nation has had, he calculated in 2002, "ten to fifteen years" of unethical culture pouring out of the executive suites, where the prevailing executive attitude among far too many white Silent males has been *absolutely anything for the company* (even if unethical and illegal), and *I've paid my dues, always did as I was told, and, by god, I'm now entitled to reward (even if I have to go dirty or lay off ten-thousand employees to hold on to it)!*"

And it's not just corporate leadership. It's also the leadership of government:

There are three methods by which the U. S. Congress may discipline a member who has behaved improperly: expulsion, censure, or reprimand. And there have been more Silents (eleven) punished in this manner than any generation in history.

One important point: as the epidemic executive scandals surface in the 2000s, there are a number of Boomers—and even a young Gen X'er or two—accused and convicted of wrongdoing, too. No generation of leaders corners the market on greed and corruption. But the corruption *erupts* during the Silent leadership era, when the policy making and decision-making are largely dictated by the unique Core Values that emerged from their generation's unique formative years' times and teachings.

And surely no one is more disheartened by this legacy than the many Silents who led their organizations and their lives honorably. Think of Martin Luther King, Jr., Ralph Nader, Phil Donahue, Gloria Steinem, and other Silents famous for their integrity and compassion towards the less fortunate.

The Great Divide Between The
Rich And Everybody Else

History will also remember the Silent-leadership decades as the period when executive compensation skyrocketed and the average American worker was kicked downward into an abyss of job and income uncertainty. The Great American Middle Class was slaughtered during the Silent Leadership Era. The richest and most powerful few became *more* rich and *more* powerful, while the masses were herded into lives of financial instability.

As a number of national surveys document, this Great Divide still alienates most Americans and—as you'll read with the young Millennials—is now giving us a generation that has come of age anti-executive-excess and pro-worker, pro-little-guy.

U. S. President Barack Obama closed calendar-year 2013 declaring this income inequality between rich and poor "the defining challenge of our time". And it is a challenge, created by Silent leaders, that is now tumbling into the lap of the generation just beginning its own two-decade leadership era, the Boomers. More on this in the Boomer chapter.

Korea: The Silent Generation's Forgotten War
1950–1953
"Somehow, we lost *our* war"

The older half, or First-Wave, Silent men comprise the overwhelming majority of troops who fight in the Korean Conflict.

This war, which ends in a divided Korea and becomes a distasteful political stalemate instead of a resounding American victory like World War II eight years earlier, has a profound impact upon the Silent generation, especially its men.

A Silent male explains:

In 2008 and 2009, PBS TV stations around the country aired the first two shows in our *America's Generations With Chuck Underwood* series. One of these hour-long shows is essentially the same Silent story you're reading here.

A physician in Florida who saw the Silent show, Dr. William Mitchell, emailed me and shared his belief that his fellow Silent males would later fail as leaders, in part because of their experience with their generation's war and the generational Core Values that emerged from this stalemate.

The Korean War, he wrote, "significantly slowed the normal course of social development, especially for the boys, far more than would be apparent to anyone who didn't experience it.

"But more important, it left us with the knowledge that somehow we had lost OUR war, that our generation was somehow lacking in the 'stuff' which characterized the American 'get 'er done' spirit; that basically, we were losers! That any success we might have (in our careers) would be more a result of good luck than to our own abilities."

Younger, Second-Wave Silents, by the way, participated in the next war, Vietnam, and also came home with a similar sense of "losing".

Indecisive Leadership
"twice as many hearings...one-third as many laws."

The Silent leadership era is further diminished by the fact that their generation lacked the decisiveness required of leadership.

The seminal book in generational study is entitled *GENERATIONS* and was published in 1991, authored by a Harvard MBA and a Yale MBA whom I will always feel honored to count as my friends, the late Bill Strauss and Neil Howe.

Here's a quote from that book:

"In politics and business, the Silents have been a proven generation of bureaucratizers. Compared with the G.I.-dominated Congresses of the early 1960s, Silent Congresses in the mid-1980s convened twice as many hearings, debated for twice as many hours, hired four times as many staff, mailed six times as many letters to constituents, and enacted one-third as many laws."

Why This Unique Combination Of Indecisive Leadership And Vulnerability To Greed And Corruption?

Throughout most of their careers, Silents had worked under the generation that Tom Brokaw's book labels *The Greatest Generation*, the G.I.s, who had passed through their unique formative years enduring and surviving The Great Depression and two World Wars and, from those unique times, formed generational Core Values of humility, character, compassion for others (*we're in this nightmare together, so let's truly take care of each other*), and the fearlessness, boldness, vision, and willingness to lead and to be accountable for their decisions that emerged from their survival of those times.

And when the G.I.s went on to become presidents of major corporations and leaders of government and education and religion, they cared as much for the janitor down in the basement as they did for their vice-presidents upstairs in the air-conditioned executive suites because, only a few years earlier, in a foxhole in Europe or a cave on a Pacific island or flying their bombers over North Africa, that future janitor had fought shoulder to shoulder with that future president and they KNEW they had each other's backs.

I call the leadership style of the G.I. Generation "Foxhole Leadership". Bosses and their employees rose or fell together; they insisted upon standing on the same side of the fence.

We're in this together. I will NOT abandon you.

No epidemic snobbery. Or arrogance. Or ruthless treatment of employees. Or *I'm more important than my employees.* Or *In order to please my shareholders I'm going to send 10,000 U. S. jobs overseas and kick my American work-ers into the streets with résumés in their hands.*

Instead, the G.I. generational Core Values delivered—overwhelmingly, if not perfectly—a lead-ership era distinguished by its humility, compassion towards others, and integrity.

The outcome of the G.I. leadership era? The great-est quality of life for the masses in the history of the United States, as well as a period of bold, confident innovation and progress.

Here's the point: as young Silents begin their work years, the opportunity for them is not to *lead*. The G.I.s are giving us plenty of leadership.

Instead, the opportunity for younger Silents is to *follow*: to facilitate, to execute, to take the big bold ideas of their G.I. bosses and make them happen.

The opportunity for Silents is to *help*. And they be-come brilliant at it, and this becomes a very admirable component of their generational legacy.

Silents give our nation and world a bumper crop of skilled helpers: teachers; doctors and nurses; religious leaders; architects; engineers; accountants; attorneys; and other professions.

And as elected officials, they are collaborative and willing to compromise.

This is the Silents' proud legacy: brilliance in the helping professions.

Silent Women In Adulthood
"Born Too Soon"

As former United Nations Ambassador Jeane Kirkpatrick once said, "We are the generation of women born twenty years too soon."

Too soon to catch two waves that younger Boomer women will catch: the invention of the birth control pill, which first hits the market in 1960 but won't receive widespread use until the mid- to late-'60s; and the feminist movement, which takes root in the late '60s and '70s.

Most Silent girls pass through their formative years fully anticipating—whether they want it or not—an adulthood of wifehood, motherhood, and homemaking. Remember, the workplace isn't letting them into the mid- and high-level positions during this time, except in nursing, teaching, secretarial work, and a few other tiny pockets. So these young girls are told by their elders (today, this is unimaginable) to be *grateful* if and when they receive a marriage proposal, because it might otherwise be financially difficult or impossible for them to live on their own. And if they live alone and never marry, they'll be labeled—gasp!—*old maids* and *spinsters.*

When their boyfriend kneels before them and asks, *Will you marry me,* Silent girls might speak the word *Yes* but are conditioned by the times to think *Thank Goodness.*

Spinsterhood is a very real fear during this time.

But beginning in the mid-1960s, two events *force* many of them into the American workplace.

First of all, The Sexual Revolution is underway. Most Silents are already married when it hits, but those younger, sexually liberated Boomer girls have given many Silent men a case of what several authors will later describe as "Jennifer Fever". And in 1971, according to U. S. Census Bureau data, marital infidelity contributes to a divorce rate that suddenly skyrockets to 165% higher than it had been only ten years earlier in 1961. Divorce especially hits the younger, or Second-Wave, Silents.

Secondly, the feminist movement is creating, especially among First-Wave Boomer couples who are now entering adulthood, the dual-career-income household, not just dual-JOB-income household, as young adult women get their first widespread shots at authentic careers. And these higher household incomes promptly drive up the cost of living for all Americans.

So many Silent women, most now in their thirties and forties, find themselves thrust into the workplace, either as divorcées on their own or happily married and simply trying to help their husbands keep pace with this sudden rise in the cost of living.

Many Silent women are educationally unprepared to compete with younger Boomer women for the skilled positions. And many are psychologically unprepared for this sudden new life: spending their days in an office or factory or retail store, rather than standing in the kitchen at home and proudly preparing tonight's family dinner from scratch. It is a jarring time for many Silent women.

"It's so nice to have a man around the house" Dinah Shore (1950)

In their generation's formative years, Silent girls had sung along with a 1950 top-twenty hit by gorgeous Dinah Shore about married bliss:

"It's so nice to have a man around the house,
A knight in shining armor, something of a charmer,
Put no one else above him,
A house is just a house without a man."

And in these years right after World War II, it WAS nice to, once again, have a man around the house.

That was the '50s. But now in the '70s, Silent women are in the workplace with these aggressive, career-minded Boomer feminists, who, in *their* formative years, sang along to Helen Reddy's starkly different lyrics:

"I am woman, hear me roar
In numbers too big to ignore....
If I have to, I can do anything,
I am strong, I am invincible,
I am woman."

Talk about a generation gap!

But an interesting thing happens. Those Silent women reach down deep, make the adjustment, and as many of them start to turn forty and fifty, they feel a couple of sensations they never could've imagined for themselves while growing up: financial independence; and, living alone but being okay with it.

They *survive.* And many of them go on to flourish in the workplace and become career role models to their own daughters and sons.

To refer once again to that television talk show Special in 2001: a twenty-ish Gen X female sat in our studio audience with her divorced Silent mother. Near the end of the show, after listening to the discussion about all of these life passages her mother's generation had gone through, the daughter stood and said, "I was a latchkey kid in the '90s and resented the fact that Mom had to find a job when she and Dad divorced and wasn't there for me like she had been for my older brothers and sisters. But until today, I never realized what she went through when she was forced to work. Now I appreciate her so much more."

Her mother then stood up beside her daughter and said, "I would rather have been at home for her after school, to give her warm milk and cookies like I had been able to do with her brothers and sisters when I was still married. But I had to go to work."

Gen X women: have you ever asked your mom what it was like, back then, being a mother and a woman?

Richest Retirees Ever
Free Spenders
Many Will Work In Retirement
Pent-Up Desire To Live
Under-Appreciated, Overlooked

In retirement, this generation is financially better off than any generation before them. And they spend their money more freely than prior generations.

I conducted formal Silent Generation focus groups in multiple states for a Denver client—the world's largest provider of escorted group travel tours—and, boy, did the Silents confirm this during those focus groups: they feel they have *earned the right* to reward themselves. They've worked hard for a lot of years, they've been devoted parents, they did what they were told, they didn't rock the boat, and so now *it's our time. We've earned it!*

A significant number of Silents are working past retirement age, at least part-time. Many are doing so not so much for the money but instead to stay plugged in and vital, while other Silents must work because the executive corruption scandals, such as Enron and WorldCom, and the nation's economic downturns of 2000 and 2008, have ravaged their retirement nest eggs.

And these extended work years will only increase their purchasing power and, hence, their generation's importance to the American workplace.

"It's Now Our Time..."

As you deal with Silents, you might detect a pent-up desire for a little adventure, experimentation, taking chances, a desire to *live life.*

Frank Kaiser, a Silent who writes for the website SuddenlySenior.com, wrote this about his generation then and now:

"We became apolitical. Safe. Silent. And boring. We didn't save the world like the previous generation, and we didn't squeeze life for all of its satisfactions the way Boomers have. Like lightning, the realization hit us that we only go around once, and it's now our time to start living it on our terms."

And there's a line in the song "My Back Pages" by Silent troubadour Bob Dylan that also says it perfectly for the current-day Silent mindset:

"I was so much older then,
I'm younger than that now."

Longevity: *What To Do, What To Do?*

We all know life has changed dramatically for the younger generations because of technology. Often overlooked is that it has changed just as remarkably for seniors.

In 2013, online search giant Google announced it is backing Calico, a start-up company that will research aging and explore the extension of the human life span. Other tech titans are triggering similar initiatives: Oracle's Larry Ellison founded the Ellison Medical Foundation, with a focus on longevity. And there are others.

AARP launched its "Life Reimagined" campaign (lifereimagined.aarp.org) to help its members rewrite the book on life after 50. As AARP CEO Jo Ann Jenkins told *USA Today* about post-50 life, "It's a time to find real meaning and purpose, to do something that you have a passion about doing. We see three simple areas: health security, financial resilience, and personal fulfillment."

As science extends our lives, what should Silents do with those additional years?

They're at their wisest and most mature. They have much to give.

As the Halftime Institute describes it, how can seniors reset their mentality and advance "from success to significant"?

Well, they can work for pay, part-time or full-time or on a project basis. Or volunteer. Consult. Mentor (remember, Silents, you are brilliant at *helping*!). Travel. Run for office. Take a college course, or three or four, for the heck of it.

AARP has a program that teaches the 50-plus gang how to use technology. It's called AARP TEK (Technology Education and Knowledge). Technology can be helpful in many ways to seniors, including its ability to reduce their sense of isolation: with email and social media, seniors can dialogue with others anywhere in the world without leaving their chairs.

What role can religion, faith, and spirituality play in helping Silents to be fulfilled, happy, productive?

Will community colleges and universities create courses for Silents and make it truly commonplace to see students in their 70s and 80s strolling across campus and sitting in classrooms? I spent a good chunk of

2015 training hundreds of community college leaders around the nation in various generational strategies and told them the Silents represent a potential gold mine for their schools: as students, employees, donors, and mentors.

At the time of this writing, the Institute for Aging Research at Albert Einstein College of Medicine in New York City is seeking funding for a unique clinical trial: it wants to enlist more than a thousand seniors in a multi-year test of a specific drug, metformin, to see if it can delay or prevent the major diseases that come with aging- heart disease; cancer; diabetes; and, Alzheimer's. And other organizations are currently testing anti-aging medicines, some with very exciting results.

Music & Memory

Born as an idea to revitalize memory in Alzheimer's sufferers, *Music & Memory* is a program that is in hundreds of elderly housing facilities and was the subject of the film *Alive Inside,* which became an online sensation; one clip from the film has been viewed more than 10 million times. It shows a man, Henry, slumped and unresponsive in a wheelchair, until a nursing home worker places a set of headphones over his ears and he instantly comes alive and sings along with Cab

Calloway. *Music & Memory* is the creation of New York social worker Dan Cohen. Silents: the music of your youth can be more than just entertainment.

D2 Architecture In Dallas

This company's president David Dillard moved his employees into senior housing for 24 hours to better understand what residents experience, with the ultimate goal of designing more resident-friendly facilities. Among their discoveries from this wonderful idea: window sills are often too high for seniors to see out; lighting should be more indirect; no ramps or steps; better acoustics to create more quiet spaces, especially because diminished hearing causes some residents to crank up the radio and TV volume so loudly that it pours out into the hallways and other residents' rooms.

Aging In Place

How can smart-home technology, healthcare, home construction, and furnishings enable us to live at home as long as possible, rather than at an assisted-living or long-term care facility?

As gerontologist Ken Dycthwald told *USA Today*, the traditional house is "a rich emotional nest". We want to stay there if we can.

Many Silents will be able to enjoy such aging-in-place innovations as these:

* Housecleaning robots;
* Heated driveways;
* Easier-to-read-and-program thermostats;
* Thermostats that increase and decrease as they move from one room to the next;
* "Alerts" to remind them to take their medication;
* Easier-to-operate window hardware;
* Anti-scald devices on showers;
* More thorough tech monitoring of their health;
* Easier and cheaper access to the Internet, which is the link that makes the smart home possible, and this will be especially valuable for lower-income seniors.

Other Silent Discussions

Sex in nursing homes: what are the moral, ethical, legal, and logistical considerations?

Should states require road tests for older drivers to renew their licenses, especially as they work into later years and become part of the heavy-traffic daily commute?

Fitness: Silents, the evidence is irrefutable. Begin a fitness regimen, either at home, outdoors, or in a fitness center. Workouts are Brain Fuel. Workouts enhance quality of life. And when done properly, experts say you can even put your body through *intense* training. Cardiovascular training aids in memory tasks. Strength training boosts higher-level brain tasks.

How about acting, directing, or playwriting? From a *Wall Street Journal* story:

In Oakland, California, Stagebridge is a senior theater company where some thirty classes are taught weekly in acting, playwriting, improvisation, storytelling, singing and musical theater, and other subjects. The school's eight performing troupes visit schools, senior centers, public theaters, and adult day centers. In Atlanta, a similar troupe calls itself the Past Prime Players. Founder Monciella Elder recently suggested the performers take a week off from their schedule; they refused. "I can't get them to go home", she said.

Silents seem to be embracing the attitude of one of their own, respected newsman Dan Rather. At age 83, Rather launched a new production company to produce interviews with high-profile guests with this comment:

"I'd much rather *wear* out than *rust* out."

The Third Stage

Silents, you have entered what AARP calls the Third Stage of Life, *the age of possibilities.*

At the moment, most members of the younger generations do not enjoy this luxury. They're scratching and clawing, trying to "make it" one day at a time. They're in the heat of the battle. But your generation has earned its way to the Third Stage.

Consider The Third Stage one big Banana Split and gobble it up.

Silents: Their Legacy

I have the privilege to present Generational Strategy to audiences in every corner of the country. But after each presentation, I then get to listen and *learn,* during the question-and-answer session that follows. I've absorbed Americans' comments about our generations for many years. And here's the "hope" that constantly surfaces when all generations discuss the Silents:

Silents, you carry something very special inside of you: a memory that younger generations don't possess, which will become clear when you read the chapters about Gen X and Millennials.

Along with the G.I.s and Boomers, you carry a first-person, direct-experience knowledge of an America that was magnificently fulfilling its promise as you came of age.

An America that took on big problems and *solved* them. An America in which neighbors helped neighbors. An America in which bosses and employees were on the same side. An America in which the family unit was rock-solid and kids grew up feeling loved and safe and guided. An America whose radio and television and music industries were wholesome and life-affirming and brought out our best instincts instead of our worst. An America whose citizens were unrushed enough to practice common courtesy with each other. An America that smiled. And laughed. An America that dared to dream big dreams and was idealistic and sassy enough to think—to *know*—it could achieve them. An America that truly believed it should pursue perfection.

It is an America that Gen X'ers and Millennials—this is difficult to comprehend, isn't it?—have not experienced in the same full glory as you did. Your kids and grandkids don't know how magnificent everyday American life can be. Their only knowledge of America is best described by a woman who has spent her career working for child services agencies, currently in Washington, D.C. "For the past twenty years," she told me in the 1990s, "it feels like America has been suffering from a low-grade flu."

And in the '90s, on his Sunday-morning network-TV news show, long-time news anchor David Brinkley concluded one episode by asking this memorable question, with disgust in his voice:

"When is the last time America solved a major problem?!"

Can you Silents find a way to impart the story of the America *you know* to your skeptical children and grandchildren so they, too, will demand that their country not rest until it has achieved the *ideal*, rather than shrug their shoulders and simply accept this low-grade flu as the American norm? If you can find a way to pull this off, it might become your generation's greatest legacy.

You have a story to tell. You have work to do.

It's time for the *Silent* Generation to *make some noise.*

Two More Silent Chapters

More to come: one chapter about Silents as consumers in the marketplace, and one about them as employees in the workplace.

THE BOOMERS

Forever Young

. . .

CHAPTER 8

The Boomers

"Your Beauty Will Be Lost With Your Peace Of Mind"

• • •

Birth Years:	**1946 Through 1964**
How Many Born:	**79,907,844**
Formative Years:	**1950s To Early 1980s**
Their Parents:	**Younger G.I.s, Most Silents**

ON SEPTEMBER 2, 2013, BOOMER Diana Nyad became the first person at any age to successfully swim from Cuba to Florida without the protection of a shark cage. She swam for 53 hours, covering 110 miles.

She had failed to complete the same journey four times before.

When she finally walked out of the water and onto the white sands of Key West—dazed, sunburned, and after hallucinating and choking on sea water and suffering jellyfish stings, and with fans on the beach applauding and news media waiting with cameras and microphones—her first words were quintessentially *Boomer*:

"I've got three messages. One is, we should never, ever give up. Two is, you're never too old to chase your dreams. Three is, it looks like a solitary sport, but it is a team."

She was 64 years old.

Her first *failed* attempt had occurred when she was 29.

* *Never ever give up.*
* *Never too old.*
* *Team.*

Hail the Boomers: forever young.

In the early 2000s, I gave a speech in Columbus, Ohio and then met an old college buddy for a beer at an outdoor café. A woman he knew came over to say hello. He introduced us, and she sat down and asked what I do for a living. When I explained and then said, "I'm guessing you're a Boomer" and then told her about the importance of "formative years" to our lives, her eyes opened wide, she leaned over the table towards me and said almost ferociously:

"We were so lucky!"

Welcome to the story of A Golden Age For Kids....

Their Formative Years And Core Values

August, 1945. The unfathomable human slaughter and agony of World War II blessedly ends all at once, after an estimated 50,000,000 to 75,000,000 people worldwide have died, including 406,000 American troops.

The last of 16,000,000 young, triumphant, and apparently quite horny U. S. troops come home all at once, step off the trains and buses in their hometowns all at once, have a welcome-home beer with hometown friends down at the corner tavern all at once, reunite with their spouses or get married all at once (the wedding industry promptly becomes a three-billion-dollar business, and this is when a billion dollars actually means something), and...

hop in the sack all at once.

Sure enough, right on schedule, nine months later in 1946, the epic, legendary American Baby Boom is *on*. And it will continue for nineteen years. As the old song goes, their parents were *makin' whoopee*.

Frequently.

And yet all these decades later, most Boomers still cannot *imagine* their parents ever having sex. And those kids who accidentally DID catch their parents in the act? Still traumatized.

The 19 birth years of the older Silent Generation had produced fewer than 47,000,000 American babies. The 19 years of the Boom are now about to deliver nearly 80,000,000 Mouseketeers.

And this generation's formative years—the 1950s, '60s, '70s, and early '80s—will bring times and teachings *profoundly* different from those of the Silents. And so Boomers will mold profoundly different generational Core Values.

The parents of the Boomers are primarily the younger G.I.s and virtually the entire Silent Generation.

First Wave, Second Wave

Each generation tends to have what is called a First Wave and a Second Wave. Older half and younger half. Typically, the two waves are slightly different but still share enough Core Values to be a single generation. And that's absolutely true with Boomers, only the differences between their waves are a little more pronounced.

First-Wave Boomers are born from 1946 to about 1954. Second-Wave'ers, from about 1955 to 1964.

"We need idealistic children"
Dr. Benjamin Spock

As the First-Wave Boomer babies are arriving, their G.I. and Silent mothers are faithfully following the parenting advice of a pediatrician by the name of Dr. Benjamin Spock, who, in his book *Baby and Child Care*—which comes out in 1946 and over the next half-century will sell more copies (some 50 million) than any book in U. S. publishing history except the Bible—writes four words that help change the course of American history:

"We need idealistic children."

Well, Dr. Spock, unbeknownst to you in 1946 as you write those fateful words, in another two decades this is exactly what America and the world will get.

Sure enough, Boomer children come of age embracing the idealism that their parents, educators, religious leaders, and others are preaching and teaching to them every day, in the living room, classroom, and house of worship: *Don't accept almost right from yourself and others; demand exactly right.*

"A job worth doing is worth doing well!" Oh, if Boomers only had a nickel for every time they heard that one from their elders...

They're also imbued by Mom and Dad with another strong message: a no-nonsense belief about what is *right* in life and what is *wrong*, what is good and what is bad, what you do and what you don't do. As Boomers come of age, there isn't much gray area—not much room for *negotiating* with Mom and Dad—when it comes to the matter of right and wrong.

And then, in the 1960s, after spending their early childhood in the carefree, innocent, hula-hoop and pogo-stick Happy Days of the '50s, this cocktail—this mixture of idealism and a strong sense of right and wrong—goes a long way in explaining one of the most tumultuous periods in our nation's history, but also one of the most socially enlightening periods...

The Consciousness Movement: 1961 To 1975

...the so-called Consciousness Movement of 1961 to 1975, but which most of us refer to as simply *The Sixties.*

I was on a flight, 40,000 feet somewhere over America, when I read an on-point description of the Consciousness Movement in Delta Airline's in-flight magazine. The reporter described the period as a time "when America remakes itself in fairer terms, beginning the process of righting our wrongs". Although I scribbled down the quote, I failed to write down the author's name. Whoever you are, *nice*.

The parents of the Boomers had battled an economic depression and then military enemies in their own younger years.

As the First-Wave Boomers come of age, and as they sit across the dinner table each night from these larger-than-life heroes who have just saved the world and are now building the greatest nation on the planet and who just happen to be named *Mom* and *Dad*, they can't help but absorb their parents' own generational Core Values of engagement (*I will roll up my sleeves and participate in this experiment called America*), empowerment (*I think I can make a difference*), patriotism, nothing-is-impossible, dream big, work hard, and most of all, work ethically and compassionately towards others.

But now, in these new times, young Boomers aim those same Core Values at a new set of enemies.

And during this fifteen-year convulsion in the United States, First-Wave Boomers deliver their passion, masses, and idealism to no fewer than eight major cultural revolutions, most considered very noble and selfless, but some considered damaging and selfish. Any one of these revolutions is big enough to define a generation forever, but as this generation comes of age there are *eight* of them flying all around at the same time!

Boomers propel forward the:

1. Civil Rights Movement
2. Feminist Movement
3. Ecology/Environmental Movement
4. War Protest Movement
5. Sexual Revolution
6. Drug Revolution
7. Religion Revolution
8. Youth Empowerment Movement

Each of these major pivots in American life earns its status as a true "revolution" because it creates change that is (A) significant, (B) widespread, and (C) long-lasting and perhaps even permanent. This definition of revolution strips away temporary and less important changes due to fads, cults, and other tweaks to American life.

And the first seven revolutions are made possible, in part, by the eighth one: Boomers become the first U. S. generation to enjoy true youth empowerment, which is granted to them by their own parents' teachings, and by the mass media that devote so much attention to them, and yes, by the "times", which place all of these epochal causes in their laps as they're coming of age.

By the way, the Boomers provide the passion, masses, and idealism, but the iconic *leaders* of these revolutions are mostly not-so-silent Silents, with even a couple of G.I.s:

The civil rights movement of the '60s is led by Silent Generation members Martin Luther King, Jr. for American blacks; by Silent Cesar Chavez for Mexican-Americans; and by Silent Russell Means for AIM, the American Indian Movement.

The gutsy firebrand of the feminist movement is Gloria Steinem, a Silent, whose legendary crusade follows G.I. Generation Betty Friedan's 1963 book *Feminine Mystique,* generally credited with sparking the awareness that a substantial percentage of stay-at-home moms might not be as fulfilled in their lives as others believed. And don't forget the remarkable impact upon women's emergence of Phil Donahue and his daytime talk show. Donahue *transformed* 51% of the U. S. population and got the other 49% to change their thinking about women.

The ecology movement begins during this time with G.I. proponents John McConnell and Senator Gaylord Nelson and Silent Denis Hayes. And six of the first seven directors of the newly created Environmental Protection Agency are Silents.

The anti-Vietnam War protests had many, many figureheads, dominated—especially in the early months—by Silents.

The sexual revolution: *Playboy* magazine founder Hugh Hefner is a "cusp'er", born right at the end of the G.I.s and beginning of the Silents.

And a primary figurehead of the drug revolution is G.I. Generation member Dr. Timothy Leary, who coins the phrase *"Turn on, tune in, drop out."*

The Religion Revolution is not a typical revolution. It does not have radicals standing on the front steps of churches and synagogues pounding their fists and demanding change. Instead, it becomes more of a personal search, a quest, by Boomers, and later X'ers and Millennials, to find a faith and spirituality that fits their unique generational Core Values. It is more a journey than a rebellion, and it continues to this day with these three generations, who profess a strong belief in some kind of God but seek...*more.*

And about the eighth revolution, Youth Empowerment? The Boomers become America's first-ever youth-empowered generation. There are so many moments that symbolize its arrival, but perhaps none as exuberant as the fabled moment on February 7, 1964 when The Beatles step off that airplane at John F. Kennedy Airport in New York City, appear on *The Ed Sullivan Show* two nights later, and create in America *The Night When Everything Changed.*

And since all family members watched the show together, Boomer kids got to hear their parents' reaction to The Beatles. Dad, skeptically: "That hair looks a little long." Mom, as peacemaker: "Well, yes, but it looks *clean.*"

Vietnam: The Boomers' War

Second-Wave Silents and First-Wave Boomers represent the overwhelming majority of our combat troops in Vietnam.

More than 3 million troops serve in Southeast Asia during the war. More than 58,000 die. The average age of the American soldier fighting there is nineteen.

Several lifelong Boomer Core Values will emerge from their generation's war, which Boomers will always refer to in shorthand, as simply *Nam*.

Core Values # 1 and # 2: empowerment *and* engagement. Their anti-war protests in cities across the nation influence the U. S. government's decision to ultimately quit the conflict. From that comes the empowerment, the belief within Boomers—even those who don't march in the streets—that the masses truly can influence their government's decisions, especially the decisions regarding military conflict. And with that empowerment comes the companion Core Value of engagement: *Yes, I will engage in the democratic process; I will live the kind of Advanced Citizenship this country demands and needs.*

Core Value # 3: skepticism of government. Before Nam, Boomers had been coming of age with an especially positive perception of their nation's government. But with its government leaders' handling of this war, they grow more skeptical.

Core Value # 4: for a number of Boomers and younger Silents, this is a hard-learned lesson. But years later, the generational Core Value will be unambiguous, and younger generations will learn from what many Boomers consider their one mistake during 'Nam:

Anti-war Boomers and Silents harshly criticize their uniformed brothers and sisters for their participation in the war. Our troops come home after nobly serving their country, only to be insulted, harassed, and even spat upon by their own generations.

One Boomer Marine told me he stayed inside his parents' house for a full month when he first came home, in order to let his hair grow longer. In the era of long hairdos for the men, his buzz-cut would announce him as "military" and he knew he would be confronted by anti-war people when he walked the streets. Instead of returning to an appreciative nation, he hid.

But now today, in sharp contrast to the way that some Boomers and some Silents felt back then, they— and most Americans—now overwhelmingly agree:

No matter how strongly we might disagree with our government's handling of military conflict, we nonetheless will ALWAYS support our troops.

And this is a very powerful legacy of Vietnam. It taught many Americans, especially anti-war Boomers, to separate their feelings about their government from those about their brothers and sisters wearing the uniform.

Decades later, in the late 2000s, Anheuser-Busch produces a very emotional TV commercial when America is in the heat of the battle in its war against terrorism. The commercial captures the lesson that Boomers and the nation learned from Vietnam:

Not a word is spoken in this commercial, which begins by showing a bustling airport concourse filled with people standing or sitting, chatting or reading, as they await their own flights and watch other passengers briskly walking up and down the concourse.

Suddenly, off-camera, we hear a single person slowly clapping his or her hands. A couple of others join in. Other heads turn in the direction of the applause. *What are they clapping about?* Then, we get our answer: de-boarding a plane and entering the concourse are a half-dozen male and female troops, dressed in camouflage and boots. One by one, the civilians in the concourse rise from their seats, applaud and smile as the troops walk past, and modestly return the smile, a bit embarrassed by the attention. The commercial ends with two words typed in the middle of the screen:

Thank you.

I show this commercial in my training seminars and, in city after city, audience members choke up and tears trickle down their cheeks.

And I have personally witnessed—and participated in—this same experience in more than one airport around the country: in Atlanta, where the black Boomer woman working our gate for her airline not only asked military personnel to board the plane first but also introduced each of them on the P. A. system and solicited our applause, which we gladly gave. And in Omaha, which is near Offutt Air Force Base and where I sat in a concourse café for four hours awaiting my flight. During that time, every single airman (and in the Air Force, females are also referred to as "airmen") who de-boarded a flight was greeted spontaneously, without any prompting, with concourse applause.

The feeling one gets from witnessing and participating in this show of appreciation?

How cool!

And to any of you readers who are active duty, veteran, or civilians who have worked in a job that supports our troops...

THANK YOU FOR SERVING OUR NATION.

"I have a dream today!"
August 28, 1963

For African-Americans during the Consciousness Movement...

This is it!

The modern civil rights movement—the Glorious Struggle, as this period will be called—now reaches full bloom and becomes an emotional roller coaster ride of historic joy and historic anguish, especially for black Boomers who are in their all-important formative years.

Here is just a very small sample of what Boomer blacks witness as their generation comes of age, and what their white, American Indian, Hispanic, Asian, Jewish, and other ethnic brothers and sisters experience with them as this idealistic and empowered generation makes the gritty decision to stand shoulder to shoulder, put themselves through the wrenching process of stripping away personal prejudices that had been handed down to them from their elders, and launch a full frontal assault on a racism that makes no sense to their generation's Core Values and has no place in their idealized vision for America.

Together, they will come of age witnessing and being molded by moments like these:

1963: Martin Luther King, Junior's historic "I Have A Dream" speech.

1964: Passage of historic civil rights legislation by Congress.

1965: The assassination of black activist Malcolm X.

1966: The founding of the Black Panther Party.

1967: The worst urban riots in U. S. history.

1968: The assassinations of Dr. King and Bobby Kennedy, and the occupation of Alcatraz Island in San Francisco Bay, which helps to popularize the American Indian Movement.

Throughout their formative years, Boomer blacks see their brothers and sisters—and in some cases their mothers and fathers—begin to make unprecedented progress in American life, especially in the American workplace and, with that, in the American economy.

And during the '60s, Baby Boomers of all hues will be pulled even closer together by a tiny factory in Detroit. The factory is actually a converted house that mass-produces not automobiles but instead... music.

Motown.

It is the creation of a Silent Generation black man with a vision: Berry Gordy.

The Temptations. Four Tops. Supremes. Marvin Gaye. Smokey Robinson. Stevie Wonder. The Jackson Five. Martha and the Vandellas. Mary Wells. And all of the other giants.

(By the way, do you Boomers know what a "vandella" is? Didn't think so. Me, neither. As co-host Dan Rowan used to say on the TV show *Laugh-In*, "Look THAT up in your Funk & Wagnalls!")

As Boomers come of age, popular music assumes a leadership role in dissolving ethnic and racial barriers.

So does sport:

In 1963, "The Game Of Change" as it would later be called, takes place in East Lansing, Michigan. It's a college basketball game in which Mississippi State University defies a state injunction designed to prevent the Bulldogs from playing a racially integrated opponent, Loyola of Chicago, in an NCAA Tournament game. The photograph of white MSU player Joe Dan Gold shaking hands before the tipoff with black Loyola captain Jerry Harkness becomes iconic. Loyola wins the game, but the handshake and racial statement advance the nation.

And throughout the 1960s, college and professional sports integrate more fully and accelerate the dizzying and dazzling progress of race relations during the Boomer childhood.

Likewise with television: from 1965 to 1968, the popular network TV show *I Spy* becomes the first American television drama to feature a black actor (Bill Cosby) in a lead role.

And politics: in 1966, Edward William Brooke of Massachusetts becomes the first popularly elected Black U. S. senator.

What a time to be a kid coming of age in the United States!

What a time to be a *black* kid coming of age.

"...an intensity we cannot name"

Keep this in mind: First-Wave Boomers have always been one of the more scrutinized and judged age cohorts. They were in kindergarten and elementary and junior high school in the Happy Days of the '50s and very early '60s, which would later be described as America's Last Innocent Decade. And when they had looked upward to those older, cooler Silent Generation high schoolers and college students, they saw joy, innocence, and carefree good times, and they fully expected their own teenage and early adult years would be just like that.

To this day, most First-Wave Boomers still can't fully explain how and why their nation erupted as it did during the Consciousness Movement.

A Popular Culture professor at Ohio State University thinks it was the actor Dennis Hopper who first uttered the famous line about the Consciousness Movement:

"Anyone who tells you he recalls the '60s clearly... probably wasn't there."

And authors Strauss and Howe, in their book *Generations,* include the comment of a Boomer college student who says it a bit more seriously in her 1968 commencement speech to her fellow First-Wave Boomer graduates at Radcliffe College in Cambridge, Massachusetts:

"We do not feel like a cool, swinging generation. We are eaten up by an intensity that we cannot name."

What they had been taught by their elders during their formative years was idealism and that strong sense of right and wrong. In the '60s, First-Wave Boomers simply react to what they're witnessing all around them in perhaps the only way a generation raised on those Core Values *can* react.

By the way, a number of younger Silents will tell you they identify more strongly with Boomers than with their own generation, in part because they recoiled from the conformity of their own generation's youth and instead embraced the nonconformity and sense of liberation that the Boomer activism brought. So they prefer to be Boomers, which is fine!

Boomers, Cars, And America

Not only are the '50s, '60s, and '70s a golden age for kids, they are also a golden age for the American automobile.

As Boomer kids come of age, they eagerly ride their bicycles to local dealerships on that one thrilling Saturday morning each September, when the dealers theatrically tear down the brown paper that is covering their massive showroom windows and reveal the new models.

And every year, these new models seem bigger and brighter and flashier than the year before.

And for Boomer kids and all Americans, our automobiles seem to reflect the magnificent afterglow of their nation's triumph in World War II: during the 1950s and '60s, we Americans are feeling "big" and "bright" and "flashy".

America Gets Connected

Boomers also pass through their childhood witnessing the largest earth-moving project in the history of the world: the construction of the interstate highway system; begun in the '50s and mostly completed in the '60s. 47,000+ miles of pavement! One description of its impact on the United States is this: "The Interstate Highway System released a perpetual motion machine."

And in response to the interstate system, the lodging industry invents roadside "motels" to go along with traditional downtown "hotels".

And in response to the baby boom in America, the auto industry invents the legendary station wagon.

And in response to the roominess of the station wagon, the parents of Baby Boomers launch the grand era of the Family Driving Vacation, with all of its adventures and misadventures that are hilariously captured years later in the 1983 film starring Chevy Chase and Beverly D'Angelo, *National Lampoon's Vacation*.

So if you're a First-Wave Boomer kid, you grow up viewing automobiles *romantically*:

- Cars are a celebration of *America*...
- of *family*...
- of *adventures* and *misadventures*...
- and *memories*.

Speaking of station wagons, which feel as if they're 18 miles in length during this era, they are designed with something quite new and novel: a third seat that faces *backwards*, which passengers easily access through the rear tailgate.

Ideal for these times of large families, yes. But what the automakers apparently failed to test is this:

It can be physically disorienting to sit in a car facing backwards, especially when the car is racing in the opposite direction at these new and higher speeds permitted by the interstate system. And if you put a young kid in a rear-facing seat and drive for any length of time at high speed, that kid's gonna throw up.

I mentioned this during an advertising seminar in Grand Rapids, Michigan and a Boomer woman in the audience started laughing. Here's the story she remembered and shared:

She's 9 years old. It's the early '60s. Dad buys a station wagon and maps out the big driving summer vacation. Because there's so much seating room in these cars, she gets to invite her best-buddy girlfriend. They plunk down in the rear-facing seat, and off they go. And because Mom and Dad seem so far away, all the way up there in the front seat, these two 9-year-old girls, looking out the rear window, decide this is the perfect time to smoke their first cigarette. It didn't take long.

Most First-Wave Boomers can recall a Station Wagon Vomit Story from their youth.

All of this fascination with the automobile will come to an abrupt halt when Gen X'ers begin to arrive on the planet. The Arab Oil Embargo of the early '70s reduces automobiles to smaller, more functional, and less flashy *conveyances*. During Gen X's formative years, cars become boring.

Second-Wave Boomers
Born 1955 Through 1964
Second Wave Boomers: *Who Are We?*

Now then, after launching all of these cultural revolutions, the inevitable occurs. The First-Wave Boomers must leave their classroom years, enter adulthood, launch their careers, and start their families. They will now disappear from the front pages of the nation's newspapers for a quarter century.

Behind them comes their generation's Second Wave. Born from about 1955 to 1964. So these are the folks who graduate from high school from roughly 1973 to 1982.

Same passion as their older Boomer brothers and sisters. Same idealism. Same empowerment. Same engagement. Same Boomer swagger. Same zest for life. But the social activism is winding down just as they're getting old enough to join it.

So: what to do with all of that Boomer energy as they come of age in the '70s and early '80s?

Well, it seems that after 15 years of serious introspection during the Consciousness Movement, Americans simply need a break. They need to exhale, have some fun, and regain their laughter. And so: enter the Second-Wave Boomers, who turn the '70s into the party decade of Sex, Drugs, and Rock 'n' Roll. Do you Boomers clearly remember that decade?

Didn't think so.

But some members of this group haven't felt like Boomers, primarily because the word "Boomer" is so strongly associated with the social activism that is winding down just as they're becoming old enough to join it. So most Second-Wave'ers don't march in the street, crash the Miss America pageant, or occupy a campus building, or get tear-gassed.

They also know this: they don't feel like younger Gen X'ers either. And to this day, some of them still ask the question, *who are we?*

Let's see if we can help them.

Nuclear Families Intact
Live Life To The Fullest
Unlimited Possibilities
Career-Driven

Like First-Wave Boomers, most Second-Wave'ers grow up with their nuclear families intact; not much divorce by their parents, either. And this alone molds a long list of Core Values similar to the older Boomers and dissimilar from Gen X.

They also pass through their childhood when anything seems possible in this marvelous nation called America. Boomers, to their good fortune, come of age during perhaps the best period in American history to be a kid. During their formative years, they witness a soaring nation, being led by a fearless, humble, visionary, and compassionate G.I. Generation that demonstrates that Americans can achieve anything they set their mind to. Families are strong, neighborhoods are safe, communities are tight-knit, jobs and incomes for most dads are stable and secure, the middle class is flourishing, our country's best and brightest are curing polio and landing men on the moon and building the interstate highway system, and Americans are generously helping less fortunate countries, thanks in part to Congress' landmark passage of the Peace Corps Act in 1961. This legislation defines the Peace Corps' purpose as follows:

To promote world peace and friendship through a Peace Corps, which shall make available to interested countries and areas men and women of the United States qualified for service abroad and willing to serve, under conditions of hardship if necessary, to help the peoples of such countries and areas in meeting their needs for trained manpower.

Between 1961 and 2013, more than 215,000 Americans join the Peace Corps and serve in 139 countries. And worldwide, citizens of other nations look to America in awe and reverence and ache to come here. America, they feel, stands for everything that is good and right as Boomer children are molding lifelong Core Values.

And the stability and security and national pride of the times liberate the American people to become introspective, take on their own worst personal prejudices, especially against minorities and women, and make historic progress against them.

As Boomers come of age, America is unstoppable. America is as magical as magical gets.

The Wonder Years

A couple of decades later, in the late 1980s, a new TV sitcom airs on national TV: *The Wonder Years,* which presents a Boomer kid (played by super-cute Fred Savage) and his friends and classmates coming of age during those remarkable times. One episode begins with the show's narrator, actor Daniel Stern, describing the Boomer formative years perfectly, as...

"a golden age for kids".

So, Second-Wave Boomers move through their formative years feeling *hope* and *opportunity* all around them. And they come to share the same powerful go-for-it, live-life-to-the-fullest mindset as their older Boomer brothers and sisters.

What's more, the American economy is rolling during *most*, but not all, of their formative years, so Second-Wave kids also feel America will offer them unlimited career and income opportunities if they just follow their parents' no-nonsense advice to work hard, work smart, and work ethically.

From all of this, they grow up feeling a strong sense of nation and patriotism. They're career driven, willing to work long hours and be loyal to the company, but also sassy enough to challenge the company if they feel it's doing something wrong. They're big dreamers, and willing to put in the necessary time and sweat to achieve those big dreams.

Oh, how drastically all of this will change when X'ers arrive on the planet!

Belief In Meritocracy
Individuality
Merging Of Black-White Cultures

Second-Wave'ers are also very-much-Boomer in their belief in meritocracy, the belief that you advance in your career by way of hard, smart, and honest work. Not by shortcuts, cheating, or backstabbing.

This is also when black Boomers, propelled by the Civil Rights Movement and the black pride movement that comes with it, begin to see their white Boomer brothers and sisters embracing their African-American culture for the first time. All of a sudden, music, movies, TV, fashion, slang, and other essential youth touchstones are now crossing over *in both directions.*

By contrast, in the '40s and '50s when *Silent* kids were in their teens, some black entertainers often had their naturally curly hair straightened—remember *Ultra Sheen* hair products and the conk hairdo?—so as to be more appealing to white audiences. But now in the '60s, some white Boomer kids are growing, or trying to grow, their own curly "Afros".

And from this comes a Core Value in *all* Boomers of taking pride in reducing the race gap in America.

Forever-Young Mentality

And finally, these Second-Wave Boomers are true Boomers in one other very important Core Value. They think young, without even knowing it, without trying. A forever-young mentality. It comes from their generation's childhood that was filled with such hope, optimism, and security; a belief that everything is possible.

To the Baby Boom Generation, life on earth is one big banquet table, and they want to sample every dish while they're here.

So that's how Second-Wave'ers are very much Boomer. Here's how they're somewhat different.

Skeptical, Not Cynical
More Money-Motivated
Less Optimistic

In the '70s, the ones born from 1955 to 1964 are still in the latter stage of their formative years. And this is when life starts to unravel in America: the Watergate scandal that forces a U. S. president to resign; a higher cost of living; more limited career opportunities; job layoffs up there in the adult world, maybe even for Mom and Dad; early signs of more cynical and vulgar commercial radio, television, and music industries; and, a rising materialism in American life.

And so these Second-Wave Boomers develop some Core Values that are slightly different from the First Wave. They become a bit more skeptical about life in America, but not hard-bitten cynical, as younger X'ers will understandably become in another decade.

Also, they become more motivated by money, as America enters what historians later label the *Decade of Greed:* the late '70s and '80s, a very materialistic period that is similar to the 1950s, when many Americans measure themselves and others by their possessions, their *stuff.*

Finally, Second-Wave Boomers become a bit less optimistic about how unlimited their career opportunities are truly going to be when they reach adulthood.

All-Volunteer Army

And Second-Wave Boomers also have a very different experience with the military: they begin to reach draft age in 1973, which is precisely when Congress ends the draft and our military becomes all-volunteer. And with relatively few exceptions, Second-Wavers do not fight in the Vietnam War or any subsequent war.

But in the big picture, the similarities outweigh the differences, and those Americans born from 1955 to 1964 are card-carrying members of the Baby Boom Generation. The Core Values they possess are overwhelmingly Boomer.

Epidemic Divorce

In adulthood, many Boomers struggle terribly with marriage and parenting, and this will scar their Gen X children. They, along with a number of younger Silents, send the divorce rate over the moon, for a variety of reasons:

Untold numbers of them "have to get married" as the sexual revolution arrives in their local communities before many teenage girls can gain access to the birth control pill. Unplanned, and largely unwanted, pregnancies proliferate. And during this time in the '60s and early '70s, abortion is not yet a legal option and seldom a moral option for this generation. So they "try to do the right thing" by getting married—hasty "shotgun weddings"—but they're simply too young and immature. Their marriages collapse, trapping their Gen X children in a bewilderment and anger that is chronicled in their own generation's upcoming chapters.

And marriage is frequently difficult even for those Boomers who don't get pregnant and do marry with all of the traditional good intentions, because the only model of marriage this generation has ever known—the model they witnessed in their parents and grandparents—largely disappears, as the women's movement suddenly opens career doors for women, and the birth control pill gives them nearly complete control over their reproduction. As many Boomer women become financially independent, and as they become just as career-driven as they are family-driven or even more so, they do not feel compelled to remain in unsatisfactory marriages. And this is a generation that also pursues the absolute ideal in life. A perfectionist mindset. *If my marriage isn't meeting my high standards, I'll end it.*

In addition, the sexual freedom created by the world-changing birth-control pill is also increasing marital infidelity and, with it, still more divorce.

And in 1971, according to Census Bureau data, the divorce rate in the United States is an astonishing 165% higher than it had been only ten years earlier in 1961.

Singer-songwriter Carole King, as she has done so often in her acclaimed career, captures—with collaborator Toni Stern—the Boomer divorce tsunami with her powerful, Grammy-winning 1971 song, "It's Too Late":

"Stayed in bed all morning just to pass the time...
There's something wrong and there can be no denying...
One of us is changing, or maybe we just stopped trying.
And it's too late, baby, now it's too late,
Though we really did try to make it.
Something inside has died...
And I can't hide, and I just can't fake it, ohhh noooo..."

The Boomer divorce epidemic raises this question: how many of their own parents and grandparents would have divorced if those generations' women had enjoyed the same freedoms afforded by The Pill and financial independence?

Parenthood

Boomers also struggle with their parenting. They usher in an era of permissive and guilt-riddled parenting and a desire to be their kids' buddies, rather than the stricter authoritarian figures their own parents had been to them.

Also, because they are divorced or dual-career, time-starved, absentee parents, they see their children struggling emotionally, as the American family unit takes a beating.

So they ease off on the scolding, correcting, and reprimanding. They allow bad behavior by their kids to slide a bit. Many of the rules become lax and negotiable. And there is less of a disciplinary and tough-love message about right-and-wrong than prior generations of kids had absorbed.

American life is changing so swiftly now! And the American family unit is undergoing seismic transformation, much of it negative, from what Boomers had known in their own childhood.

They *want* to be perfect in their marriages, parenting, and careers, but there's no manual to tell them how to accomplish it in this new model. Boomers thus become the generation that must write the new manual. Translation: they must be the generation that conducts the *trial and error* to discover what will and won't work. They get some things right, they get some things wrong.

In The Workplace: The Golden
Generation Continues The Fight

But if they struggle with marriage and parenting, Boomers will be nothing short of brilliant in the American workplace. And they will continue their generation's clench-fisted crusade for a more ethical, compassionate, and ideal America.

Boomers have been, and will continue to be, The Golden Generation in the American workplace.

Ambushed
Fierce Competition

The Silent Generation's white men, remember, have enjoyed that uncommonly smooth career passage.

The Boomers, conversely, will forever be the Ambushed Generation, because they enter adulthood fully expecting their careers to proceed as smoothly as those of the just-older generation, but then get bushwhacked in early- to mid-career with a spate of corporate downsizing, rightsizing, re-engineering, consolidation, outsourcing, off-shoring, and the executive corruption and greed meltdown of their Silent bosses, and all of this on a colossal scale.

Not only are they ambushed by the cutbacks and corruption, but Boomers also are so massive in number that they will face fierce, lifelong competition *from their fellow Boomers* for the same jobs and promotions. The Silent Generation and Gen X, both much smaller in number, will never have to endure such competition. Millennials, another big generation, will.

Not only are Boomers so much more numerous but also, with their arrival in adulthood, the competition for jobs and promotions is—*for the first time in U. S. history*—no longer restricted to white males, as it had been with all prior generations.

Now, the competition also comes from women and minorities, two subsets of Boomers who are thrilled by the hard-earned opportunities *finally* being extended to them, but who also feel extraordinary pressure to perform *perfectly,* because they sense, and in many cases, know, that their older white bosses, sitting upstairs in the executive suites, probably felt pressured to hire them and don't like it one bit.

Not only that, but these Boomer minorities and females also are acutely aware that they carry the weight of history on their shoulders. In the '60s, '70s, and '80s, they know they are *the first.* They know the entire nation is watching. And they simply cannot fail. So they must work longer and harder and smarter. Unlike white men, they cannot be merely "good". They must be better than good.

In 1969, James Brown accurately expresses the feelings of minorities and females when he sings:

"I don't want nobody to give me nothin'.
Open up the door, I'll get it myself."

And with the Boomers' arrival at adulthood, that door opens.

But once again with this generation, there is no manual, no guidebook, to tell them how to handle it.

Boomers must write still another manual.

This means their females and minorities must conduct the trial and error to learn how to step into a white man's world and find their place.

So, in these thrilling, terrifying, bewildering early years:

How do we women dress for work? Like our male bosses? Well, on this matter, fashion designer Yves San Laurent comes to the rescue when he popularizes the legendary pantsuit.

How do we act? Like our white male bosses? Or can we women be feminine, and can we minorities be true to our cultures?

Which sexual remarks and racial remarks from our white colleagues and bosses do we tolerate, and which ones do we challenge?

And if we are the victims of sex discrimination or race discrimination, do we dare complain?

And the constant question as Boomer females and minorities are beginning this uncharted journey:

How fair or unfair to us will our white male boss be?

Boomer Women: Here They Come

And now today, it's happening. The seeds planted a half-century ago are blooming. Boomer women, in their careers, are reaching the top and will bring profound, permanent, and surely positive transformation to the leadership and governance of American business, government, education, and religion:

⚜ Thirty-two years after graduating from the Air Force Academy, and after facing resistance and sexual harassment in her career, Boomer Lt. Gen. Michelle Johnson in 2013 is appointed the Academy's first female superintendent.

⚜ Boomer Janet Yellen, in that same year, becomes the first female top cop on Wall Street as chairwoman of the Federal Reserve.

⚜ Big Four accounting firm Deloitte chooses its first female CEO in 2015, Boomer Cathy Englebert, as the *Wall Street Journal* writes that the glass ceiling has "sprouted a few more cracks".

⚜ In law enforcement, the Drug Enforcement Administration, Secret Service, U. S. Park Police, the FBI's Washington Field Office, and Amtrak

Police Department are all headed by women by 2014.

⯈ Boomer Mary Barra becomes the first female CEO of General Motors.

⯈ Boomer Denise Morrison: CEO at Campbell's Soup.

⯈ Boomer Carly Fiorina: CEO at Hewlett-Packard (but the tech industry has had a disappointing overall track record of systemic hostility and discrimination in its treatment of female employees; in the latter half of the 2010s, industry leaders are beginning to address the problem);

⯈ And, many others. Still not enough. But on the right track.

Many American blacks and other minorities have experienced the same passage as women. Progress, yes, but still, unfair treatment lingers. So America is still falling short of its promise. But Boomers, famously persistent and idealistic, are likely to keep pushing.

In this book, there is more to come on Boomer women and minorities and their present and future impact upon leadership and governance and the workplace.

Great Expectations

There's one other stress-builder for Boomers that few of them fully comprehend, to this day:

History had marked them, from an early age, as a *special generation* that came along at a *special time* in American history; and thus, *special achievement* would always be expected from them. And this generation does not want to disappoint.

Boomers appreciate the struggle and sacrifice that their parents' and grandparents' generations suffered during The Great Depression and World War II. They know they've been given uncommon opportunity by their elders, and they want desperately to deliver. Remember that Radcliffe College quote from 1968?

"We are eaten up by an intensity that we cannot name."

A reporter for the daily newspaper in Phoenix called me to discuss a story he was preparing as to "which generation has the greatest sense of entitlement". And he asked, and tried to simultaneously answer, his own question by phrasing it this way:

"Surely it's the Boomers, isn't it?"

And I said, "Boomers probably have the *least* sense of entitlement when compared to Silents, X'ers, and Millennials."

I conducted a formal focus-group session with ten Boomer men, each of whom had come of age in a different region of the country. For two hours we discussed a long list of topics. At one point we discussed the notions of entitlement and pressure. And I asked them, "are Boomers the most pressured generation?"

And they all shook their heads. *No!* One guy said it for most Boomers: "You want pressure? Try The Great Depression. Try World War II. Compared to our parents and grandparents, we've had it easy."

So with these times and teachings and generational Core Values regarding career and work ethic, Boomers enter adulthood the only way they can: career-driven. This is the generation that always has, and always will, define itself by its work, by its contribution to something bigger than just a paycheck.

Boomers make long-hour workweeks the norm. They take work home. Work on weekends. Willingly pack up their families and accept job transfers and promotions to other cities and states and nations. They've been described as the generation that lives the motto T-G-I-M.

Thank God It's Monday.

Boomers feel little sense of entitlement. One day, their generation will leave this planet probably feeling they spent their entire lives trying to fulfill the promise bestowed upon them by the elders they revere.

Layoffs
Age Discrimination
Eldercare And Extended Childcare

Layoffs begin hitting many Boomers in mid- or even early-career, and then once again in late career when The Great Recession of 2008 staggers the country. And now today, they also face illegal but rapidly disappearing age discrimination, which is forcing some of them to search for new jobs and careers.

Not only that, but Boomers are also feeling the bookend pressures of eldercare, as their beloved parents live longer than parents have ever lived, and extended childcare, as many of their Millennial adult kids remain at home longer or their Gen X kids return home, again in part because of the Recession.

And many, many of their adult kids have turned to them with their hands out, seeking financial help, which has diminished Boomers' savings and is jeopardizing their retirement.

The Aging Of The Boomers

This massive generation is now entirely north of age 50. And its aging is now having momentous impact on our nation.

Such issues as longer and more flexible careers, Social Security, pension plans, healthcare and wellness, housing, politics, financial security, philanthropy, volunteerism, advocacy, community planning, and the American marketplace, workplace, and lifestyle are about to undergo staggering transformation.

Retire? *Why?!*

And about retiring? This is the generation, the men and the women, who in unprecedented number won't.

Why?

We're in a golden era of anti-aging science and medicine. As evidence of the "burgeoning science of extending the human life span" (*Wall Street Journal*), technology colossus Google announced in 2013 it is throwing its financial muscle behind a new company that will research aging and try to improve the human life span and health of the aging.

Boomers who take care of their health genuinely have no idea how long they'll live. So how can they possibly know when they can afford to retire? They can't. So they won't.

In 2010, when he left his position after a heralded run as Chief Executive Officer of mighty Procter & Gamble, Boomer A. G. Lafley, then about age 63, was asked by a reporter if he would now fully retire. And Mr. Lafley's answer captures the mindset of his entire generation:

"I have lots of runway left."

Sure enough, three years later when Procter was struggling under his successor, the Board of Directors asked him to return. He did.

1. The Great Recession ravaged Boomers' retirement nest eggs. Many of them can't retire.

2. In addition, many of them have not saved adequately for retirement. They've been an instant-gratification generation and came of age certain that their good hard work would always keep the money coming in.

3. There's also this: the fathers of many Boomers worked in physically demanding manual-labor jobs—factories, construction, and the like—because America was primarily a manufacturing economy during their work years. Understandably, those fathers retired as soon as they could, because the physical grind became increasingly difficult as they aged. And many Boomer kids saw their fathers retire, lose their sense of purpose, grow old, and die. And so Boomers say today, "Not us."

4. Boomers LOVE to work and need to be vital. And they are too skilled, dedicated, and productive for smart bosses to let them get away. And this includes their younger bosses, who might be sick and tired of living in the Boomers' shadow, or who might selfishly want their Boomers to depart so they can climb the ladder faster, or who might

feel it's wise to kick out higher-paid Boomers and go younger-and-cheaper. So I say this to management-level audiences in my training program in Generational Workforce Strategy:

If you want to drive away your Boomers for any of these reasons, then I want to consult your competitors, because your stupidity is going to make me look extra good in their eyes.

The Baby Boom Generation is delivering the death-blow to the traditional model of retirement.

As you'll read in the chapter on Boomers In The Workplace, they are creating a New Workplace Reality that is significant and permanent.

And as you'll read in the chapter on marketing to this generation, the use of the word *retirement* is being removed from advertising that targets Boomers.

Rewriting The Book of Life

Yes, Boomers have rewritten that good ol' *Book of Life* every day of their lives. They've done so many things so differently from the ways they had been done before.

And to the other generations who had assumed, and in many cases hoped, that Boomers would one day slow down, become a bit more conservative, and go gently into their next life passage...

guess again.

As this generation becomes empty nesters, and as their careers strike at least a more reasonable balance, their social activism—their sense of right and wrong— is beginning to re-emerge. They see an America that isn't fulfilling its promise. An America whose leadership culture has been a cesspool for a long time.

Boomers are pissed. And so they aren't done.

They're getting active again on causes. And this activism is gaining momentum. The Boomer masses are discovering that the Internet can be the same gathering point that the college campuses and courthouse steps were in the '60s.

One powerhouse example is the political activist organization MoveOn.org, founded by Boomers and X'ers. Here is a copy-and-paste from its website; notice how it gushes with Boomer Core Values of idealism, we-the-people empowerment, engagement, and compassion for the little guy, while also harnessing the power of modern technology:

> *For over 14 years, the MoveOn family of organizations have used online tools to lower the barriers to participation in our democracy, so real Americans have a voice in a political process where big money and corporate lobbyists wield too much influence. Increasingly, MoveOn members and progressives are stepping up as the leaders of their own campaigns for social change, using MoveOn's cutting-edge technology, such as MoveOn Petitions, to tap into our collective people power by enlisting other MoveOn members' support. The MoveOn family of organizations is not-for-profit and funded by small dollar donations from our more than 8 million members—no corporate contributions, no big checks from CEOs. And our tiny staff ensures that small contributions go a long way.*

Classic Boomer.

"The country is starved for integrity."
Colleen Rowley

When we think of Boomer activism, we tend to think back to the mass protests of the '60s.

But one of the more overlooked stories of this generation's imprint on history is the incalculable number of quieter, one-on-one battles that individual Boomers have fought in adulthood, usually in the workplace, and frequently against their Silent bosses, for their generation's values-driven and ethics-driven beliefs. An overlooked story. But every now and then, such stories bubble up to the surface:

May 21, 2002. Colleen Rowley, Boomer mother of four, sole breadwinner in the family, and only two and a half years from retirement from what everyone agrees is a distinguished career, nonetheless makes the very personal decision to risk losing all of that.

She testifies before the U. S. Senate Committee on Intelligence that her employer, the FBI, deliberately ignored alerts and obstructed investigations by its Minneapolis office that might have helped to uncover the terrorist attacks of September 11, 2001 before they occurred.

When asked later why she was willing to risk everything, Rowley's reply was classic idealistic, empowered Boomer: "It was the right thing to do," she said. "The country is starved for integrity."

Sherron Watkins

Same response by Boomer Sherron Watkins, who risks everything to reveal the accounting fraud and corruption at Enron, an energy/commodities darling of the 1990s. Board chairman Ken Lay, a white Silent male, and CEO Jeff Skilling, a Boomer, will later be convicted. Lay is ordered to prison but dies before serving any time. Skilling goes to prison. Employees who entrusted their life savings and futures to these men, by saving through the company, see their retirement nest-eggs diminished or wiped out by executive corruption.

Cynthia Cooper
"I'm not a hero."

Same response by Boomer Cynthia Cooper, who risks everything to reveal the executive corruption within the company that employs her, WorldCom. And she does so, despite being angrily ordered by then-golden-boy CFO Scott Sullivan to back off. Cooper keeps digging. By the end of 2003, the company confesses it inflated its total assets by billions, the largest accounting fraud in history until the Bernie Madoff (yes, sadly, another white Silent male) scandal topped it. Sullivan goes to prison. Cooper's white Silent male boss, CEO Bernie Ebbers, also goes to prison.

Cooper tells *TIME*, "I'm not a hero; I'm just doing my job."

Enron and WorldCom, whose scandals come to light in the early 2000s, become the two poster children for the greed, corruption, and executive excess of the Silent leadership era.

TIME magazine selects Rowley, Watkins, and Cooper its 2002 Persons of the Year.

In a *Des Moines Register* story about Rowley a month after the *TIME* tribute was published, reporter Mary Challender sums up Rowley's courage this way:

"When you're called to stand, you stand, even if your legs are shaking."

Three Boomers. Risking everything in order to do the right thing.

Three Boomers, simply being true to Core Values burned into them during their generation's unique formative years' times and teachings.

Idealism. Empowerment. Engagement. Right and wrong. Ethics. And yes, fearlessness.

"Mommy Loudest"

Boomers truly are the forever-young generation; they really do think young, without trying, and without being especially aware of it.

In the mid-2000s, the *Wall Street Journal* and *People* magazine write stories about a wave of Boomer and older X'er mothers who are forming their own garage bands and scheduling performances around their career and mommy schedules. One Boomer rocker, Judy Davids, says she looked around at her suburban Detroit housewife life one day and found herself thinking, *"This can't be all."* The Boomer Core Values at play here? *Forever young*; and, *squeeze life for all of its satisfactions.*

Some of the names of these Mommy-Loudest bands:

* From Detroit, *The Mydols.*
* From New York City, *Housewives on Prozac.*
* And only from our sisters out in wonderfully wacky California would we get a mother band that chooses to call itself *The Lactators,* also known as (brace yourself) *Placenta.*

This mommy-rocker movement launches its own three-day music festival in New York. It's called

Mamapalooza. Among the original songs they sing: *Eat Your Damn Spaghetti* and *Vasectomy.*

And *Mydols* lead singer Kara Rasmussen made this announcement to the crowd one night at a Detroit club as her group stepped on stage:

"We're an all-mom band, so we don't have time to practice. If you don't like what you're hearing...go to your room."

What About Their Future?
Growing Old Is Optional!

To Boomers, the battle cry from this moment forward is simple:

Aging is mandatory. But growing old is optional, and we've decided against it.

Modern science and medicine, and their own Core Values, are permitting Boomers to continue to rewrite the *Book of Life.*

We're entering this era of increasing longevity in part because Boomers are a massive generation, with massive spending power and a forever-young mindset. And pharmaceutical companies, government research agencies, and individual scientists know this: whoever among them wins the race and discovers the Magic Pill that will slow, stop, and someday actually reverse the aging process will enjoy a spectacular return on their investment.

But Boomers, as always, aren't waiting. They are finding the new outer limit for the endurance of the human body at their age. They are:

* hiking up mountains and skiing down them;

* skydiving from the heavens and scuba diving to the depths;

* and, running or bicycling or fulfilling a lifelong dream by purchasing their first-ever motorcycle and promptly crashing it.

To orthopedic surgeons, Boomers have become a Joint-Replacement Jackpot.

And at every future age marker—80, 90, and yes, 120—this playful, Mouseketeer generation will alter the lifestyle, career, and consumer models from what they've always been before at those ages.

But:

Here Is A Big "But" Or, More Accurately, A Big "Butt"

As *AARP The Magazine* documents in a story head-lined "The Rise and Fall of the Fitness Generation", many Boomers are out of shape. The brutal sub-header to this story: "Once-buff boomers confront the blimp in the mirror and ask: What the hell happened to us?"

This is the *Jane Fonda workout in her leg warmer video* generation. Olivia Newton-John's fitness song *Let's Get Physical*. Richard Simmons. Boomer Frank Shorter's 1972 Olympic gold medal in the marathon, which ignited the nation's running craze. Twiggy, the British model who made skinny *trés chic*. Gold's Gym. The surf culture.

And this fitness revolution has its roots in a 1950s New York University study revealing that American youths were less fit than their European contemporaries. Later, U. S. president John Kennedy authors an article for *Sports Illustrated* entitled "The Soft American" and the government begins to promote physical fitness. Boomers respond with their customary all-in mentality, and the movement is underway.

Physician Kenneth Cooper, author of the 1968 best-seller *Aerobics,* writes, "Baby boomers led an unprecedented fitness revolution into a kind of golden era of health."

But now today, one big belly flop:

The *Journal of the American Medical Association* recently reported that Boomers are less fit at their current age than their parents were! Only 35% of Boomers exercise regularly, and 52% have no routine.

Has the lifelong Boomer passion for wellness and good appearance been steamrolled by America's fast-food, couch-potato, time-poor lifestyle?

Or perhaps by the theft of their—and other generations'—energy and enthusiasm that the slaughter of the middle class has caused?

Or has their generation simply not yet rebounded from the fitness downturn that usually begins in one's 40s and 50s, when most of us are at our busiest with careers, kids, home upkeep, and financial pressures, and thus with regular workouts backburner'ed until we complete that stretch of our lives? Gen X'ers, you're now in that passage; how are you doing with your wellness?

And, although Boomers are pushing the human body to new outer limits, even they cannot escape the slowing metabolism and muscle atrophy of aging.

But many of them, as a result of those unique Core Values that came from their unique formative years, will continue to push themselves and, by doing so, demonstrate what can and cannot be achieved by the human body.

Americans: Erase Some Obsolete Retirement Tapes Playing In Your Heads

The research is convincing:

- Increasing the retirement age will increase a nation's productivity.

- Working later in life improves health and general well-being.

- The notion of a fixed retirement age is dying.

- Boomers love to be productive, are coveted by employers, and still have much to give.

With Boomers standing center-stage as America rethinks the notion of retirement, American Enterprise

Institute scholar Nicholas Eberstadt and Global Coalition on Aging Executive Director Michael Hodin recommend this:

* A tax credit and other incentives for firms and individuals who invest in training and educating older workers;

* Encouraging what Japan calls "silver entrepreneurs" who want to start new businesses later in life;

* Portable pensions across the life-span, as Americans move through different employers;

* Corporations should change their hiring, training, and retention to capture the eagerness, wisdom, success, and productivity of older workers, as AARP's programs and companies like CVS and BMW are doing;

* Employers should audit their workplaces to identify how the facilities can be age-friendly (for example, softer factory flooring, better lighting, and sound acoustics);

* And finally, we must purge our brains of the inaccurate assumption that retention of older

workers prevents younger workers from getting jobs and advancing. Authors Eberstadt and Hodin say this: "Similar arguments were once made about women entering the workforce, but it is now clear that their contributions have been a tremendous economic boost."

"America's aging population is a great untapped economic resource," they conclude. Especially when that population includes the forever-young Mouseketeers who became, and remain, The Golden Generation In The American Workplace.

And especially when there aren't enough X'ers to replace them.

There is a magnificent opportunity awaiting America's employers if they will understand and embrace this New Normal.

Swinging Singles

Based upon the behavior of the older Silent Generation just before, the housing industry had guessed Boomers would enter adulthood, swiftly marry, have kids, purchase homes, and settle down as they entered adulthood. And so it launched a home-building boom.

Oops.

Young-adult Boomers had little desire for home ownership. They wanted to remain single, work hard, play hard, and visit every corner of magical America and beyond. They wanted to spend their money on experiences, not houses. They wanted the freedom to pack up and move elsewhere and not be burdened by the albatross of a mortgage.

And so apartment construction replaced home building. "Swinging Singles" complexes flourished around the country when Boomers crashed young adulthood in the 1970s. And those rental communities added bars, swimming pools, tennis courts, and *ohmygod* yes, hot tubs. A national magazine planned for Boomer homeowners instead became *Apartment Life.*

Decades later, Boomer stand-up comedian Jeff Foxworthy would describe Boomer starter apartments:

"They all had shag, green-and-gold carpets. In your bedroom you had the mattress on the floor, milk crates for nightstands, stolen road sign on the wall, a blanket for a curtain, out on the balcony it was the rusted-out hibachi grill. In the den you had the *spool*, and next to that, the nine-thousand-dollar stereo. We're going hungry but we've got tunes!"

Well, here we are some forty years later. One in three Boomers is unmarried and, of them, about 3 of 5 live alone. The divorce rate among age-50-plus Americans is at its highest, as empty-nest Boomers— especially females who enjoy financial independence like no previous generation of women at this age— feel they can now dissolve unfulfilling marriages and move on to whatever's next. In the U. S., these are unprecedented numbers at this age and life stage. And according to Bowling Green State University professors I-Fen Lin and Susan Brown, authors of *Unmarried Boomers Confront Old Age: A National Portrait*, only 10% of Boomer singles are widowed. Overwhelmingly, they are divorced or never married.

Unmarried Boomers will generally struggle more than married Boomers with their finances and their physical health. Some will be lonely. Others will be alone but not lonely. Many are single by choice and will enjoy the freedom.

And this communal generation is already adjusting to its singleness:

Boomers are signing formal contracts with close friends or even not-so-close friends, pledging to care

for each other when they're ill and to oversee the settlement of their estates when they die.

The generation that popularized cohabitation is
doing it again and living with friends and compan-
ions; today, two Boomer women or men living together does not necessarily mean gay.

And some are selling their suburban houses and
moving in to residential communities of like-minded
unmarried Boomers. And savvy real-estate develop-
ers are beginning to create new residential communities with this Boomer lifestyle in mind.

They're dating. And so online dating services for
age-50-plus are emerging. In their 80s and 90s and
beyond, Boomers will have *boyfriends* and *girlfriends*.

This unique Boomers' singles life will create new
marketplace opportunities in such industries as travel,
dining, recreation, residential living, and many others.

Granny As Nanny

Also in their future, Boomers and Silents will continue to change grandparenthood.

They are heavily involved in the PRIMARY care of their grandkids.

And they seem to like the idea of helping to re-build the family unit that took such a beating when they were parents in the '70's, '80's, and '90s. Some are moving in with their adult kids to help them with their parenting. This change is creating more house-holds with MULTIPLE adult generations. It's also creating new opportunities for the travel industry: multigenerational vacations, sometimes with eight, twelve, or twenty family members renting large man-sions instead of staying in hotels.

As you'll read in the Gen X chapters, Americans are very focused these days on re-strengthening the no-tion of "family". This bodes well for today's toddlers.

Boomers And Religion: Searching For A Spiritual Home

In research studies, Boomers say they possess a strong faith and spirituality, but they have not embraced tra-ditional religions in the same percentages as older generations. They continue to search for a spiritual "home".

A number of them right now are sampling different religions, attending services in different houses of worship from one week to the next.

And because Gen X'ers and Millennials feel pretty much the same way, the traditional religions of this country are struggling to maintain their membership levels.

This challenge is a generational challenge. And we're finding that training religious leaders in Generational Faith-Based Strategy can often help them find the best possible generational solution.

Controlling Their Lives, Controlling Their Deaths

It's very simple: Boomers have always famously insisted upon living life their way. It is quite likely they will also demand to die on their own terms.

When they become infirm or worse, when they feel they are becoming an irreversible burden to family or friends or society, when their lives are moving towards a wretched existence of physical incapacity or mental dementia, when a nursing home is looking like the only option, Boomers will want to end their lives

(1) nonviolently, (2) painlessly, and (3) without feeling moral guilt.

They will not want to be indefinitely warehoused in a nursing home merely because modern medicine now knows how to keep their hearts beating.

Many Boomers have witnessed all of this in the deaths of their own parents and grandparents. They've seen the emotional and physical suffering. And most importantly, they know many of their elders wished they could have ended their lives, rather than being forced by society to endure the torment. They saw their parents lie in bed, sad and suffering and trapped: powerless to do anything about it.

Boomers do not exactly do well with the notion of "powerless".

And so over the next few decades, look for rising pressure from this generation on lawmakers, physicians, and the pharmaceutical industry to develop and legalize a pill or cocktail, accessible without hassle, that will enable all of us to simply go to sleep and pass peacefully *whenever we damn well decide,* instead of being forced by law and society to wrap our lips around a gun barrel and blow our brains out.

Boomers In Congress

The buck stops here. Thus far in the 2010s, Boomers represent an overwhelming generational majority in the U. S. Congress, which has become, by most measurements, a mess.

535 popularly elected people. 435 in the House of Representatives, 100 in the Senate. And most American citizens are disgusted with, and ashamed of, the performance of these elected officials and their uncompromising combativeness. The public's approval rating of Congress is shamefully low.

What the hell happened? The Boomers happened.

Yes, the nation itself is especially divided by unique times. With major issues like gay marriage, immigration, and the assault on our nation by so-called Islamic terrorists, it's understandable that Americans and their elected officials would have especially different, and passionate, opinions as to how each issue should be handled.

But beyond that, there is also this:

As they were entering adulthood a half-century ago, young Boomers achieved remarkable and positive change in America by refusing to back down, refusing to slow down, *refusing to compromise.*

Civil rights. Women's rights. The environment. The Vietnam War.

When older generations who held the power and wealth pushed back at these "kids" on these issues, Boomers refused to slow down or bend. Possessing no financial clout and holding no positions of power, their unyielding commitment was all they had.

And lo and behold, it worked.

And so their generation molded powerful and permanent Core Values that, all these years later, do not work very effectively in a legislative body that relies heavily upon compromise and meeting the other side in the middle.

In the mid-2000s, a number of congressmen and congresswomen announced they would not seek re-election, saying they were sick of the contentiousness and extremism. Almost all of them are members of the Silent Generation, which is famously good at collaboration and compromise. Silents remember earlier years on Capitol Hill, when adversaries went to lunch, talked quietly with each other, and worked things out.

Today? Gone. And a big part of the explanation is generational.

Now, here's the upside of that Boomer aggressiveness, and it explains why America SHOULD be at the front door of a magnificent couple of decades:

The Boomer Leadership Era

In the late 1990s, a local public-television show in Cincinnati inadvertently showcased the differences in leadership values between Silent and Boomer corporate executives.

In front of a "live" theater audience of several-hundred people, two powerful and locally based executives sat onstage, discussing modern-day business and then answering audience questions: Fifth Third Bank's Silent CEO George Schaefer, Junior; and, Procter & Gamble's Boomer CEO A. G. Lafley.

Towards the end of the show, a Gen X male audience member asked them, "What do the two of you look for when hiring Gen X'ers?"

Schaefer gave the true-to-form *Silent* answer: "I'm looking for capitalists."

Lafley gave the true-to-form *Boomer* answer: "I'm looking for integrity."

Many Americans assume we've *been* a Boomer-led nation for some time now.

We have not.

In the mid-2000s, while reading an *Ad Age* magazine article that was not generational in nature, I nonetheless connected some dots and came upon the notion of "the generational leadership of America"; that is, what happens to America while one generation is dominating the executive suites and leading business and government and education and religion according to their generational Core Values?

I found no information on this application of generational study. So I took it on myself, starting with zero and taking several years to create a credible body of knowledge. To test it, I gave a 2010 keynote speech to about sixty members of the Columbus Metropolitan Club, an organization of leaders, influencers, and intellectuals in Ohio's capital city. Thankfully, it worked. Their response was quite positive.

Then I got my ultimate test: a keynote speech in Washington, D. C. to an audience of 1,300, the ultimate Power Crowd: the annual conference of NACD, the National Association of Corporate Directors, whose members sit on the Boards of Directors of American companies. Despite my warning early in the speech that "some of this content is likely to be rather sensitive to some of you", the message nonetheless resonated with them, according to their written evaluations afterwards. And soon afterwards, NACD local chapters in Chicago, Dallas, Atlanta, New Jersey, Southern California, Washington, D. C., and Fort Worth booked me to repeat the same speech at their local meetings.

And one of the audience members in Washington was the former Chairman of the Joint Chiefs of Staff, General Hugh Shelton, who founded the Shelton Leadership Center on the campus of his alma mater, North Carolina State University. General Shelton is a two-tour Green Beret, heavily decorated for his bravery in the Vietnam War. The center that bears his name focuses upon values-led leadership training.

And I received an email from the Institute, requesting the same speech at its 2015 Leadership Forum, which I gave to an audience of 550 past, present, and future leaders.

For what it's worth, the content of that speech is the most important generational message I will have ever presented anytime, anywhere, to any audience. By far.

Which is why I have included the entire script of it near the end of this book.

In a nutshell:

The Generational Disruption Of Leadership

Each generation takes its turn at the top of America. Its members enter adulthood in their late teens and early twenties and begin their career passages at the bottom: entry level. The brightest and luckiest of them methodically advance as they pass through their twenties, thirties, and forties. Then, they steadily replace the retiring older generation of leaders. And for about two decades, *their one generation overwhelmingly dominates the decision-making positions throughout the nation.*

And while they enjoy such dominance, they install their generation's unique Core Values throughout their organizations and all of American life; and when this happens, America turns in a new direction that is notably different from the path of the prior generation's leadership era, which was guided by different Core Values.

And we now understand this: a generation's leadership era roughly begins when its oldest members reach retirement age—traditionally around 65—and the rest of the generation trails downward in age through its early 60s, 50s, and late 40s. Over several years, that generation's leaders will usually fill their organizations' other executive and top-management positions with colleagues who embrace their own basic Core Values. And after a few years at the top, when their generation has finally and completely disentangled from the two decades of leadership by the prior generation, their new Core Values finally take hold and send America on its new path.

In my first career, as a sportscaster, I announced college football and basketball games on radio and then TV. I interviewed Ohio State Buckeyes' football coach Earle Bruce, who said this:

"If you want to judge a college football coach fairly, then wait until his fifth year on the job because, until that time, the seniors on his team were recruited by the previous coach. But in his fifth year, the new coach will be putting seniors on the field he personally recruited during their senior year of high school."

Same basic idea with generational leadership. It takes a few years for the new generation to gain full control of its leadership era.

In 2011, the oldest Boomers turned 65. Their leadership era began. But years from now when we look back, it will probably have been in the 2020s when we noticed a substantive pivot in the direction of America. And the Boomer leadership era will end around 2030, when Gen X'ers will begin their era.

And thanks to the women's movement and civil rights movement of a few decades ago, Boomers become the first American generation to take its turn at the top with significant numbers of females and minorities adding their unique sensibilities and skills to leadership and to the governance of that leadership as they sit on boards of directors.

The entire American history of leadership being a fraternity of white men comes to an end with the retirement of the Silents. With the Boomer era, American leadership, for the first time, becomes multi-gender and multi-ethnic.

And here is just a partial list of what we should expect from the influence of female leaders in the c-suites and boardrooms:

1. along with Boomer men, a more clench-fisted commitment to ethics;

2. decision-making that includes emotional considerations, not just business intelligence;

3. long-term thinking, not just the current short-sighted quarter-by-quarter mindset;

4. risk-taking that will also be weighed by social benefit, not just monetary profit;

5. less complacency towards the decisions of the corporation's executive team and a greater willingness by women to challenge and to ask "Why are we doing it this way?", which recent Boards of

Directors so frequently failed to ask, with the epidemic executive corruption being the outcome;

6. a heightened people orientation towards employees and customers and the community, instead of a narrow orientation only towards profit;

7. on corporate boards and among investors, a push for social responsibility, not just shareholder value;

8. and obviously, a better knowledge than white-men-only executive teams and board members of how to serve female and minority customers and clients and employees.

I suggest to my clients and audiences that they store in the backs of their minds the year 2020, by which time we should *begin* to see the effects of Boomer Nation. At that time, let's all look around at our nation and ask ourselves if American leadership, and hence America, is better or worse than it was in the 1990s and 2000s.

Message To Boomers

Boomers, you now enjoy a generational majority atop America. In corporate America's executive suites and board rooms and investment firms. In government's elected offices, including the U. S. Congress. At the top of higher education. And religion. Just about everywhere.

It's your turn to lead. Your one and only turn. And it will end before you want it to.

And when it does end, your generation will then become something it has never been: unimportant and irrelevant.

So this is the final important life-chapter your generation will ever write.

And here's what generational study tells us:

History called the G.I. Generation to greatness twice: in World War II; and then, in building a nation afterwards. And most agree the G.I.s delivered greatness.

As it turns out, history never called the Silent Generation to greatness. The "times" simply didn't demand it.

But Boomers, history will have called your generation to greatness twice in your lives.

The first time occurred in your young adulthood. And your generation delivered greatness by propelling forward civil rights, women's rights, the environmental movement, and yes, by forcing your government to re-examine its decision-making when it comes to the matter of war.

You achieved all of this despite holding no positions of power, possessing no financial clout, and facing a thick granite wall of resistance from the older people who did have the power and the money.

Well now today, Boomers, for one brief shining moment, you have it all.

You have it ALL.

And because you are inheriting a leadership and governance culture that the overwhelming majority of Americans believe is the moral equivalent and compassionate equivalent of a Toxic Waste Dump, your generation is being called to greatness a second time.

Without exaggeration, history is asking you to save the nation that has given you such limitless opportunity but is now quite ill.

And my god, isn't this the precise moment that your passionate, idealistic generation has been pointing towards its entire life? The chance to do America your unique way, according to your highest principles and boldest vision?

So...

What are you going to do?

The unique times and teachings of your formative years, *beyond your control,* molded in you virtually every key value and quality needed for truly *great* leadership. The stars and heavens were perfectly aligned for it, as they were for the G.I. Generation, and as they were NOT aligned for Silents and X'ers.

Those times and teachings cemented in you Boomers a special boldness of vision, selflessness, compassion for the little guy, team play, idealism, ethics, a willingness to lead, a courage to tackle the difficult task because *it's the right thing to do,* a willingness to make the tough decisions and be held accountable for them, a passion to dream the biggest dreams, a remarkable sense of empowerment and engagement, and the confidence that you will make a big positive difference in life on Earth.

And nothing less than the future of America—and almost surely the *fate* of America—rest upon your generation's answer to one question. It goes like this:

You once had your idealism: your demand upon yourself and your world to always pursue the absolute best and not settle for simply *good enough.*

Do you still?

You once stood up for the little guy and the less fortunate, and you believed in bettering life for the masses, not just for the privileged few. Well, now that your generation's leaders *are* the privileged few...

Do you still?

You once believed in the power of we-the-people, not just the aristocracy. Now that your generation's leaders are the aristocracy...

Do you still?

You once were fearless.

Are you still?

You once were ethical.

Are you still?

And about your belief back then that America is the one nation on Earth with the best chance to *get everything* right...

Were you wrong? Or, is it still?

Or:

In order to advance your careers while working all these years for older-generation bosses, have you surrendered or compromised or changed your own values in favor of pragmatism: going along to get along in a workplace culture dictated by a different generation's Core Values?

More bluntly, have you sold out? Now that the power and the cash are rolling in, are you in it for "me" instead of "we"?

Have you been seduced by the trappings?

Remember what your Boomer sister and 2002 *TIME* magazine co-person of the year Colleen Rowley said?

"The country is starved for integrity."

Americans think far too many of their nation's leaders, corporate and government, are one big pile of unethical and ruthless shit. They're disheartened. *The bad guys are winning.*

They have witnessed and endured the slaughter—by those corporate and government leaders—of The Great American Middle Class, from which so many of you Boomers emerged all those years ago.

They feel stripped of the wonderful empowerment and control over their lives that the masses enjoyed in the decades after World War II.

The epidemic executive corruption and greed and callous indifference to American workers that marked the Silent Leadership Era make most Americans sick to their stomachs.

So Boomers, you're up.

And in a few years, when you've fully disentangled from two decades of Silent-led culture, your generation's Core Values will fully emerge and determine the path and trajectory of America.

And only then will all Americans learn for certain your generation's answer to the final important question your generation will ever answer; the one question upon which the future and fate of this nation rest.

And the question, Boomers, is this:

How much of you is left?

America Is In Position For A Great Run: The Generational Alignment Is Right

In the 2010s and 2020s, America's generations are lined up as they were during the magnificent post-World War II decades:

1. Back then, the generation that was in charge and leading the country was meant to lead. The G.I.s.

2. The just-younger generation, whose task was to execute their bosses' ideas, was excellent at execution. The Silents.

3. And the young-adult generation, whose job was to work hard and deliver new ideas and passion and not let their bosses get too set in their ways, was doing just that. The Boomers.

But then in the 1990s and 2000s, it all went sideways:

1. Silents were leading and weren't prepared to lead.

2. Boomers were following and weren't prepared to follow.

3. Gen X was in young adulthood and, after that difficult childhood, was bringing negative baggage to its early career years.

But from now until around 2030 or so:

1. Boomers are leading and have no excuse for anything but greatness.

2. Gen X is delivering new ideas, which is its strength.

3. Millennials are bringing positive spirit, eagerness, and ideas.

If American business, government, education, religion, and our families at home understand how generational dynamics guide the direction of our country...

and if each generation understands its unique strengths and shortcomings, and those of the other generations, too...

then this current alignment of generations is perfect for a wonderful run of idea generation, productivity, ethical and compassionate behavior, and a high quality of life for the American masses.

As Boomers now lead the nation, three new buzzwords have emerged and are championing this return to executive responsibility:

1. Conscious Capitalism: *I am conscious of the effects of my decisions upon society and will decide in favor of the greater good.*

2. Compassionate Capitalism: *I will run my organization with compassion for others as my top priority; our employees are our greatest asset.*

3. Servant Leadership: this concept has been around a long time, but Robert K. Greenleaf is credited for popularizing it in modern times in an essay that he first published in 1970, entitled "The Servant As Leader", in which he writes:

"The servant-leader is servant first… It begins with the natural feeling that one wants to serve, to serve first. Then conscious choice brings one to aspire to lead. That person is sharply different from one who is leader first, perhaps because of the need to assuage an unusual power drive or to acquire material possessions…The leader-first and the servant-first are two extreme types. Between them there are shadings and blends that are part of the infinite variety of human nature."

Boomer leaders can, should, and in many cases will benefit from the mainstreaming of these three concepts. But Gen X'ers, with more time to learn and assimilate them before their generation takes its turn at the top, should *really* enhance their leadership.

"Your Beauty Will Be Lost With Your Peace Of Mind" Johnny Mathis

If you're wondering where this chapter's subtitle comes from, and what the heck it means, here it is:

Legendary singer Johnny Mathis recorded a 1967 song entitled "Misty Roses". I didn't hear it until decades later, and when I did, one line of the lyrics instantly rammed me as quintessential Boomer.

Boomers, you have spent your entire lives willing to be uncomfortable.

In your teen years and early adulthood years, you forced yourselves to look in the mirror and re-think the values your elders had handed down to you regarding race, women, sex, war, religion, the environment, marriage, parenting, and others; values that you decided to change, given the unique times of your youth.

It was a gut-twisting process, wasn't it? It would have been so much easier to look the other way—on racism, sexism, the Vietnam War, the trashing of the environment—and accept what you had been taught just to feel *comfortable.* Instead, you chose to take the path less traveled.

So you've never permitted yourself to get comfortable, kick back, and adopt the passive attitude that *I know it's wrong to feel this way but that's just the way I am, and I'm not going to change."*

Here's the point:

Boomers, you can get a good night's sleep when you die.

Until then, America and the world need your generation to *continue* to toss and turn and fret, and continue to push yourself beyond your comfort zone, and continue to lead your country to *what's right*, even when it means wrenching discomfort for you.

The country is starved for integrity.

So, don't get comfortable, Boomers.

Your generation's beauty will be lost with your peace of mind.

Three More Boomer Chapters

More to come: one chapter about Boomers as employees in the workplace; and one chapter about them as consumers in the marketplace.

And then, the final chapter of this book: the script of one specific speech that I present around the country, which puts Boomers front-and-center and calls them to action.

GEN X

58,541,842 Armies Of One

. . .

CHAPTER 9

Gen X

America's Least-Understood Generation

• • •

Birth Years:	**1965 Through 1981**
How Many Born:	**58,541,842**
Formative Years:	**1970s To Early 2000s**
Their Parents:	**Younger Silents, Boomers**

IN PALM SPRINGS, I WAS presenting a training seminar in Generational Workforce Diversity and Leadership Strategy at the annual conference of the California Professional Firefighters. The audience was comprised of 150 lean, clean-cut, well-built guys and one tall, gorgeous, blond Gen X female who, much to my dismay, chose to sit in the very last row of seats in the hotel banquet room.

But after the session, she walked up to me and asked, "Could you see me when you were presenting the story of my generation?"

I told her, "I saw you when you first walked in because, in a room of buzz-cut guys, you stood out with your long blond hair and your very good looks. But when we darkened the lights so all of you could clearly see the slides on the projection screen, no, I couldn't see you."

And with that, it came pouring out of her:

"When you walked us through the childhood years of Gen X, it all came back: my parents' divorce; the confusion in my mind; the hurt and anger and sense of betrayal. I started to cry. And I was embarrassed, being surrounded by all of these macho firefighters, and at a business seminar, no less. So I subtly pushed my chair back from the table so the guys on either side of me couldn't see me crying, and I stared straight ahead until I regained control. Finally, I dared to look slowly to my left and right to see if anyone had noticed me crying, and I saw two Gen X guys crying, too."

Similar story from a 40-something X'er guy in an audience in Toronto. "I thought I was over it, but it all came back and I started choking up."

And from a Gen X female newspaper reporter in Ohio, after a training session in Generational Newspaper Strategy: "My parents divorced when I was young and (she swallowed, paused, and steeled herself as the tears arrived) and it never goes away, does it? Thank you for letting others know what it was like for so many of our generation."

Generation X.

Misunderstood. Overlooked. Under-appreciated. Sensitive. Smart.

Prepare yourself for one of American history's most fascinating roller coaster rides: the story, thus far, of Generation X.

A roller coaster ride of extreme ups and extreme downs.

And if you're wondering, the answer is "no". "Gen X" is not meant as a derogatory label. It was popularized and cemented for all time in 1991 when Bill Strauss and Neil Howe published the first important book (and to my knowledge, the first book, *period*) on generational dynamics, entitled *Generations: The History of America's Future.*

And on that previously mentioned PBS live-audience TV talk show I hosted, with Strauss and Howe and four others as my onstage guests, Strauss explained the story behind the name:

In the late 1980s and early '90s when he and Howe were writing their book, several events brought the name to the front: Canadian Douglas Coupland authored a 1991 fictional book entitled *Generation X*; punk rocker Billy Idol fronted a band called *Generation X*; some Britons born in the early 1960s and who didn't feel like British Boomers were calling themselves Generation X; and, the Hollywood movie *Malcolm X* was released and was heavily merchandised, with T-shirts and ball caps sporting the letter "X". All of these disparate events coalesced, and Strauss and Howe formalized the name in their seminal book.

And the premise behind the name is this:

The members of this generation were coming of age so individualistic in their thinking, and so diverse in their ethnicities and lifestyles, that they tended to resist any *group* label and resented attempts—especially by marketers and advertisers—to pigeonhole their 59 million members into a single cohort.

That was then.

Today, with generational study now firmly in place, X'ers understand their 58+ million members do possess a shared center, a common core. They recognize that they embrace similar Core Values that arose from the unique times and teachings of their formative years.

They acknowledge they ARE a generation.

And they are an "island" generation, way *out there* and like no other generation because of a childhood passage quite unlike that of any other generation before or since.

Boomers and Millennials have a lot in common. Silents and G.I.s do, too. But X'ers are pretty much on their own.

After reading about the joyous childhood passage of the Boomers, you'll find this chapter is now going to get a bit dark. But the Gen X story *will* have a happier ending.

Their Formative Years And Core Values

Born from 1965 through '81. And the all-important formative years for Gen X are the 1970s, '80s, '90s, and very early 2000s.

Fewer than 59 million X'ers born, according to the U. S. Census Bureau. Like the Silents, this is a small generation. For every 8 Boomers born in this country, there are only 6 X'ers. And in 2015, Millennials also surpassed them in size, and in two fewer birth years. So Gen X is a population trough. And this will always benefit them in their careers: less competition for the better jobs and promotions.

Why so small? Because their birth years occur:

1. just as the revolutionary birth control pill is gaining widespread use in America, giving females their first reliable opportunity to delay or completely forgo child-bearing;

2. just as abortion is legalized in 1973, the ninth of this generation's seventeen birth years; according to the Centers For Disease Control And Prevention, abortion will cost this generation about 9,000,000 members during its final eight birth years, roughly 1.1 million U. S. abortions per year;

3. just as the feminist movement is opening career doors for women on a widespread basis, and so a number of them postpone motherhood or choose to bypass it entirely;

4. and, Gen X will have only 17 birth years; Silents and Boomers each had 19, the G.I.s had 26, and Millennials are still coming.

"You Called Us Slackers. You Dismissed Us..."

No American generation will grow up more isolated from, and misunderstood by, older generations than Gen X.

A *TIME* magazine cover story from 1997, when X'ers are aged 16 to 32, says it all, as far as many X'ers are concerned:

"You called us slackers. You dismissed us as Generation X. Well, move over. We're not what you thought."

Now, here comes that roller coaster ride:

Good news: as a generation, X'er children experience the most materially comfortable childhood to that point in American history. Thanks to the women's movement, their parents are the first to enjoy widespread dual-*career* household incomes, not just dual-*job* incomes. And thanks to the civil rights movement, minority households, especially American blacks, also see their incomes begin to climb. So, more households enjoy more income.

Bad news: but X'ers also experience the most emotionally difficult childhood in American history, as

(1) the divorce rate among their parents skyrockets, (2) those time-starved dual-career parents become absentee parents, and (3) many of their nation's leaders regularly lie and cheat and fail to deliver on their promises to them.

"All About Survival"

As a guest on my first public-television Special about the generations, author Neil Howe said this: "Generation X has been all about survival."

Survival, because their formative years are influenced by four dramatic changes up there in the adult world:

Change # 1—widespread divorce: according to U. S. Census Bureau data, in 1971 as the oldest X'ers turn six, the nation's divorce rate is suddenly 165% higher than it had been only ten years earlier in 1961. And the divorce rate will climb through the 1970s, peak around 1980 and level off, but still at a very high plateau. According to a study released in *American Demographics* magazine in the mid '90s, a staggering 40% of X'er kids come of age in divorced or single-parent households.

I presented generational training workshops to the management, marketing, and human resource teams of Zondervan, then the world's largest publisher of Bibles and Christian books and gifts. One of its employees, a Gen X woman named Jen Abbas, had just co-authored the book *Generation EX: Adult Children of Divorce and the Healing of Our Pain.* Jen mailed a copy to me, signing it with a handwritten note that hints at this generation's strong desire to be understood by older generations: "Chuck, thanks for all you're doing to tell our story."

Here's a passage from Jen's book, as she writes intimately to her fellow X'ers whose formative years were turned upside-down by their parents' divorces:

"Can you identify?

* You're afraid of falling in love but really want to.
* You've turned into a perfectionist.
* You're afraid that even though someone says 'I love you', ultimately that person might leave you.
* For you, trust comes in hard-earned degrees.
* You're not sure where home is, or you aren't so sure you want to accept the home that society has defined for you.
* You wonder if you will ever have your entire family in the same room without fighting or awkward silence.

❀ You have holes in your history.

❀ You aren't sure what a healthy marriage looks like…

"Betrayal. Rejection. Fear. Anger. Abandonment."

And she adds this:

"Society is now beginning to realize what we have known all along: divorce is not simply a bump in the road for the children affected by it."

Well, the one piece of good news here is this: if 40% of X'er kids experience divorced or single-parent households during their youth, it means 60% of them come of age with their nuclear families *intact*. And this is a good time to explain…

How Nationwide Generational Core Values Are Created

Do the math with this 40%-60% thing. It means that in every Gen X classroom of twenty students, 8 of those 20 are coming to school each day from divorced or single-parent households. And the other 12 are coming from traditional, intact households. The 8 sit with the 12: shoulder to shoulder, class after class, cafeteria lunch after cafeteria lunch, social event after social event, month after month and year after year, throughout all of their formative years. And from this constant connection and constant conversation, they *all* become sensitized to the consequences of divorce. And so *all 20* tend to mold similar Core Values and beliefs about such matters as marriage, divorce, family, parenting, and other aspects of life.

Remember: the *classroom period of our lives* is the great incubator of coast-to-coast, generation-wide Core Values. Then, we leave the classroom years and enter adulthood and our career years. Suddenly, we're immersed in coworkers ten years older than us! Forty years older! Yes, we'll evolve and change, but we now begin to lean heavily upon those Core Values we've just formed in the classroom years to guide our decision-making for life.

Now, back to those major changes in American life as X'ers are arriving:

Change # 2—widespread career moms: during Gen X's childhood years, women are getting their first legitimate and widespread career opportunities. They know they carry the weight of history upon their shoulders. And many of them sense that, upstairs in the executive suites, sits an older male boss who is against this "experiment" of women-in-the-workplace and perhaps even hoping it will fail. The women, under intense scrutiny and pressure, *must* work harder and longer and smarter, in the same way minorities who are getting their first chance must also do. *Good* won't be enough; they must be *better than good.*

And with this reality, driven and dual-career parents create our first generation of widespread latchkey kids, the X'ers, who come home after school to an empty house because Mom and Dad are still at work.

And in this era of the time-starved family unit, many X'er kids lose a daily ritual that, all these years later, child experts say is so central to the healthy development of a child: they lose the nightly, sit-down-together, family dinner *at home.*

The good news? The women's movement and civil rights movement are enabling more Gen X children to live in greater material comfort. And these kids are also benefitting by witnessing the emergence of women in the workplace, household, and American economy.

During this time, Latchkey is not so new to American minorities, especially African Americans, whose prior generations of kids had often come home after school to empty houses because so many of their mothers and fathers had to work evening or overnight hours, perhaps in multiple jobs, to survive the low wages and limited opportunities available to them in racist America.

That's the bad news. The good: from those tough times, blacks create tight-knit neighborhoods and communities and extended families, where neighbors and grandparents and friends helped working, absentee moms and dads look after the kids.

The Silent and Boomer parents of X'er kids *want* to get everything right: parenting; marriage; careers. But they are the first spouses and parents of post-feminism America.

Translation? They have no "manual" to guide them through these dramatic changes to career, marriage, and family. So they become the generation of parents who must *write* the manual, through trial-and-error experimentation. And this trial and error is taking place as a generation of children is coming of age and molding Core Values that will guide their decision-making for life. Their parents get some things right and they get some things wrong. They're making more household income than prior generations, but it's costing them time with their children. As more than one parent of Gen X children has said in hindsight:

"We gave them everything but ourselves."

Change # 3—a new era of guilt-ridden and permissive parenting: during this time, there is a new desire by Gen X's parents to be their children's buddies and friends rather than strict disciplinarians. Not only that, but divorced and time-starved parents also become the most guilt-ridden parents ever. They see their children struggling with anger and bewilderment in their broken families, and so they back off on the scolding and correcting. They feel they just cannot pile even more pressure on their stressed and depressed kids by constantly enforcing the million-and-one rights and wrongs that parents should teach and preach. And in their rushed lives, they're in the physical presence of their kids less often and cannot monitor them as closely. From all of this, many of the rules become negotiable, and there is much less of a stern parental message of right-and-wrong than prior generations of kids had absorbed.

And there's also this:

When the parents of X'ers had been children themselves, American neighborhoods were safe and nurturing, and the mass media of radio and TV were clean and wholesome and reinforced the parents' own high values. Pop music did the same, and education also echoed parental values. So now in adulthood, these parents of X'ers feel they can loosen the reins a bit and give their kids more freedom, more input, more choices than they were given.

But as bad luck would have it, this is when American culture swiftly spirals downward: neighborhoods start to become less connected (see "mobile society", coming up next); commercial radio, TV, and music that target children become more exploitive and vulgar and cruel; and education relaxes its classroom discipline.

And so America drifts into an era of permissive parenting just as external forces begin to assault children and demand even stricter parenting!

Who could have seen all of this change coming?

Change # 4—mobile society: America becomes a more mobile society just as X'ers are born. A *TIME* magazine cover in 1976, when the oldest X'ers kids are 11, shouts it out: "Americans On The Move!" Here's what happens:

As America's business model evolves from locally owned companies to national conglomerates, the parents of X'er kids often are forced to advance their careers, or simply keep their jobs, by accepting company promotions or transfers to other cities or states or nations. In addition, it is at this time that America's economy shifts from a manufacturing to a service economy and many job opportunities migrate from the industrial Northeast quadrant of the country to the Sun Belt states. Not only that, but as television—which is only about 15 years old when the oldest X'ers are born—now brings moving images of America and the world right into our living rooms, many parents of X'er children leave their hometowns because they want to experience life elsewhere.

As the leading edge of Gen X reaches age 6, the lyrics of a popular Carole King song from 1971 reflect this increasingly mobile society:

"So far away...
Doesn't anybody stay in one place anymore?
It would be so fine to see your face at my door...
It doesn't help to know that you're so far away..."

And so, a significant number of X'er kids will be uprooted and come of age geographically separated from their relatives, and their neighbors who knew the family's life history, and their educators who had also taught their parents, and from their communities that possessed the special "glue" of hometown roots.

And because of this, their generation also will attend fewer family reunions, fewer weddings, and fewer funerals while living in new cities where they know fewer people.

In this newly mobile society, the cozy, nurturing, and protective cocoon of the American hometown becomes nothing but a final glance out the car's rear window for many X'er children.

A Nation At Risk (1983)

Sure enough, in this era of divorce, latchkey kids, time-starved and absentee parents, permissive parenting, a less clear message of right and wrong, and loss of hometown roots, the classroom performance of Gen X does indeed dip below that of prior generations.

Teen social pathologies increase: crime; substance abuse; pregnancies.

And in 1983, as the older Gen X'ers begin to graduate from high school, the landmark report *A Nation at Risk: The Imperative For Educational Reform* is published.

It is compiled by an elite 18-person committee, authorized by President Ronald Reagan, and guided by Secretary of Education T. H. Bell.

The report describes "a rising tide of mediocrity (emerging from America's schools) that threatens our very future as a nation and as a people" and adds this: "More and more young people emerge from high school ready neither for college nor work."

And with that, X'er bashing begins: scathing news stories, editorial columns, and personal opinions down at the corner tavern about these youngsters being a lost generation, an underachieving generation…

a slacker generation.

But *A Nation at Risk* also points out that the education system is letting X'er students down, describing "disturbing inadequacies in the way the educational process is conducted".

And this will become a recurring theme of Gen X's childhood: the adult world letting them down. This is part of their roller coaster childhood, and they have no control over it.

Extreme ups, extreme downs.

Core Values

From all of these formative-years' times and teachings, X'ers will mold strong and distinctive Core Values and beliefs. As with all other generations, some values are considered positive, some not so positive. They develop:

* Core Values of independence and self-reliance; *I am a Gen X Army of One; I'll take care of me, you take care of you; survival of the fittest;*

* a noteworthy emotional distance from older generations, because they spend less time with them and develop a certain distrust of them;

* a belief, with divorce swirling all around them up there in the adult world, that marriage must be something that is disposable;

* and, an attitude of *okay, looks like it's gonna be us against them; us X'ers against those older people who are constantly badmouthing us.*

Years later, cable television channel VH1 airs a documentary about grunge rock band Nirvana, whose angst-filled lyrics from such songs as 1991's "Smells Like Teen Spirit" become anthems for Generation X:

"With the lights out, it's less dangerous,
Here we are now, entertain us,
I feel stupid and contagious."

Gen X's sense of self-worth is taking a beating during this very difficult time to be a child. (With the next generation, this will change sharply, as American parenting changes and Millennials grow up to overflow with self-esteem.)

And in that TV documentary, a reporter for *Rolling Stone* magazine sums up the childhood of many, but not all, X'ers when he says, "Older people just didn't understand how badly kids were hurting."

Media Isolation

In addition to career moms, divorced parents, workaholic parents, and that uprooting from hometowns, Gen X's sense of distance from older people is also the result of another phenomenon—a major pivot in American life—occurring for the first time in history. And it just happens to be occurring during their generation's formative years: media isolation.

In the 1970s and '80s, in cities nationwide, the number of local radio stations suddenly increases, as FM radio surges. Lots of choices on the radio.

The good news for Gen X: they are America's first generation of kids to have their very own radio stations that are programming to them only, advertising to them only, disc jockeys talking to them only; *Hey, this radio station is just for us!* They don't have to share one or two AM radio stations with their parents and grandparents, as prior generations had done in childhood.

More good news: beginning in the 1980s, the same thing occurs with television as cable TV arrives, and X'ers—mostly the younger or "Second-Wave" X'ers—become the first children to have their very own TV channels that program and advertise only to them. *Hey, this TV channel is just for us!*

And because television can now offer kid-customized programming, it becomes an important companion to Gen X kids, with shows like *Sesame Street, The Brady Bunch,* a new burst of African-American programming, and many others.

More good news: as their parents now enjoy greater career opportunities, thanks to the women's and civil rights movements, many American households, for the first time, can afford multiple TV sets. So a good number of X'er kids come of age watching their favorite shows on TV set # 2 in room # 2, while Mom and Dad watch different shows on TV set # 1 in room # 1.

By contrast, many Boomers will never forget their own childhood suffering (not really) when their beloved Grandma and Grandpa, owning just one TV set that offered only three channels, occasionally babysat them on a Saturday. The visit was going great until the dreaded evening hour when Grandma and Grandpa insist they all sit down together and watch...

The Lawrence Welk Show.

Noooooooooooooooooooooooooooooooooooo!!!

Losing *The Little Moments*

But here comes that Gen X roller coaster ride again. There is also an insidious downside to Gen X's experience with mass media: for their generation, radio listening and TV viewing become a more *solitary* experience or a peer-only experience, an *isolating* experience, that separates them from older people because they no longer share the same radio and TV shows.

So X'er kids miss the kind of multigenerational TV-viewing experience of February 9, 1964, February 16, 1964, and February 23, 1964.

The importance of these three consecutive Sunday nights is not just that every Boomer kid who is old enough to walk is flopped on the living room floor and watching the Beatles' three historic appearances on *The Ed Sullivan Show*. No, the importance is that Mom and Dad, sitting behind the kids in the big easy chairs, are also watching. And a few miles away, Grandma and Grandpa are also watching the Beatles because, in a three-channel TV universe, television programming must be multigenerational in its appeal. And Grandma and Grandpa know that the act that follows the Beatles will be targeting *them*.

And the next day, and next week, and next family reunion, Boomer kids and their parents and grandparents have a television experience to share and discuss. And by doing so, Boomer kids learn *another inch of information* about their elders, and their elders learn another inch about Boomer kids, and their generations draw another inch closer.

X'er kids, by having their own radio and TV channels, lose thousands and thousands of these precious and invaluable Little Moments, these "inches" of connection to their elders. And so, beyond their control, they come of age more distanced from elders and do not assimilate all of the important and wonderful nuggets of knowledge that prior generations of kids had soaked up by sharing millions of these moments with their elders.

Radio and television had always brought younger and older people together and strengthened intergenerational understanding and bonding. But suddenly, in the '70s and '80s as Gen X kids grow up, these two mass media, for the first time ever, are *pushing the generations apart.*

A female Gen X audience member at one of our Los Angeles seminars shared this memory:

"I can remember *only one time* during the first 17 years of my life when our entire family sat down together and shared a significant moment on television. It was the 1984 summer Olympics."

The lifelong impact on Gen X of the loss of so many Little Moments with their elders during their formative years is incalculable.

And a vital question all these decades later is this: as parents, are X'ers sharing lots and lots of Little Moments with their own children, or not?

Commercial Radio, Television, And Music: Their Race To The Bottom

In addition to media *isolation,* X'ers also are the first generation of kids who will come of age absorbing an all-out bombardment of vulgarity, violence, celebrity bashing, and sexual titillation by commercial radio and television and the music industry, which comes from the desperation by the executives and creative people who lead those media.

In the '70s and '80s, as the number of radio stations and TV channels sharply increases in America, competition among them for advertising dollars becomes brutal. And not all stations can win the ratings-race competition. Some shows are simply not as good as others.

And so the people producing and performing on the shows that are losing the "ratings war" must find ways to turn the heads of radio listeners or TV viewers to *their* shows. They lack the talent of the winning shows, so they resort to their only option:

We will SHOCK people into listening to our radio show. We will SHOCK people into watching our TV show. How do we shock people? Not by being clean and nice. No. Clean and nice does not turn heads and get ratings. Instead, we will be more cruel than the winning shows, we will be more vulgar, we will be more sexually graphic, we will be more violent. In other words...

We will race to the bottom.

When this media transformation begins, I experience it from the inside. I'm working in major-market radio when it begins in that medium, and I move to television when, a few years later, *that* medium becomes desperate. At the time, I'm a sports play-by-play announcer for college football and basketball, so I'm not involved in shock radio and shock television, but I witness it—and the management strategy behind it—firsthand.

And so shock radio enters American life, begun by desperate and under-talented disc jockeys and approved by station managers who conveniently look the other way because *it's working*: people ARE tuning in; it's getting ratings; and better ratings mean *bigger revenues!*

Instead of bringing out the best instincts in American radio listeners, let's increase our station's ratings and revenues by bringing out their worst instincts with Shock Radio.

Same thing with television. Suddenly, those dozens of cable channels need enough shows to air 24/7, but there is not enough first-class creative talent to go around, and not every show can survive the ratings battle. The less-talented executives, show producers, writers, and actors cannot compete with the more-talented shows. Solution? Race to the bottom.

Let's shock viewers into watching our show by giving them more violence, vulgarity, cruelty, and sex scenes than they've ever seen. Instead of bringing out the best instincts in American TV viewers, let's get ratings and money-money-money by bringing out their worst instincts with Shock Television.

And it works! Howard Stern and other radio shock jocks earn fortunes. Ditto, shock television. For years, the legendary *Phil Donahue* daytime talk show had brought out viewers' best instincts. But now, shows hosted by Geraldo Rivera and Jerry Springer and Maury Povich and many others get big daytime ratings by bringing out viewers' worst instincts. So, too, does MTV, with its relentless bombardment of Gen X children, and then Millennial kids, with sexually titillating images, coarse language, cruelty, and so-called "reality" shows.

And there's more. It is during this time that these desperate commercial media executives begin *rewarding the bad guys:*

* Radio gives G. Gordon Liddy, the mastermind of the Watergate break-in, his own nationally syndicated show. Crime pays!

* Women who have sexual affairs with married politicians or religious leaders, but get caught, become media darlings and cash in. Home-wrecking pays!

* Have you done something really, really bad? Our publishing company will give you a book deal. Scandal pays!

Executives figure that, in the very crowded media landscape, a well-known "name", even if well-known for all the wrong reasons, can "cut through the clutter" and deliver increased listenership, viewership, or readership and, thus, increased *revenues.*

And this race to the bottom—this sweeping media abandonment of integrity and moral obligation—is occurring as one generation of American children is passing through its formative years, looking around at America and planet Earth for the first time, assuming *this is just the way it is,* and molding Core Values that will guide their decision-making for life.

X'ers have never known any other media environment. To them, and beyond their control, vulgarity and violence and sex and celebrity-bashing and bad-guys-get-rewarded ARE American commercial media.

Trivialized And Marginalized

The net effect of all this? Youth-targeted media *trivialize* X'er kids by overwhelming them with the relentless message that fame and wealth and sex are important in life, and our nation's leaders are meant to be bashed and mocked by radio and TV.

This trivialization delivers the inevitable consequence: in large part because of the media messages to them in childhood, X'ers will enter adulthood *marginalized* to the outer edges of American life. And they will feel less influential upon, and less critical to, the elements of life that *are* important.

The outcome? Instead of reading the main section of the daily newspaper and the weekly news magazines, as most other generations begin to do in early adulthood, X'ers make successes of celebrity-focused publications like *People* and *Us Weekly*, and TV shows like *Entertainment Tonight* and *Access Hollywood*, which dish the celebrity gossip. And they'll watch the TV shows that mock "the system" instead of the shows that earnestly try to explain and improve it.

All of this comes from their formative years' experiences with the commercial media, over which they have virtually no control.

They were kids.

The night before I gave a training seminar in Salt Lake City in Generational Marketing Strategy, I was taken to dinner by four Gen X women who worked for the trade association that hosted the event. Wonderful, dynamic, intelligent women. At one point during our conversation, I asked them, "If you go to a Gen X party on a Saturday night, what does everybody talk about?" Their unanimous answer, without hesitation: "Celebrities. J-Lo and Ben!" (at the time, the romance between Jennifer Lopez and Ben Affleck was the celebrity topic du jour).

The mass media hammered a message into the brains of X'er kids: *celebrities are very, very important to your lives.*

By contrast, when Millennials arrive, the technology revolution will give them a different message: instead of celebrities-are-important-to-you, the new message is:

YOU are the celebrity, by posting your life story on My Space, and then Facebook, and then Pinterest and Snapchat and the other social media that deliver every detail of your day to the entire world!

The Quarter-Life Crisis

I first heard the Gen X term *quarter-life crisis* in 2004, when *Atlanta Journal-Constitution* reporter Don Fernandez called me for generational insights into a story the paper would headline this way:

"Get-rich-fast ideal, celebrity culture lead twenty-somethings [Gen X] to frustration."
Atlanta Journal-Constitution

The quarter-life crisis refers to the delayed negative influence of MTV and other media on coming-of-age X'ers when they reach adulthood. This crisis is also summed up in a single line of dialogue spoken by actor Brad Pitt in the 1999 Gen X-targeted movie *Fight Club:*

"We've all been raised on television to believe that, one day, we'd all be millionaires and movie gods and rock stars. But we won't. And we're slowly learning that fact. And we're very, very pissed off."

This is a line in a Hollywood movie. But in the Atlanta newspaper story five years after *Fight Club* was released, real-life Gen X comments repeat the same sentiment:

* X'er Cathy Stocker, then thirty-four, calls the relentless TV presentations of the luxuries and excesses of wealthy young adults the "American idolization of career expectations". Stocker runs the website quarterlifecrisis.com.

* X'er Russell Tanton, then twenty-five, told the *Journal-Constitution,* "I don't think anyone was straight with people my age about how low our expectations actually should have been."

* X'er Leslie Wright, then thirty-one, added, "You turn on the TV, and you see *The Apprentice,* the super-fab restaurants, the designer clothes. It's telling you that's what you should aim for. But I know that in twenty years, I won't have done anything better for the world."

❋ As then twenty-eight-year-old X'er Jason Shepherd told the *Journal-Constitution,* "Two years ago, there would not be a day when MTV was not on... Now I can't remember the last time I watched it."

In this news story, the quarter-life crisis is described by X'ers themselves, as is their own wising up to the reality of adulthood and the emergence of a new generational attitude to judge their personal happiness by what they think of themselves, not what society thinks. But it's not easy for the members of any generation to shrug off the media influences, good and bad, of their formative years.

X And Sex

The Silent Generation had come of age before the birth control pill and had to be careful about casual sex because of the fear of pregnancy. Boomers had come of age just after the pill's arrival and before the HIV virus (AIDS) and so frolicked with sex, but still experienced a very large number of unplanned pregnancies.

Ask X'ers what comes to mind when they think of sex during their generation's formative years:

Condoms. Date rape. AIDS. Death.

AIDS, or Acquired Immunodeficiency Syndrome, which is caused primarily by unprotected sexual intercourse and was first diagnosed in Africa decades earlier, arrives in the U. S. in the early 1980s and becomes an avalanche of death, especially within the gay male community. But it's not just unprotected sex that transmits it. Thirteen-year-old Ryan White of Kokomo, Indiana is a hemophiliac who contracts the disease because of a contaminated blood treatment he receives and dies from it at age 18. His story, along with those of basketball star Magic Johnson, tennis star Arthur Ashe, actor Rock Hudson, and others draw attention to the disease. And in 1990, when X'ers are aged 9 to 25, the U. S. Congress approves legislation in Ryan's name to provide funding of medical treatment for AIDS patients who lack the financial resources to pay for it themselves.

And their experience with AIDS becomes part of Gen X's formative years' experience with sex and, thus, influences their Core Values about it.

Speaking of sex: pity the X'er male. The remarkable Internet, and with it email, become popular in the early '90s when X'er males stretch in age from about 12 to 28, their age of puberty and sexual awakening.

But the moment these guys open their first email accounts, they're spammed with constant messages conveying the same alert:

You need to buy our product because your penis is too small! Enlarge, enlarge, enlarge!

Jees!

The Computer Generation!

Very good news for Gen X:

They are the first generation to grow up with another brand new mass medium to go along with radio and TV: the revolutionary and almighty personal computer!

X'ers are developing a positive Core Value: a sense of pride that they are the computer generation. And they are. *TIME* magazine declares them so with a cover story in 1982, when the oldest X'ers are 17, describing them as "A New Breed Of Whiz Kids".

And as we all now know, X'ers' ease with technology will benefit them their entire lives, especially in their careers. Boomers did not have the benefit of classroom instruction on the basics of hardware and software and have had to learn technology in patch-quilt fashion, a piece here and a piece there.

Good timing for Gen X: they hit the computer era perfectly. In fact, they hit it even better than Millennials, as you'll read in the Millennial section of this book. Mils have actually been damaged by tech's dominance in their lives, but X'ers hit the Sweet Spot.

But once again, the Gen X roller coaster childhood of "a down for every up" rears its ugly head:

The new and exciting PC has one drawback during the formative years of all but the very youngest X'ers. The Internet is not yet attached to it. This box is not yet connected to other human beings. And so the computer becomes still one more *isolating* activity, just as radio and TV have now become. As *New York Times* reporter James Fallows reflects in his 2006 story about the PC, "In the beginning, personal computers were for loners."

So, in contrast to prior generations, many X'er children are spending more time in individual, solitary, or peer-only pursuits and less time in the presence of other, and especially older, human beings.

Collectively, all of these formative years' experience will mold Core Values and attitudes—such as self-reliance, independence, individualism, a diminished sense of closeness to elders, and a comfortable embrace of technology—that will guide their generation's minute-by-minute decision-making for life.

Gen X And Wellness

The Gen X roller coaster ride is especially pronounced in the matter of fitness, nutrition, and wellness. Big highs, big lows.

Good news: X'ers are the first generation in history to come of age with fitness as front-page news.

In the '70s, the fitness craze begins, driven by forever-young and now-adult Boomers. Coast to coast, fitness clubs are constructed. By 1981, *TIME* magazine's cover story captures the frenzy of the past decade: "The Fitness Craze: America Shapes Up."

More good news: X'er schoolgirls enjoy greater sports-participation opportunities than older girls had experienced, thanks to the landmark 1972 legislation known as Title IX. More on that in a few pages.

Bad news: but despite the fitness opportunities, a significant number of Gen X kids, especially the boys, come of age sedentary: sitting or standing for hours in front of these new and seductive video games (from *Pong* to *Tetris* to *Grand Theft Auto,* and all the others), whose lure can be overpowering.

Prior generations of kids had raced outdoors after school, after dinner, and on weekends and burned off the calories. But many X'er boys sit down, lie down, or stand in front of a video game and exercise their fingers. And as you'll read, the impact of gaming on child obesity has gotten worse with Millennials.

More bad news: beyond their control, X'ers are also the first generation of school kids to eat lunches in cafeterias that now offer greasy and fatty burgers, fries, pizza, and sugary soft drinks every single day, instead of the nutritionally balanced (but not exactly *yummy*) plate lunches that older generations had eaten in their school years. During this time, schools are eager for new sources of revenue. So they lease cafeteria space and vending-machine space to high-fat, high-sugar outside vendors. And it won't be until years later, for the most part after X'ers have departed the classrooms for adulthood, that schools will recognize the youth-obesity calamity and slowly begin to make the necessary corrections.

And it's not just the schools that are shoveling junk-food into X'er bodies:

Time-starved, dual-career parents of Gen X kids, perceiving themselves to be too busy to cook, succumb more and more to fast food for family meals. And during X'ers' formative years, most fast-food chains are not yet offering many healthy alternatives to their mainstay menu of burgers, fries, and colas.

According to a *New York Times* report: in 1970, near the beginning of Gen X's formative years, Americans spend $6 billion on fast food. By 2000, near the end of their formative years, Americans now spend $110 billion on fast food. *18 times more fast-food expenditures in 2000 than in 1970!*

And especially for X'er boys, the revolution occurring with electronic video games and the personal computer gives America a generation of kids who are Suddenly Sedentary: much more so than prior generations.

Leisure-time physical activity plummets.

Thus, it is with Gen X, and especially its younger half or Second Wave, that the crippling youth-obesity epidemic begins and continues to this day with Millennials.

Good news: many X'er girls, who seize the new sports opportunities at their schools and do not fall under the spell of sedentary gaming, become very fit and remain that way today, thanks to the good habits and Core Values they developed during their youth.

Premature Wealth And Refined Tastes

A significant number of X'ers also comes of age experiencing what sociologists call "premature wealth".

In part because so many households now have more income thanks to the women's and civil rights movements...

and in part because so many of those divorced parents feel guilty...

and in part because many concerned grandparents are witnessing the struggle their X'er grandkids are experiencing and want to do something—*anything*—to help them through this difficult passage...

a number of X'ers go through their formative years being showered with expensive *stuff.*

Designer-label clothing, expensive sneakers, their own TV sets, their own stereos, their own telephones, their own computers, their own unshared bedrooms, travel; and as teens, their own cars, which beginning in the 1980s forces many high schools to find extra acreage in order to create *student* parking lots, which had never before been necessary.

And this part of their formative years creates a generational consumer value of refined and expensive tastes. *X'ers know quality.* And in adulthood today, to the greatest extent that their incomes permit, X'ers demand quality in the goods and services they purchase.

But there's another side to this premature wealth. Here's what a 36-year-old Gen X male emailed to me after attending my speech on Generational Marketplace Strategy in St. Petersburg, Florida:

"If we are the divorce generation, we are also the original 'Deadbeat Dad' generation. My dad still owes my mom money. What is it like to wear a $150 pair of shoes? I have no idea."

Appreciate Their Parents' Hard Work

On another matter, a lot of X'ers also say this:

Yeah, Mom and Dad weren't around as much I would've liked during my childhood, but I do know how hard they worked to provide for me, and I appreciate that hard work.

African-American X'ers: Thrilling, Historic Times

The formative years' experiences of African-American X'ers are closer to those of white X'ers than any prior generation. There are still differences, but the Civil Rights Movement has shrunk the gap, and the positive changes these black kids see are exciting and happening quickly.

Suddenly, African-Americans are no longer one big "monolith", one big homogeneous group with similar jobs, similar incomes, living in similar neighborhoods, leading similar lives. Instead, that monolith is now breaking up:

- A significant number of blacks are landing better and higher-paying jobs than people of color had previously enjoyed;

- Some are moving from the inner cities to the previously all-white suburbs;

* Their nation's government is finally passing legislation to try to erase centuries of suffocating discrimination;

* X'er kids now see blacks in high-visibility jobs, as elected officials, news anchors and reporters, doctors and lawyers and professionals in other fields, and they see them flourishing in sport and entertainment;

* School busing occurs during the school years of Gen X and intermingles young black and white kids more thoroughly than ever before; and although busing isn't always easy, Gen X blacks and whites learn more about each other than any prior generation of American kids. And from this comes a powerful and proud generational Core Value of inclusiveness and anti-racism.

In 1990, while a tiny handful of us were trying to develop the field of generational study and push it into the daylight, I hosted a half-hour television Special for the ABC-affiliated station in Columbus, Ohio. It was my first attempt, and I imagine *the* first attempt, at getting the topic of "generations" on television. It was a talk-show format, with a studio audience of 55 hand-picked high school juniors and seniors who had been born in the mid-1970s and who were not yet formally named Generation X. For the heck of it, we named this teen-oriented TV Special *Sneakers,* not to be confused with the Robert Redford movie of the same name, which came out soon after.

It was not a "live" show. We taped it in advance for later airing. And I simply asked these high school X'ers-to-be questions, nonstop for 2½ hours, and then edited the footage into a 30-minute finished show.

We talked about all-things-their-generation, and at one point deep into the taping, I threw this one out to them:

"Are you racists?"

Their response, a one-word *chorus,* was the most passionate response of the entire taping. "No!"

One white 17-year-old Gen X boy stood and said with pride, "I think we're the first generation to *come of age* as a non-racist generation." 54 other heads, a mixed-ethnicity audience by design, nodded in enthusiastic agreement.

Inclusion. Racial and ethnic color blindness.

Television Plays A Leading Role

And television plays a very important and positive role in this national awakening during the breakthrough decades of the '70s and '80s:

* *The Jeffersons;*
* *Sanford And Son;*
* *Good Times;*
* the Saturday celebration *Soul Train;*
* *A Different World;*
* the epic mini-series *Roots;*
* and, the remarkable *Cosby Show*, which simply knocks one out of the park when it presents an African-American family with parents who are happily married and successful in their careers and whose trials and tribulations with their kids are not ethnic but simply "normal".

Television, for the first time, is portraying and celebrating the rich variety of African-American life.

And it is doing so as one American generation is coming of age and molding Core Values that will affect their decision-making for life.

And in 1986, smack-dab in the middle of Gen X's formative years, Congress approves legislation creating a national holiday in honor of civil rights icon Dr. Martin Luther King, Jr.

Gen X comes along at the right time to absorb racial awakening in America.

Crack

But amid all of this sudden optimism, the formative years of X'er blacks are also scarred by some negatives, among them the horrible impact of crack cocaine, which begins ravaging black (and white) communities in the early '80s and grows into a full-blown monster by the end of the decade.

Rap

With the emergence of gangsta rap in the music industry, many older blacks, who had fought The Glorious Struggle to change the perception and treatment of their people by the non-black American masses and to create better opportunities for their young kids, become disheartened as rap's cruel, vulgar, female-denigrating lyrics and its baggy-clothed fashion represent, in their minds, a major step backwards for the Struggle. But for those many angry and frustrated X'er kids, there is a market for this kind of musical message.

As you'll read in the Millennial chapters, rap finally gets so negative in the 1990s and early 2000s that it misses the mark with many upbeat and optimistic Millennials, and its sales plummet.

Gen X Kids And Activism

During their formative years, social activism in America shifts from longer-lasting protests and "movements" to shorter "events", often coming from the music industry, with the masses contributing their money but otherwise being mostly passive spectators instead of active participants.

Television, now with all of those additional channels, assumes a larger role in such events. And 1985, when X'er kids are aged 4 to 20, is an especially busy year for cause-related events, with:

* *Live Aid,* a satellite-connected one-time colossus in cities in the U. S. and abroad, created by Bob Geldof and Midge Ure to fight famine in Africa and seen "live" in roughly 150 nations by some 1.9 billion people;

* *We Are The World,* a single musical recording by a collection of famous singers and promoted by a television Special covering the taping session,

championed by Silent Harry Belafonte and fundraiser Ken Kragen to fight famine in Africa; 20,000,000 copies are sold;

❧ *Farm Aid,* an annual concert launched that same year by singers Willie Nelson, John Cougar Mellencamp, and Neil Young to help struggling U. S. family-owned farms;

❧ One year later, in 1986, *Hands Across America,* when approximately 6.5 million people DO actively participate and hold hands in a human chain for fifteen minutes along a path across the continental United States; many participants donated ten dollars to reserve their place in line; the proceeds were donated to local charities to fight hunger and homelessness and help those in poverty;

❧ And apart from music, in 1987 Boomer Lynne Cox swims the frigid two-mile waterway of the Bering Strait, with water temperatures at 38 degrees, and helps to ease Cold War tensions just as U. S. President Ronald Reagan and his Soviet Union counterpart Mikhail Gorbachev are developing the friendship that would lead to the momentous fall of communism a few years later.

So youth-targeted activism in America evolves into this new format of live events, which lessens *mass participation* during X'ers' formative years.

X'ers, Military Service, And Community Involvement

From 1940 to 1973, the U. S. military had drafted its troops. Younger G.I.s, Silents, and First-Wave Boomers knew they might be called to mandatory service for their nation.

But the younger Second-Wave Boomers, all of Gen X, and the Millennials thus far, reach traditional military draft age, 18, with no draft in place and, instead, an all-volunteer force.

And with the end of conscription, as the draft had been called, X'ers come of age with a weaker sense of nation and community service. To them, America's wars—Serbia, the Gulf War, and war against terrorism—are not fought by "us" but instead by "the Army": *other people, not me.* And this is a direct consequence of the draft's end.

With this diminished sense of nation and community, especially when coupled with their generation's individualism, X'ers also are not joining local volunteer organizations that have delivered such enormous "good" to their local communities through the decades: Rotary; Kiwanis; Lions; Optimists; Sertoma; Moose; Masons; Elks; National Organization For Women; PTA; American Legion; Veterans of Foreign Wars; and others. These membership organizations are hurting today because Gen X hasn't joined.

Off and on through the decades, U. S. presidents and Congresses have suggested the value of one or two years of mandatory public service by young adults, and most agree such a program would help raise more advanced citizens and benefit the country in numerous ways, but no such mandatory program exists at this time.

Gen X's Unique Gender Dynamic: Females Surging; Males Searching

In adulthood, and this will usually ignite a lively discussion at a Gen X party, X'ers have emerged as an especially confident and assertive female generation, while some of the guys—the evidence is convincing— are still searching for their identity, for their masculinity, for their focus.

Here's what happened:

* During this generation's formative years of the '70s,'80s, and '90s, young Gen X girls come of

age soaking up the full force of the feminist message that is all around them, in the classroom and the living room. They hear it from Mom and Dad and their educators: *You can grow up and do whatever you want to do, be whoever you want to be, go wherever you want to go. There are no limits. You go, girl!* And so, girls' confidence? Up!

» Just as X'ers begin their classroom passage in the early 1970s, the education industry, for the first time, begins to place a special focus on girl-friendly education. Informally labeled The Girl Project and initially designed to eliminate girls' traditional weaknesses in math and science, it achieves much more. Gen X females methodically surpass the classroom performance of the boys in elementary school and later in the nation's college classrooms. The girls' confidence grows even more; the boy's confidence takes a hit.

» In 1972—again, just as the leading edge of Gen X is entering its school years—Congress passes the landmark legislation Title IX that, among other things, mandates that American schools must offer equal sports opportunities for boys and girls. So, many X'er boys go through their school years seeing some of their sports diminished or completely eliminated in order to make budgetary room for the girls, while X'er girls see their athletic opportunities mushroom. Thirty years later, in the early 2000s, the TV show *60 Minutes* produces a segment on Title IX, asking now-adult Gen X'ers to reflect upon the impact of this legislation on their lives. One X'er woman speaks for her entire generation when she says, "We know we're the lucky Title 9 babies."

❧ Also during Gen X's formative years, and this is The Big One in explaining their unique gender dynamic, our nation's suddenly busy divorce courts are overwhelmingly awarding child custody to Mom, not Dad, *not back then*. So millions of X'er boys will try to make that difficult climb to manhood while living in a mom-supervised household and spending time with their divorced Dad only "every other weekend", if that. And if one Gen X boy has just one sister living with Mom and him, then—*jees!* — he is also growing up in a female-*dominated* household!

Title IX: A Difference Maker In American Life

Here's more on the impact of Title IX. In a word... *wow.*

According to the NCAA, which governs intercollegiate sport at our nation's larger universities:

During Gen X's college years, from the late 1980s to the mid 2000s, the number of men's sports offered by the bigger universities decreases by 245 while the number of women's sports increases by 703!

In addition to the classrooms and athletic fields, television also is celebrating this era of the surging female:

* In the 1976 Summer Olympics, young Gen X girls, riveted to their TV screens, see Nadia Comaneci become the first female Olympian ever to score a perfect score of 10 in women's gymnastics;

* From 1976 to 1981, X'er girls watch the three female leads in the popular action-adventure show *Charlie's Angels* every week. When star Farrah Fawcett dies of cancer nearly three decades later (and on the same day Michael Jackson dies, June 25, 2009; a very dark day for X'ers), reporter Caryn Brooks writes an Associated Press newspaper tribute in the form of an open letter to Farrah, whose character on *Angels* was named Jill Munroe:

"Gen-X women are talking about Jill Munroe, the character you played on 'Charlie's Angels' and how you taught us to kick butt. For an entire generation of girls, that was your legacy. And even some of the girls born later who are fans of Sigourney Weaver in the 'Aliens' franchise, Carrie-Anne Moss in 'The Matrix' and even 'Xena'..."

* In 1978, when the oldest Gen X girls are 13, the United States Army disbands its Women's Army Corps and for the first time welcomes females to its regular army;

* In 1983, X'er girls see Sally Ride become the first woman in space;

* And in 1984, Geraldine Ferraro becomes the first-ever female candidate from a major party for Vice President of the United States. *TIME* magazine captures the importance of her selection on its cover: "A Historic Moment."

What a glorious, magical, sky's-the-limit time to be a young Gen X girl coming of age in America! Wow! Wow! Wow!

Fight Club

The understandable frustration by X'er guys with all of this female dominance shows up in the 1999 movie mentioned earlier about the disillusioned Gen X male in early adulthood: *Fight Club.*

In an early scene, two Gen X guys, portrayed by actors Brad Pitt and Edward Norton, are sitting together in a run-down bar in a run-down section of town, reflecting on their disenchantment with adulthood and trying to figure out this frilly, feminine, pro-girl era in which they were raised.

Brad Pitt asks Edward Norton, "Do you know what a duvet is?"

Norton answers matter-of-factly, "Yeah, a duvet is a comforter."

In disgust, Pitt says it for all Gen X men, "What are guys like us doing, *knowing what a duvet is?*"

Sensing a demand for movies that will help Gen X guys find their masculinity, other Hollywood producers return the macho, super-male hero to prominence, after the genre had been somewhat abandoned in the 1970s during the soaring Feminist Movement. X'er boys come of age seeing multiple films from Sylvester Stallone's *Rambo* and *Rocky* franchises; Charles Bronson's two-decade stretch with his blow-'em-to-hell *Death Wish* series; and, Arnold Schwarzenegger's *Terminator* flics (*I'll be back* and *Hasta la vista, baby*).

Music also rushes to the aid of Gen X guys, with heavy metal and rap that frequently denigrate women.

But despite this boost from pop culture, it is still a difficult upward climb for X'er guys.

So Gen X females and Gen X males, in some important ways, have divergent childhood passages. The girls: surging. The boys: searching.

A note to you Gen X ladies: many of your Gen X guys came of age taking some pretty big hits and trying to climb a steep hill. And now in adulthood, they are also trying to re-define the American male, especially as husbands and fathers. They love it, but their lives still carry the kind of uncertainty and trial-and-error that always accompanies pioneering work. A suggestion: ask them to tell you about this fascinating journey.

The Gen X Gender Dynamic Today

And how does this generational gender dynamic show up decades later?

In 1960, according to a Pew Research Center study, females were the primary breadwinners in only 11% of U. S. households. By 2013, 53 years later, the figure was 40%. And a growing number of wives are higher-paid than their husbands, in part because The Great Recession especially hammered traditionally male-worker industries like construction and manufacturing.

From all of this, we also see, in Gen X, an increase in the number of stay-at-home dads.

This female ascent in the workplace has enabled many of them to be, by choice, never-married single mothers. By 2015, 40% of all U. S. births, according to the Census Bureau, were to single mothers. What does this mean for their children's lives? We'll begin to see the results around 2030, when all of these single-parent kids enter adulthood, become a member of a generation, and show us their Core Values, strengths, and weaknesses. And if you're reading this book as part of a book club, I'm guessing you could fill your next meeting by discussing this issue alone.

You read earlier in this chapter about the impact of X'er boys growing up without the constant presence of their divorced dads. But after one of my recent speeches, one Boomer father in the audience added this, "The negative impact is not just on boys growing up without their father; it's also on *girls* growing up without their father."

"My Best Friend"

Here is one of the very positive outcomes of the women's movement and its impact upon Gen X's Core Values:

X'er husbands and wives are demonstrating a true sense of equality in their marriages. More than any prior generation, they are *sharing* responsibilities rather than dividing them.

And as I zigzag around the country for seminars or speeches, Gen X clients and audience members constantly share the same sentiment: *My husband—or my wife—is also my best friend.*

Formative Years:
Unimpressed With Authority
Cynical Towards Older Generations
Distrustful Of Major Institutions
Disempowerment And Disengagement

Because of what's going on up there in the adult world during their formative years, both male and female X'ers are developing another set of Core Values that, in many ways, are toughening them in the right manner for the adulthood that awaits them.

They are growing up to be pretty unimpressed with authority, cynical towards older generations, and distrustful of many of our nation's major institutions. And in 180-degree contrast to all other generations, they're also developing a deep sense of disempowerment and the twin Core Value that often accompanies disempowerment: disengagement.

Think about it: all around them, as they come of age in the '70s and '80s and '90s, X'er kids see one adult institution after another fail to deliver on its promise.

Gen X's Experience With Government

Take the biggest institution of all, the federal government:

Ask G.I. Generation members about their own formative years' memories of government, and they'll tell you about an FDR administration that leads them out of The Great Depression and then to victory in World War II.

And they remember a U. S. Congress that in 1935 passes the landmark legislation called Social Security, which will give their generation a true opportunity for a dignified and financially stable retirement.

And after 16,000,000 of them had just served their nation in uniform, saved the world, and come home from World War II, G.I.s will recall their government's passage of the Servicemen's Readjustment Act—or more popularly, the *G.I. Bill*—which delivers wonderful benefits to returning veterans such as low-cost mortgages, low-interest loans to start a business, cash payments of college tuition and living expenses, and one year of unemployment compensation.

And this is the government of The United States to the members of the G.I. Generation during their formative years.

Ask the Silent Generation what government means to them and they'll tell you about "their generation's president": a war hero named Eisenhower, who served as U. S. President in the 1950s and presided over an America of integrity and world leadership, and whose masses were enjoying a quality of life higher than the world had ever seen.

This is the government of The United States to Silents during their formative years.

Ask the younger Silents and the older Boomers what government means to them, and they'll recall a charismatic and idealistic G.I. Generation presidential candidate named John F. Kennedy, whose overdue campaign bus reaches the campus of the University of Michigan at 2 a.m. and who gives the speech that changes the direction of their lives. It is remembered, simply as "The Peace Corps Speech":

"How many of you who are going to be doctors are willing to spend your days in Ghana? Technicians or engineers: how many of you are willing to work in the Foreign Service and spend your lives traveling around the world? On your willingness to do that—not merely to serve one year or two years in the service, but on your willingness to contribute part of your life to this country—I think will depend the answer whether a free society can compete. I think it can! And I think Americans are willing to contribute. But the effort must be far greater than we have ever made in the past."

And within a year, the Peace Corps is launched, and thousands of younger Silents and Boomers fan out around the planet to help the less fortunate.

And soon after this speech, that same man, now our nation's President, puts America's scientists and engineers on the spot in front of the whole world when he challenges them to achieve the unthinkable: land a man on the moon, and do so *before the end of the decade.*

And we do!

And they remember a Congress that somehow comes together to pass one of the more contentious and important pieces of legislation in U. S. history: the multiple parts of the Civil Rights Bill.

And this is the government of The United States to younger Silents and older Boomers.

Well:

The positive perception of government begins to unravel as younger Boomers are coming of age, and it pretty much falls apart for Gen X.

Here is the government of The United States of America that X'ers grow up with:

* In 1973, as the first X'ers turn 8, their parents tell them one day, *The Vice President of our country has just resigned in scandal;*

❧ One year later in 1974, as they turn 9, their parents tell them one day, *The President of our country has just resigned in scandal and his replacement has decided to not hold him responsible for his misdeeds;*

❧ In 1975, they turn 10, and their parents tell them one day, *Our government has decided to quit and lose a war;*

❧ In 1979, they are now 14, and they watch as our nation begins a 444-day count of Americans held hopelessly hostage by activists in Iran;

❧ One year later in 1980, they're 15, and they share the national embarrassment of a *failed attempt* by their government to rescue those hostages;

❧ For several years in the mid '80s, they witness congressional hearings into their government's *Iran-Contra scandal;*

❧ On January 28, 1986, most X'ers today can remember where they were when they learned that NASA's Challenger space shuttle had just exploded. And this particular failure is especially deep within Gen X for two reasons:

1. Cameras were able to capture the actual explosion "live" because it occurred soon after lift-off.

2. And the shuttle was carrying, for the first time ever, a school teacher, Christa McAuliffe. And 1986 just happens to be the only year in history when Gen X filled every level of American classroom, from kindergarten to college senior. And because a teacher was aboard the Shuttle, many classrooms took time to lay down the textbooks and watch the launch—and witness the explosion—on television;

❧ X'ers' negative experience with their nation's government continues in the '90s with the impeachment of President Clinton over the Monica Lewinsky sex scandal, in which the president confesses he "misled" Americans in his sworn testimony about his sexual improprieties;

❧ And, X'er children also witness and endure political campaigns that abandon the notion of using advertising to educate *We The People* about a candidate's qualifications and beliefs and, instead, use the advertising to launch unprecedented dirty-tricks campaigning and unethical and inaccurate attack ads on the opponent. The era of *sleaze campaigning* escalates in the 1990s and overruns the democratic process as this American generation of children is passing through its formative years.

And this is the government of The United States of America during the formative years of Generation X.

And these kinds of one-after-the-other events solidify in Gen X children the understandable Core Values of *distrust* of government and, with the distrust, *disinterest* in government.

During generational-strategy training seminars around the country, I've asked X'ers in the audience to try to identify a single federal government event during their formative years that molded a positive Core Value about their government. They can't.

Some say, "The fall of communism in 1989 and '90!" I respond, "Great, but what positive Core Value about the U. S. government did it mold in you?" They think for a second and then concede, "Oh, none I guess. Yeah, our president said 'Mr. Gorbachev, tear down this wall' at the Brandenburg Gate, but communism fell because of the actions of people and governments in *other* countries."

By the way, the memory of President Reagan's "tear down this wall" sentence is the closest Gen X equivalent to the Boomers' experience with "Ask not what your country can do for you, ask what you can do for your country" from President Kennedy.

The one positive experience with government that some X'ers mention: the gentle, upbeat personality of President Reagan. One Gen X man recently told me, "When our generation was growing up and having such a hard time of it, President Reagan came across almost like an uncle or grandfather, and a lot of us somehow felt a sense of *comfort* from him."

Mr. Reagan aside, here's how these negative experiences during their youth show up in their adulthood:

Gen X Kids And Big Business

Not only do X'ers come of age distrustful of, and disinterested in, government, but they also have the same experience with another major American institution: big business.

In 1973 and 1974, the oldest X'er children are age eight and nine when they learn that an oil embargo by a few obscure nations on the other side of the planet is bringing America, supposedly the world's economic superpower, to its knees.

And throughout their formative years, many X'ers will see their fathers and mothers laid off from their jobs in massive numbers, despite their hard work and loyalty to their employer, as America enters a lengthy period of corporate downsizing, rightsizing, consolidation, outsourcing, offshoring, and all those other polite euphemisms for "firing" because of industry shifts, incompetent management, and cost cutting to appease shareholders.

And corporate bosses receive unprecedented bonuses and pay raises from their Boards of Directors, in part because they eliminated those jobs.

The 1970s and '80s are the era of so-called Merger Mania, when "corporate raiders" invest lots of money in publicly held corporations and then force executives to merge the company with another or to cut costs, both of which often lead to worker layoffs. Today, when we think of the slaughter of the middle class, we tend to point the finger at corporate executives or our federal government. Investors, however, have been able to do their corporate raiding more invisibly to the masses.

Beginning with the formative years of Gen X, and continuing to this day in the mid-2000s, the rich get much richer while The Bottom 85% takes a beating.

And these kinds of events mold Gen X Core Values of:

⁕ a pretty healthy distrust of employers, especially publicly-held corporations;

⁕ a strong belief among X'er kids that they're gonna have to look out for themselves when they enter the workplace because two-way loyalty between boss and employee is clearly dead, again especially at the publicly held corporations;

⁕ and, a hardened Gen X attitude *of I'll be darned if I'm going to pledge blind loyalty to a company and then get blindsided with a layoff like Dad and Mom did.*

I Can Trust Dirt—Literally

Another outcome—a minor ripple, but intriguing nonetheless—of the disgust that younger X'ers and Millennials feel towards corporate executives? A growing number are becoming farmers, helping to reverse a three-decades-long drop in the supply of young farmers.

According to the U. S. Agriculture Department, the number of Americans under age 35 running farms increased 10% from 2007 to 2012, to about 55,000. Gary Matteson, vice-president of the Farm Credit Council, told *USA Today*, "There's a very full pipeline of people that are going into [farming]."

Once such new farmer, Kate McNellis, a young X'er, left a New York City fashion designer career, saying, "I felt just like a cog in the big wheel of a consumerist mentality. It just felt claustrophobic. Now I'm outside every day, into the dirt. To me, it's about having the life I want."

This is good news for the agriculture industry, which is facing a shortage of farmers as Boomers retire.

And in 2014, Congress allocates $100 million for farming apprenticeships, land-matching programs, and financial assistance to purchase the real estate and heavy equipment. And technology is beginning to deliver robots that will reduce the cost of farming.

Maybe it's time for television to resurrect the hit series *Green Acres* (1965-1971) about a New York City attorney who longs for a simpler life, buys a farm, and finds himself and his aristocratic wife surrounded by a cast of hilarious down-home zanies.

Religion, Sport, And Other Disgraces

X'ers experience similar formative years' disappointments with other major American institutions:

❧ High-profile *religious* televangelists fall in disgrace: Jim Bakker goes to prison; Jimmy Swaggart breaks down in front of the cameras and confesses to sin; and numerous Catholic priests are revealed as child molesters.

❧ And high-profile *sports* heroes fall in disgrace: Pete Rose, the all-time hits leader in major league baseball, initially lies and says he did not bet on baseball games while serving as manager of the Cincinnati Reds but then later admits he did and is banned from the sport for life; and other athletes get caught using banned steroids to unfairly boost their performance.

And so these young Gen X kids pass through their formative years, looking up at the adult world and constantly asking themselves, "Is there ANYONE or ANYTHING I can truly trust?

And by their actions, the leaders and heroes send back this reply:

No.

But like all generations before them, X'er kids think, "Well, by golly, at least we can trust the MUSIC of our generation!" Until along comes *Milli Vanilli,* the music and dance act of Fab Morvan and Rob Pilatus in the late 1980s and '90s whose international blockbuster album wins a coveted Grammy Award, which soon after the Grammies' telecast is taken back when it's learned they actually weren't the singers on the album! Oops! Ironically, the album is entitled *Girl You Know It's True.* As it turns out...no, it isn't.

Gen X's Self-Focus

Why do X'ers possess such a strong Core Value of self-focus: a "me" orientation rather than a "we" orientation? Because during their unique formative years:

1. They grow up more home-alone than other generations;

2. More of them do not have to "share" with siblings, as family size shrinks during their birth years, thanks in large part to the arrival of the birth-control pill;

3. More parents can afford bigger houses, thanks to the feminist movement, and so more X'ers grow up not having to share a bedroom;

4. Because of more radio and TV stations, they have their very own stations;

5. More households have two or more TV sets, so X'er kids do not have to patiently sit through and share Dad's or Mom's or a sibling's favorite show;

6. More absentee or divorced guilt-ridden parents shower them with "stuff" because of the guilt: their own TV sets, stereos, computers, telephones;

7. They are not forced into military service, thanks to the transition from the draft to an all-volunteer force by the time they reach draft age; thus, a diminished Core Value of serving others, little sense of "something bigger than myself", and a weakened sense of "we" and "us" and a stronger sense of "I" and "me";

8. They attend fewer weddings and funerals, where *other* people, not themselves, are the focus of attention; especially those many X'ers whose

parents move from their hometowns as part of America's more mobile society;

9. Computers are not yet connected to the Internet, and so PCs isolate America's first computer generation;

10. And, video gaming is new and older people show little interest in it, so it too becomes just one more isolating, separating activity.

The impact of these shifts in American life show up the moment Generation X begins pouring into adulthood:

Employers complain that X'er employees are not good team players and will not "go the extra mile" for the good of the company if it means inconvenience—staying at work an extra hour, for example—to them. *I agreed to work from 8 to 5, and so I'm leaving at 5. If there's still work to be done, it'll have to wait until tomorrow.*

Marketers find that, if their advertising messages aren't created solely for Gen X, they won't get this generation's attention. *If this isn't about me, I'm not interested.*

It's very simple: beyond their control, Gen X children come of age during unique times, and self-focus is a generational Core Value that emerges from these times.

First-Wave And Second-Wave

Like the other generations, Gen X has a First Wave and Second Wave. Older half, younger half. They're still a single generation, but with some notable differences.

First-Wave'ers are born, roughly, from 1965 through about 1973.

Second-Wave'ers: born from about 1974 through 1981.

Most First-Wave X'ers grow up sharing TV viewing with Mom and Dad because there are only 3 channels to watch and, often, only one TV set in the house. They also share a single telephone line.

Second-Wave X'ers: cable TV, with lots of channels and, in many households, a second TV set. And, these are the kids who are also beginning to have their own private telephone lines at home (still landlines; no cells yet) and phones in their bedrooms.

First-Wave: popular music is optimistic and upbeat during most of their formative years in the '70s and early '80s.

Second-Wave: in the late '80s and '90s, the anger and female denigration and increasing vulgarity of Heavy Metal and Rap and Grunge move in and dominate the charts and minds of young kids.

Most First-Wave X'ers learn to type on a typewriter.

Second-Wave: computer keyboard.

There are other differences. First-Wave X'ers tell me their parents developed in them a good work ethic, and they feel it's the younger members of their generation who are responsible for the negative rap their generation received in early adulthood from employers.

Bottom line: as with other generations, the differences in Gen X's two Waves are overwhelmed by the similarities, and those Americans born from 1965 through 1981 are very much Generation X.

Gen X And *The News*

From this understandable disappointment with just about every corner of the adult world as they're coming of age, X'ers' Core Values of distrust, disempowerment, and disengagement help explain why they haven't followed the *hard news* of the day and, until very recently, haven't voted in elections in the same high numbers as other generations.

I have consulted and trained dozens of television stations and newspapers in generational media strategies because media research documents that Gen X is not watching local TV news and network TV news, and they're not reading their daily newspapers' main section, which traditionally has presented the "hard news" of government and big business.

This is a crisis for the legitimate news industry because X'ers will be a major target of advertisers through the 2020s because they're at the age when they're buying lots of stuff.

Who's to blame for the low ratings for TV news and low readership of daily newspapers?

In the mid-1970s, just as the older X'ers are entering their middle-school years, local TV news becomes shallow and "slick".

News anchors are hired not for their reporting abilities and journalistic integrity but because their hairdos and faces are pretty; they became news READERS instead of *journalists.*

Outside "news consultants" now penetrate newsrooms and make a lot of money if they increase the stations' news *ratings,* not if they improve the journalism. Suddenly, news stories become shorter, the sports anchor is ordered to become a showman, and news stories are chosen because of their visual impact, not their newsworthiness. Fires! Car crashes! Violence! Blood! In many newsrooms, the first story in the newscast is chosen because it fits the mantra, "if it bleeds, it leads".

Local TV news and the 24-hour cable news channels, throughout all of Gen X's news-watching years, have been superficial, manipulative, and irrelevant to their lives. Most of these stations and channels are owned by publicly traded corporations, whose shareholders demand the biggest possible return on their investment; they don't give a damn about good journalism. So money, not journalism, is everything. And the competition for ratings and revenues reduces TV news.

Constantly throughout the day, we see these words splashed across the screen of CNN: *BREAKING NEWS*. And then we see that it really isn't legitimate breaking news, after all. It's just that those two words are designed to get us to stop channel-surfing and stick around for a while. And the news anchors and reporters relentlessly use hyperbolic adjectives to try to hold on to us viewers: "incredible", "amazing", "disturbing", and "shocking". After he had retired, legendary CBS newsman Walter Cronkite—known as "The Most Trusted Man In America" —was interviewed on The Larry King Show and asked about today's TV anchors and reporters. He spoke volumes when he softly said, "They use too many adjectives."

I had just finished training executives and salespeople at the Dispatch Media Group (a respected and *privately owned* company that owns Ohio's Columbus Dispatch and local radio and TV stations) in Generational Advertising Strategy. It was time for questions and answers. One executive asked, "What about news and Gen X?" I replied, "How honest do you want me to be?" He said, "Very." So I told him:

"To Gen X nationwide, local TV news is a joke. Your stories—superficial, and too often cops-and-robbers stories, because they're easiest and cheapest for you to cover—don't matter to them. Your stories are irrelevant to their lives. Your anchors are plastic. Their chit-chat (it's called *by-play* in the industry) is moronic. The pace of your newscast is way too slow and is bogged down by poor writing and too many "teases" and "bumpers" going into and out of the commercial breaks. "Other than that," I sarcastically concluded, "you're doing just great."

And the moment my seminar ended, several X'er employees of this news organization swiftly came to the front of the room and said, "You're exactly right!"

So television news has mangled its opportunity with Gen X.

All of this airheaded superficiality emanating from the TV newsrooms of America is captured in the blistering 1982 song *Dirty Laundry* by Don Henley, which skewers news anchors and gives us insights into why X'ers don't put much faith in local TV news. Here a couple of stanzas:

"I make my living off the evening news
Just give me something, something I can use

People love it when you lose,
They love dirty laundry

We got the bubble-headed-bleach-blond who
Comes on at five
She can tell you 'bout the plane crash with a gleam
In her eye
It's interesting when people die
Give us dirty laundry."

And on February 6, 2015, the Associated Press newspaper story is headlined, "NBC's Williams fighting for his reputation."

It seems the NBC Nightly News anchor of the prior ten years, Brian Williams, lied when he claimed during a newscast that he had been in a helicopter hit by a grenade while reporting from the Iraq War.

Not hit. No grenade.

According to this AP story, "Williams apologized... [and] speculated online that constant viewing of video showing him inspecting the damaged helicopter 'and the fog of memory over 12 years made me conflate the two, and I apologize.'"

Williams' newscasts had gotten good ratings. So instead of firing him, NBC suspended him for a while and then brought him back in to the fold. In television, when the decision is between ratings or integrity, guess which one TV executives choose.

And so the principles of journalism take another big punch to the belly.

And we wonder why Gen X has unplugged from so many large pieces of American life. As Simon and Garfunkel might have sung about this loss of integrity in America:

Where have you gone, ~~Joe DiMaggio~~ Walter Cronkite?
Our nation turns its lonely eyes to you...

Newspapers

Newspapers have faced a different problem. They remain The Best Obtainable Version of the Truth and maintain a strong culture of journalistic integrity, which X'ers want. But newspapers are very poor at marketing their product. Here's why:

Newspapers began in the U. S. in the early 1700s, some three-hundred years ago. For 290 of those 300 years, they had no competition for the comprehensive reporting they provided, so they didn't need to demonstrate a lot of marketing and promotional savvy. They were the Big Newspaper; the money was rolling in; who needs to *market?*

But then, in the mid-2000s, just as I was training and consulting newspapers on Generational Newspaper Strategy, the world-changing phenomenon of New Media arrived, and suddenly the young adults whom advertisers crave migrated from hardcopy newspapers to the social media sites on their computer screens and mobile devices. Like many industries, newspapers were blindsided and brought to their knees with astonishing swiftness. Ad revenues plummeted. Layoffs ensued.

The industry that had never needed to be any good at marketing now had to be. But it wasn't. And isn't, to this day.

Newspapers' editorial content needs to be generationally sensitive, generationally strategic, and generationally relevant, but it isn't.

In these times when America is struggling horribly, the highest principles of journalism are urgently needed to explain the problems accurately and comprehensively, and to investigate all possible solutions. These should be golden days for newspapers.

But I find their executives and reporters to be too often arrogant and insular; they tell me they understand generational dynamics.

No, they don't.

And they're blowing a magnificent opportunity.

Gen X And Disempowerment

Well, from all of this, X'er kids are coming of age with a Core Value of disempowerment, a sense of powerlessness to do anything about all of these major negative things swirling around them during their youth:

* *My parents are divorcing and I can't do anything about it.*

* *Or, my parents are happily married, but my best friend's parents are divorcing and I can't do anything to help my hurting friend.*

* *My dad got laid off—and his boss received a bonus because he laid him off—and I can't do anything about it.*

* *My mom accepted a transfer and is moving us a long distance from my friends, and I can't do anything about it.*

* *My country's leaders and heroes are lying and cheating and failing, and I can't do anything about it.*

* *My radio stations and TV channels are exploiting me instead of serving me, and I can't do anything about it.*

Reality Bites

This distrust of older generations and this sense of disempowerment are vividly presented in a 1994 X'er movie that is all about Gen X'ers' life passage from college into an unfriendly adult world and job market. It's entitled *Reality Bites*. When it is released, X'ers are aged 13 to 29.

And the movie begins with a college graduation speech by an X'er valedictorian portrayed by the actress Winona Ryder who, in her valedictory address to her fellow Gen X graduates, says this:

"And they wonder why those of us in our twenties refuse to work an 80-hour week just so we can afford to buy their BMWs; why we aren't interested in the counterculture they invented. But the question remains, what are we going to do now? How can we repair all the damage we inherited? Fellow graduates, the answer is simple. The answer is, I don't know."

The *Wall Street Journal* And Gen X

The *Wall Street Journal* crafted an impressive advertising campaign to enhance readership and circulation among Gen X'ers. Rather than try to convert X'ers from disengaged to engaged and from cynical to trusting with heavy-handed messages, the print ads instead acknowledge this generation's cynicism and offer its product as a path to empowerment and engagement.

Each full-page ad shows a photograph of a Gen X'er reading the *WSJ*, while the typed copy includes a sentence in which one cynical word or phrase is crossed out in favor of a more optimistic one.

One ad shows a young X'er professional sitting in an airplane seat, reading the *WSJ*. The ad copy reads: "My boss is ~~impossible~~ a sitting duck."

Another ad shows an X'er female at her breakfast table, sipping coffee, and reading the *WSJ*. Copy: "The boys' club keeps me ~~down~~ fighting."

Another ad in this series shows a Gen X guy sitting in his small and cluttered cubicle: "My cubicle is a ~~black hole~~ launch pad."

This is good generation-specific messaging by the *Wall Street Journal,* acknowledging the unique Core Values that emerged from the unique formative years of an American generation.

X'ers In The Voting Booth

About Gen X's low participation rates as voters:

After I had presented multiple training sessions on Generational Newspaper Strategy to staffers of *The Columbus Dispatch,* its research department got curious and reviewed Central Ohio voting data from the 2004 general elections. What it found is surely symptomatic of the entire generation: X'ers, then aged 23 to 39, were out-voted by older Silents and Boomers *and even the younger Millennials* as a percentage of registered voters who actually voted.

Gen X'ers passed through their young adulthood unplugged from government and the democratic process. *Disempowerment* and *disengagement.* Their low voter turnout is a direct and predictable consequence.

But in the 2012 elections, a nice ray of sunshine: for the first time, more than 60% of eligible Gen X voters did vote. Still skeptical, but they're now at that life stage—home ownership, family, career, their children's futures—when they see how the decisions of elected officials directly impact their lives. So it seems they're finally engaging.

Adulthood

Well, let's take a look at X'ers today in adulthood and see how their unique formative-years' experiences and teachings are influencing their decisions.

And you'll find that many positive beliefs and positive values have been forged from those comparatively difficult childhood years.

And you'll see the remarkable resiliency of the human spirit, and the special spunk and moxie of this generation.

Pragmatic
Self-Reliant
Not A "Joiner" Generation
Make Marriage Work
Be There For Children

Gen X is not a generation of any sweeping idealism. They do not espouse many universal causes.

They grew up trying to understand and survive their sometimes bewildering childhood and didn't have a lot of time to think about saving the world, as G.I.s and Boomer and Millennials did. So their attitude towards life is one of pragmatism:

It's up to me. Feet on the ground. I'll do what it takes to get through my life as best I can. One day, one decision at a time.

They're self-reliant and independent:

I'll sweep in front of my door, you sweep in front of your door. And if we all do this, the whole world will be clean.

Gen X is not a generation of "joiners". As mentioned, they are not joining local membership and volunteer organizations in their communities and nation: civic groups; service clubs; professional trade associations; military veterans' organizations; and, other established organizations that have done so much good for America through the decades. And they're not creating their own new organizations to replace them, which is creating a crisis—a shortage of participants— in these groups.

Their generational argument for their drop-out mindset has always been "We're too busy". Perhaps now that their older members are becoming empty-nesters, they'll begin to volunteer and participate more in the Advanced Citizenship that this free country requires.

Rebuilding The American Family Unit

They are especially eager to make their marriages work and to *be there* for their kids because, in their own childhoods, so many experienced the opposite: broken homes and absentee parents.

And they are especially sensitive to the career-versus-parenthood, career-versus-personal-life decision.

A good number of them had entered adulthood wanting to rule out all-consuming careers, especially during their children's pre-school years but also as single adults who wanted a predictable work schedule and active after-work personal life.

Today, X'ers still try very hard to prevent their work from getting in the way of the rest of their lives.

And some married X'ers have been able to choose at least temporary financial sacrifice to accommodate that Core Value of their generation: *I'm gonna be there for my kid.*

Many other X'er parents want to do this but simply can't afford it.

And The Great Recession has forced many couples to keep working and put in longer hours. And this is making it difficult for Gen X to be what it wants to be:

The Family-First Generation.

Holder Construction Company brought its supervisory people from around the nation to Atlanta, where I trained them in Generational Workforce Management Strategy.

Afterwards, a Gen X gentleman told me this story:

"I joined Holder a year ago after quitting another firm that had not told me it expected me to work 60 to 70 hours during the summer months. My son plays Little League baseball, and I want to be there for my son. So I quit. When I interviewed with Holder and asked if they could help me with this, they said, *'You've chosen construction for your career and you know we have to work more hours when the days are longer and the weather is better; so we can't guarantee you a 8-to-5 40-hour week in the summer. But now we understand what's important to you, and we'll do our best to help you.'* It's still not perfect, but I believe they really are trying to help me be there for my kid, and that will keep me at their company."

One consequence of this Core Value of family-first: certain industries report a diminished interest within this generation of "moving up" in the workplace. Law firms, for example, are finding that some of their Gen X attorneys do not aspire to the position of "partner". Too much work, too many hours. Instead, they want to stay on the same rung of the career ladder in order to preserve their quality of life. And X'ers, more than prior generations, have avoided professions that require evening and weekend work, such as healthcare and retailing.

The American Psychological Association reports that working moms tend to be less depressed and happier with their lives than full-time-at-home mothers who lose financial freedom and the intellectual stimulation and companionship of the workplace, and who endure the thankless and repetitive tasks at home that can diminish their self-esteem and challenge their patience.

But the counter-argument is equally powerful: the children, especially pre-school infants, and in a way they are incapable of expressing, benefit from the re-assurance and emotional comfort that their mother's and/or father's *constant* presence provides.

So what to do? Whose welfare comes first, the child's or the parents'? Is there a way to have it all? Gen X parents are the trial-and-error generation trying to answer these questions.

Judith Warner, a senior fellow at the Center for American Progress, makes the point that stay-at-home motherhood is often not the "choice" that many claim it is, especially for lower-income moms:

"A woman who ends up staying home with her kids because her work pays so badly that she can't afford decent child care really has no choice. Ditto for a woman who has a special-needs child… and whose husband earns more than she does, making her the natural, if not necessary, primary parent."

Gen X'ers As Parents—Or Not

How to sum up Gen X's attitude and track record when it comes to parenthood?

Alpha parents. Or non-parents.

Alpha Parents

X'er parents are proving to be protective and nurturing, but trying to not be as permissive as their own parents had been with them. Instead, as G.I. parents did with their Silent and Boomer children, X'er moms and dads seem to be giving their kids pretty clear boundaries and responsibilities and enforcing them.

I sat on a plane with a Gen X mother, who told me her son was in his freshman year of college. She and her husband asked the son to sign a contract, which he did, stating that if he stays in school for each full school year and makes satisfactory progress towards a degree, the parents will pay for that year of school. If he screws up in any way, he pays for the year, even if he has to take out a loan to do so.

And that same woman told me of another Gen X couple who do it this way: their kids secure year-by-year loans to pay for college; if they finish each year satisfactorily, the parents pay for the loan.

X'er families are also the most time-stressed of our living generations. Driving the kids to and from school has become a milk-run, with stops along the way at the post office, dry cleaner, drugstore, and drive-through coffee shop.

Not enough time, not enough time!

They're obsessive about giving their kids every possible positive experience and advantage. Soccer Moms and Nascar Dads play chauffeur and spend lots of time and money to get the kids to unending structured activities, day after day, especially in sport. Summer camps? Learn, learn, learn!

They're going online to gather advice from others about parenting. And websites on the topic have proliferated.

When Gen X women became the dominant "mom generation", Procter & Gamble launched a massive campaign of product advertising and online advice sites to help them and advertised heavily in the Winter Olympics telecasts because the sports of the winter games tend to be popular with female viewers.

But their generation's individualism and self-reliance also show up in their parenting: they'll gather advice but then do it their way.

Dads are more heavily involved with their kids than prior generations. A *Wall Street Journal* story headlined "Are Dads the New Moms?" calls today's Gen X dads "rock-solid fathers".

X'er dads are the pioneers who are re-defining the roles of father and husband. Less division of duties with the wife; instead, more sharing. And dads are changing diapers, taking paternity leave from work, even becoming full-time stay-at-home dads while the moms have the careers and make the money. This is uncharted territory for most men, and some employers are trying to help the guys by providing fatherhood seminars—maybe lunch-and-learn sessions at work—and more generous leave policies, and by keeping them plugged in to the company during their paternity-leave absence with regular communications.

In their careers, this "Daddy Juggle" of work, life, and family is sometimes posing a dilemma: some dads fear they'll lose face with their bosses and coworkers if they take extended paternity leave. And as Millennial men now begin fatherhood, their generation is also facing these challenges.

But this is changing rapidly: tech giants like Netflix and Microsoft have announced mega-generous parental leave policies for their highest-level employees. Netflix, in 2015, declared that new parents may take up to a year of leave, and Microsoft—competing against Netflix and other tech employers for the best talent—instantly expanded its leave, too.

Although this can create serious workplace problems when the program is not designed properly, the workplace bias against Daddy Leave and Mommy Leave is steadily dissolving. And the Family-First Generation is making it happen.

The American family unit took a beating during the 1970s, '80s, and '90s. As it did, one generation of children was passing through its formative years and forming lifelong Core Values. Today, that generation is now America's moms and dads, with kids living at home. And they possess the one human quality needed to significantly change the direction of parenthood and family.

Passion.

A hundred years from now, it is likely that Gen X will be remembered as the generation that re-strengthened the American family, with substantial help from Boomer and Silent grandparents. Note to X'ers: your passion for parenting is the same powerful force that compels Boomers to try to save their nation. Different formative years, different generational purposes, same emotion.

And hopefully, they will find ways to create those Little Moments, when their children learn one more tidbit of information about life on earth—and about older people—by spending relaxed, unhurried, and undistracted time in the presence of Mom and Dad, instead of growing up rushed, with their brains locked myopically on their mobiles.

X'ers As Grandparents

This should be very interesting: how will Gen X'ers behave as grandparents, which their older members are now becoming?

As parents, they have been passionate, driven, and *family-first*.

Will they "grandparent" the same way? Or, will their helicopter/alpha parenting have caused burn-out, and will they tell their own adult children, "We raised you with fanatic devotion; now it's *our time*."

Stay tuned.

A 2013 *TIME* magazine cover story shouted out another New Normal:

The Child-Free Life
When "Having It All" Means Not Having Children

G.I.s, Silents, and all prior generations had come of age when it was largely assumed *everyone* gets married and *everyone* has kids. If women went unmarried, they were derisively labeled as spinsters or old maids; *something must be wrong with them.*

But a number of Boomers and younger Silents—especially because the Feminist Movement created the opportunity for financial independence for their generations' women—discovered they actually prefer to be single. *And child-free.* The women and the men. And so they began to advance the argument that such a life is OKAY.

Today, Gen X and the Millennials are pushing this lifestyle further along, and American life is slowly shifting to a new value:

Marriage and parenthood are optional, not mandatory. And it's perfectly healthy to think that "having it all" means *not* having children.

Or as someone once said, "Everyone with a womb doesn't have to bear children any more than everyone with vocal cords has to sing opera."

After giving a presentation to the faculty and staff at Edmonds Community College in Seattle, I watched and smiled as I saw generational differences about this issue play out during a question-and-answer session with a few hundred employees. A Millennial female in the audience said, "I really don't want to be a mother", and a Silent male smiled at her and said in a comforting paternal manner, "One day, you will." Afterwards, she came up to me and privately said, "No, I really won't."

Two generations. Two sets of Core Values. Neither is right, neither is wrong; just different.

Some people want and are suited to be spouses and/or parents. They're simply right for those roles.

Many are not. Among the higher-profile Non-Moms:

Oprah Winfrey, who said this in an interview with Barbara Walters: "I have none—not one—regret about not having children because I believe that is the way it's supposed to be [for me]."

Feminist crusader Gloria Steinem: "I'm completely happy not having children. I mean, everybody does not have to live in the same way."

Comedienne Margaret Cho: "Babies scare me, more than anything."

According to a 2010 Pew Research study, childlessness has risen quite suddenly across all racial and ethnic groups in America. In the 1970s, 10% of our nation's women did not have children. By 2010, it was 20%, meaning one in five American women was ending her childbearing years maternity-free.

There is some lingering pressure on women to marry and bear children, but X'ers and Millennials—after Boomers began to break the mold—will push back on this mindset.

The likely and hopeful outcome?

Married couples will be people who SHOULD be married.

Parents will be people who SHOULD be parents.

Singles will be people who SHOULD be single.

Happier, better-adjusted adults.

Happier, better-adjusted children.

Gen X And Religion

Gen X'ers, like Boomers and Millennials, are searching for a religion, a faith, a spirituality that suits their core values.

Various studies document that most members of their generations do believe in a higher power but aren't sure what that is.

In an effort to connect with them, some of our nation's religions and local houses of worship have re-worked their traditional services. Some even offer separate services that are generation-specific, such as Gen X-oriented services with ministers who dress more casually and offer live music and PowerPoint presentations for this very visual generation.

The religious beliefs of a good number of X'ers seem to be summed up in the 1987 song, a spiritual message, sung by Bono and his group *U2*, entitled "I still haven't found what I'm looking for":

"I believe in the Kingdom Come
Then all the colours will bleed into one
Bleed into one.
But yes, I'm still running.

You broke the bonds
And you loosed the chains
Carried the cross of my shame
Oh my shame, you know I believe it.

But I still haven't found
What I'm looking for."

X'er Nation: The 2030s And 2040s

As mentioned in our Boomer section, each generation's best, brightest, and luckiest steadily work their way to the top during their 20s, 30s, and 40s. And then they spend about two decades as the dominant decision-makers for American business, government, education, and religion, applying their unique Core Values and beliefs to their leadership.

And when they do, they move America in a different direction from that of the prior generation's leadership era.

Each generation produces good leaders. Each generation produces bad leaders.

In the late 2010s and 2020s, Gen X will begin to penetrate the leadership positions, but America will still be a Boomer nation.

Especially in the 2020s, there will be a significant overlap of Boomer and Gen X Core Values at the top.

But it won't be until around 2030, as the youngest of the Boomers fully retire (if they ever do; remember, this generation likes to work) that we'll become a Gen X Nation for fifteen to twenty years before X'ers themselves pass the leadership baton to the Millennials, who will then take their turn at the top in the 2050s and 2060s.

The American Society of Foundation Engineers, a national trade association, asked me to conduct a single 2-hour focus-group session during its annual leadership conference in Las Vegas. Fifteen (male) superstars of that industry—1 Silent, 7 Boomer chief executives, and 7 promising middle-management Gen X'ers—gathered in a private room with an audio-visual crew that video- and audio-taped the entire session.

The purpose? Identify ways for older, successful owners of engineering firms to work more closely with X'ers to prepare them to move up in their firms and deliver good leadership and future success.

For two hours, with the X'ers and Boomers sitting on opposite sides of a long table, I guided them through the generational issues: their challenges in working together and the opportunities their two generations create when they do work together, and what actions should be taken to help X'ers.

At the very end, a Boomer gentleman looked across the table at the X'ers and asked, "What can we Boomers do to help you X'ers?" One Gen X man, without hesitation and with the others on his side of the table nodding in agreement, said, only partially tongue-in-cheek:

"You can retire."

Don't hold your breath, X'ers.

Idea Leadership And People Leadership

Generation X is already proving itself to be brilliant at "finding solutions". So they will give our nation and the world exceptional Idea Leadership: they will create new products, new services, new workplace processes and efficiencies. Where the rubber meets the road, they will create solutions. It is their generation's brilliance.

But their leadership might lack in People Skills and in compassion towards the people they lead; that is, employees. When I present Generational Leadership seminars around the country, X'ers say things like this:

I don't think our generation especially WANTS to lead. As we came of age, leadership wasn't very cool.

I don't like all the headaches and hassles of dealing with the people I manage.

Yes, there are brilliant Gen X People Leaders. But the idea of managing other human beings just doesn't come as naturally to this generation as it does to others.

At a training session for about 150 leadership personnel at several San Francisco-area hospitals, one Gen X woman told me this story:

"I recently took a managerial position at my hospital. I came from the outside, not from within the hospital. I manage Boomers, X'ers, and Millennials and they don't seem to accept me as their boss, and they won't let me in. What do you think I should do?"

"Why don't you call them together and discuss it," I suggested.

And her reply was classic, no-nonsense, efficient Gen X:

"That seems like such a waste of time. It seems like we should be *working.*" And I quietly told her, "This is what 'management' is. It's about people." She crinkled her nose. She didn't get it. But she smiled and said, "Okay. Thanks!" And I'm guessing she gave it a try with her staff.

Will You X'er Leaders Ask For Help?

I hadn't thought of this until a seminar participant raised the question:

"If Gen X is so self-reliant and independent, will its leaders freely ask for help when they need it, especially those confident, competent, and assertive Gen X females?"

X'ers, how do you answer that one?

When I heard the question, a thought swiftly came to mind: I was watching brilliant Boomer movie producer and director Ron Howard on David Letterman's late-night show. Ron—who is still "Opie" to the generations who watched *The Andy Griffith Show*—told Dave that, in directing a recent movie, he had come to a scene that he just couldn't figure out how to direct. The director of a movie is a czar and controls everything; movies are a director's medium, not an actor's medium. But rather than try to come up with a solution on his own, this Oscar winner gathered his cast and crew and said, "Guys, I'm stuck here. Anybody got any ideas?"

Classic Boomer-think and Millennial-think: we; us; team; group. But X'ers how about you? Will you men ask for help? You women?

Here are two additional and vital questions about your upcoming leadership era:

1. When you lead America, will you be extremely ethical or extremely unethical or average in your executive ethics?

2. And, will you treat your employees—especially U. S. employees who have taken such a pounding the past quarter-century—compassionately

and make executive decisions that will give them a true shot at financial stability? If the decision is to either lay off employees or make less money for the company or yourself, which will you choose?

You entered your work years when too many White Silent Male leaders were creating an executive-suite culture of unethical, greedy, and corrupt behavior and triggering the dismantlement of the American middle class, kicking millions of U. S. workers into the streets with résumés in their hands and sending their lives crashing downward into financial uncertainty and instability.

Usually, American children who grow up during any kind of "extreme" like this either fully embrace the extreme or recoil from it and defiantly do the opposite. They seldom settle in the middle.

So, when you take your turn at the top, will your generation be extremely unethical and selfish and greedy because you assume it's *simply the way it's done in America because this is all I've ever seen?* Or will you go the other direction and be extremely ethical and compassionate towards employees?

I gave a speech about Gen X leadership in Grand Rapids, Michigan. 55 of the 60 attendees were X'ers.

These dynamic people had already distinguished themselves in their careers and were serving as presidents of companies of a certain significant size, which enabled them to become members of the local chapter of an international association called Young Presidents Organization, which hosted my speech.

When I finished, I asked the X'ers for a show of hands to answer this multiple-choice question: when it is your generation's turn to lead America, will your generation's leadership era be: (1) ethical; (2) unethical; or, (3) about average with its ethics.

These X'er presidents voted...

unethical.

Why?

The leadership era that has prevailed over most of Gen X's career years is the Silent Generation era. Translation: an understandable belief within Gen X that this is way leadership works.

And when you couple that experience with their own "survivalist" childhood that molded in them the additional Core Values of self-reliance and self-focus...

And when you then add the financial uncertainty of their generation's adult lives…

You get a very powerful cocktail that might—repeat, *might*—position X'er leaders to be uncommonly vulnerable to extreme self-focus and less compassion for employees and customers because, to this generation, life in America is Survival of the Fittest; I'll take care of me; you take care of you.

Thus, as leaders, this generation will be especially vulnerable to behavior such as this:

If I have to lay off employees in order to please shareholders and receive a bonus this year, I'll do it.

If my corporation is failing and going under but I can save it and preserve my own financial security by going dirty, I'll do it, just like I saw it done before by my elders. I'm going to take care of me.

Boomers To The Rescue?

But if Boomers, who are now underway as America's leadership generation, can clean up the c-suites cesspool of greed, corruption, and the slaughter of the "Bottom Percents", X'ers will see that leadership can be performed differently.

They'll have a new model.

Key Point: I am not stating that Gen X will behave this way as leaders. Instead, I am saying they will be *vulnerable* to it, because of the unique Core Values that came from their unique formative years, over which they had no control.

But here's the very good news for you X'ers:

Silent leaders, who performed so poorly, did not have the field of generational study to alert them to their generation's unique leadership vulnerabilities and strengths. Boomers are learning about their leadership strengths and weaknesses on the fly, right now as they lead.

But your generation can use generational leadership study to get your leadership strengths and weaknesses and vulnerabilities in front of you *in advance,* years before you run America, if only you'll take the time to learn about them.

With such wisdom, you will be the first generation with enough lead time to maximize your leadership performance.

Someday in the future, I can foresee executive conferences that are generation-specific and designed to prepare each generation for its leadership era: *The Gen X Leadership Conference.*

One more piece of good news: your generation will get a full turn at the top. As I meet members of your generation during training workshops throughout the country, they tell me they're tugging at the leash, eager to move up, and waiting restlessly for Boomers to retire. Yes, Boomers will work significantly longer than prior generations, but we're ALL going to be working to later years in our lives. So you X'ers will enjoy a long tenure in the c-suites. It's just that it will probably arrive at a later age.

And more good news: X'er females will continue to surge. They will stand on the sturdy shoulders of the women who came before them and poured the foundation, and they will contribute enormously and uniquely to American leadership.

What Will Your Kids Be Like In Adulthood?

The *oldest* children of Gen X—the Millennials born generally between the late 1980s to mid-1990s—are now in early adulthood, and we're just starting to get a clear "read" of their values and behavior.

And it looks mostly good. Those young adults are demonstrating many, many positive Core Values from the unique times and teachings of their formative years, and much of the credit goes to their Family-First, *I'm-gonna-be-there-for-my*-kids moms and dads. But as you'll read in the Millennial chapters, this generation also is demonstrating some shortcomings.

X'ers, have you passed on to your children your generation's best values or your worst? All generations possess some of each.

Optimism instead of pessimism? Hope instead of hopelessness? Empowerment, not disempowerment? A healthy skepticism instead of cynicism? Ethics?

Compassion for the less fortunate? Strong work ethic? The importance of family and community and nation? "We" and not just "me"? Volunteerism? Participation? Engagement instead of disengagement? Advanced citizenship instead of drop-out citizenship?

Will your kids laugh freely?

And your children are the first in history to be fully slammed by The Technology Revolution. And because they're the first, there is no manual to tell you parents how to handle it. You must conduct the trial and error to see what's right and wrong.

So, will your children be damaged by the "bad" that is going along with the "good" of technology while they pass through their all-important formative years?

Your children, very soon, will provide the nation and the world with the answers to these questions.

And What About You?

X'ers, will you vote in elections, and will you cast intelligent votes by doing your homework about the candidates and ballot issues?

Will your generation's best or worst members aspire to elected office and lead our national, state, and local governments?

As you empty-nest and enjoy more time to yourself and more money, will you volunteer and give your time and money to charitable causes, as all prior generations have done? Will you ever join a civic organization—your local Rotary, Lions, Kiwanis, Optimist, and others—that contribute so quietly but so enormously to local communities, or might you create new models for your generation to deliver the same contributions?

Where will you get your information? Will you seek factual, comprehensive, and unbiased reporting on your world? Or will you go with the noisemaking, personal-opinion blogs and mocking TV shows that the mass media force-fed you during your youth?

Will you ever feel empowered and believe you truly can make a difference?

Or will you go down in history as a Dropout Generation that chose to never fully participate in the Advanced Citizenship that America needs?

Go Get 'Em

Your generation is now chalking up major victories in life, after that comparatively bumpy childhood passage.

You're solidifying your careers, building strong families, owning homes, and saving a few bucks.

You're finally gaining control.

Quite a journey, huh?

Your generation brings unique and positive values, attitudes, skills, and ideas to American life. It seems your members *want* to contribute, *want* to plug in, *want* to make a positive difference, *want* to do the right thing.

And our discouraged nation urgently needs for you to do so. You have a lot to give.

What will it take—from yourselves, and from others—to get you to fully plug in to all aspects of American life and deliver the substantial contribution of which you're so wonderfully capable?

Two More Gen X Chapters

Still to come in this book: one chapter about Gen X'ers as consumers in the marketplace, and one chapter about them as employees in the workplace.

THE MILLENNIALS

The New World

. . .

CHAPTER 10

The Millennials

"Helicopter-parented, trophy-saturated, and abundantly friended"

• • •

Birth Years:	**1982 Through 1998 So Far**
How Many Born:	**66,168,000 So Far**
Formative Years:	**1980s To ??**
Their Parents:	**Boomers, Older X'ers**

IN DALLAS, I WAS PRESENTING a workshop in Generational Leadership Strategy to a national-conference audience of several hundred interns and leadership candidates—Silents, Boomers, X'ers, and Millennials (or "Mils")—who work for the country's largest health-care system, the Veterans Administration medical centers and clinics.

I presented the Silent Generation. Then the Boomers. Then Gen X. As I introduced each generation's segment, the room was attentive but quiet; everyone was taking notes. When I finished with X'ers and simply said, "Now for the Millennials", the Mils in the audience instantly threw their hands above their heads and gave themselves a raucous, whooping, ovation.

I love myself and there's nothing wrong with that!

As more than one observer has expressed ever since this generation began to enter adulthood at the turn of the millennium with such spirit, optimism and, yes, over-the-top narcissism:

Hail The Millennials.

After training many of the executives at one of our nation's more prominent retail companies (sometimes in this book I can identify the company, and sometimes I've signed confidentiality agreements with them and cannot), they asked me to conduct a formal research study, internally, to help them retain their beloved Boomer employees and recruit the best Millennial job candidates.

One of my first interviews for this study took place with the corporation's highest-ranking Human Resources executive, a Boomer female, in the company's skyscraper headquarters in New York City.

I placed the tape recorder on her desk, hit the "record" button and asked her, "Since you've been hiring Millennials, what has been your experience with them?"

She burst out laughing.

"You and I are sitting on the executive floor of our building", she said. To get on to this floor, a person must enter a secret code on a keypad located beside the door. This floor is supposed to be impregnable. But since we started hiring Millennials, I'll be sitting at my desk on any given day and reading or typing, when suddenly I sense this "presence" on the other side of my desk. I look up, and there's a newly hired Millennial who somehow cracked the code, walked into my office, and is now sitting at my desk and grinning from ear to ear, because she has just come up with THE idea that is going to make our corporation a billion more dollars, even though she's only been working for us for eight minutes.

"She has a boss, who has a boss, who has a boss, who reports to me, but she and other Millennials consistently ignore our company's chain of command in order to take their great ideas to the highest possible level.

"When this happens, my first instinct (she's still laughing) is to lunge across my desk and strangle them.

"But then I look in their eyes. And I see this incredible spirit.

"They're driving us nuts, but they're gonna be great."

About Their Total Number

As of 2016, we don't yet know when the Millennial Generation will end and our next generation will begin.

And we won't announce the arrival of America's next generation until we see America's high school graduates, for several consecutive years and coast to coast, demonstrating Core Values that are markedly different from those of the Mils.

So...

As of January 1, 2016, the Millennial Generation's population is just above 66,000,000, according to U. S. Census Bureau data. By January 1 of 2017, if they continue, they'll total some 70,000,000. To surpass Boomers, their generation's birth years will have to extend through about 2002.

When I wrote my first book in 2007, it bothered me that we generational pioneers had not adequately defined the point in time when an individual actually *becomes a member of a generation.* It was a missing piece of generational study. So I waded in. And it took a couple of years to verify the principle that you read earlier in this book and to correct the size of the Millennial population:

We do not join a generation until we leave our high school years, essentially at age 18. And so 16-year-olds and 9-year-olds are no longer simply tossed into the youngest generation at any given moment (as even I wrongly did in my 2007 book).

I alert my clients to this, and I've turned down prospective clients who wanted to use generational strategy to market a product or service to the twelve-to-seventeen or six-to-eleven age demographic. I tell them point-blank: generational values don't become crystallized and reliable until we're out of high school. So if you want to understand high school kids or younger, you cannot use generational strategy; you must use *age* strategy, which is very different.

Millennials inched past Gen X in total population by the end of 2014, and they did so in two fewer birth years. And by the end of 2015, their population stood at 66,168,000. But it is likely the Millennials will end before they surpass the Boomers in size.

Many news outlets are parroting what some others are saying, that the Millennials are the largest U. S. generation ever. No, they're not. Beware the flawed generational content floating around out there.

Here are the Census Bureau's average annual birth rates for each of the four generations included in this book:

- Millennials: 3.89 million births per year, so far.
- Gen X'ers: 3.44 million per year.
- Boomers: 4.21 million per year.
- Silents: 2.45 million per year.

The Millennials will end for the same reason that all American generations end: *there will be substantial changes in the times and/or the teachings that children absorb in their formative years; changes that will create in them substantially different Core Values from those of the Millennials.*

Their Formative Years And Core Values

The Millennial Generation. A dramatic departure from the Core Values and attitudes of Gen X, because

Millennials experience dramatically different formative years.

Where Gen X children had been the least adult-supervised generation in U. S. history, Millennials are the *most* adult-supervised, by those omnipresent, protective Helicopter Parents who hover above their kids' lives, ready to swoop in and rescue them from any kind of harm or setback.

And their Core Values, as a result, are notably different from those of X'ers.

Optimistic And Enthusiastic
Uncertain About USA
Respectful Of Authority
Focused On Their Education
Close With Their Parents
Compassionate

Here's what we've learned about *Mils*. They are proving to be:

* optimistic and enthusiastic about their own future;

* much less certain, but still hopeful, about their country's future, in light of such negatives as

The Great Recession, polarized and paralyzed politicians, epidemic executive corruption and ruthless treatment of U. S. employees, and the war against terrorism;

* respectful of authority—they're eager to change some things, but they'll work within the system and are not a rebellious generation;

* focused on their education, because they must be; like Boomers, they're a large generation that will always face fierce competition from each other for jobs and promotions;

* very close to their parents and grandparents;

* and, compassionate towards others and, in contrast to Gen X, outwardly, rather than inwardly, focused.

Just as the oldest Millennials were reaching adulthood, I received a morning phone call from *NBC Nightly News*. They wanted to send a film crew to my Cincinnati house that afternoon to tape a quick comment that would be included in a story in that same night's newscast:

The Northwestern University women's lacrosse team, which had just won the 2005 national championship, was invited to the White House to be honored by the President. These young Millennial women created a fashion-industry uproar when they wore flip-flops to the ceremony. *Egads! Fashion Faux pas! Disrespect! An insult to the presidency!*

The *Chicago Tribune* headline screamed, "You Wore WHAT To The White House?!"

So I was asked to present "the generational angle" to the incendiary Flip-Flop Flap. I asked, "How many seconds do you want?" "Eight", the reporter said by phone. "And say it about ten times and vary your wording, and we'll select the best take."

So, in about eight seconds, my comment on that night's newscast was, "These are the Millennials; they're not a rebellious generation; all we witnessed in the White House was a fashion statement, not an insult."

And at the time, some of those flip-flops cost more than a nice pair of heels.

And what happened next is so wonderfully "Millennial":

Because of the publicity, the team members auctioned their famous flip-flops and donated the proceeds to the Friends of Jaclyn charity, named for Jaclyn Murphy, a young girl battling a brain tumor.

Mom And Dad: *My Best Friends*

At about the same time as the Flip-Flop Flap, the acclaimed CBS television show *60 Minutes* produced a segment on the Millennial Generation. Mils talked about their fast-paced lives, grade-pressured lives, tech-dominated lives, and the spending power they were given in their youth by their parents. And then the reporter (Steve Kroft, I believe) asked a group of Millennial kids to talk about their parents. And these 20-somethings *gushed* with praise and gratitude. And subsequent research studies have affirmed their generation's feelings towards their parents:

Mom and Dad: my best friends. My weekend buddies. My role models. My confidantes. Always there for me, always there for me, my parents are the BEST.

An unmistakable generational Core Value of gratitude towards their parents.

Coca-Cola promptly showcased this generational Core Value with a humorous and memorable TV commercial:

In this 30-second spot, we see a Millennial teen-age boy open the refrigerator door and reach for the last Coke on the shelf just as his Dad, off-camera in another room of the house, shouts out, "Chris, is there any more Coke?" As Chris ponders whether to keep the Coke for himself by lying and answering "no" or to give the last one to Dad, the spot cuts to three flashbacks as Chris recalls some recent events between Dad and himself:

1. Dad is teaching him how to drive. They sit in the car, which is backed into the driveway, and Dad instructs him to put the car in "drive" and go forward, but Chris mistakenly shifts into "reverse" and backs the car right through the closed garage door. Dad calmly sighs and gives him a comforting pat on the shoulder.

2. Next, Dad is sitting at the kitchen table doing some paperwork as Chris, practicing golf in the backyard, drives a ball right through the window, showering dad with broken glass, but again, Dad reacts calmly.

3. Finally, Dad opens the bathroom door just in time to see his son shaving half of his scalp in order "to get the right look for graduation" but

looking hideous. Dad quietly closes the door and respectfully leaves his son to all of his teenage goofiness.

The spot ends by returning to a shot of Chris at the refrigerator, making his decision to give Dad the last Coke, "Yeah, got one right here," with the word "gratitude" typed on the screen.

Excellent messaging to the Millennials' Core Value of gratitude towards their parents.

"Why Young Voters Care"
TIME (2008)

On the cover of its February 2, 2008 edition are the fresh young faces of ten, multi-ethnic Millennials with the subtitle "Why Young Voters Care and Why Their Vote Matters".

Millennials are very involved in the democracy. They vote. They participate.

They are a significant factor in the 2008 election of America's first black president, Barack Obama. Two of every three Millennials vote for him. And even those who vote for Senator McCain are heavily involved in the campaign process.

In the *New York Times*, columnist Gail Collins describes the Millennials' memory of President Obama's historical inauguration day on January 20, 2009 as their generation's "Woodstock...but without the mud".

A few months later, I'm giving a speech somewhere, and when I share that quote, one Millennial female in the audience stands and says with a laugh, "I was there. And it WAS muddy!"

On National Public Radio the morning after our nation has elected its first African-American president, a reporter asks a black father what he had said to his 9-year-old son when the voting results were final. The father answers that he had turned to his son and simply said:

"No more excuses."

What an impact on Millennials, and what a wonderful message to African-American kids coming of age!

This Millennial engagement is very different from Gen X, which for a long list of reasons during their formative years unplugged from the political process in their young-adult passage.

Strengthening these Core Values of citizenship and participation even more? Along with some younger Gen X'ers, Millennials are our front-line combat troops in our war against terrorism.

In the 2012 elections, Millennials' voting numbers drop a bit; their discouraged generation is now being battered by high unemployment and high underemployment rates, compliments of banking executives' gift to America: The Great Recession.

"America Isn't Easy"

Nonetheless, their generation understands what the actor Michael Douglas means when he says the following, as part of his acclaimed monologue at the climax of the 1990s Hollywood film entitled *The American President*:

"America isn't easy. America is advanced citizenship. You gotta want it bad, 'cause it's gonna put up a fight."

Millennials get that. They're up for the fight. They're willing to wade down into that arena where, every day, this messy and magnificent experiment called *America* is being fought out eye to eye. Like Boomers during the Consciousness Movement, their generation views this fight as a celebration of their country. As the Godfather of Soul James Brown had sung in 1985:

"Livin' in America: eye to eye, station to station
Livin' in America: hand to hand, across the nation
Livin' in America: got to have a celebration"

Millennials think they're going to change the world for the better, so they probably are.

And they're about to get some big help with this because, in the 2010s and 2020s, Millennials are going to be living and working in an America whose leadership generation, the social-activist Boomers, feel exactly the same way. The conservative, don't-rock-the-boat Silents are now largely retired.

And what that powerful Boomer/Millennial combination of engagement and empowerment, and with big contributions from solution-finding Gen X in the middle, MIGHT accomplish in the next 20 years is astonishing. The view from generational study is unmistakable:

America is just now getting back in position to enjoy a magnificent run after a wretched two decades in the '90s and 2000s (which *TIME* magazine's cover in December, 2009 described as "The Decade From Hell").

Mils And Their Music: Declining Sales Of Rap

The Millennial Generation's optimism and closeness with their parents might also explain a March 2007 Associated Press story that states, "After 30 years of popularity, rap music is now struggling with an alarming sales decline and growing criticism from within about the culture's negative effect on society."

According to this Associated Press account, from 2005 to 2006, when Mils were aged 18 to 25 and in their peak record-buying years, rap sales decreased a whopping 21%. And mathematically speaking, if rap simply had *held steady* with Millennials, sales should have *grown*, because Millennials are about 25% larger in population that Gen X.

Rap's rage and cynicism and violent lyrics and video images had fit perfectly with the emotions of Gen X kids in the troubled '80s and '90s. But it doesn't translate well with the soaring positivism of Millennials.

Rap insider Chuck Creekmur told Associated Press reporter Nekesa Mumbi Moody, "A lot of people are sick of rap...the negativity is just over the top now." And a study by the Black Youth Project showed a majority of black youth feel rap has too many violent images.

The American marketplace, including the music industry, must understand shifts in generational Core Values. And Millennials are a pretty upbeat group.

Rap And Rape

Many music videos and lyrics, especially beginning with early '90s rap (just as younger X'ers and older Millennials were coming of age), delivered a mega-dose of female disparagement and denigration by using music-video images and song lyrics that relent-lessly present women as sex instruments.

Here are lyrics from some leading rappers like Eminem, Ja Rule, Notorious B.I.G., Tyler The Creator, and Cam'rom. This is what younger X'ers and Millennials hear as they come of age. <u>Warning</u>: very, very violent and vulgar lyrics...

* *Pistol whip the kids and rape your stray ho*

* *You're the kind of girl I'd assault and rape*

* *Kidnap kids, f__ em in the a__, throw 'em over the bridge*

⁂ *You call this sh__ rape, but I think rape's fun*

⁂ *We kill girls, rape 'em, bury their skirts*

There are additional examples of rape lyrics in rap. And the generations of young boys and girls who grew up with these lyrics are now pouring into adulthood. And suddenly, the United States Military (the Army, Navy, and Air Force are clients of mine) is reporting a serious problem with sexual abuse within its ranks: rape; molestation; sexual harassment. I'm aware of this because of my work with the military and in training mental-health counselors at our Veterans Administration hospitals in Generational Behavioral Healthcare Strategy.

But in the 1990s, female rappers begin to push back on this female denigration and draw a line in the sand. The four-women-group En Vogue's lyrics in 1992:

"The only thing you changed was love to hate
It doesn't matter what you do or what you say
She doesn't love you, no way
Maybe next time you'll give your woman a little respect
So you won't be hearing her say, No way
No, you're never gonna get it (not this time)

Never ever gonna get it (my lovin')
No, you're never gonna get it (had your chance to
make a change)
Never ever gonna get it..."

Grade Pressure And Time Pressure

Millennials come of age feeling intense pressure to get good grades. They're a big generation, like the Boomers, so the competition among them has been, and always will be, ferocious to get admitted into their colleges of choice, land the best jobs, and win the best promotions. Gen X, much smaller in number, will never have known this level of competitiveness.

As Millennials reach college, a new phenomenon occurs among this generation's top academic performers: the triple major, the quadruple, and in some cases the quintuple major, just to gain an advantage when it comes time to enter the job market.

Millennials also feel time pressure and tend to schedule their days like efficiency experts.

When I hosted that previously mentioned generational talk show for public TV, one of our featured guests was Myrtis Powell, Vice President of Student Affairs at Miami University. When asked about the Millennials, she didn't hesitate: "These kids schedule everything. If they have a one-hour square on their electronic calendars that doesn't show some activity filled in, they panic!"

Us-Think

Gen X had come of age during times that molded them as a "Me" generation: individualistic; independent; self-reliant.

Millennials, conversely, grow up in different times that mold them as a "We" generation. Group-think, team-think, us-think.

Where X'ers had come of age with the media isolation mentioned earlier, the media of the Millennials' youth connects them to other people 24/7. X'ers are the Computer Generation. Mils are the world's first full-blown Tech Generation.

What's more, Millennial students' classes have been more frequently structured for group projects, in which all members of the group receive the same grade based upon the team performance. And this experience reinforces the Core Value of "group-think".

The teachings change. And so the Core Values change.

I ran that group-project concept past a group of ten Gen X women in a formal focus-group session. They crinkled their self-reliant, independent X'er noses at the thought of *their grade being at the mercy of other people!* Not Millennials, who love the group dynamic.

There's no right or wrong here. Just different. And this is an important message from generational study:

Those Generation Gaps that so frequently irritate and divide us, within our own families and on the job and down at the corner bar, are often not a matter of one generation having it right and the other generation having it wrong. It's just different ways of doing the same thing.

With the tech revolution, coming-of-age Mils change the social activity of movie-watching, often preferring to watch it at home on DVD with groups of friends, rather than going to a local theater. In this manner, they can pause the movie at any time to talk about it and thus make it more of an interactive and group experience than when sitting quietly in rows at the theater. It is a more "we-friendly" environment in a house, made possible by changes in technology and the fact that this generation of kids, with their friends, are so fully comfortable in the presence of their moms and dads.

The times change, and the Core Values change.

September 11 And Katrina

Several historical events will always define this generation and give its members a *shared center*:

* the terrorist attacks of 9/11;

* the devastation of New Orleans and other parts of the Gulf Coast by Hurricane Katrina;

* the big oil spill in the Gulf of Mexico;

* the tsunami and nuclear meltdown in Japan;

* and, Millennials also know they are The School Shootings Generation: Columbine; the massacre at Virginia Tech University; Northern Illinois University; Red Lake, Minnesota; Craighead County, Arkansas; and nearly a dozen others and, sadly, still occurring. And away from the classrooms: the Oklahoma City bombing and

the movie-theater killings in Aurora, Colorado (of the 12 people killed that night, 9 were Millennials).

It's often difficult for other generations to understand, but these shootings give Millennials, the generation that walked into school each day by passing through a metal detector, a *diminished sense of personal safety on U. S. soil.*

But the shootings also have brought them together as a generation: within hours of the Virginia Tech shootings, other colleges around the country used email and social networks to send messages of sympathy and support to the Virginia Tech students, as technology once again enabled the MySpace and Facebook Generation to reinforce their sense of "us".

Generation Give

As a result of these *events*, these *times*, and because most schools now make it a priority in their *teachings*, Millennials also grow up molding a Core Value of community service and volunteerism.

They've been labeled "Generation Give". Sound familiar, Boomers?

For many, it began at their schools in the immediate aftermath of the 9/11 terror attacks, with blood donations, school fundraisers to send money to the victims' families, pillow and blanket collections to ship to the relief workers working 'round the clock to search for survivors and pull bodies from the rubble of the three crash sites.

Remember: the classroom years are the great compressor, the great incubator, of generation-wide Core Values.

And Millennials were the ones discussing 9/11 and Hurricane Katrina and the shootings in the classrooms, cafeterias, buses, and locker rooms after each disaster.

These are value-forming historical events for this generation, just as the Great Depression, World War II, Cold War, Kennedy assassination, man on the moon, Consciousness Movement, Watergate scandal, space shuttle Challenger explosion, epidemic executive corruption, and similar events had been for other generations.

A *USA Today* newspaper story, "Kids trade spring break for a chance to help", chronicles the new wave of alternative spring breaks among Millennial collegians, a wave coordinated by Campus Compact, a coalition of a thousand colleges committed to community service. Instead of heading for the traditional spring break of beaches and beers and babes and boys, Millennial students, in noteworthy numbers, help others. An estimated "tens of thousands" of college students pour into the Gulf States during spring break 2006 to assist Katrina victims, even volunteering for the nasty clean-up work. 88-year-old Rosemary Doran, whose New Orleans house sits in eight feet of water, is helped by a group of Kansas collegians and tells the *New Orleans Times-Picayune* afterwards, "I wish I could adopt them, they're so adorable."

In 2006, when the oldest Mils are 24, applications to work for *Teach For America,* which recruits college grads to teach in underserved urban and rural areas, is triple the number of 2000, when the youngest X'ers were graduating. The Peace Corps took in the largest number of volunteers in thirty years (since the high-spirited Boomer heyday), up more than 20% from 2000. And VISTA (Volunteers in Service to America) enjoys a similar surge in volunteers with Millennials.

Portland, Oregon Millennial Elizabeth Jones gives up her career in corporate banking to join the Peace Corps. As she is about to leave for service in Panama, she sums up her own—and her generation's—Core Value: "There's a lot of need in this world, and it wasn't doing anything in my heart to help make the rich people richer."

This *Generation-Give* mentality is further reinforced in Millennials' minds because, during their classroom years, American schools are stressing community service more than ever before. And yes, there's also this healthy selfish motive: community service looks very good on a college or job application form, and this is a massive generation competing fiercely among themselves.

High School Community Service:
1984:   900,000 U. S. Students
2003:   6,200,000 U. S. Students

Here's a comparison, and this is not a knock against Gen X; it's simply a reflection of changing times:

In 1984, as the older X'ers were graduating from high school, 900,000 American high school students participated in volunteer community work as part of their school activities. In 2003, as the first Millennials are graduating, the number is seven times higher: 6,200,000 high school students.

59 Of The 60 Made It Up The Hill

As I write this book, I'm trying to find the funding to produce a training video for our nation's religions in Generational Faith-Based Strategy. This program about a secular strategy, which I've given in-person, helps leaders of all faiths to understand generational dynamics and use this knowledge to connect more fully with each generation of members and potential members. I want to put this training on video because it will be much more affordable for local houses of worship to purchase the video than bring me in "live".

Because of this project, I met a dynamic Gen X'er: Dr. Todd Marrah, a minister and Superintendent of a thriving K–12 Christian school system in Ohio, Tree of Life Christian Schools. Dr. Marrah focused his doctoral thesis on generational dynamics.

When we met, he shared this story, which so vividly demonstrates the sharp contrast between Gen X's Core Value of self-focused "survival of the fittest" and Millennials' Core Value of "we/team/group/us":

It is 2006. Dr. Marrah is leading 60 8th-graders through an outdoor obstacle course during a retreat.

Four years later, after high school, these 8th graders, born around 1992, will officially become Millennials.

At one point on the obstacle course, the kids must walk down a hill, jump a small creek, and then climb up the steep embankment on the other side. It's been raining. The grass is tall, wet, and slippery. 59 of the 60 kids successfully reach the top of the slope. The one who doesn't is a pudgy, un-athletic boy, new to school, shy, and barely known by the others. He tries to climb the hill but slips and falls onto the wet grass and mud, and slides back down. Tries again. Fails. Again. Fails. He's mud-covered and wet.

And this is where Dr. Marrah gets excited as he tells the story:

"I'm an X'er", he says. "If that's me on that obstacle course and I make it up the hill, and another person can't handle one of the obstacles, *that's too bad. Tough luck.* I don't look back; I'm on my way to the next obstacle. *Survival of the fittest. I don't ask you for help; you don't ask me for help.*

"But do you know what these Millennials-to-be do? All 59 of them stop at the top of the hill. Not 58. *All 59.* And without even discussing it—without even THINKING about it!—I watch from a distance as 20 of them grab each other's wrists, form a human chain down the slippery slope, lock hands with their classmate at the bottom, and everyone at the top joins hands and pulls them all up the slope!"

And that's not the end of the story.

"The boy who can't handle the hill is obviously grateful for the help, but he is also *mortified*. He is the only one who needed assistance, and he also is the only one who is wet and muddy. And he's in the *eighth grade*.

"Needless to say, on an obstacle course the unofficial leaders are the jocks, the athletes who best handle the obstacles. So do you know what these 8th-grade jocks do? They take off running and dive into the mud so their buddy won't be the only one!"

Hail the Millennials.

Formative years' times and teachings mold Core Values that influence lifelong decision-making.

This little anecdote, and others like it that I hear regularly from my clients and audience members around the nation, give us a good idea of how the Millennial Generation is going to pass through its life.

Positive Celebrity Influence

Another phenomenon of sorts is occurring during Millennials' formative years and is reinforcing even more this generational value of helping others.

When Gen X'ers were coming of age, America was much more materialistic, and MTV and other teen-targeted media were hosing down X'er children with constant stories and images of *conspicuous consumption and self-indulgence by the rich and famous:* actors, singers, CEOs, and other glitterati were showcased by TV for spending lavishly on *themselves.* Mansions, fur coats, diamonds, weddings, travel, limousines, $6,000 shower curtains, and on and on.

Remember the TV show *Lifestyles of the Rich and Famous With Robin Leach,* which aired nationally from 1984 to 1995, when younger X'ers were growing up? Wikipedia describes the weekly series this way: "The show featured the extravagant lifestyles of wealthy entertainers, athletes and business moguls."

That was then.

By the middle of the 1990s and thereafter, what do Millennials, in their formative years, hear and read about the nation's wealthiest people?

The Bill & Melinda Gates Foundation. Warren Buffett adding his own billions to the Gates Foundation mission. George Clooney, Oprah Winfrey, Brad Pitt and Angelina Jolie, Silicon Valley tech billionaires, and other celebrities using their fame and wealth to help the less fortunate, by being we-focused instead of me-focused; by feeling a sense of responsibility to do a greater good.

Mr. Buffett and Mr. Gates also create The Giving Pledge, which encourages billionaires to pledge more than half of their wealth to charity, either while they're still alive or in their estate settlement when they die. The year 2016 begins with some 138 billionaires worldwide joining the pledge. And Millennial billionaire and Facebook founder Mark Zuckerberg and his wife Priscilla Chan announce they will give away 99% of their company shares, which at the time of their announcement are valued at $45 billion.

And as this era of celebrities creates such a high-profile culture of philanthropy, one American generation of kids comes of age and forms lifelong Core Values.

For this reason, philanthropy faces a promising future in the U. S., if only its professional practitioners will use Generational Strategy in their fundraising and development. If you're requesting a donation, you should make your pitch differently to a Boomer than to a Silent or to an X'er or to a Millennial. The generations have different hot buttons and frames of reference when it comes to giving.

Core Values

All of these experiences have created Millennial Core Values of patriotism, a sense of nation, empowerment and engagement, volunteerism, charity, and teamwork.

Cause Marketing To Millennials

Some prominent companies are aiming "cause marketing" at Millennials. As a *Business Week* magazine story about this strategy is headlined, "We're Good Guys, Buy from Us."

Target stores, American Outfitters, Timberland footwear, Nike, Macy's, American Apparel, Starbucks, and others are in sync with research that says many Millennials are more likely to buy brands that support charitable causes.

And as a noteworthy number of young-adult Mils continue to live at home with their folks after their classroom years, in order to dig out from college and credit card debt, marketers know these young people also influence many major purchases by Mom and Dad, which adds to their generation's influence in the marketplace.

Declining Social Pathologies

And finally, many but not all teenage social pathologies have declined with the Millennial Generation. During their formative years, the teenage birth rate reaches a sixty-year low; teen crime drops; likewise for teen smoking.

Drug and alcohol use by junior high and high school Millennials-to-be is generally down, according to a study by the University of Michigan, although their improper use of the painkiller OxyContin reaches a record high in 2006. And research by The National Center on Addiction and Substance Abuse at Columbia University compares collegians' drug use in 1993, when X'ers filled our nation's campuses, and 2005, when Millennials dominate enrollments. And the study documents that the use of cocaine, marijuana, and illicit drugs in general is once again on the rise.

So, all of these decades after the Boomers launched the Drug Revolution, we are still a junked-up nation of kids and young adults.

Spirituality Rising

Millennials are demonstrating a significant interest in their own spirituality, faith, and religion. They haven't found a "home" for their generation's beliefs and thus join Boomers and Gen X in a search, a quest, for the right fit. Various research studies document that America's generations profess a strong belief in "God" or at least some higher power, but they're *not sure what that higher power is.*

According to U. S. Department of Education data, from 1990 (X'er college years) to 2004 (Millennial college years), enrollment at the nation's "faith-centered colleges" rose more than three times faster than enrollment at all four-year colleges. As one college senior told *TIME* magazine about his emerging generation:

"Young people want to know something bigger than themselves."

And yet, most Millennials say they do not belong to a specific religion and do not regularly attend religious services.

And hence, a crisis for America's traditional religions. Our training program in Generational Faith-Based

Strategy makes this simple point: religion's problem is generational, so its solution is generational.

A Perfect Generation, Right?

So, based upon what you've read so far, you parents of Millennials have darned-near succeeded in raising The World's First Generation Of Absolutely Perfect Children, right?

Brace yourself.

The Millennials are a normal generation. Like all others, they have their problems and challenges.

Threats To Their Wellness

Yes, overall drug use IS down. But the abuse of pharmaceuticals and marijuana escalates with young-adult Mils.

And our *next* generation is going to be growing up in an America where pot is legal in some states, not just for medicinal purposes but also for recreational use. What will be the impact on them of this new frontier?

Binge drinking by eighteen- to twenty-year-old females shoots upward when Millennial females begin to pass through those ages.

From my work with our nation's military and mental-health community, and with tremendous contributions from them, I developed a training program for mental-health clinicians—psychiatrists, psychologists, social workers, doctors, and nurses—on the subject of Generational Behavioral Healthcare Strategy to help them better understand and treat their patients from each generation. And from my homework and research for that application of generational study, here are SOME of the serious health threats to Millennials:

- High rates of suicide—highest among American Indians and Alaskan Natives;

- Homicide—highest among Millennial Blacks;

- Depression, anxiety, and panic disorders—higher in Millennial females than males;

- Substance abuse;

- Sexually transmitted infections like gonorrhea and chlamydia;

- And here's the big one—obesity. Epidemic Millennial obesity.

Fat Millennials

By the mid-2000s, the percentage of First-Wave Millennials who are obese is TRIPLE what it was forty years ago with Boomers at that age: 24% of Millennials are obese; not merely overweight, but *obese*. With Boomer kids, it had been only 8%.

Nearly 2/3 of Mils do not engage in regular, leisure-time physical activity.

Many of them have been made sedentary by the seduction of the Technology Revolution, where the only body parts getting a workout are their thumbs. They also grow up with a regular diet of fast-food and high-salt, high-fat, high-sugar foods and beverages in their school's cafeterias and vending machines.

And so Millennials are the first generation that will likely face, sometime down the road, *early-onset*, obesity-related diseases that will kill them at a younger age than prior generations who did not grow up obese.

Health experts worry that Millennials might become the first-ever generation to live shorter lives than their parents because of what happened to them nutritionally during their youth.

To give you an idea of how obese and unfit this generation is:

In 2011, when Millennials are aged 14 to 29, 27% of them do not meet the physical requirements to be admitted into the United States Military.

And of those who do gain admission, the Military then loses 12,000 of them each year—men and women—before they complete their first term of enlistment because they don't meet the medical requirements.

Gary Player

In 2013, Gary Player, one of the all-time great professional golfers, poses nude—very discreetly (no private parts showing; only his very toned 77-year-old arms, legs, and torso)—for the annual Body Issue of *ESPN The Magazine*. In a subsequent interview with *USA Today*, the native South African who has now lived in the U. S. a long time, said:

"I love America, but...America is maybe the most unhealthy nation in the world because they live on *crap*. They've got the best food in the world, the best farmers...but 55% of the greatest country in the world is obese? If I can encourage young people to look after their bod[ies]...I will have achieved something greater than 18 major championships."

And this is why he agreed to the attention-getting photo, showcasing the 77-year-old body that puts many 20-year-olds to shame. If you haven't seen the photo, search online for "Gary Player Nude Photo".

American obesity—all ages, now—is so bad that architects are now designing office buildings and the spaces inside them in a way that will encourage healthy lifestyles, especially during the often-sedentary work-hours. The concept is called "Active Design", which encourages the use of stairs instead of elevators, makes employees walk farther to get to the coffee machine or office printer, and provides outdoor space—trails and paths—that mobilizes employees.

And one of my clients, Steelcase Manufacturing, which makes office furniture, gave me a tour of its headquarters building, which houses their experi-mental office furniture prototypes. One such piece: a collection of four treadmills, facing each other and connected tightly together. The idea is for four em-ployees to have a meeting with each other, eye to eye, while walking on the treadmills.

But the concept of "chicken soup for the soul"—the argument that we look to food for comfort, especially during stressful times—suggests that obesity won't go away until a major change occurs in America: employers must provide more job stability to U. S. workers. We eat when we're stressed. And sure enough, the nationwide rise of *adult* obesity began just as corporate executives began their slaughter of the middle class in the late 1980s and Americans realized they were losing control of their own lives, losing their empowerment. And so they headed to the refrigerator.

By the way, it is no accident that the decade of the '90s also witnesses another symptom of this loss of control, to go along with the obesity: a phenomenon called Road Rage, when American motorists suddenly turn on each other: aggressive driving; sudden acceleration and braking; close tailgating; cutting off other motorists or preventing them from merging; chasing them; assaulting them; sounding the horn; yelling, threatening, and intentionally colliding with them; and even shooting and killing them.

Struggling Americans, it seems, are reaching an emotional breaking point. Road Rage is not merely a consequence of greater traffic congestion; it is too pervasive and too sudden for such a simple explanation. Rather, Americans are losing control of their lives and futures. Angry and bewildered and power-less, they boil over and lash out.

And in the midst of this, a generation comes of age.

When a prior generation of business and govern-ment leaders had so passionately nurtured workers' job stability in the post–World War II years, Americans were willing to take on their own weaknesses: racial prejudice; sexism against women; and, their trashing of the environment. They had their security, they felt good about themselves, they had room in their hearts and heads to take on major self-improvement.

Such feelings have been largely absent from America, for all but the richest and most powerful few, since that time. And younger X'ers and all of the Millennials have never experienced those positive feelings and behavior.

Sex Bombardment By Mass Media

Another concern about Millennials: commercial tele-vision—in its pursuit of Millennial spending dollars amid the brutal competition from digital media—has increased both the volume and the boldness of its vul-garity and sex content in its desperation to hold on to young viewers. So, too, have books, music videos, mu-sic lyrics, video games, Hollywood movies, magazines, the Internet, the apparel industry, the pornography industry, professional sport, and virtually every other teen-targeted medium except one:

The one medium that has thus far refused to join this "race to the bottom," as the media vulgarity and sex bombardment have been described, is the daily newspaper.

In puberty, Mils become the "hooking-up" generation: promiscuous sex, often oral rather than vaginal. And ubiquitous pornography sends out a message to their generation that sex is a *performance*, not an intimate act of love and procreation.

We still don't know the long-term impact on this generation of this sex assault by commercial media.

And as the media vulgarize the language, employers say they are frequently shocked and disappointed by Millennial employees' use of the more vulgar cuss words on the job, especially in front of clients and customers.

Dirt Up There In The Adult World

Just like Gen X'ers, Millennials have gone through their formative years witnessing what they perceive to be the ethical and moral failures of some trusted adult institutions:

* the Catholic priest sex-abuse scandals;

* the epidemic executive corruption atop corporate and government America;

* President Clinton's affair with Monica Lewinsky;

* and, athletes like disgraced cyclist Lance Armstrong using banned, performance-enhancing drugs.

How this perceived moral failure by the adult world will affect the Millennials is not yet fully measured.

Helicopter Parents

Here are additional concerns about this generation's upbringing that are attracting significant attention:

Millennials come of age so heavily supervised by adults that child experts are now pretty certain they've been over-parented: they've grown up too dependent upon always-present and protective parents and other adults to develop the necessary (1) independence of thought and (2) mental toughness the adult word is now demanding of them. You know the nickname for these over-protective elders: Helicopter Parents, who constantly hover over their children, ready to swoop in and rescue them from any setback or solve a problem the kids should've solved on their own.

Here is a chorus that I hear from many of my clients around the country, when I'm consulting them on Generational Workforce Management:

Millennials want their bosses to also be their parents; they're constantly asking for help and not standing up on their own two feet and taking responsibility for their tasks. What should we employers do?

The more extreme of these parents have now been nicknamed after a more extreme model of military helicopter and are called Blackhawk Parents. An example:

After I had presented Generational Workforce Diversity and Human Resource Strategy to the Ontario Nurses Association conference in Toronto, one Boomer mother in the audience confessed, "I've been a helicopter parent of my nine-year-old son. I knew I was over-protecting and over-nurturing him, knew he needed to learn and correct mistakes on his own, but I couldn't help myself. So I asked my husband to help me give our boy some breathing room but that didn't work either, and I didn't know how to stop my excessive attention to my son, so I bought a puppy."

She added with a giggle, "I now have the most nurtured dog in Canada."

Narcissism

This generation comes of age with parents convincing them that *you, my darling precious Millennial child, are the center of the entire universe. The world revolves around you.* The Millennial formative years are marked by a parental focus on building their children's self-esteem.

So, during their youth, in any kind of competition, everybody gets a trophy.

Free Play

This is also a generation that grows up with much less free play than prior generations enjoyed. Their childhood is the most structured, scheduled, and supervised in American history.

Because of his concern with this, California psychiatrist Stuart Brown creates the Institute for Play. And in a magazine interview, he scolds parents, saying:

"When you rush around delivering them to all those structured activities, it tells them you want them to be hyperactive, over-achieving, over-scheduled workaholics and that's what they could very well become as adults."

Bicycles?

So many Millennials never learned to ride a bicycle in their youth that "adult beginner classes" have now popped up in Los Angeles, San Francisco, Chicago, Minneapolis, Nashville, Atlanta, Washington, D. C., and New York.

Despite the bicycle's appeal as a healthful, cheap, and environmentally friendly conveyance, Millennials grew up with video games, cable TV, heavier automobile traffic on U. S. streets, and over-protective parents, all of which kept them indoors rather than outdoors. A San Francisco–area Mil named Amy Wang Hernandez listed "learning to ride a bike" on her "30 Before (age) 30" bucket list. And when interviewed by the *Wall Street Journal*, Robert Prinz, education director of the Bike East Bay club, said there was a waiting list for its adult sessions.

According to a 2015 national survey by research company YouGov, 5% of Americans age 55 and older don't know how to ride a bike, while 13% of Millennials don't know.

What The Heck Happened To Parents?!

How and why does American parenting swing so sharply when Millennials begin to arrive on the planet? From generational study, here is the (very) short explanation:

Gen X children had been raised in the most permissive parenting era in U. S. history. Their parents, suddenly time-starved as the women's movement enabled two full-time careers, were often absent. So X'er kids became latchkey kids and spent more time alone.

Not only that, but divorced parents also felt strong guilt about their failed marriages. They saw their Gen X kids struggling to understand: bewildered; angry; depressed; battered self-esteem. Parents didn't want to pile more pressure on them. So many moms and dads backed off, no longer preaching and scolding and correcting their X'er children as relentlessly as prior generations had done.

It was an experiment. It was brand new. Parents were conducting the trial and error to discover what did and didn't work within this new model of marriage, family, and parenting. They got some things right; they got some things wrong.

Parental guilt is a prominent feature of Gen X's childhood.

But in the early '80s, parenting in America shifts. And because it does, Gen X ends and the next generation begins.

Parents now get their first long look back at the way they had been raising their X'er children. And based upon what they see, they reach a couple of conclusions:

1. Children need more boundaries and rules than X'ers had been getting;

2. And, they need for their mommies and daddies to be more physically present in their hour-to-hour, day-to-day lives, especially in their pre-school years.

After Gen X kids had come of age in what generational author Neil Howe described as an "anti-kid" era, we now begin to see—in the early '80s—that little yellow sign dangling from cars' rear windows. Remember? The sign said:

Baby On Board

And mothers now become omnipresent Soccer Moms. And dads who behave the same way will be labeled Nascar Dads. It is a stark shift in American parenting in the direction of *I've gotta be a bigger presence in my children's lives.*

A number of Boomer parents bore Gen X children, divorced, remarried and then bore Millennial children. Having learned from their first go-round, many of them say they are quite different parents the second time.

And all of this means that young kids coming of age with this transformed parenting will develop different Core Values from those of Gen X.

And so begins, with the births of 1982, the Millennial Generation, which will formally become a generation eighteen years later when they begin to graduate from high school.

The teachings (parenting) change, and so the Core Values change.

In 1982, we do not yet know if the *times* will also change for young kids, but oh my, will they ever!

"Girls are on a tear."
"Boys are falling behind."

Here is another concern about Millennials, which continues a problem that had begun with Gen X: overlooking the boys.

In the early '70s, educational experts launched what was informally called the Girl Project to try to wipe out girls' historical weaknesses in math and science. Schools focused on girl-sensitive education. It worked then and continues to work today.

Here's a quote from Thomas Mortenson, a senior scholar at the Pell Institute:

"Girls are on a tear through the educational system. [Since the early '70s], nearly every inch of educational progress has gone to them."

And Harvard professor William Pollock adds:

"It's not just that boys are falling behind girls. It's that the boys are falling behind their own functioning and doing worse than they ever did before."

And the downward spiral by boys and young men is especially severe with African-Americans, which is heartbreaking to older Blacks who fought the courageous battle for people of color in the latter half of the twentieth century, achieved such spectacular progress, and thought they were creating better opportunities that future generations would seize.

Some X'er and Millennial black men *have* seized the opportunity. But too many others have fumbled the ball. Maybe it's education's fault, maybe it's society's fault, maybe it's the parents'. But maybe it's also time for young male blacks to look in the mirror, *man-up*, and embrace Michael Jackson's lyrics:

"I'm gonna make a change for once in my life,
It's gonna feel real good
Gonna make a difference, gonna make it right
I'm starting with the man in the mirror
I'm asking him to change his ways
And no message could have been any clearer
If you wanna make the world a better place
Take a look at yourself, and then make a change."

The road to manhood changed course with Gen X boys and Millennial boys, who are receiving mixed messages about manhood and relationships with women. As psychology professor Andrew Smiler at SUNY-Oswego told

USA Today, "Guys know they're supposed to treat women as equals, but we haven't changed masculinity, and we haven't taught boys and men how to deal with these women. We still tell boys and men they should be in charge and wear the pants."

And family physician Leonard Sax, in his 2007 book (when Mils were aged 10 to 25) *Boys Adrift,* suggests that many young men are becoming slackers, in part because their motivation is being undermined by too many hours of video games and a shortage of male role models.

These X'er and Millennial males have carried their search for their *identity* and *focus* into adulthood and the workplace. In my work with employers around the country, their comments as bosses and parents reinforce a single theme:

Our X'er and Millennial women are confident, competent, and focused, while the guys—not all, but some—from those generations seem to be lost. They can't find themselves.

As older X'er men have now demonstrated, the younger members of their generation and the Millennials will one day hit their stride and find their focus. But because of the unique times and teachings of their two generations' formative years, that focus is coming later in life than it did for prior generations.

Families And Little Moments

Since the 1970s, when the women's movement gave us dual-career, fast-paced, and time-starved parents—or unmarried parents—two generations of children have missed out on, as one Associated Press newspaper story described them, the "little moments": the million-and-one tiny instances in a child's life when she or he learns another *inch*— one more tiny morsel—of information about life, just by spending lots of *relaxed* and *unhurried* hours in the physical presence of Mom and Dad, listening to them, talking with them, sharing with them, *absorbing them.*

In their generations' family environments, many Millennial and X'er children are not exposed to the Million Morsels that most Boomer, Silent, and G.I. kids had sponged from their elders.

And over 17 or 18 years of childhood, those morsels from those little moments accumulate into a substantial body of knowledge.

The UCLA Center On Everyday Lives Of Families

In the mid-2000s, as the older Millennials are entering adulthood, the Alfred P. Sloan Foundation commissions a sizable study by UCLA to examine the intersection between American family life and work.

The findings point to the biggest change in family dynamics in the last half-century: mothers working outside the home. From an Associated Press news report about this study:

"Parents and children live virtually apart at least five days a week, reuniting for a few hours at night."

Study director Elinor Ochs concludes, "We've outsourced a lot of our relationships...there isn't much room for the flow of life, those *little moments* when things happen spontaneously."

And Ochs is especially concerned about this: "Returning home at the end of the day is one of the most delicate and vulnerable moments in life. Everywhere in the world...there is some kind of greeting. But here (in the United States), the kids aren't greeting the parents and the parents are allowing it. They are tiptoeing around their children."

Prior generations of kids didn't take this punch to the belly. X'ers and Mils did.

Families are in flux. Their lives together are cluttered.

Little moments. Lots of them. Lost. Which future generation of parents will correct this?

Campus Counseling

According to a survey of college counseling center directors, as the Millennial generation begins its campus years in the late 1990s and early 2000s, there is a sudden escalation of students seeking psychological counseling, which experts feel is directly related to their over-structured, over-parented, hyperactive schedules.

Here's the list of diagnosed behavioral problems: severe psychological problems; anxiety; panic attacks; substance abuse; eating disorders; self-inflicted injury; and, even withdrawal from college.

At some colleges, the wait-time for students to schedule a *second* counseling appointment is four to six weeks.

Wealth And Fame And Millennials

In 2006, a study by the Pew Research Center finds that 81% of those Millennials aged 18 to 24 rate their top two priorities in life as becoming (1) rich and (2) famous. The study has a ± 5% margin of error.

Blame the worldwide web.

Millennials come of age with MySpace and Facebook and Pinterest and Snapchat and other social media permitting Millennials to *present their life stories to the entire world.*

With Gen X'ers, who had come of age mostly pre-Internet, the mass media of their youth—radio and television and magazines—pounded their generation with the message that celebrities are important to their lives.

With Millennials coming of age with the web, the message is *YOU are the celebrity.*

The times change. And so the generational Core Values change.

But in a *USA Today* story about these generational values, consumer psychologist Kit Yarrow of San Francisco's Golden Gate University worries that

Millennials are in for "a sense of emptiness and depression" as they "put their validation and self-worth into what people who aren't close to them think of them".

Mils And LGBTQ

It is during the formative years of the Millennial Generation that a decades-long crusade by older generations for equality for lesbians, gays, bisexuals, transsexuals, and queer (with the "q" also referring to people who "question" their own sexual preferences) scratches its way upward. And by the time Mils are in young adulthood, it achieves its greatest triumph.

The historic date for the LGBTQ Movement: Friday, June 26, 2015. The Supreme Court delivers its landmark ruling permitting gay marriage in all fifty states.

Two days later, Gay Pride parades take place and *USA Today*'s front-page headline, above a photo of New York City's parade marchers, proclaims "PRIDE NATION". The most frequent chant in the parades: "50 States!"

A month later, Boy Scouts of America approves a resolution ending its system-wide ban on gay adult leaders and permitting individual scout units to set their own policy.

And in Congress, the Democratic Party begins to craft legislation that will outlaw LGBTQ discrimination in the workplace, education, credit, federal programs, housing, jury service, restaurants, and hotels.

For Millennials, this movement—and moment—are similar to what Boomers had experienced with the Civil Rights Movement of the 1960s.

America's more conservative religions lose a major battle with the Supreme Court ruling on gay marriage, while other faiths accept and even embrace it. In the *Dayton Daily News*, two days after the ruling, twenty local houses of worship, of various faiths, take out a full-page ad that says, "As communities of faith in the Miami Valley, we do support marriage equality and celebrate the spiritual values of justice, equality, hospitality and peace."

But the issue of gay marriage continues to be a wrestling match in American society, especially the debate about the impact of gay marriage on the children who grow up in a same-sex household. In fact, some of those children file an "amicus brief" with the Supreme Court in support of traditional male-female marriages. One of them, Katy Faust, raised by her mother and same-sex partner, wrote this:

"Most kids will tell you that if they could order their own world, it would be one in which they are being loved and raised by their mother and father. We should never encourage fatherlessness or mother-lessness. Children do best, and by extension society flourishes, when kids have a relationship with both their mother and father whenever possible."

And as Americans know, there are others who dis-agree and argue that same-sex couples can raise children who do just as well.

And Other Changes In The Family Unit

According to government data, some 40% of new births in the United States are to single women who either live alone or cohabit. And according to the Centers for Disease Control and Prevention, more than a quarter of births to women aged 15 to 44 in the early 2010s were to cohabiting couples, the highest on record and nearly double the rate from a decade earlier. Why?

Earnings of less-educated American men have fall-en in recent decades, while education levels among women have risen, making marriage less economically desirable and necessary for women.

The traditional benefit of marriage—that is, delivering greater financial security—has proved to be elusive to this generation. So some young couples cohabit, knowing how tough it is to make relationships work, postpone marriage until they're more financially stable, but then get unintentionally pregnant.

Affluent, highly educated Americans still tend to marry before starting families. Single motherhood remains most common among the poor.

Their generation has delayed marriage and parenthood to the latest ages ever in the U. S. In the mid-2010s, the men have been marrying at 28, the women at 26.

But with Millennials, the number of births that occur within traditional marriages—as opposed to single mothers or cohabiting unmarried couples—is increasing. In 2010, after the worst of The Great Recession, the birthrate among married people increased, while the rate among unmarried declined. Demographers predict this trend will continue with Millennials.

Mils, Marriage, Motherhood, And Fatherhood

How will Millennials shape their marriages? How will they parent?

A *TIME* cover story in late 2015, entitled "Help! My Parents Are Millennials", sets the stage for Millennial parenthood this way:

"Until now, members of the millennial generation... have mostly been busy following themselves. Helicopter-parented, trophy-saturated, and abundantly friended... and cast as the self-centered children of the cosseting boomers who raised them...millennials have a new challenge that has shifted their focus: raising kids of their own."

So what are the early signals?

The sense of equality and task-sharing between Mil spouses will build upon what Gen X began.

Mils will probably divorce less because they will have more years, and presumably more maturity and wisdom, under their belts before they marry.

Hopefully, that same maturity and wisdom will also make them better equipped to handle the jarring life-change of parenthood.

Like all generations, they'll imbue their children with many of their own generational Core Values. In their case, this means: optimism; idealism; a sense of nation; self-esteem; individualism and yet a sense of "we"; inquisitiveness.

Their generation, predictably, is turning to search engines and social media for parenting advice. And as they post the daily lives of their kids on those social media and subject themselves to online opinions as to how they're doing, they will feel pressure and competitiveness with others to be perfect parents.

Where X'ers proved to be achievement-obsessed helicopter parents, Millennials are being described more as "drone" parents who, as that same *TIME* story wrote, "still hover, but they're following and responding to their kids more than directing and scheduling them".

Hopefully, they'll be more financially secure before they marry.

And with all of this, hopefully, their children will come of age in happy and stable households.

Millennials also have a strong "be-there-for-my-child" Core Value. A comparison:

In 1999, according to Census Bureau figures compiled by Pew Research, 23% of mothers with kids younger than 18 (essentially, Gen X mothers) did not work outside the home. By 2012, as Millennials were just entering parenthood, the number had climbed to 29%.

And during the same period, stay-at-home fathers nearly doubled, from 1.25 million in 1999 to 2 million in 2012.

One current problem: working Millennial couples are struggling to either find or afford daycare for their children. There's a shortage of daycare workers, and daycare costs have increased.

Millennials' Children And Tech

And what will be the impact of technology on their kids? A story published in the *Austin American-Statesman* raises red flags. The headline: "Are we raising kids to have 'digital dementia'?"

The 2-year-old who can nimbly use an iPad could be en route to trouble with memory and thinking, according to psychiatrist and neuroscientist Dr. Manfred Spitzer: "When you use the computer, you outsource your mental activity."

While computers can be fine tools for adults who are using their minds all day long, they're poison for kids, he said, adding, "The more you train kids with computer games, the more attention deficit you get." He sees kids with high frustration and stunted social skills, and says the minimum age for media consumption should be between 15 and 18. Young people look at their smartphones about 150 times a day, and Spitzer feels this raises stress and anxiety in all ages, but especially in kids.

And the Academy of Pediatrics urges no TV for those under 2.

We know Millennials are damaged, probably permanently, by the Technology Revolution. As mentioned earlier, when we're in the middle of a true *revolution*, there is no manual to guide us through it, and so trial-and-error occurs. Who knew how to handle tech when it arrived and changed just about everything?

We know Mils are making heavy use of tech for advice on parenting, and they're posting every aspect of their children's lives on social media. But what we don't yet know is how Mils will permit their kids to use technology. Will they have the big-picture awareness to harness its good and shield their kids from the bad? Or not?

Mils And Marijuana

The phone call came from an entrepreneurial Gen X gentleman in Las Vegas. He creates and manages major business conferences and trade shows. He had booked me twice before for keynote speeches to his international tea conferences. Yes, as in iced tea; generational strategy goes *everywhere*.

But this call for a keynote on Generational Marketplace Strategy focused upon a new product. The conference is called Marijuana Business Conference & Expo, which is informally nicknamed Cannabusiness. As he explained, "Don't worry; your audience won't be a bunch of stoned potheads. These people are suit-and-tie Wall Street investors. They want to know if pot is The Next Big Thing."

Famed consumer advocate Ralph Nader had key-noted the group's 2015 convention; I was booked for the 2016 keynote.

Just as the legal barriers to gay marriage are coming down after decades of steady campaigning, so is America's resistance to the legalization of pot. As with the legalization of casino gambling, state lawmakers see legalized pot as a new source of revenue for their coffers. And so pot legalization for recreational use begins to make its way, state by state, to the ballot box.

One by one, beginning with California's approval of it in 1996, states stick their toes in the water and approve it first for medicinal use only. A few years later, Washington state and Colorado approve it for recreational use, too. With that, pot retail stores—with cannabis infused in foods and beverages—flourish.

And now, the nation waits and watches to see if stoned Coloradans will be less productive in the workplace, and can bosses fire them if they fail a pot drug test? Will they be more dangerous behind the wheel? Will drug traffickers take it across state lines and sell it where it's still illegal?

Will Mom and Dad help "turn on" their kids, with the argument *if you're going to smoke this stuff we want you to do it safely at home with us?* Will children eat pot-laced cookies and candies, either intentionally or unintentionally?

In the aftermath of Colorado voters' approval of the issue, emergency room physician George Wang of Children's Hospital in Denver says his ER is treating one to two kids a month for marijuana reactions, mostly from laced brownies or candies.

Will taxes from pot sales be the windfall that is predicted?

Will children go to school stoned? The answer to this one is "yes". Within a few months of Colorado's legalization on January 1, 2015, twelve middle-school students in suburban Denver were suspended for eating loaded candies at school, supplied by two students who were expelled. "A couple of our teachers noticed some kids who weren't acting right", said a school spokesman.

A Denver man, hours after buying marijuana candy, began ranting about the end of the world, pulled a handgun from the family safe, and killed his wife.

Law officers in states that surround Colorado complain of stoned drivers leaving Colorado and driving through their towns.

Kevin Sabet, executive director of Smart Approaches to Marijuana (SAM), which opposes legalization, told the *New York Times*, "By any measure, the experience of Colorado has not been a good one unless you're in the marijuana business."

In 2015, Ohio voters resoundingly reject marijuana legalization for both medicinal and recreational use: 64% to 36%. The *Dayton Daily News* prints this clever headline the next day:

NO-HIGH-OH.

So, Millennials and the young kids behind them pass through their formative years with the marijuana debate raging. They hear it's bad for them, but then they also hear it reduces nausea in cancer patients undergoing chemotherapy and relieves the symptoms when smoked by glaucoma patients.

So their generation comes of age wondering, *is pot good or bad, or both? Should we, or shouldn't we?*

Race In America: Are We Back-Sliding?

Millennials are two generations removed from The Civil Rights Movement that bloomed in the 1960s. By the time they begin to arrive on the planet, blacks and whites are thoroughly enough intermingled that most Mils come of age color-blind: it isn't white, black, brown, red, yellow; it's just "us". Skin color is now like wallpaper in the bathroom: unnoticed.

Racism, for all the right reasons, is not showing up on this generation's radar screen as prominently as it had with prior generations.

But then in the mid-2010s, the nation experiences a flurry of white police officers killing black crime suspects in Missouri, New York City, Chicago, Cincinnati, and elsewhere; and the slaughter of nine African Americans at Emanuel African Methodist Episcopal Church in Charleston, South Carolina by a 21-year-old professed white supremacist.

But then comes this, in the same year: the shooting and murder of a white Memphis cop by the black passenger in a car the officer had stopped because it was parked illegally. As it turns out, the passenger was on probation for a prior armed robbery and was not permitted to be in possession of the gun he used to kill the cop by shooting him multiple times. Later, it was determined that officer Sean Bolton had unknowingly interrupted a drug deal.

So where are we with race in America?

Mils And Their Money

Unprecedented college debt. Unprecedented credit-card debt. Restless job-hopping. The Great Recession. Unemployment and underemployment. Postponement of marriage. Postponement of parenthood. Living with Mom and Dad. Borrowing from Mom and Dad. Damaging Mom's and Dad's retirement nest-egg and forcing them to delay retirement. Postponement of saving money: they want to save, but can't.

Millennials and money. *Yow.* What a ride it has been in their early adulthood.

And their precarious financial position influences such industries as automotive, house building, travel, banking, healthcare, insurance, and many other sectors. And economists say it will be many years before their generation digs out and begins to spend in a normal manner.

Employers are considering different types of compensation, benefit, and retirement plans that are crafted for the unique needs of this generation.

It seems all of our generations are more financially illiterate than we should be. According to the 2011 Survey of the States, only 13 of our 50 states require high school students to take a personal finance class. And according to the National Foundation for Credit Counseling in 2012, 60% of 18- to 34-year-old Americans (Millennials and the youngest X'ers) do not even keep a budget.

Millennials' money woes create challenges and opportunities for the American workplace and marketplace. Financial-services firms, employers, and colleges might find a receptive audience if they offer guidance on personal finance to this debt-saddled and Recession-scarred generation: employers can offer lunch-and-learn workshops; community colleges and universities can offer courses; and, banks and investment firms can teach Mils by posting information on their websites and social media.

Immigrants: The Hispanic Tsunami

After World War II, Silent kids came of age with a wave of mostly European immigrants.

Boomer kids? Southeast Asian immigrants, especially Vietnamese.

Gen X and Millennials? The influx of Hispanics from Mexico and Latin American countries. Some of this immigration is legal and some is illegal. And so these two generations grow up with immigration as a front-page news item and with immigrants sitting next to them in many classrooms, especially as Hispanics spread from primarily the southern and western Border States to America's interior.

Millennials are generally accepting of immigrants but they're not sure how they feel about those who are here illegally and receiving healthcare and other benefits and paychecks that are costing money and jobs to legal U. S. citizens. Immigration is a major issue in America as Mils pass through their formative years.

The Tech Effect: Very Good And Very Bad

Gen X is America's first Computer Generation.

Millennials are America's first Technology Generation.

We know the *good* from this: Mils understand technology, they're fast with it, they learn it easily, they're empowered by it, it offers many time-saving efficiencies in their work and personal lives, and it gives them instant access to much of the world's information.

But we're just beginning to identify the *bad*, as this generation now has delivered more than a decade of track record in adulthood and the workplace:

⚜ cruelty and bullying: technology has permitted Millennial kids to communicate anonymously, and the result of that anonymity has been more public and vicious cruelty towards and bullying of others, with instances of suicide by victimized kids;

⚜ gaming addiction: one Millennial male flunked out of the University of Iowa because of his addiction to video gaming (the game *World of Warcraft*, in his case), entered an expensive treatment center in Seattle ($14,000 for 45 days), and described tech addiction "as destructive as alcohol or drugs";

⚜ FOMO (Fear Of Missing Out): Mils' constant connection to everything and everyone has created the FOMO phenomenon, the fear of missing out on *any* tidbit of information and—*OMG!*—being the last to know; and so arrives the 24/7 tech addiction and the desire to leave their cells/mobiles turned on while they sleep;

* short attention span: Mils have grown up getting their information in tiny little "mini-bursts"; and the information has come to them so relentlessly that their attention spans are detrimentally shorter than older generations. I have the privilege to conduct Generational Leadership training at some of our military bases. And after a session at Spangdahlem Air Force Base in Germany, I received an email from a woman stationed there and who attended our briefing and wrote: "I listened to a song this morning by the Black-Eyed Peas that I think describes the Millennials perfectly:

> "I need it immediately, and I just can't wait.
> I want it immediately 'cause time can't wait.
> I ain't got no patience, I sure can't wait."

The name of the song: *Now Generation.*

As one Pew Research study concluded, Mils have "a remarkably superficial knowledge of complex subjects", as well as:

* difficulty in completing long-term projects;

❧ limited creativity (when asked to "create", Mils turn to their technology and wonder, *What are my hardware and software capable of creating?* instead of beginning with a truly blank canvas and asking themselves what their *minds* are capable of creating);

❧ abuse of technology on the job; using it for personal pursuits when they should be working;

❧ a certain awkwardness and lack of skill in "live" conversations, either in person or on the phone; for example, I received a phone call from a woman who handled the college internship program at a San Francisco area hospital. She had attended one of my training seminars in Generational Strategy and wanted to share this story and ask a question:

"A very bright and charming Millennial student at the nearby University of California-Berkeley came into my office on the first day of her internship. She was supposed to report to another person but she got lost and came to me. I said 'No problem, I'll call the person you're supposed to report to, and she'll guide you to her office.' I called the person and handed the phone to the intern, who immediately *fell apart.* As I watched and listened, I saw this intelligent and charming college student suddenly stutter and stammer as she talked on the phone, and her face flushed. I truly thought she was either having a stroke or on drugs. She hung up, looked at me, and said very sheepishly, 'I'm not very good on the telephone.' Was that generational?"

I told her I imagined it was, to a certain extent. Perhaps an extreme example, but here's the point:

Millennials have come of age communicating via texting and social media, instead of "live" and eye-to-eye. This means they type their message and are able to check it before sending it. If they don't like the way they've phrased it, they can change it. *They get a second chance.*

They do not enjoy this luxury with a "live" telephone conversation or a "live" in-person dialogue. NO SECOND CHANCE. You have to get it right the first time.

This is similar to what an actor experiences: if Tom Hanks is shooting a film scene and flubs a line, it's no problem: "Take two." But if he's performing on Broadway before a live audience and flubs a line? No second chance.

The "live" phone chat is no problem with prior generations, who had to learn how to think and speak spontaneously. But technology can make it a pressurized situation for Mils;

❀ Technology has also diminished Millennials' ability to read body language, a skill that has been described as *silent fluency*. Other generations are fluent in reading another person's body language, which gives so many clues as to what that person is thinking and feeling, a major advantage especially in a business situation. Mils, with their faces in their mobiles, are proving to be less skilled at silent fluency.

Nicholas Carr, author of "The Shallows: What the Internet Is Doing to Our Brains", writes this for the *Wall Street Journal* in a piece headlined "Automation Makes Us Dumb":

"Worrisome evidence suggests that our own intelligence is withering as we become more dependent on the artificial variety. Rather than lifting us up, smart software seems to be dumbing us down."

The Stanford Study Of The-Internet-Of-Things

The Tech Revolution is too transformational for us humans to fully grasp, too massive for us to understand its impact on our lives. And because our devices are about to become our personal confidants and counselors, Stanford University researchers, in December 2014, launched a *100-year-long* study (!) to assess the implications "of systems that can make inferences about the goals, intentions, identity, location, health, beliefs, preferences, habits, weaknesses, and future actions and activities of people".

Findings from this century-long study will be released every five years.

One debate that will affect the generation that follows the Millennials centers on this question: to what extent does technology belong in the classroom? Until we decide our answer, tech trial-and-error will occur with youngsters' minds and skills.

Millennials Are The Guinea Pigs of the Tech Revolution.

The "Extremes" That Mold Each Generation

Each generation comes of age during some kind of unique EXTREME:

- G.I. Generation kids come of age during the extremes of The Great Depression and two World Wars.

- Silent kids come of age during the extremes of the depression and war, and an era of extreme conformity and postwar materialism.

- Boomer children come of age during the extremes of youth empowerment, social activism, and prosperity for many.

- Gen X kids come of age during the breakdown of the family unit, the dramatic increase in the number of mass media outlets, and the computer revolution.

- And now Millennials come of age in the extremes of the technology revolution, protective parenting, and epidemic executive corruption.

While each generation of kids is in the middle of one of these hurricanes, there is no guidebook to tell them or their elders how to deal with it.

And so they must undergo the trial and error to find out how to deal with it; what works, and what doesn't.

They get some things RIGHT in handling these extremes and they get some things wrong.

It seems that it's not until maybe ten or fifteen years later, when we have hindsight, that we finally get a clear look at each extreme and identify the good and bad that have come from it.

And we are only just now getting an idea of the likely long-term effects, good and bad, on the Millennial Generation of their childhood extremes of tech, over-parenting, and executive corruption.

Big Picture

The big picture?

Millennials are going to be great. They're just pushing traditional adulthood to a later-than-ever age.

They *feel* like a generation, much like the G.I.s and Boomers do, because they know their age cohort shares very unique formative years' times and teachings and Core Values. In other words, they're aware that, from coast to coast, people their age have a common core.

They've been imbued, by their formative years, with a long list of positive Core Values: optimism; empowerment; engagement; ethics; compassion; assertiveness; and yes, like the Boomers, a definite swagger and cockiness that will probably be a good thing and not a bad thing.

Do Not Call Us Gen Y!

Millennials make one request: *don't call us Generation Y, and don't call us Echo Boomers,* as some marketers and media are doing.

To them, Gen Y sounds like their generation is nothing more than a continuation of Generation X; the tail at the ass-end of the Gen X dog. And they'll tell you, *we're not them; we're different from Gen X.*

And they're right. BOY, are they different!

ABC News commissioned a national survey about this, just as leading-edge Millennials were entering adulthood, and before this generation had been formally named. And *Millennials*, not *Generation Y*, was their top choice.

Got that, news media? And for print publications that sometimes struggle to fit the lengthy word "Millennials" into headline space and lazily settle for Gen Y, there is a very simple alternative that is an unambiguous reference to this generation. And unlike your use of Gen Y, this one won't insult them:

Mils.

U. S. Army Recruitment Campaign

In the early 2000s, the U. S. Army creates a new advertising tagline for its recruitment campaign: "An Army of One."

That tagline—*An Army of One*—is excellent Gen X messaging. Self-reliant, independent, individualistic. X'ers are 59,000,000 armies of one.

But then, America goes to war in 2003 after the September 11th attack. And the Army now needs to recruit both me-generation X'ers and we-generation Millennials, who are growing up more patriotic and more nationalistic in their thinking than X'ers did.

In one TV commercial, the Army does a nice job of creating two-generation appeal:

As we view video footage that constantly switches from *individual* soldiers (Gen X appeal) to *groups* of soldiers (Millennial appeal), here's part of the narration we hear:

"An American soldier serves more than his army. He is a selfless defender of our rights and our freedoms. (This is good messaging to the September 11th, patriotic Millennials). He is proof that one soldier can and does make a difference (good messaging to X'ers)."

So with this single TV spot...*multigenerational* appeal.

The Revolution: Extended Adolescence

Millennials have launched a revolution. It is profound and probably permanent. It has an informal name: "Extended Adolescence."

This generation is re-defining what it is like to live life in one's twenties. In significant numbers...Millennials are using their first decade of adulthood to:

*   sample different jobs and careers and employers;

*   have a little fun before settling down, perhaps travel;

❋ and, postpone the serious adult commitments of career, marriage, and parenthood.

In 1970, according to the U. S. Census Bureau, American women married for the first time at age 20. Today, Millennial females have pushed that beyond age 26. And the men are 28.

In 1970, American women bore their first child at age 20. Today: beyond 26.

And how are Millennials financing this Extended Adolescence?

Yep, by living at home with *my best friends, my weekend buddies, my role models, my confidantes: Mom and Dad.*

What Is Causing This Extended Adolescence?

1. Millennials face unprecedented credit card debt.

2. Millennials face unprecedented college debt.

3. Millennials are hit hard by The Great Recession of the late 2000s and early 2010s. When the national unemployment rate peaks around 9%, it is double that—18%—for Mils only. Many have

been, and remain, unemployed or significantly underemployed.

4. Not only that, but this generation of young adults is the most frequent job-hopping generation in American history. In 2014, the average 26-year-old Mil had already worked for seven employers since leaving the classroom years. Although some have genuinely advanced their careers and income in this manner, this restlessness is hurting the chances of many others to improve their financial positions and job security.

5. Millennials are using their first decade of adulthood to have some fun, maybe travel a bit, and remain single before beginning their long-long-long career commitment and family track.

And they're not purchasing houses. Instead, they're renting. In the question-answer session after I delivered a speech to the annual conference of the National Association of Corporate Directors in Washington, D. C., a gentleman from a mortgage-lending company asked, "If our industry lowers the mortgage interest rate, will we entice Millennials to buy houses?" And I gave him the discouraging list: college debt; credit-card debt; job and income insecurity;

job-hopping; don't want to be burdened by a mortgage; and besides all of this, the mortgage-lending and banking industries crashed our economy with their executive greed and corruption, and so Millennials view them about as highly as they view cigarette companies: *your industry ruined my grandparents' retirement savings; you knocked my parents, my friends, and me out of work; you ravaged our nation and caused coast-to-coast suffering!*

6. And finally, we are entering a golden era of anti-aging science and medicine. And young Mils know they're going to live beyond 100, which means they're going to have to work eighty or ninety or one hundred years, or longer, so:

What's the rush?!!

With Mom and Dad paying the rent, utilities, and food bills, there are a number of twenty-somethings who DO enjoy some discretionary income. And some Millennials are making lots of money, especially those working in the technology sector. As a result, marketers of some higher-end products and services— jewelry, alcohol, apparel, and others—who previously targeted 30- and 40-somethings are now advertising to 20-something Mils.

I received a call from a distiller of a pricey brand of Kentucky bourbon, seeking information about Millennials. The company had always targeted one specific $40-a-fifth brand for people in their late 30s and older, but it now wanted to learn how to appeal to a younger target demographic, given this shift.

Pro-Labor? Pro-Union? Anti-Rich-Ruthless-CEO?

It is likely Millennials will be a pro-worker, pro-little-guy, and pro-labor-union generation, and perhaps with an anti-executive attitude.

Why? Millennials' formative years have occurred during the era of *very rich celebrity CEOs*. This generation has come of age regularly hearing and reading the countless stories of American executives receiving unprecedented compensation packages and massive bonuses.

And the way many Millennials see it, those executives—particularly the ones leading the massive, publicly held corporations—received this astonishing wealth because they pleased shareholders by cutting costs and increasing profits by laying off thousands of American workers or sending their jobs to cheaper labor overseas.

And those laid-off workers just happen to be the Millennials' moms and dads.

In this well-documented era of the richest and most powerful few getting much richer and more powerful, the once-great American Middle Class being slaughtered, and the bottom 85%-the average worker- struggling to survive...

a generation of American kids has come of age and molded Core Values that will guide their decision-making for life.

And when you layer that perception of *executive excess* over the epidemic *executive corruption* in this country during the 1990s and 2000s, it's pretty easy to forecast a generation that is going to be pro-worker and anti-executive.

And a national-award-winning radio commercial, a public service announcement that targets Millennials, captures and reinforces this generational Core Value.

The sixty-second spot is actually an anti-smoking message. It was part of the anti-smoking campaign in the state of Minnesota. But it's easy to understand how it also solidifies that anti-CEO Millennial Core Value.

This radio spot begins with a traditional "man-on-the-street interview", except it's a young woman on the street.

She walks up to a couple of Millennial girls standing on the sidewalk, as we hear the noise of cars passing by them on the street. Here's the dialogue:

Female interviewer: "All right, you mind answering some questions for me?"

Teenage girl: "No, not at all."

"Alright. For 25.4 million dollars, would you go to school naked for one day?"

"Oh, yeah. Yeah, definitely." (the girl's female friend giggles in the background).

"Would you eat road kill for 25.4 million?"

"I think so, yeah." The sidekick exclaims, "But you're a vegetarian!" And the girl says, "Well, I know, but that's a lot of money."

"Would you end every single sentence with 'That was a stupid thing to say' for 25.4 million dollars?"

"Yeah, I could do that. That'd work."

"Here's your final question: For 25.4 million dollars, would you hook 3,000 kids a day on something you know will eventually kill a third of them?"

"Never."

"Well, the CEO of the tobacco company that makes Marlboro cigarettes doesn't have a problem with it. Last year, he made 25.4 million dollars in salary with stock options."

"That sucks."

(Voiceover tag): "Corporate tobacco won't tell you the truth, so we will…"

A radio public service announcement. Anti-smoking? Anti-rich-executive? Or both?

Piece-Meal Careers And On-Call Scheduling

For too many Millennials—and X'ers and Boomers—temporary jobs are the New Normal.

The ride-sharing service Uber is emblematic of a new and precarious career path that Microsoft

Research's Danah Boyd calls the "piecemeal labor force".

Along with other recent startups like Lyft, Instacart, Task Rabbit, and others, Uber offers minimal wages, minimal benefits, and virtually no promise of income to those who work for it. And in the post-Recession era, many otherwise unemployed or underemployed workers must accept this no-security offer.

Even more established firms like clothing retailer Abercrombie & Fitch, Victoria's Secret, and others had been practicing "on-call scheduling", which—as documented in a *Wall Street Journal* report—"requires workers to make themselves available for shifts that may be cancelled by the boss at the last minute and forcing workers to show up or stay home with little notice. Workers whose shifts are cancelled don't receive pay, even if they had blocked out that time and made child care or other arrangements."

As New York State Attorney General Eric Scneiderman said, "Unpredictable work schedules take a toll on all employees, especially those in low-wage sectors."

Under pressure from Schneiderman's office, and in response to a lawsuit filed by a Victoria's Secret employee, Abercrombie, "Vickie's", and others are ending on-call scheduling in their New York state workplaces.

But this is the treat-employees-like-dirt culture that Millennials have walked into as they've begun their career passages.

We all are the products of our formative years' times and teachings. And Millennials have come of age during an era of executive greed, corruption, and punishing treatment of U. S. workers. Now in adulthood, Mils are making decisions guided by the Core Values that came from those times, which helps to explain this:

"Sorry, Corporate America"

In late 2014 in our nation's capital, as mentioned earlier, I gave the luncheon keynote speech to 1,300 people who serve on Boards of Directors of American corporations. The event was the annual conference of the National Association of Corporate Directors. Here's a tiny snippet of what I shared with them:

"I apologize in advance. I'm about to quote a cussword from a headline posted on a Millennial-oriented news website, *elitedaily.com.* The headline reads, *50*

Things About Millennials That Make Corporate America Shit Its Pants (note: the actual headline spelled it "Sh*t").

"Sure enough, the column lists 50 reasons why Millennials are sickened by the corporate leadership culture they've witnessed thus far in their lives. In addition to the list of 50 reasons, the article delivers this generational warning to America's executives:

'Sorry, corporate America. We're just not interested. We gave you a shot, tried you out, and decided you weren't for us. We saw how you treated our parents, grandparents, and the bottom percents and realized you weren't that good of a guy.'"

I then went on to make this point:

Unless the Boomer leadership era of the 2010s and 2020s cleans up the ethics mess and the heartless and unmerciful treatment of American employees that Boomers have inherited from the Silents, big corporations are going to attract the *worst* members of both Gen X and the Millennial generations—the ones who will embrace that culture of greed and corruption and *employees are my puppets*—instead of attracting the best and brightest, who already are finding careers elsewhere.

We saw how you treated our parents, grandparents, and the bottom percents…

And this generational Core Value creates…

A Major Opportunity For Labor Unions

After the hard-earned gains that workers achieved with their unions during the post–World War II decades, after many workplaces had often been dangerous sweatshops, who could have predicted that it would all implode in the '80s, '90s, and '00s? Workers went backwards in job and income stability, and union membership plummeted.

Today, life is so uncertain for so many U. S. workers that labor unions face a tremendous future if they will only understand the needs and preferences of each generation in the workplace, expand their narrow vision beyond wages and working conditions, and then market themselves using generational strategy.

But I don't see much evidence that unions are training their leaders around the country in generational strategies and widening their focus. So they might blow the opportunity.

Millennials: The Future

Well, Millennials, here you are in adulthood. We don't yet know which year will be your generation's final birth year, so you're still coming.

And, like all previous generations, you're arriving with unique Core Values, which were molded during your unique formative years.

Here's what Americans still wonder about your generation:

It appears you're very much like the G.I. and Boomer generations and very different from Gen X. You seem to feel empowered (*I think we can make a difference*), engaged (*yes, I will participate fully in America's advanced citizenship*), ethical, compassionate (*sorry, corporate America, we just aren't interested*), with a strong sense of *we're all in this together so let's take care of each other*, and wanting to make a positive difference in life on earth. And you're sassy enough to think you can do all of this.

Is this accurate, or not? And if it is, will you succeed in pulling it off, especially when the going gets tough, which it will?

You came of age surrounded by lots of competition from other members of your massive generation: in the classroom; on the playing fields; and, in just about every other endeavor. In your careers, will you demonstrate competitive fire and thus give America another golden era of innovation, hard work, and productivity? Do you appreciate that people your age in emerging countries are *hungry* and *driven* and have their sights set on surpassing you and your nation? So, just how hungry are you in your careers?

Like X'ers, your formative years bombarded you with a lot of ethical and moral failures by your nation's leaders in business and government and religion and media. Do you simply accept this as *the way it is* and plan to behave the same way? Or do you envision an America without these shortcomings and ask, *How do we get this country right?*

Don't fret too much about these questions, Millennials.

All that's at stake with your answers is the future of the United States of America.

CHAPTER 11

When Will Millennials End And Our Next Generation Begin?

When Significantly Different Times And Teachings Produce Significantly Different Core Values

• • •

THE MILLENNIALS WILL END, AND our next generation will begin, only when we see high school graduates, coast to coast *and for several consecutive years,* clearly demonstrating a set of Core Values that is not just mildly different, but instead *notably* different, from that of Mils.

The next generation's unique Core Values will have been molded by unique formative years' times and teachings, which are difficult, if not impossible, to forecast. Over the past century, who could have predicted:

* World War I?
* The Great Depression?

- World War II?
- Postwar prosperity, the invention of television, and America's ascent to world leader?
- The invention of the birth control pill?
- The social activism of the '60s?
- Epidemic divorce beginning in the '70s?
- The demolition of the American middle class and executive corruption?
- The tech revolution?
- The terror attacks of 9/11?
- The Great Recession?

All of these events helped to begin and mold and end generations.

But remember, we mold our Core Values by the times and *teachings* of our youth. And the teachings are somewhat more predictable than the times:

Those kids born from roughly 1990 to 2010 have mostly Gen X parents. And at least partially, all of us *are our parents.* So we're just starting to witness the emergence of Gen X's kids and learn how much *Gen X* they have in them. Stay tuned.

Yes, some irresponsible noisemakers out there are declaring today's school-age teens are the next gener-ation—"Generation Z" or the iGeneration (*they are not yet members of a generation)*—and the news media are parroting this nonsense.

But I'll wait until valid research clearly documents that a significantly different set of Core Values, again, over several years, is present in America's high school grads; different enough from Millennials' to confirm and accurately declare that America's Next Generation has genuinely arrived.

With that said, here's a brief list of what we're witnessing in today's younger teens in their pre-generation years:

- decline in teen pregnancy, but continued unsafe sex behavior;

- stronger family units that also involve the grandparents;

- healthier foods in the school cafeteria and fast-food joints, and the childhood obesity continues but is diminishing with infants;

- a lessening but continuing sedentary lifestyle;

- continuing tech addiction, whose true ugliness will soon come out from the shadows;

* continued female denigration by video games;

* continued cruelty and bullying (as commercial television continues to rely upon cheap-to-produce "reality" shows, which survive on argument and confrontation);

* continuation of technology's wild-west, trial-and-error revolution;

* texting while driving;

* e-cigarettes instead of traditional cigarettes, although we're just starting to see sales figures level off;

* slight drops in alcohol and illegal drug use;

* stress and fatigue, especially as schools stubbornly cling to early start-times that clash with children's body clocks;

* continued lack of skill in math and reading, but improvement;

* skepticism towards the U. S. workplace and the executives who control it;

❀ and, continued fear for their physical safety on U. S. soil (shootings at schools, movie theaters, and elsewhere).

What Can Parents And Educators Do With Our Next Generation?

In 2014, *TIME* magazine published "ten requirements for teens that won't get them into college but will make them better people", a gentle nudge authored by Kristin van Ogtrop, editor of Time Inc.'s lifestyle brand Real Simple, and shortened here:

1. Write a letter that doesn't begin with "Hey" and is written on real paper.
2. Learn to cook a good meal for the entire family.
3. Hold down an unpleasant job that makes you hate your parents a little because they won't let you quit.
4. Go somewhere for the weekend without your phone.
5. Every time you get a new toy, give an old toy to someone who doesn't get new things as often as you do.
6. Take care of someone or something other than yourself.

7. Write a heartfelt thank-you to someone over the age of 70.
8. Read a book for pleasure.
9. Do something nice for a neighbor without expecting any credit for it. Keep your identity secret after doing so.
10. Don't race to the top. Get there slowly, deliberately, without knocking everyone else out of the way. Or missing the beautiful view.

Two More Millennial Chapters

Still ahead: one chapter on Millennials as consumers in the marketplace, and one chapter about them as employees in the workplace.

The Generational Disruption
Of The Workplace

. . .

CHAPTER 12

Generational Workplace Diversity And Strategy

Recruitment, Onboarding, Training, Management, Communication, Retention, Harmony, Teamwork, Fulfillment, Culture, Productivity

• • •

BY FAR, THE MOST WIDESPREAD usage of generational business strategy is in the management of the American workforce. Two groups benefit from this training:

1. Employees, when trained in Generational Workforce Diversity, learn to understand, appreciate, and work smoothly with coworkers from other generations, even though they might bring different values, skills, and methods to the same tasks;

2. And, when employers and supervisory personnel are trained in Generational Workforce Management Strategy, they are better able to:

A. recruit the best employees from each generation;

B. onboard them smoothly, in the critical first few hours, weeks, months and years;

C. train each generation appropriately;

D. manage, motivate, and lead each one according to their unique needs and preferences;

E. communicate with each one effectively;

F. retain employees from each generation;

G. enhance intergenerational understanding and harmony among all employees;

H. maximize their sense of fulfillment with their work and thus their bottom-line productivity;

I. and, create a permanent, comprehensive, and nimble workplace culture of generational diversity and strategy.

Generational Workforce Strategy helps to guide an organization's:

- Overall Culture
- Manpower Planning
- Compensation and Benefit Planning
- Job Recruitment Advertising
- Candidate Screening and Interviewing
- Recruitment and Retention
- Employee Training and Development
- Leadership Training and Development

- Internal Communications
- Mentoring, Employee Advocacy
- Team Building
- Talent Management
- Innovation
- Performance Assessment
- Succession Planning
- ...and more.

What Do ALL Generations Want On The Job?

Naturally, this book showcases generational *differences*.

But as we all work shoulder to shoulder each day with members of other generations, let's remember that, when it comes to jobs and careers, *all* generations seek—and hope for—the same core of experiences and outcomes:

- An employer that is honorable and a good corporate citizen in its community and nation;
- Executives who are ethical, compassionate, and talented; the new buzzwords towards that end are Compassionate Capitalism, Conscious Capitalism, and Servant Leadership;
- Executives who are as dedicated to the welfare of employees as they are to the bottom line and shareholders;

- Executives who will place themselves on the same side of the fence as their employees so that *we all rise together or we all fall together* (this is the most significant missing piece in the American workplace today);
- Meaningful, fulfilling work;
- Positive relationships with coworkers;
- Respect, leadership, and recognition from the boss;
- Opportunity for advancement; or,
- Opportunity to *stay put* and not be pressured to climb the ladder;
- Opportunity to be heard and provide meaningful input into the organization's success;
- A fair wage and relevant benefits; and,
- Long-term job security and a stable, high-quality life with career/personal-life balance.

If an employer delivers all of this, it is well on its way to being a desirable destination for all generations of employees, which means it can attract and retain top talent and enhance overall productivity and profitability.

So that's the big picture.

Now, here are tighter-focused and generation-specific guidelines:

CHAPTER 13

Silents In The Workplace

Tips, Tactics, And Guidelines

• • •

THE EMPLOYEE BENEFIT RESEARCH INSTITUTE conducted a controlled survey of older Millennial workers who then were age 25 to early 30s. The top two reasons why these Mils said they plan to work deeply into later life:

1. Want to stay active and involved;
2. Enjoy working.

Not "need money" or "keep insurance benefits", which ranked lower in their responses. They say they will *want* to work.

As do all generations. So:

Employers, erase any old tapes playing in your heads about age, employment, and retirement. The notion of retirement for most of us at age 65? Dead. Forever. Which bring us to...

The Silent Generation worker.

Unique skills that younger generations don't possess. Wisdom. Maturity. Experience. Loyalty. Magnificent work ethic. And thanks to modern science and medicine, more physical and mental vigor than any prior generation at this age.

A recent study documents that older workers are usually (1) better than younger ones at *problem solving* but sometimes (2) need more time than younger workers to *learn complex new tasks.* So, employers should help older workers maximize this strength and minimize the shortcoming.

Key Point: the Silent Generation's primary workplace shortcoming? Knowledge of technology. But they can eradicate it easily if only employers will understand they need a somewhat different hardware/software training session than younger generations; today, this is one of the biggest failings of employers. More detail on this key point in a few more pages.

Home Depot And AARP
"This is a gold mine of resources for us."

In what the *Wall Street Journal* described as the first-ever attempt to target thousands of mostly Silent workers, Home Depot and AARP launch a national hiring partnership in the late 2000s.

AARP recruits and trains Silent workers (and the very leading edge of Boomers), and Home Depot hires them in all departments. Think about it: if you walk into a Home Depot or Lowe's or local hardware store and need assistance with a DIY project, who gives you more comfort: a Gen X or Millennial employee, or a Silent or Boomer? Thought so.

Robert Nardelli, then chairman of Home Depot, said this in an interview: "When you look at the skill set, the knowledge and career experience, and the passion of these members of AARP, this is a gold mine of resources for us to draw upon."

The Silent Generation will be working energetically for a number of years, and they bring a unique set of Core Values and attitudes, skills, and wisdom to the workplace that other generations don't possess and will thus welcome the opportunity to learn.

Consider the title of a *Business Week* cover story about Silents:

"Old. Smart. Productive."

This story states, "High-level work is getting easier for the old. Internet search engines serve as auxiliary memories...And these people are also creative, drawing upon a lifetime of observation and experimentation."

Urban Institute senior fellow C. Eugene Steurerle addressed the U. S. Congress House Ways and Means Committee about the growing pool of retired Silents and said they "have now become the largest underutilized pool of human resources in the economy."

So, with their unique formative years that you read about in this book, and with the unique generational Core Values and attitudes that were molded in those formative years, who are Silents in the workplace?

Silents At Work

* Strong work ethic.
* Disciplined.

* Energetic and productive and smart.
* Courteous and diplomatic; good manners and interpersonal skills.
* The company comes first.
* Don't rock the boat.
* Loyal/less attrition.
* Respect for authority and company history.
* Team players.
* Consensus builders.

One of the reasons Silents have distinguished themselves in the so-called helping professions is their Core Value of inclusiveness. If ten employees are seated around the conference room table and the discussion is led by a Silent, you can be fairly certain all ten will have a generous opportunity to be heard. And if there is disagreement, the Silent will skillfully find consensus.

* More private than younger workers.

In casual conversations with their bosses and coworkers, Silents are probably less likely than X'ers and Millennials to share the intimacies of their personal lives. They tend to be more private and discreet than younger generations while at work. X'ers and Mils, you should be alert for this generational difference and sensitive to it when conversing with Silents. Probably not a good idea to ask your Silent male boss how the Viagra's working or whisper to a female Silent coworker about your sexting.

* Probably more flexible than younger generations on work hours (they're empty-nest: fewer family entanglements).
* Fountain of wisdom. Think of all they've experienced in their lives and careers!
* Valuable mentors to younger generations.
* *Stick to it.* Often more patient and focused with long-term tasks than shorter-attention-span Mils.
* Especially good social and interpersonal skills; deal well with customers and clients. The customers' needs come first.
* Good "front" people for an organization; less likely to make a politically incorrect blunder.
* Would some of your clients and customers *prefer* to deal with Silents rather than younger employees? Trust? Courtesy? Maturity? Experience? Wisdom? Helpfulness?

I presented a training program in Springfield, Oregon. Afterwards, the president of a regional bank shared this thought:

"I'm the president, but I'm not the face or personality of our bank. At banks, *tellers* are the faces. And many of our bank's older customers, and some young ones, are put off by younger tellers who are tattooed and body-pierced and cold and simply not 'warm'. Is there any reason we can't hire retired Silents, who are so skilled at customer service and emit such a strong vibe of trustworthiness and courtesy, on a part-time or even job-share basis?"

He asked this question precisely at the moment in time when Generational Strategy was first suggesting that this is an excellent idea. Look around today: in banks; department stores; hardware stores; and elsewhere where customer interaction is vital. Do you see Silents in selling and customer service? Do you feel a certain sense of comfort and relief when a member of their generation walks up and asks, "Can I *help you?*"

Recruiting Silents

* Identify and eliminate obsolete thinking and age bias in your HR and management culture and throughout your organization.

* Identify the best channels to locate and recruit this generation. They're probably different from the younger generations' channels.
* Review the copy for your job recruitment ads; is it tilted towards younger employees, with words like "eager" and "energetic," or does it emphasize "experience" and "maturity"?

From an Indianapolis engineering company comes this alert: the VP of Human Resources participated in our training workshop and said his organization had screwed up. His people had discovered that, in their recruitment of candidates, they had fallen victim to Buzzword Bias. As he explains it, the engineering industry is regularly creating, as most industries do, new buzzwords: the latest hip and trendy jargon, usually created by younger employees. These buzzwords aren't especially important, he added, but their recruiters had been evaluating candidates partially—and subconsciously—by whether candidates were familiar with them. Younger candidates tended to know the buzzwords, older candidates often didn't. And the recruiters finally realized they had allowed some very talented older candidates to slip right through their fingers, and for the stupidest of reasons. The lesson: put your entire recruitment process under the microscope. Are you guilty of needless Buzzword Bias in your recruitment ads, resumé review, candidate screening, interviewing, evaluation, and final selection?

* Explain the company's history. Silents will want to know.
* Explain the organization's big picture and goals and processes.
* Be creative and flexible with schedules, compensation, benefits, and perks. Be as generation-specific as possible. A simple example:

A Florida insurance agency re-hired a retired Silent gentleman to work as its accountant. The Silent was the perfect candidate, didn't need the work or the money but enjoyed working and *knew everything*, and his request to the agency was simple: "I'll work for you if it won't disrupt my Wednesday round of golf with my friends." Done! The boss says the Silent's wisdom and experience are irreplaceable and the work always gets done accurately and on time (natch, he's a Silent!). And his weekly golf outing is preserved. Generation-specific scheduling.

Managing Silents

* Train Silents in Generational Workforce Diversity.

  Life in America changed profoundly just as this generation left its formative years for adulthood, so there is a significant cultural and lifestyle gap between Silents and the three younger generations. What's more, Silents began their career years when the American workplace was a very different culture from what it is today. Teach them why the workplace values and attitudes of Boomers, X'ers, and Millennials are often not the same as their own, and teach them how to understand and work harmoniously with the other generations. This training, incidentally, is essential for *all* generations.

* Identify, respect, and utilize their generation's unique strengths.
* Help them overcome their primary shortcoming: they will probably need technology training.

  Key Point: If at all possible, find fellow Silents, Boomers or, if necessary, VERY sensitized and understanding X'ers or Mils to train them in tech.

Silents and some Boomers will need and want to ask many basic, ABC-type questions about hardware and software because they never received Computer 101 training during their classroom years, like X'ers and Mils enjoyed. Instead, they had to learn technology on the fly, and usually piecemeal in small mini-blasts of instruction. They might be self-conscious about asking "dumb questions" of a younger instructor who gets frustrated when they *don't know something so simple!* Silents will probably be more willing to open up to an instructor who truly understands where they're coming from. And what too many younger bosses still don't understand is this: the reason tech training often doesn't *stick* with Silents—the reason they say "now tell me again how to do this"— is because they were never taught the basics of what happens inside that computer when they click that mouse or touch that screen. If Silents understand the *logic* behind the hardware and software—in other words, if instructors allow extra time to teach the logic instead of jumping right into a specific program or application—then Silents will "get it" and remember it. But if you can't provide a Silent or Boomer instructor, sensitize your X'er or Millennial instructor to this need of Silents. Give the Silents

their pride, acknowledge their career track record, pro-actively solicit "the dumb questions",
don't make them feel rushed or embarrassed,
and make it fun.

If the younger generations need 60 minutes
for tech training, make it a 90-minute session
for older workers.

If you train them properly in tech, you will
then get that long, long list of coveted workplace
values and attitudes that Silents deliver.

* Give them personal attention. Their America is
  much more human-touch than the America of
  X'ers and Mils.
* Don't mistake silence and courtesy for disinterest.

In a group meeting, their silence and calm-
ness and unwillingness to interrupt others or
talk loudly to make their point is a result of
Silents' Core Values of courtesy and inclusiveness. Silents usually listen—and think—before
they talk. You might experience a pause before
Silents respond to a question. This is not a slowing brain. It is a very thoughtful and intelligent
brain preparing its best response before talking. Younger generations could learn a lot from

this approach. Silents tend to be less aggressive than Boomers and Millennials, *but they're fully engaged.*

♦ Be sensitive to their age: especially the hearing and sight diminution that X'ers and Mils will one day experience.

Is your workplace lighting adequate, right down to the individual workstation? Are your chairs comfortable for all ages? Floors solid and even? In lengthy meetings, are you scheduling frequent-enough restroom breaks? What time of day are you scheduling those meetings? Is your type size large enough? What about extraneous noise, including that humming air duct in the ceiling that might make it harder for them to hear? With hearing loss in mind (and by the way, hearing loss is now occurring at younger ages), have you conducted an employee lunch-and-learn to teach everyone how to recognize body language in another person—the slight head-turn or the squinting eyes that are trying to read lips—that is trying to convey to the speaker, *Please speak up, I can't hear you clearly.*

♦ Consider new work arrangements: job sharing and leave sharing; part-time; flex-time;

telecommuting; phased retirement; creative compensation, benefit, and pension plans; and more.

After lopping off higher-paid older workers in favor of cheaper and younger ones for years, American business now recognizes it must do everything it can to *retain* the workplace values and wisdom and skills of Silents and Boomers, especially because Gen X is a small generation and will not deliver enough warm bodies to replace Boomers when they move on to What's Next. Age discrimination in the workplace is dying a very swift death. So we're just now entering a golden era of creative workplace accommodations.

Key Point: in Human Resources from this day forward, there is no such thing as a bad idea. The complexity of the multigenerational workplace demands a culture of receptivity to new ideas and doing things differently than before. So we all must be willing to step outside the box and be excited about the wonderful possibilities when we do so. As we all live and work longer, the workforce will one day become 5-generational. And then 6-generational.

I know. *OMG!!*

❀ Don't let staff meetings conclude without giving your Silent employee, probably sitting quietly and listening intently, the opportunity to share years of experience and wisdom.

CHAPTER 14

Boomers In The Workplace

Tips, Tactics, And Guidelines

• • •

IN FLORIDA, I CONDUCTED A training seminar in Generational Workforce Diversity And Leadership Strategy at a national conference of about 200 people who work at hospitals around the nation. They were Silents, Boomers, X'ers, and Millennials.

Each of them was given a wireless remote-control device that enabled them to electronically answer my multiple-choice questions and see their answers instantly tabulated and presented on the big screen in the front of the room.

Here was one question:

"What is your individual opinion of the OTHER generations with whom you work?"

And here is how they answered:

When I asked Boomers, Gen X'ers and Millennials for their opinions of their Silent Generation coworkers, 42% felt positive about Silents and 25% felt negative, and the others had no strong opinion either way.

When I asked Silents, Boomers, and Millennials about their Gen X coworkers, 37% replied positive and 32% negative.

With Millennials, the other generations were 34% positive and 40% negative.

And now here is how Silents, X'ers, and Millennials feel about Boomers on the job:

68% positive, only 18% negative.

Many employers, especially the ones trained in Generational Workforce Strategy, now understand that most Boomers—not all, but most—deliver such an exceptional work ethic, energy, maturity, sense of team play, ethics, commitment to the organization, and skill that they should be aggressively recruited and retained.

They are The Golden Generation in the workplace.

And in massive numbers, they will never fully re-tire and go flop on the beach for a couple of decades. They don't want to. And many cannot afford to.

And because we're entering this new frontier of breakthrough anti-aging science, Boomers become the first generation to truly have no idea how long they might live if they take good care of themselves. So how can they possibly know how much money they'll need to retire? They can't know! So:

How can I possibly know WHEN to retire?

They can't. Which leads us to this:

**The New Reality In The Workplace:
Finish Current Career And Launch *Career Next***

Here is the new Boomer-driven reality, the new mod-el, in the workplace, and it is probably permanent for future generations:

1. work as long as possible in your current job; or,

2. retire from that job and launch a full-time, full-blown Career # 2, perhaps going to college to

get the training for it (a spectacular opportunity for community colleges); or,

3. finish one career and then take an assignment with the same employer or elsewhere that might be a lower-rung position with lower pay but also fewer hours and less pressure, and it might be full-time or part-time; or,

4. consult, train, take on project work; or,

5. start your own business, possibly working from home (in the mid-2000s, more new businesses were started by Boomers than any other generation); or,

6. volunteer.

Boomers, can your generation do ANYTHING without turning American life inside-out??

Why are Boomers doing this? Why this New Model? Answer:

1. To supplement retirement income;
2. Remain productive, stimulated, and involved;
3. Experience another fulfilling type of work, perhaps for a worthy cause;

4. Help and mentor younger people with their careers;

5. And, give employers adequate time to capture their knowledge, skills, values, and productivity.

Boomer Core Values On The Job

⁜ The career-driven generation. Excellent work ethic.

⁜ Willing to care about the entire organization and their coworkers, not just themselves.

Boomers, like Silents and the G.I.s, are a socially skilled "people" generation. When you couple that with their career drive, you can understand why Boomers frequently socialize with, and become personal friends with, their coworkers. Gen X'ers are more likely to compartmentalize and separate their work and personal relationships. A Gen X woman, in a recent seminar audience, shared this story with me, with shock and bewilderment in her voice: "I had just begun to work with an insurance company, and a Boomer coworker came up to me on my *first day* with two cups of coffee, and do you know what she wanted to do? She wanted to *have a chat!!*" X'ers generally like to come to work, do the job, and go home at quitting time. Yes, they're friendly, but they're not schmoozers. Boomers like to take time to get acquainted, and if necessary they'll gladly work past quitting time to make up for it. No right or wrong here. Just different generational Core Values. Not a problem if managers and all employees are trained in generational workforce diversity.

* Willing to go the extra mile, work the extra hours.
* "Work" to them means *vitality* and *contribution*.
* Ethics and values are very important.
* Assertive, aggressive.

Boomers, a massive generation, *had* to grow up competitive with each other and thus are pretty aggressive and outspoken. They'll fight hard for their beliefs, and they want others who disagree with them to push back just as assertively. And if they're unhappy with their work, they'll discuss it with the boss and try to work it out, rather than fold up the tent and quit. One client of mine put it this way: "If a Boomer employee is dissatisfied for some reason, she'll come right to the boss and fight for what she believes in and try to resolve the issue. When

X'ers become dissatisfied, we don't hear about it until, one day out of nowhere, they give us their two-week notice. Dissatisfied Millennials simply don't show up one day."

Note to Boomers: be careful that your natural assertiveness doesn't overwhelm, dominate, and suffocate those X'ers who might not fight back as vigorously as you fully expect and *want* them to do. Don't fall into the trap of dominating the dialogue around the conference table. Again, there's no right or wrong with either style. It's just important to understand why the generations bring different values, attitudes, and preferred ways of working to the job each day.

* Willing to lead and be accountable for their actions.
* Demand fair treatment for everyone, not just themselves.
* Willing to pay their dues.
* Play by the rules, but willing to vigorously challenge them, too.
* Outgoing, dynamic personalities.
* Comfortable with technology.

X'ers and Millennials enjoyed an early and wide lead in the race to understand and use technology. But now, predictably, the older generations are catching up and becoming as skilled with it. The Tech Gap was a gaping one during the 2000s, and it still exists, but it is shrinking. And with the proper type of tech training for older generations, it will soon disappear.

❧ Usually comfortable with change.

Boomers: don't dig in your heels and resist change at work just because you've done it one way for many years and it has always worked just fine. This is the classic older-employee trap. Be willing to be uncomfortable. Don't get so set in your ways that you become a burden.

❧ Team builders.
❧ Wisdom from varied experiences.
❧ Loaded with practical intelligence.

The white Silent male enjoyed that smooth career passage. But many Boomers have endured more rough-and-tumble careers. The good news from this: Boomers have seen so much, experienced so much, and been forced to create and survive and think outside the square. And this kind of practical intelligence is now cherished by American business.

From four separate research studies of Boomers on the job:

1. They're willing to learn and try new things (AARP study);
2. They're as mentally agile and quick as younger generations (Sloan Management Review study);
3. Boomers waste less time on the job than X'ers and Mils (Salary.com study);
4. Their motivation is actually increasing with age (Towers Perrin study, since renamed Towers Watson).

Many Boomers are now at peace with their compensation and benefits, their job titles, and their lives. This contentment frees them to simply enjoy their work and their coworkers, which enhances their motivation and creativity.

* Their generation is creative. A study by the University of Chicago and Ohio State University explains: younger people tend to discover new ideas by way of "lightning bolts"; that is, ideas that come to them from out of nowhere. Older people discover new ideas more as a result of their accumulated wisdom, knowledge, and experience. No right or wrong; just different.

- At this stage in their lives, Boomers might seek *personal growth* from their work, not just income. A *challenge.* Learning something new.
- As empty nesters, they might be more mobile and flexible with their time than younger generations who must deal with their family commitments.
- Boomers are usually skilled "front" people for an organization.

   Articulate, streetwise, sensitive to other people, comfortable in the spotlight's glare. They can take the heat. Sometimes, though, their generation's assertiveness might not be as politically correct as that of Silents. Boomers might be a little more spontaneous, blunt, and less calculating than Silents.

Recruiting, Managing, And Retaining Boomers

Does your workplace culture truly seek out, welcome, and *understand* the Core Values and current life stages of Boomer workers and prospective workers? Or does it not?

- Retirement security is now a priority to Boomers. Recruit them with this in mind. Discuss it during the interview process. And consider generation-specific compensation and benefits.

- Explain your organization's big picture. Boomers will care about your total success, not simply their own paycheck.

- Discuss short-term and long-term goals, both for the organization and them.

- Discuss fulfillment and personal growth, not just the ABC's of the position they're applying for.

- Is your organization guilty of age bias in the wording of its job ads and descriptions, and in its interviewing and screening?

- Consider new work arrangements: part-time; flex-time; job sharing; leave sharing; telework or "portable jobs"; phased retirement; part-time projects; consulting assignments; full benefits for part-timers; and others.

- Offer them choice and flexibility.

- Consider a referral program that pays a bonus to employees who help land Boomer (and yes, other-generation) recruits. One of my Milwaukee hospital-clients set aside $30,000 for such referral bonuses. And the bonuses were weighted: if an employee successfully referred a surgeon, the bonus was larger than if she referred a lesser position.

- Adopt a mindset that, during these times of generational differences, "there are no bad ideas" when it comes to Human Resources. Consider everything.

- Prove to Boomers—don't just say it, prove it— that your organization is ethical.
- Train Boomers, especially those in supervisory positions, in Generational Workforce Diversity And Strategy.
- Employee satisfaction surveys: capture and stratify the results of these surveys along generational lines to reveal possible generation-specific needs and wants.
- Consider new and customized compensation and benefit packages: match them to Boomers' current and future life stages. (Do the same for the other generations.)
- Don't overlook the Grandparent Connection; consider how you can turn this generation's passion for their grandkids into a recruiting, management, and retention advantage for your firm. Lunch-And-Learns on grandparenting? *Bring Your Grandchild To Work* days?
- Don't lower performance standards for them: "coasting towards retirement" is unacceptable to most Boomers.
- Include them in all new training, even if they're near to retirement. Boomers want to go out at 200 miles an hour.
- Promote or move them laterally. Not all employees need to pursue an upward path. You can sometimes re-invigorate long-time employees by

moving them sideways to a new assignment, department, team, and environment.

❧ Review your physical spaces and work schedules for possible aging unfriendliness. Don't patronize Boomers as they age. But with respectful discretion, accommodate their likely need for larger type size, good lighting, comfortable seating, regular breaks during long meetings, a quieter environment so they can more clearly hear telephone and in-person conversations, and so on. Do your phones have good clarity and volume-boost controls? Are you forcing employees to use cell phones—or to listen to you or others while you're using your own cells—with their notorious poor audio quality? Are you arranging a conference call? If so, ask all who can do so to use a landline phone, not a mobile.

❧ Can you offer a comprehensive "wellness" program: education and services that will satisfy this generation's desire to remain physically, mentally, and emotionally fit? Lunch-and-learn lectures, fitness club memberships, a regular wellness article in employee newsletters, on-the-job health screenings, and so on.

❧ Many members of this instant-gratification generation have not saved adequately for retirement.

Can you help them make up for lost time: more pay for longer hours? Creative benefit plans? More reward for more risk?

To Avoid The Boomer Brain Drain

Unavoidable mathematical problem: for every 8 Boomers born in the U. S. A., only 6 X'ers were born. Similar ratio in Canada. So whenever it is that Boomers retire from their current positions, there will not be enough X'ers to replace them.

In addition, Boomers possess workplace values and skills that younger generations do not.

Solutions:

* Retain Boomers as long as possible. And recruit Boomers—yes, even in their sixties and beyond—from the outside.
* It's not enough to "try" to recruit and retain Boomers. A half-baked effort will flop. It must be a refined, well-thought-out, Boomer-specific program.
* Can you help reduce their stress and burnout?
* Phased retirement (but not phased *performance*), for those who want to retire over several years.

* Create a program to *systematically* capture and transfer Boomers' (and Silents') knowledge to the next generations; ask Boomers/Silents to develop this program. Capture their wisdom in print, but also consider recording them: both audio and video tapings. "Alumni reunions": bring back retirees to impart their wisdom to employees.

* Identify promising Millennial leadership candidates to overcome the shortage of X'ers; fast-track them with (1) leadership training and (2) Boomer job-shadowing and mentoring. Leadership will come to Mils as comfortably as it has to Boomers. They'll lead differently, but it will come to them pretty comfortably, because of the times and teachings of their formative years. (You'll see that this bullet point also appears in the Millennials' workplace chapter).

CHAPTER 15

X'ers In The Workplace

Tips, Tactics, And Guidelines

• • •

WHAT'S ESPECIALLY IMPORTANT TO GEN X on the job?

- Training, education.
- Advancement based on merit, not some arbitrary time period.
- Security, stability.
- Women: mentoring; equal pay; opportunity.
- Work-leisure balance.
- Creative opportunities: products; services; methods.
- Positive relationships with coworkers.

- They will be the generation that eventually replaces the Boomers at the top.

Is your organization training them to replace Boomers and become leaders (which will not come as effortlessly to X'ers as it will to Millennials)? Are you devising a method to transfer Boomers' intellectual capital and practical intelligence to them? If not, contact me.

* They're creative, entrepreneurial.
* Self-reliant and independent. Sound ordinary? Take it for granted? Wait 'til we get to the Millennials.
* At ease with change: adaptive and nimble.
* Technologically savvy.
* Brilliant at finding solutions.

Boss, got a problem, opportunity, new idea? Need to find the best solution? Turn your X'ers loose on the project, give them the time and tools to complete it, and give them credit when they achieve it. "Finding solutions" is a Gen X strong suit.

* Efficient.
* Linear mind-set, task-oriented.

Gen X'ers demonstrate a unique no-nonsense, high-efficiency approach to work. Their preference is to view each task as a straight line from A to Z, and they want to cover that distance as smoothly and rapidly as possible. This is a very good quality in many occupations.

And as X'ers move into the executive suites at publicly-held companies, shareholders will love this efficiency. But in such disciplines as selling, customer service, patient care, and others that involve the "human factor", the task is usually a more twisting, winding, up-and-down journey, not a straight line, and X'ers sometimes struggle with this.

- Career gender-benders; the first generation, in such big numbers, in which women successfully pursued traditionally male jobs, and men took on previously female professions.
- Willing to work hard.
- Want to make money and be secure.
- But also seek work-leisure balance and have frequently avoided careers with unpredictable hours or shifts: healthcare; firefighter; police officer; retailing; and others where the work involves evenings, weekends, or rotating shifts.
- Global perspective. They came of age during the early years of the global economy.
- Seek a workplace culture that embraces new ideas. All they request, boss, is that you'll be open to their suggestions and give them a chance. And as Boomers now take their turn at the top and lead with more openness and flexibility than Silents did during the 1990s and

2000s, X'ers should find more receptivity by the boss to trying something new.

* Individualistic, results oriented.
* Survival of the fittest. *I'll take care of me; you take care of you.*
* Self-focus comes more naturally than group focus.

The adult world failures that X'er kids witnessed during their formative years engendered in many of them a self-protective inclination: *me first.* Millennials and Boomers? 180 degrees opposite: *we; us; group; team.* No inherent right or wrong to these values; just "different". Employers need to be aware of it.

* Entered adulthood not expecting or promising loyalty.
* *Every job is temporary. I assume I'll get laid off someday.*
* Every company, every job, is a stepping-stone to something better.
* Career free agents. But as X'ers age, they're "churning" less and digging in with one employer.

X'ers and Millennials have job-hopped much more than Boomers, Silents, and G.I.s did at the same age. X'ers are not genetically programmed to job-hop. They would love to enjoy stimulation, fulfillment, and advancement with one employer, but they came of age seeing too many bosses unilaterally dismantle the traditional two-way loyalty with employees, so this "stepping-stone" attitude is an acceptance by X'ers that they can't count on loyalty from, and longevity with, any employer. So they must always be ready to move on and seek other opportunities.

There is a unique Gen X gender dynamic in the workplace:

- The girls came of age during the era of the Surging Female and, all these years later, sure enough, they're surging in their careers. Confident, competent, focused.
- A noteworthy percentage of the boys had a more difficult childhood because it was, in some ways, an anti-boy era. And so today, a number of them seem to be searching, trying to find their focus and identity. My clients around the country confirm this dynamic in their own workplaces.

What about these aspiring Gen X women? Surveys by Pew Research Center and the Business And Professional Women's Foundation indicate that the key needs and wants of professional women include:

* Advancement opportunities;
* Job-sharing or part-time work;
* On-site daycare for moms;
* A variety of work styles; these women are not all alike;
* Evaluation by productivity, not hours;
* They want to self-manage;
* Seek autonomy, not just flextime;
* Want to identify where and when they work best;
* Big pay is more important to women than to men;
* If they take maternity leave, keep them up to speed during their absence.

Some Gen X and Boomer mothers who left their jobs to raise children and then tried to come back are frequently having a tough time because of that hole in their résumés. And so some companies are trying to accommodate motherhood better. Consulting firm Deloitte developed a "Personal Pursuits" program that permits employees to take various kinds of un-paid leave, including maternity leave, for several years. The company offers periodic training sessions and assigns mentors to keep them current so they can return and hit the ground running. It hopes to cut down on turnover costs by rehiring these people after their leaves expire.

A *Wall Street Journal* story explained Accenture's "Future Leave" program, whereby the company helps employees to set aside, in advance, part of their pay to finance up to three *extra* months of leave, with benefits. But there's also an employee backlash to this. If not developed properly, generous "leave" programs will stick other employees with the task of picking up the slack for the absentee moms and dads. This causes resentment. So, develop such programs with all employees—and the good of the organization—in mind.

For Gen X men, remember that the number of single dads with child custody is growing. According to the Census Bureau, in 1970, when Silents were the dominant generation of parents, there were only 393,000 single-*father* families in America. By the 2000 census, when X'ers were aged 19 to 35 and beginning their turn as parents, there were more than 2 million, a five-fold increase in thirty years.

Because of the newness of single *dads* having child custody, and because Gen X has been a mobile generation and moved away from hometown friends and relatives, they don't have the same social support system that single moms have been able to develop over a longer period of time.

Here's what we're finding:

- Many dads are reluctant to take paternity leave;
- They fear career setbacks for using company benefits related to child-rearing;
- They're often teased or insulted because of their caregiving;
- They're often viewed as distracted, less dedicated to the job;
- But we're now starting to see a greater acceptance of paternity leave.

So, how can you help them?

- Keep them connected while they're on paternity leave;
- Educate—sensitize—other employees to dads-with-custody;
- Provide information/education to help them with their fatherhood and work-dad balance;

* Can you organize a "dads" affinity group at work?

And for both dads and moms:

* Flexible schedules?
* Extended maternity/paternity leave and pay?
* Transfers, perhaps temporary, to positions with less travel or better hours for new parents?

Boomer bosses: please remember that the joyous years when your generation came of age stand in stark contrast to those of Gen X's youth. Try to understand how their formative years shaped these kinds of values and attitudes:

* X'ers might be skeptical of elders, big corporations, and government; if you've read the earlier Gen X chapter, you now know why;
* Might prefer start-ups and smaller firms: fewer layers; less bureaucracy and workplace politics;
* X'ers don't blindly buy into a "pay-your-dues" philosophy (it requires two-way loyalty between boss and subordinate, and X'ers have constantly seen bosses unilaterally break that deal).
* Demanding attitude: want it fast;
* Seek respect from the boss and want their input to count;

* Generally not as aggressive and assertive in a face-to-face discussion as Boomers and Mils.
* Might choose a city first, and then find a job.

Some X'ers—and now Millennials, too—seek a certain way of life in adulthood. So they move to a city that offers it and *then* try to establish their careers. In the 1990s and 2000s, a number of U. S. cities launched formal initiatives to attract the young professionals of Gen X. This is why my client list includes local and state economic development departments that want to craft recruitment initiatives and community planning and lifestyles that will appeal to them. Some cities are succeeding, some aren't.

Recruiting, Managing, And Retaining X'ers

* Explain the time demand up front.

If, in an average year, there will be certain peaks and valleys in the hours required, outline those peaks and valleys with X'er job candidates *during the recruitment period,* right away! In as much detail as possible! This is one of the regular complaints I hear from my clients. Managers say, "Our business is not always a perfect 8-to-5 or 9-to-6 world. Sometimes, we face a crunch and we need our people to put in extra hours. But our X'ers draw a harder line on start-and-stop times than our Boomers, and when the clock strikes normal quitting time, they're gone, leaving us high and dry." So if necessary, discuss this during the interview.

One General Sales Manager at a major-market TV station said, "There is a period, in the spring months, when the advertising sales team at a television station has only a couple of weeks to sell advertising for the upcoming Fall TV season. It's now or never. Consistently during those crunch weeks, our Boomer salespeople are still at their cubicles at 8 or 10 p.m.; they understand. But all of my X'ers left at 6."

In Texas, after I had presented a training session to the Texas Society of Certified Public Accountants, a principal in one firm shared this story. "We recently had a Gen X female accountant time her pregnancy so she would be on maternity leave during tax season, which is our crunch time!"

And a physician's group affiliated with a hospital in South Carolina shared a similar story. When it was her turn in the rotation to be on-call when patients needed help after normal hours, a Gen X female physician was consistently refusing to take the calls, and her Boomer colleagues were forced to cover for her.

But here's a positive anecdote, which I mentioned earlier. It comes from another client of mine, one of the country's larger commercial construction companies, based in Atlanta, Holder Construction. An X'er employee and I were discussing this same workplace dilemma after my presentation to that company's management team, and here's what he said:

"I quit my previous job with another construction company because, in the summer months, the work mushroomed up to seventy hours a week, and I want to see my son's Little League baseball games. So, I started looking around and interviewed with Holder. I told them about my commitment to my kid and they did their best to explain, up front, when the peaks and valleys would occur, and we're trying to find the middle ground. I know I can't have it perfectly because I've chosen construction for my career and that means lots of work in the warm-weather months. But the company is demonstrating good faith and I figure they're doing the best they can to help me with my work-life balance. The key is, we talked about this potential conflict and got it on the table at the right time: during the recruitment process."

* Can you explain long-term career paths?
* Be technologically forward.
* Reward individualism, creativity.
* Key Gen X perks and incentives: cash and flex-time.
* They seek skill-building opportunities. Want to retain an X'er? Then train an X'er. Train them constantly. With X'ers, this can build loyalty. So build their toolbox.
* Offer mentoring.
* If a restless X'er leaves, remember that you might get him or her back, down the road; make their departure cordial and maintain contact.
* Quantify their performance, don't just pat 'em on the back; measure their performance and put it in writing.
* Give them constant feedback.

Some companies practice the 360-degree performance review, in which employers and employees review each other anonymously. And X'ers appreciate the sense of input and involvement this policy permits.

❧ Give them bountiful opportunities to provide input.

Open up communications lines between X'ers and senior personnel: ask-me-anything lunches; regular meetings; and, online dialogue; all designed to give X'ers authentic input and, hence, a true stake in the outcome of the organization.

❧ They're time-starved and stressed. Help them.

Gen X is passing through that period of life that, for all generations, is the heat of the battle: career advancement; marriage; parenthood; home ownership. They want to get all of this *right*. So, help them with these aspects of their lives and you will win their loyalty and productivity. Provide expert information, perhaps with lunch-and-learn lectures or printed content or downloadable/streaming audio and video on such matters as:

❧ Personal finance;
❧ Time management;
❧ Parenting;
❧ Marriage;

* College-selection counseling to help them help their kids;
* And for their oldest members, grandparenthood.

As you've undoubtedly seen, heard, and read, the wildly profitable tech companies in America are hosing down their employees with a long list of extravagant benefits. They're doing so because there is a shortage of the elite, super-skilled coders and programmers, and so the competition to win them is ferocious. Other industries, not rolling in as much cash, cannot offer the same luxuries. But these perks give us an idea of what appeals to time-stressed X'ers and Mils:

* On-site healthcare counseling;
* On-site daycare and perhaps on-site eldercare;
* On-site fitness centers, with full spa services;
* Errand-running services;
* Take-home dinners, with an on-site gourmet chef and deli;
* In the San Francisco Bay area, fleets of customized buses that pick up and drop off employees so they don't have to drive and can conduct their work in these high-tech vehicles;
* One non-tech manufacturer offers a basketball court;

* If you can afford a few perks, ask your employees from all generations to identify and prioritize the ones they like most.

Beyond their control, X'ers came of age during a time of widespread executive corruption and unethical behavior in so many corners of American business. They might assume this is the norm. They might also possess a strong self-focus that doesn't fit with your organization's team focus because, as generational author Neil Howe said, "Gen X has been all about survival." Ditto with this generation's possible cynicism, pessimism, and distrust. So:

* Be alert for their ethics;
* Be alert for their self-focus;
* Be alert for cynicism, pessimism, and distrust and understand where it came from.

I've phrased these caveats with the words "be alert for" because you shouldn't a*ssume* them. Many X'ers share the same high ethics, sense of team, and optimism as other generations. But because of their generation's unique experiences, these caveats are "possibles" you'll simply want to remember. And X'ers will welcome your guidance and help in doing the right thing.

- Make training visual. This is the MTV generation that grew up with rapidly-changing images on the TV screen and is vulnerable to swift visual boredom.
- Teach application—where the rubber meets the road—over theory.
- Teach hard and soft skills: accountability; business courtesy; interpersonal skills.

Training in common courtesies: after a seminar in Generational Human Resource Strategy at a big-city hospital, a male Gen X employee shared this: "I have two close friends, and we've talked about this. We were lucky; our parents drilled courtesy into us as we grew up. And whenever we're competing against other X'ers for jobs or promotions, we actually use our own courtesy as a competitive weapon against our fellow X'ers because we know most of them didn't have it pounded into them as we did." X'ers, in your fast-paced, no-nonsense approach to work, you can sometimes come across as a little blunt and sharp-edged to the others. Not a matter of right and wrong; just be aware of it.

After I had mentioned this during a presentation to faculty and staff at Passaic County

Community College in New Jersey, a Gen X female audience member nodded in agreement and told me, "I'm married to a Boomer (who was sitting right beside her at that moment). When he comes home from work and starts to tell me a story in his usual Boomer way with lots of detail and flourish, I hold up my hand to stop him and say 'Give me the short version'." She and her husband laughed; they've obviously made their peace with this difference.

* Train X'ers in Generational Workforce Diversity. They are an "island generation", like no other. The gaps between the other generations and their own are pretty substantial.
* Judge X'ers by merit, not seniority.
* Create a fun atmosphere.
* Reward individual achievement, not just team, group, department, or organizational success.
* Try to avoid last-minute, after-hours, pop-up meetings.
* Let them discover solutions their way and don't micro-manage them.

X'ers are skilled problem solvers and solution finders. This emanates from a long list of their unique Core Values, but especially from their independence and self-reliance. After I had given a speech about

Gen X to the national conference of the Community Leadership Association, the Executive Director of its Toledo chapter, a Boomer, walked up to the podium, carrying a hard copy of his chapter's Annual Report and beaming with pride. "I did just what you mentioned in your speech today," he said. "It wasn't easy because I'm a Boomer perfectionist. But when it was time to create and lay out the Annual Report, I gave the project to a staff of Gen X writers, editors, and designers. I spelled out the broad parameters, but then decided—and as a Boomer, this isn't always easy to do—to back off and let them run with this project on their own, and look at this! It's spectacular, and I wouldn't have done it as good myself!"

The Magnificent Marriage

There is a magnificent marriage waiting to happen in the American workplace.

Boomers: you're brilliant at leadership. X'ers: your generation's wheelhouse is execution. If you will both recognize your unique generational strengths, then you will grasp the enormity of the magic you can create *together.* And if you ever make that connection, America will soar.

Boomers: X'ers *want* you to lead.

X'ers: don't worry, your generation will get to lead, too, in a few years, and you will get a full turn at the top.

But seize the current moment: *together,* you're in position to knock one outa the park. And as Millennials start to establish themselves in their careers, they are nicely positioned to deliver the eagerness, enthusiasm, and fresh ideas that young adults should. Three generations. Lined up perfectly. It's time for America to dream big once again. And to *deliver* big.

X'ers As Leaders

Gen X will lead the nation, but at a later age then they might think because we're all living and working longer. After World War II, "normal" retirement age actually dropped for several decades, but now it is increasing and will presumably do so for a long time.

X'ers' strength is "idea" leadership: new products, services, workplace efficiencies and processes.

But they tell me, around the country, that they are struggling with the other part: "people" leadership. The Human Factor. Managing Boomers, Millennials, and their fellow X'ers.

This is a generation that came of age more roughed-up than prior generations by the adult world's failures, and more isolated and solitary in their lives. As a result, some of them just don't possess the basic interpersonal skills, persuasive skills, trust, group-think, and front-runner dynamism that leadership requires.

That pesky Human Factor.

Example: Travis Air Force Base, between San Francisco and Sacramento. We take a break in the middle of our Generational Workforce Management Strategy seminar for supervisory personnel at several Bay Area hospitals. Gen X woman comes up: "I recently took a management job at my hospital. I came from the outside, not from within the organization. I have a team of Boomers, X'ers, and Millennials and they're not responding to my leadership. They won't let me in. What should I do?" I asked, "Have you sat down with them and discussed it?" And her reply was classic, no-nonsense, work-should-be-a-straight-line X'er: "Oh gosh, that seems like such a waste of time; it seems like we should be working!" And I explained that, in leadership, the Human Factor is an integral and inseparable part of "work". She looked at me as though that thought had never crossed her mind, smiled, and said, "Ohhhhhhh, okay. Thanks, I'll do it!"

Similar seminar in Washington, D. C. for a national group of sixty elite leadership candidates. Gen X woman: "I'm not sure our generation even wants to lead. When we were coming of age, 'leaders' were dirty, rotten liars. Leadership is not appealing to a lot of us."

Key Point: there are many members of Gen X who DO want to lead and will be skillful at it. But generational leadership is defined by what the generation, as a whole, does during its reign. For Gen X, that reign will take place primarily in the 2030s and 2040s. Which means now is the time to give them the generation-specific leadership training that will maximize their strengths and minimize their shortcomings.

So, you employers, professional associations, and leadership organizations should provide generation-specific, not generic, leadership training to X'ers (give me a call; this is what I do).

Because of their generation's unique formative years, leadership doesn't come as naturally to them as to G.I.s, Boomers, and Mils; and, because of their generation's small population, you'll have to reach down deeper into their talent pool to replace all those departing Boomers, and you will probably be forced to promote under-talented X'ers to leadership positions.

Besides the generation-specific leadership training, here are two additional strategies to handle this shortage:

1. Fast-track younger Millennial leadership candidates;

2. And, hire military veterans, who—from their training and experience serving our country—have been taught the skills and values required of good leadership.

More than one X'er has asked during our seminars, "If the Millennials are lining up as a good leadership generation, is it possible we'll be working for them someday? Will they leapfrog us?"

Answer: American employers will probably fast-track Millennial leadership candidates, in part to cover the warm-body shortage from Gen X and in part because Mils will probably demonstrate leadership talent. But thus far, Mils have been job-hopping relentlessly, which might slow their advancement rather than help it. So, if X'ers stay put with one employer, their knowledge of the organization will give them a wider lead over come-and-go Millennials.

CHAPTER 16

Millennials In The Workplace

Tips, Tactics, And Guidelines

• • •

THEY HAVE A GREAT CAREER spirit, and they're going to be terrific, but right now they're driving us nuts.

I hear this repeatedly from managers and supervisors in every corner of the country and across all industries.

The Millennial employee.

What Their Generation Has Witnessed And Is Facing

Mils came of age when the richest few were getting much richer and The Bottom 85% in America were struggling. Mass layoffs by the bigger corporations were rampant. Corporate raiders were buying chunks of companies and then forcing executives to cut costs by downsizing the workforce. Loyalty from employers to employees was largely absent.

And then there was the war against terrorism, The Great Recession, and unprecedented college and credit card debt for their generation.

Unique formative-years' times molded unique generational Core Values regarding career, employer, financial stability, and nation.

Extended Adolescence

Remember, they're re-defining young adulthood, often sampling employers and professions and demonstrating little loyalty, having some fun, postponing long-term commitment to a single employer and to marriage and to parenthood and to home ownership, and living with their parents in higher numbers than prior generations.

No, not all of them. But this is the shift in American life that their generation has created.

From one year to the next, it varies slightly but remains relatively steady: by age 26, the average Millennial has already worked—full-time, and since the classroom years ended—for 7 employers.

They are the most frequent job-hopping generation in history.

In 2014, Mils aged 20 to 24 stayed on their jobs an average of only 16 months, according to the Bureau of Labor Statistics. For ages 25 to 34, the median tenure was three years, far below the 5.5-year median tenure for all workers 25 and older.

This track record has become a serious dilemma for employers in many industries, especially those in which employers hire highly educated college grads and instantly invest significant time and money to provide high-level training, only to lose them soon after as Mils add the prized training to their résumés and use it to "try something else".

For law firms, CPA firms, financial-services firms, healthcare, and other categories hit hard by this train-them-then-lose-them merry-go-round: might they need to shift their target recruiting age from the early or mid-twenties to the late twenties or early thirties? Yes, this would be a substantial paradigm shift, and the answer is probably industry-specific. *But twenty-something in America is undergoing profound and probably permanent change.*

When the oldest Millennials are about age 26 and delivering a generally negative performance to the U. S. workplace, I receive a phone call from an editor at the world's leading blog site, HuffingtonPost.com. He asks if I would like to author a regular generational blog for the site. I ask, "How did you learn about my work?" and he says, "You're quoted on the front page of today's *Metro* newspaper here in New York City, saying that employers—in order to survive Millennial job-hopping—might need to let twenty-somethings flip hamburgers for a few years until they're ready to settle down."

They're going to be terrific, but right now they're driving us nuts.

Millennials, X'ers, and even Boomers are going to be working deeply into their seventies and eighties, and perhaps beyond, as life expectancy shoots upward. So if Millennials' attitude towards commitment is *What's the rush?*, maybe employers should adopt the same philosophy about hiring them—*What's the rush?*—and allow this generation to finish its career-sorting process and mature a bit.

But wouldn't older generations love to have done this same kind of career shopping before settling down?

When Mils finally do dig in with one employer, they will bring with them a valuable variety of experiences and methods and ideas. And presumably, they'll be less restless because they'll now know what they want. It's like taking time to date around before marrying.

Older generations should also acknowledge this reality:

Millennial job-hopping is, in part, a direct response to an American workplace whose employers (especially the big publicly held companies) have so frequently demonstrated ruthless treatment of employees during the past quarter-century and thus forced many U. S. workers to become career free agents and string together a *series* of employers, often flying by the seat of their pants. This is the only culture Mils have ever known!

Right now, Millennials say their goal is a work-leisure balance (I despise the phrase "work-life" balance; work IS life). But they also want to change the world for the better. And overwhelmingly, they'll do so through their careers. So at some point, and it should be soon for the older Mils, they will kick in. And when they do, the rest of us can grab on to their shirttails and enjoy the ride.

They're gonna be great.

The Boomer Leadership Era is underway. Boomer bosses are likely to be more receptive to bold new workplace ideas than Silents were, and so they should create nimble cultures that will be a good fit for Millennials' needs, wants, and their big-dream, big-idea Core Values.

With this backdrop, what are American employers currently observing in Millennials at work?

The Good

* Idealistic, empowered, engaged.
* Upbeat, enthusiastic.
* Inquisitive.
* Environmentally *green*, socially conscious, and they demand that their employers be the same way; beginning in 2007, the nonprofit organization B Lab certified for-profit companies that demonstrate sustainable business practices, treat employees fairly, and contribute to their local communities' well-being; such companies may use the B Corp logo.
* Good "career spirit"; want to achieve; want to do the job right.

One college-graduating student at Miami University expressed it pretty accurately for his entire generation's career goals: "I like the intersection of money and meaning."

* They like an entrepreneurial culture. This does not merely mean starting their own businesses. The term *entrepreneurship* now means a workplace environment that is (1) truly receptive to new ideas and willing to change and (2) nimble enough to quickly take advantage of the best ideas.
* Job security appeals to many of them.
* Stable, old-line employers appeal.
* They want their work to "count", which is why they sometimes demonstrate restlessness with less important entry-level assignments.
* They're comfortable with older coworkers because they grew up with adults being such a constant presence.
* Love a group/team work dynamic.
* Collaborative: like to share information.
* Dislike bosses who hoard their knowledge and don't share it.
* Prefer decisions by consensus, not strictly from the top down.
* They possess an especially robust self-esteem, which is good and...

The Not-So-Good

This is the generation that came of age with parents who focused intensely on building their self-esteem. Thus:

* Narcissism.
* Flawed sense of entitlement.
* Unrealistic expectations about entry-level pay, position, and promotion.

In order to get their heads out of the clouds and feet on the ground, a Boomer female executive who managed a major department store on Long Island, New York during the years when Mils were entering adulthood, tells the same story to Millennial job candidates because, as she told me, "Millennial job candidates think they can come right out of school and be ready to manage one of our department stores in six months!"

Here's the story she tells them:

"I was driving to my store on Long Island on a beautiful September morning. Good weather for shoppers, so I figured we would have a good revenue day. I arrive at 8 a.m., two hours before we open at 10 a.m., turn on the *TODAY* show on the TV in my office for background noise, and begin my busywork. At 8:30, 90 minutes before opening the store, everything's fine. 8:45, everything's fine.

"A few minutes later, I glance at my TV and see live coverage of a major fire in nearby Manhattan. I recognize the building: one of the World Trade Towers. Wow, I think; big fire. Do I have any friends working on those floors where the fire is raging? No. I must continue with my work. 9 a.m., one hour before opening our doors, everything's fine. At 9:03 a.m., with network cameras trained 'live' on the fire, I see an airplane crash into the second tower.

"And now we know. Our nation, and my city, are under attack.

"When the second plane hits, my phone instantly lights up with calls from anonymous people saying *your company is a symbol of American greed, and we're gonna bomb your store today.* I wonder: are these crank calls or real threats, especially as I watch what's unfolding on TV, not far from my store? I now have about 45 minutes before the store opens. Do I open it and possibly risk the lives of customers and employees, if these phone threats happen to be legitimate? Or do I close it and perhaps needlessly lose a day of sales? I'll call in extra security but quickly learn there is no "extra" security available anywhere near New York City. There's no manual to tell me how to handle this; my professors didn't cover this in Management 101. I'll call our senior executives in our Manhattan headquarters and ask what to do. Wait, all the New York City phone lines are jammed! I'm cut off!

"This is going to be my decision. And the stakes might be life or death for my employees and customers."

In telling this story, the store manager then explains to Millennial job candidates the mental checklist she went through—and under extreme pressure—on that fateful day of September 11, 2001 to decide whether to open the store or not: every conceivable option and combination based upon her decades of experience. And when she finishes the story, those Millennials with their unrealistic expectations are thinking precisely what she wants them to think: *I'm not ready to manage a department store;* and, *I want a career in retail because someday, when I AM prepared, I want a job with that kind of importance and responsibility."*

By the way, she opened the store that day and nothing bad happened.

Mils And Technology: The Good

❧ They know it, they're fast with it, and learn it easily.

Mils And Technology: The Not-So-Good

❧ The immediacy of technology has created impatience.
❧ Tech has given them short attention spans.
❧ Tech has unquestionably addicted many of them, in a psychologically damaging sense:

From an Associated Press story: "[Millennial] Ben Alexander spent nearly every waking minute playing the video game *World of Warcraft*. As a result, he flunked out of the University of Iowa. Alexander, [then] 19, needed help to break an addiction he calls as destructive as alcohol or drugs. He found it...in high-tech Seattle..." which opened the first residential tech-addiction center in the U. S.

It is likely that tech addiction is going to diminish the performances and mangle the careers of some

Mils. In a biennial survey of some four-hundred Human Resource professionals coast-to-coast, conducted by York College of Pennsylvania, improper use of technology on the job by Millennials is one of the strongest criticisms of their generation. And it's on the rise: in 2009, 39% of HR professionals in the York study reported an increase in IT etiquette problems; by 2013, the percentage was up to 50%.

* Their knowledge is superficial; they've come of age getting information in mini-blasts instead of depth. One Pew Research Center about religion concluded that Mils have "a remarkably superficial knowledge of complex subjects". As the Tech Generation, Mils know a gazillion things *one-inch deep.* But in true depth? Much less.
* They're often not "in the moment".
* Because of the social-media culture of *everybody knows everything about everybody else,* be alert for this generation's attitude towards secrecy, if secrecy is important to your organization. Notorious "leakers" of private documents Edward Snowden (fled the U. S.), Bradley Manning (convicted of Espionage), and Aaron Swartz (committed suicide while under federal indictment) are Millennials.

⁕ More likely to be tech-discourteous; what is not offensive to Mils is offensive to X'ers, Boomers, Silents, and G.I.s.

⁕ Less-developed "silent fluency" (the ability to read body language, which is often very important in business).

Millennials And The Great Recession

The Great Recession ravaged our economy beginning in 2007 and continuing into the mid-2010s. During this window, the oldest Mils went from their mid-20s to their mid-30s.

Boomers lost the most savings. Gen X'ers, then in middle management, had a ton of extra work heaped upon them as subordinates and superiors were laid off and X'ers had to pick up the slack. And Millennials either couldn't land a job or had to settle for under-employment. When the national unemployment rate peaked at about 9%, the Millennial unemployment rate was twice that: 18%.

In 2012, *Business Week* magazine headlined its story about the Millennials' plight this way: "Generation Screwed".

To survive the Recession by cutting costs, some employers might have considered laying off higher-salaried X'ers and Boomers and replacing them with lower-wage young adults. But Millennials were already job-hopping and leaving the job each day promptly at quitting time. And so they shot themselves in the foot. During the Recession, employers needed reliable and experienced employees willing to *go the extra mile* and do more with less to get the company through it.

Millennials are scarred by the Recession, but they have decades to recover. And they will. Their generation's soaring optimism has taken a hit but remains intact. Short-term: uncertain. Long-term: positive.

But management personnel should be on the lookout for emotional stress among Millennials; the serious kind of stress that can devolve into behavioral problems such as anxiety and depression and even suicide. Mils face enormous college and credit-card debt, and The Great Recession heaped even more weight onto the financial pressure they feel. Most of them have no master plan to pull themselves out of this hole because there are no easy solutions. So, employers might want to consider offering on-the-job psychological counseling to these employees.

Other Millennial Values And Attitudes

Millennial college graduates are accepting job offers and then not showing up for their first day.

Gordon Miller, former senior recruiting manager at Procter & Gamble Company, told the *Wall Street Journal*, "We want to believe that an accepted offer is an agreement." But he and other hiring managers say Millennials accept offers but continue to look elsewhere during the interim between acceptance and start date. And if another offer is better, they simply blow off that original commitment.

* Less respect than older generations for the traditional workplace hierarchy and chain of command.
* Don't embrace seniority systems.
* Don't embrace annual job reviews; prefer continual updates.
* Will challenge the status quo.
* Will devise new ways to do business.
* Seek an advocate, not just a mentor.
* Seek access to senior management.
* Seek relevant, meaningful work NOW.
* Want in on the creative decisions NOW.

But:

The Great Recession was a needed reality check. The new reality for Mils: they cannot "flit" from job to job with no regard for the damage it's doing to employers. Looks bad on résumés.

Millennials also know they might never be able to retire. Social Security was never meant to support retirees for twenty or thirty years. When it was enacted in 1935, Americans died at the average age of 65, so Social Security benefits only needed to cover the final three-or-so years of a retiree's life. Today, we can receive those benefits beginning at age 62, but our average life expectancy is now 78 and climbing rather swiftly.

Millennials: Their Work Ethic

A number of insurance companies conduct generational surveys. From one such survey by Fidelity:

In a story in *The National Law Journal,* Bruce McLean, chairman of Akin Gump Strauss Hauer & Feld, says that new Millennial associates, even with mounds of college debt, often are not willing to make the sacrifice that is required to become partners and land the big money. And one managing partner at a New York City firm said of Millennial attorneys, "They are more willing to sit back and wait for things to happen to them instead of making them happen for themselves. They are (brazenly) willing to turn down work they don't want to do. They don't volunteer for committee or other firm work."

And to refer once again to that biennial York College survey of Human Resource professionals, in its 2013 study 45% reported a "worsening of work ethic" among recent Mil college grads and "no clear trends indicative of improvement" in a list of workplace performance measures.

Mils Are Getting *Smoked* By Their Foreign Contemporaries

Headquartered in Princeton, New Jersey, the nonprofit Educational Testing Service purports to "advance quality and equity in education for people worldwide by creating assessments based on rigorous research". From a report on one of its 2015 global assessment tests:

"The skills of America's so-called 'millennials' are comparatively weak in relation to their international peers.

Even the top-scoring and 'most-educated' U. S. millennials are trailing behind similarly situated millennials in most other participating Organisation for Economic Cooperation and Development nations (34 nations in all, both advanced and emerging nations) when it comes to skills in the realms of literacy, numeracy, and problem-solving in 'technology-rich environments'."

Two specific findings from its report:

1. "U. S. millennials with a four-year bachelor's degree were outperformed by all other participating OECD countries except Poland and Spain."

2. "U. S. millennials whose highest level of educational attainment was high school or less were lower than those of their counterparts in almost every other participating country."

Work-Leisure Balance And Employer Benefits

* The benefits package influences their decisions and loyalty.
* "Must" benefits: health insurance; paid leave; retirement savings plan.
* Don't like "accumulation" vacation plans.
* Many Mils *expect* flex-time; but some experts advise employers to keep flex-time as an *earned*

perk; that is, *prove yourself first.* Some employers bowed to Mils' demands but did not create a well-thought-out flex-time policy, and it created resentment and hostility among employees who had to take up the slack.

⚜ Like X'ers, Millennial mothers want opportunities for job-sharing, part-time hours, and on-site daycare.

Recruiting Millennials

⚜ Internships can help build future loyalty and slow their churn.

⚜ Campus recruiting and job fairs: "speed networking" and smaller groups seem to work nicely with Mils. Also, consider sending a Millennial employee with an older recruiter.

⚜ Use your digital media not just to recruit them but also to offer career advice to them.

⚜ Don't let social media replace in-person communication; this generation has been surrounded by living, breathing people its entire life. Mils are not as impersonal and robotic as you might think.

⚜ One employer told me his company has a "Ten Touches" policy: when job candidates visit the company, at least ten employees must make personal and meaningful contact with them.

❧ Give them access to senior management, especially during the recruitment period.

College Recruiting: Their Strategy

When job-hunting, Millennials will use:

❧ your company's website;
❧ campus career-services offices;
❧ LinkedIn and other social media;
❧ internships; sometimes multiple internships;
❧ networking: with friends, and at events. Mils rely upon Mils.

College Recruiting: Your Strategy As An Employer

❧ Create a "careers" link on your website: post job openings, application forms, videos of testimonial comments from satisfied employees and greetings from senior executives; and so on.
❧ Millennials love to hear "stories". So tell inspirational and emotional stories, concisely but completely, and even record and post them online as videos or audio clips.
❧ Build relationships with colleges' career-services offices.
❧ Speak on campus.

❧ Host Open Houses. And invite them to bring Mom and Dad.

Your Organization's Message To Millennials

❧ They seek challenging roles and advancement opportunities, so speak to this.
❧ Can you offer rotations? Mentorships? Special projects?
❧ Stress your culture of transparency.
❧ Stress organization's stability.
❧ Stress commitment to individual.
❧ Stress your civic involvement and good corporate citizenship.
❧ Manage their expectations immediately, during the interview.
❧ Make flex-time policy clear.
❧ Make vacation policy clear.
❧ Make any tech use policies and dress codes clear.
❧ Allow all generations to provide input on such policies.

Recruiting Millennials' PARENTS

Yes, if you're recruiting Millennials, most of them are going to turn to their parents for guidance and advice. So recruit Mom and Dad, too, with:

- Information kits designed for parents.
- Webinars, orientations, emails for them.
- Frequently Asked Questions on your website: answer parents' questions about benefits, retirement, continuing education opportunities, and others.
- Conference calls, visits, meet-the-boss events.
- Invite parents to annual employee meetings.
- "Bring Your Parents To Work" days.

Onboarding Millennials

Onboarding is a concept that emerged out of necessity, when this generation of heavily adult-supervised children entered the workforce and needed—and wanted—more guidance than prior generations had requested in those first few hours, days, weeks, and months on the job.

Today, onboarding programs have become refined.

And in those organizations that have undergone formal training in Generational Workforce Management Strategy, the onboarding has also become generation-specific, with different programs for different generations.

A solid Millennial onboarding program should include the following:

* Before their first day, assign to them a "Connection Coach". The coach is an employee close to their own age who stays in touch from the time the New Hire accepts the job to the first day on the job. The Connection Coach is more a "buddy" who texts or emails the New Hire in a casual tell-me-about-yourself manner and describes the "vibe" of the company. This is especially important for government agencies whose vetting of new hires sometimes takes months. And Millennials have demonstrated that they will make a verbal commitment to an employer, keep looking for something better, and ignore their commitment if they find something during the interim that is better. The Connection Coach can often prevent this behavior.
* Once on the job, assign a traditional mentor, someone older and more experienced and higher up the ladder.
* They'll need a strong orientation to ensure a good start.
* And, a fast start, to immerse them in the process before they get bored.
* How can you make their first day unforgettable?

In my training seminars, this question is usually a work-session assignment. When I ask them, "How can you make a New Hire's first day on the job absolutely unforgettable?", most of them think about it and then slap their foreheads in astonishment, saying, "Ohmygod! We have a BORING first-day orientation, with paperwork, dreary tours of the building, and other drudgery!"

And then they get excited about what an unforgettable first day *can* be:

At hospitals, for example, I ask participants, "What magic do you do here?" and they answer, "We save lives and make sick people well, and we help wounded military veterans walk on their new artificial legs", and I say "Then show your new recruits THAT on their first day; take them to where the magic is! The paperwork can WAIT!"

And at one large architecture/engineering/construction firm in Detroit, the president of the company slapped his head with sudden understanding and said, "We build bridges and dams and highways and skyscrapers! We create communities! We help people's lives! And right now, our New Hires spend their first day in our *offices* instead of outdoors where we create this MAGIC! Ohmygod!"

How can you make a New Hire's first day on the job absolutely *unforgettable*?

Mentors, Advocates, Sponsors

The mentoring model is changing. With Mils, it is sometimes evolving to a concept of multiple mentors, either sequential or all at once. And the relationship with those mentors might be shorter and less formal.

A 2012 survey of Millennial graduates by Bentley University found that, when asked, "Who provides you with the most career encouragement?", they answered:

* 33% spouse/partner
* 25% mom
* 16% dad
* 2% mentor at work

Employers need to get that 2% up to a higher number.

* Mils might have several specialist mentors.
* They view a mentor like a brief tweet, a mini-blast, rather than a long-term relationship.
* They seek a sponsor, someone with access to senior management who will advocate for them and be more than a traditional mentor.

- Peer-mentoring gatherings are an option.
- Speed-mentoring gatherings are an option.
- Reverse Mentoring is popular, whereby the mentee and mentor reverse roles.
- But Mils are developing a reputation of not holding up their end of the bargain. *Business Week* magazine headlined a story on this problem "The Misery of Mentoring Millennials". Mils need to recognize, and perhaps be told by the boss, that they must contribute to the mentorship, be on time for meetings, communicate properly and promptly, and respect the time and energy the mentor is devoting to them.
- Teach older mentors how to use social media.

Mils rely upon Mils for support and guidance; hence, the notion of "peer mentoring". And "speed mentoring": brief conversations with numerous mentors. And "reverse mentoring", in which Mils actually help older employees, especially with technological changes.

Beyond the traditional mentor model, Mils also like the idea of an "Advocate" or "Sponsor", usually an older and higher-up coworker who goes beyond "advice" and pro-actively promotes the mentee in her/his career.

Alert: Millennials are sometimes fumbling the ball with their mentors, failing to treat the mentors respectfully by arriving on time for meetings, replying to communications promptly, and by texting or calling the mentor after hours. Man-up, Mils! Be a responsible mentee.

Managing Millennials

* Internal communications: your organization should develop a Generational Gearbox; Mils might prefer texting, X'ers might like email, Boomers might enjoy face-to-face. This is a very complex era when it comes to communications, so conduct trial-and-error and find out what works best. Again, gather input on this from all employees and then establish any communications policies: if they feel they've contributed to the policies, they're more likely to support them. But in the end, do what's best for the organization.

* Bosses: don't hoard your knowledge; share it.
* Teach realistic expectations about pay, position, promotion.
* Enable your Mils to make a big contribution as swiftly as possible. It's important to them.
* The Short-Attention-Span Generation might struggle with long-term projects and get restless if there is no instant gratification. Some companies are creating more promotional

stepping-stones—usually a change in title only, but perhaps more than that—to give Mils a sense of making progress with long assignments.

* Give them freedom, but within a DETAILED framework. They need, and like, lots of structure, guidance, and clear rules. This is quite different from Gen X.

When you bring new Gen X'ers into the company, you can usually tell this very independent and self-reliant generation, "Your job is to do A, B, and C" and they'll get it and gladly figure out the rest on their own. With Millennials, you usually need to provide much more specificity and tell them, "Your job is to do A, B, C, D, E, F, G, H, I, J, K, L, and M."

There's no right or wrong to these approaches; this is simply two generations who came of age absorbing different times and teachings and thus molding different Core Values that they now bring to work each day. Once again, managers must develop a Generational Gearbox.

* Eliminate uncertainty in the task and the overall direction of the organization. Millennials struggle with ambiguity and broad concepts. X'ers and Boomers, by contrast, revel in it.

- Give them constant and specific feedback.
- But be careful with criticism.

Beyond their control, Mils came of age with their elders hosing them down with constant praise. One senior HR executive at a well-known corporation that employs about a quarter-million Americans told me after our training session, "We find we have to handle Millennials with kid gloves and criticize them as gently as possible. They're emotionally soft."

- Consider a sideways ladder. Millennials are usually a half-inch away from boredom. To keep this generation engaged, you might consider promoting them sideways rather than upward, giving them a different assignment at the same level to re-stimulate them.
- Reward them with more responsibility as soon as they're ready. They'll eat it up, and it will prevent boredom.
- To evaluate them, request a self-assessment and compare it to your own.
- Create a vibrant learning atmosphere.
- Stress punctuality.

I constantly ask Millennials in our training sessions, "Why are you guys so notoriously

LATE to meetings and appointments?" And they are; this is a common complaint by employers. Interestingly, I have yet to hear an answer Millennials agree on. Instead, they tend to giggle and say "Yep, that's us!" but they can't explain why. I'm still searching on this one. During a seminar with a state dental association, one Millennial female dentist, with a twinkle in her eye, gave her playful generational answer: "We don't worry about being late to meetings because we know no important conversation can begin until we're in the room."

Did someone say *self-esteem?*

* Can you offer them flexible, multiple, customized career paths?

It's been described this way: offer them a "tree". Tell them:

Like climbing the trunk of a tree, we want you to start out with us by proceeding along a single, proven path that all employees follow. Do it our way to begin. But then, as you gain experience, our organization can offer you many branches that go in different directions, and you can decide which ones to follow.

- Empower them and give them some space, but be accessible when they need you; and they *will* need you.
- They're the tech generation, but they also love face-to-face interaction. Again, this is a by-product of always-present elders during their youth.
- Can you offer variety and rotations to help them find a "home" somewhere at your organization? One Texas hospital created an 18-month on-boarding program in which new hires spent six months in three different jobs. By exposing a restless generation to various options, the hospital hoped to enhance retention.
- Consider informal Generational Affinity Group sessions, whereby your Millennials (and X'ers and Boomers and Silents) get together every now and then—lunch?—with their own generation just to chat about where they are in their lives and how the job's going. No bosses; this is informal. But, the groups might come up with new ideas for the company, so open a pipeline from these sessions to leaders.
- Generational Focus Groups. In order to help management understand each generation of employees, schedule generation-specific focus groups and chat sessions. One of my larger clients sent a young Millennial employee around

the country to chat with her fellow Mils at regional offices and came back with five specific ideas for improving Millennials' experience with the company.

  ❧ Give them as much ongoing access to senior management as possible.

  ❧ Explain the "why" behind company policies.

I was in a St. Louis hotel room preparing a speech when a client called and said, "We're thinking of instituting a tech-use policy because our younger employees are wasting time online and misusing technology while on the job. But we're afraid if we make the policy too stringent, even though it's the proper policy, we might chase away our Millennials. What should we do?"

My reply: "Form an employee advisory committee, with representatives from each generation, to work with management to develop the policy. If Millennials know they had input into the creation of the policy, they're much more likely to honor it. But don't turn over company management to them just to kiss their butts: do what's best for the company. And if you burn off some Millennials, so be it."

Millennials As Leaders

* Identify promising Millennial leadership candidates and fast-track them with (1) generation-specific leadership training (like the other generations, they have generation-specific strengths and weaknesses) and (2) job-shadowing and mentoring. Why fast-track? Because there aren't enough X'ers to replace Boomers.
* Leadership should come to Mils as comfortably as it has to Boomers. But when their generation leads America in the 2050s and 2060s, they'll lead differently. One likely difference: the prevalence of multiple CEOs for one organization; Mils seek the comfort and wisdom of multiple opinions before deciding.
* As leaders, their generation will struggle with accountability and the pressure of "the buck stops here" because they grew up with Mom and Dad constantly guiding them, deciding for them, and bailing them out *before* they got in trouble. But they will mature and overcome this shortcoming, just later than prior generations.

A Few Additional Ideas

* Personalize their work: make them *clearly* accountable and give them credit or criticism

depending upon the outcome. Don't give them an opening to come up with an excuse for failure. Pin them down.

❧ Millennials are negotiators; they began to demonstrate this during their school years, especially at the college level. When they failed to turn in a paper by the deadline, they tried to negotiate a deal for themselves. Ask just about any college instructor; they'll roll their eyes and say "Oh, yeah; Millennials want to negotiate every time they screw up!"

❧ Be alert for coarse language. It's simple: Mils came of age as commercial (not public) radio and TV, movies, music, video games, and the Internet were bombarding kids with more vulgarity than prior generations had experienced. To Millennials, some cusswords are not cusswords. This has embarrassed more than one employer, especially when a Millennial employee has cussed in front of a client or customer. Boss, handle this however you feel you should. And it continues with today's younger kids. Kindergartners swear at their teachers with the F-word. And two high schools in Hartford, Connecticut became so frustrated when detentions, reprimands, and even suspensions didn't stop students from aggressive cursing that they began to issue fines.

* Some companies offer cash bonuses or a Points Program for good work and for referring new job candidates. Employees accumulate points and later trade them in for merchandise or other rewards.

* Google has a 70/20/10 Rule, which asks employees to spend 70% of their time on the job to which they're assigned, 20% thinking of ways to innovate and make their task and company more productive, and 10% thinking completely outside the square to discover brand new ideas for the company.

* How about Leadership Alumni Reunions at your company? Bring back former leaders to meet with and advise Mils.

* Start your department's or company's day with a To The Point Meeting, when each employee presents her "personal commitment for the day".

* How about a "core hours" flextime policy? It goes something like this: employees must spend, say, 36 hours each week arriving and departing at times designated by the company, but the other 4 hours can be "flexed" with the boss' advance approval.

* How about a "Vision Committee", on which employees may participate in exploring new

horizons for the company while on company time? Remember, Mils are big dreamers.

* Community Service: permit employees time from their work to volunteer for charitable work.
* Allow all employees, not just the management team, to designate the charitable cause(s) the company will support.
* Stay in touch with Millennials who leave. As with Gen X, restless Millennials might leave for another job they feel will be better but then, six months or a year down the road, will wish to return.

The Technology Industry And Perks

The tech giants are rolling in cash and competing fiercely against each other to recruit and retain the best employees.

Hence, extravagant perks for their employees.

This combination of cash and competition has produced a list of innovative Perk Strategies that less profitable employers might not be able to offer but can perhaps emulate with lower-cost knock-offs.

As one example, the *Wall Street Journal* chronicled, as its headline read, "Google-Style Perks for a

Pest-Control Firm." The firm is Alterra in Utah. And indeed, other industries are now taking cues from Silicon Valley with perks, if do'able, like these:

* Relaxed dress code;
* Flexible hours;
* Basketball court, squash court, lap pools, TruGolf simulator;
* Pool table, ping pong table;
* 90-inch TV;
* Free meals, either all day every day or periodically;
* Free snacks;
* Gourmet meals that are prepared in an on-site kitchen and that employees can grab when leaving for the day and take home for dinner;
* Concierge services: dry cleaning; pharmacy; car wash and oil change; dog walks and washes;
* On-site day care for kids and pets;
* Paid vacations and employee retreats and trips;
* Employee rest areas, even nap rooms, with sofas and soothing music;
* Special events (ask your employees what they'd like);
* A plant-covered "living wall";
* A roof deck with a grill and refrigerated beer dispenser;

* A bus, or fleet of buses, to transport employees to and from work, especially helpful in traffic-congested cities with long commutes; Google converted bus interiors into high-tech work spaces.

Distinctive perks, done properly and strategically (and they CAN backfire and fail):

* help distinguish and elevate companies in unglamorous industries;
* help attract higher-quality job candidates and retain employees;
* boost employee pride and morale;
* and, create a cool factor that will intrigue customers and other visitors.

But if your executives treat employees poorly, no perks will save the company. The culture of reverential treatment of employees, which is a part of the emerging movement of Conscious Capitalism and Servant Leadership, must be systemic throughout the organization. One Gen X gentleman who owns a successful company in Columbus, Ohio spoke just before I did at an executive roundtable and said, "We truly consider our employees our greatest asset and back up the talk with our treatment of them."

The bottom line:

After more than a quarter-century of American employees being treated like pawns on a chessboard, smarter employers now understand their employees are their greatest assets. And the perks being offered by the tech sector have helped to promote this mindset.

Today, there is no such thing as a bad idea in Human Resources.

The Generational Disruption
Of The Marketplace

. . .

CHAPTER 17

Generational Marketplace Strategy

Generational Core Values = Hot Buttons

· · ·

THE MEMBERS OF THE SILENT Generation (1) possess more spending power, (2) are less brand-loyal than any prior generation at their age, and (3) are living life differently. Too many marketers mistakenly ignore them.

Boomers (1) control a disproportionately large percentage of America's wealth, (2) aren't brand-loyal, (3) spend freely, and (4) continue to re-write the book on living and spending. Too many marketers mistakenly ignore them, too.

Gen X is in its Spending Life Stage right now: (1) marriage; (2) parenthood; (3) home buying and furnishing; (4) the kids' college; and, (5) its early years of grandparenthood. How do marketers pitch their products to a generation that is especially difficult to persuade?

Millennials (1) are transforming—probably permanently—what it is like to live life in one's early adulthood. They also (2) will require years to recover financially from The Great Recession, which rammed their generation uncommonly hard. (3) Where do marketers find the world's first Technology Generation? And when they do find them, (4) how do they "message" to them?

The generational disruption of the American marketplace is registering a 10-out-of-10 on the *YIKES!* Meter.

Here's how we execute generational marketplace strategy:

1. Identify the generation you wish to target.
2. Identify that generation's current life stage; for example: young adulthood; marriage; parenthood; career advancement; empty nest; grandparenthood; retirement; loss of spouse; infirmity. (Remember, we don't become a member of a generation until we leave high school around age 18).
3. Identify one or more of that generation's Core Values.
4. Develop your product or service, and craft your marketing messages, in ways that will resonate

with that generation's Core Values and its current life stage.

Key Point: generational Core Values are the equivalent of marketing Hot Buttons that marketers should push with their products and messages.

With this in mind, generational strategy should be a permanent component of each step of the marketplace process:

1. Consumer And Market Research

This is the upfront research that helps you to: (1) identify and understand your consumers along generational lines, rather than traditional age brackets (the 1950s is the final decade when age was a fairly reliable predictor of adult consumer behavior); and, (2) identify and understand market opportunities and challenges for your products and services.

Consistently, such opportunities and challenges emerge whenever a generation advances to its next life stage. Examples:

* Millennials are living the life stage of young adulthood differently from prior generations. New marketplace opportunities, new challenges.

❧ Gen X'ers are parenting differently.

❧ Boomers are empty-nesting differently.

❧ Silents are retiring differently.

Generational research is different from traditional demographic research. When generational Core Values and influences are included in the upfront concepting and design of a research study, and then in the actual execution of the study, and then included in its Final Report, it can consistently deliver richer findings and interpretations—and suggested actions—than purely demographic research.

Example: the International Association of Exhibitions and Events—that is, the trade-show industry—asked me to guide a sizable research study that they wanted to be generationally designed, not age designed. The goal of the study: learn what trade shows must do to (A) attract Gen X'ers and Millennials to their events; and, (B) deliver such a relevant and valuable experience to them that they will return to future events.

The research was both qualitative and quantitative. Multiple firms conducted the qualitative; for the quantitative segment, I collaborated with highly regarded research firm Burke, Inc. My role was to explain the Generational Core Values that would guide both the upfront design of the study and its execution, and to then add an additional chapter to the Final Report, based upon my generational work, that compared the study's Findings and Interpretations with my own generational research and knowledge and then recommended specific actions for trade shows to take in order to connect with X'ers and Mils.

2. Development Of Products And Services

Whether you provide a product (from automobiles to underwear) or a service (from architecture to patient care), generational strategy should help guide the development of your offering.

A few examples:

* Florida retirement communities alter the amenities they offer when the Silent Generation becomes their primary target and brings its unique generational Core Values to retirement.

* Cadillac designs the radically different CTS model and dramatically changes its advertising

approach (TV commercials featuring music by rocker Led Zeppelin) with Baby Boomers in mind.

* In the 2000s, hotels re-design and re-furnish their lobbies and guestrooms to attract Gen X business and family travelers. The hotel chain "W" is an early example.

* In the 2010s, with Millennials now taking both business and leisure travel in young adulthood, hotels undergo another generationally strategized evolution in physical design, marketing, and attitude to embrace Mils.

* The Gap apparel chain brightens the color palette of its scarves to embrace joyful young Millennials as they move into its target demographic, after decades of Gen X'ers preferring muted colors.

* Walgreens and CVS pharmacies undergo a long list of changes in their store designs, product lines, positioning (CVS takes the bold and visionary step to no longer sell cigarettes in order to cement its image as a destination for health and wellness), and services with the aging Boomer

masses in mind: more stylish eyeglasses; more linear feet of shelf space for vitamins and other wellness products; and, Boomer-era music playing in the stores.

3. Marketing Research

After your upfront market and consumer research helps you to understand your target generation(s) and marketplace challenges and opportunities and then helps you create your product offering, marketing research then guides the creative development and testing of your actual marketing and advertising messages. There's a distinction between "market" research and "marketing" research.

4. Marketing, Advertising, Public Relations

And it continues: once generational strategy has guided your internal research, the development of your products and services, and the creation of your marketing and advertising messages, it is then time to let this strategy go *external* and work for you out there on the front line: it's time to roll out your products and messages to your targeted generation(s). This involves media placement, frequency, special events, news releases, and so on.

Multigenerational Messaging

Key Point: Yes! A single message can work for multiple generations, because our generations DO have many common Core Values. But in today's cluttered marketplace, generation-specific messages are often preferable, because *generational* messaging consistently achieves what every marketer seeks but doesn't always get:

It cuts through all of the clutter "out there".

TV viewers, newspaper and magazine readers, online visitors, radio listeners, motorists glancing at outdoor billboards, and other consumers instantly recognize when a generation-specific message is meant for *them*.

And digital media now make the creation and placement of *single-generation* messages easier and cheaper—even by small firms with small budgets—than they had been pre-web, when traditional print, television, and radio were the primary and more expensive media.

5. Generational Selling

I train sales teams in Generational Selling and Customer Service Strategy because, even in this impersonal age of digital communication, selling still boils down to this: one seller is trying to persuade one buyer to purchase a product or service. *And that buyer belongs to a generation and possesses unique generational Core Values that are going to influence her/his final decision.* And understanding generational Core Values is a window into the mind and soul of the buyer.

In selling, generational Core Values are Hot Buttons.

Bottom line: you will consistently find that you need to pitch your product or service to a Gen X buyer differently from the way you'll sell it to a Boomer or Millennial or Silent or G.I., whether the customer is in your department store, auto dealership, financial services office, online, or anywhere else.

Different generational Core Values. And so, different consumer preferences, needs, expectations, and hot buttons that you, the salesperson, must consider.

And different generational preferences and expectations in the way they want you to sell to them and then serve them as your customer.

What About B2B Selling?

I was retained by Pittsburgh-based manufacturer PPG Industries to provide identical training sessions, one on each coast, to the distributors who comprise its sales force for a certain line of its products.

PPG is largely a business-to-business—"B2B"—company; it sells its industrial products to other companies; for example, the paints it manufactures and then sells to automakers to apply to their vehicles.

So the question arose just as generational study and strategy were first emerging, "Does generational selling strategy apply to B2B selling as it does to B2C (business to consumer, or final end-user)?"

Answer: yes.

Why? Once again: because ultimately, a human being is making the buy or no-buy decision. And that human being belongs to a generation and possesses unique Core Values that guide his/her decision-making.

Within seven days of our training session in Generational Advertising Strategy, an account rep for the *Quad-City Times* newspaper (Davenport, Iowa), which sells advertising space to local businesses (B2B, in other words), emailed her boss, Publisher Michael Phelps: "This has already meant more dollars!" I had trained not just the newspaper's advertising-sales staff but also its local advertisers, who embraced the idea of creating generationally strategized ads and thinking of their customers in generational terms rather than age brackets.

B2B selling is generational.

And here is another example:

Key Point: marketers, ad agencies, PR firms, salespeople, and others should give serious consideration to including generational strategy in their formal pitches—their dog-and-pony shows—to land accounts. Such inclusion can be a tie-breaker, a differential advantage, in their favor in a competitive situation:

I trained a Cincinnati ad agency in Generational Marketplace Strategy. Soon after, the owner called to say the firm had been short-listed as one of the final five firms to land the Sunglass Hut national advertising account. On a single day, all five finalists would present 90-minute pitches to Sunglass Hut's reviewing committee, and the agency I trained was to be the last one on the list, late on a Friday afternoon. The agency's owner, who made the pitch with a small team beside her, told me this a few weeks later, with joy in her voice:

"We were pretty sure we wouldn't get the account, and we didn't. But when you're short-listed you pitch, hoping to get the account in the future. By the time we pitched at the end of the day, the review committee's eyes were bloodshot and glassy, and their shoulders were drooping; they had just endured four other 90-minute, high-intensity presentations—6 straight hours!—and understandably were brain-dead. In our pitch, they were lifeless *until we got to our 10-minute segment on generational strategy.* It became instantly clear that the other agencies had not included generational strategy in their pitches. When we presented it, they straightened up and took notes furiously."

In St. Petersburg, Florida, I presented Generational Marketplace Strategy on the first day of the annual statewide conference of the Florida Public Relations Association. The head of one PR firm left for the airport right after my speech to make a pitch in another city and emailed me the next day:

"Chuck, I had to miss the next day of the conference...to be part of a presentation to a client in the travel industry; and I quoted you. There's one member of the review team who started in on the need for us to more closely measure clips. I said, "You know, I had the most fascinating conversation yesterday with Chuck Underwood, the leading authority on generational marketing, and I think, based on what I heard him say, *I'd be more concerned that we need to first be figuring out what values and interests of the five living generations we can appeal to... and how.* It changed the direction of the entire conversation; it sure made for a more positive discussion."

Someday, the entire American marketplace will understand and use generational strategy, and it will be less of a differential advantage. But right now, it's still possible for you to use it to elevate yourself above your competitors.

5. One-on-One Interpersonal Skills

We all need to develop a "Generational Gearbox": the ability to smoothly and swiftly shift gears from dealing with a member of one generation to a member of another generation.

If you develop a generational gearbox, you will enjoy comfort and success in your interpersonal dealings with customers and clients.

6. Customer Service/Patient Care

Each generation has somewhat different expectations and preferences for the customer/client service they receive because they came of age, and formed lifelong Core Values, during different times and teachings.

As customers, they have different attitudes regarding such customer-service staples as communication, courtesy, and efficiency.

And in the healthcare industry, customer service primarily means "patient and family care".

As the healthcare industry makes the monumental shift to electronic record-keeping, doctors and nurses are learning that many of their G.I. and Silent patients are put off when their doctor enters the exam room or hospital room staring at her laptop for the first minute or two, in order to refresh her memory of the patient's condition and history. These two generations came of age during different times. They prefer instant eye contact and personal attention. They recoil from the coldness of *that damned computer.* Boomers, X'ers, and Mils? Less so. Clinicians need to be sensitive to these generational differences and develop a Generational Gearbox.

CHAPTER 18

Marketing To Silents

Tips, Tactics, And Guidelines

• • •

THE SILENTS' PASSION FOR LIFE, substantial purchasing power, and willingness to spend open up a banquet table of marketplace opportunities in such industries as:

* leisure travel;
* residential living;
* dining;
* grandchildren;
* financial services;
* wellness and healthcare;
* philanthropy/giving;
* education (yes! formal classes to learn something new);
* volunteerism;
* and, other sectors.

Connect With Grandchildren
Think And Act Young
Love To Travel

As consumers, Silents have many hot buttons that marketers can push. Here are just three:

1. Silents are especially passionate about being a regular and meaningful presence in the lives of their grandchildren and great-grandchildren.

When Silents became the dominant grandparent generation in the 1990s, Del Webb, a division of Pulte Homes and the builder of massive Sunbelt retirement communities like Sun City, Arizona, made the strategic shift to build communities in the cold-weather states, an acknowledgement of research that said many Silent retirees were staying put in order to be near their kids and grandkids, instead of retiring to distant warmer climates. The company's first such cold-weather community is near Chicago.

2. Silents feel they conformed and played it safe when they were young, so today they're eager to think and act young. One research study found that 78% of Silents feel that being receptive to new products and services is an important part of "thinking young". This indicates that Silents are not as brand-loyal as

previous generations had been at the same age. And this means Silents are "in play" in the marketplace.

3. Silents love to travel because, when they were children, America did not have the interstate highway system for easy ground travel, and air travel was prohibitively expensive for all but the wealthiest.

Five months after the airplane terrorist attacks of 9/11, I was speaking in Washington, D. C. While in town, I read a newspaper story written by a reporter who had contacted travel agents around the country and asked if Americans were returning to air travel yet, in the near aftermath of the terrorist airplane hijackings and crashes. The agents told the reporter that Boomers and X'ers were not yet flying, still uncertain about the safety. But Silents were jumping right back in to leisure air travel. They were even flying right to violent hot spots such as the Middle East for their vacations.

So, who's tapping into just this short list of Silent hot buttons?

Walt Disney World
The Grandparent Connection

How about Walt Disney World in Orlando, Florida?

In an advertising campaign celebrating the 100-year anniversary of the birth of founder Walt Disney, one TV spot shows a Silent grandfather and his pre-teen grandson at Disney World, staring up at an enormous statue of Walt Disney standing beside Mickey Mouse.

Here's the dialogue:

Silent Grandfather: "Do you know who that is?"
Grandson: "Mickey!"
Silent Grandfather: "What about the man?"
(Grandson shrugs, shakes his head).
"That's Walt Disney, the guy who came up with Mickey Mouse. He dreamed up this whole place. He could take an ordinary day and turn it into magic. He was full of fun ideas."
"Oh...kinda like you, Grandpa."
(They smile and hug).

This spot does not show Grandpa and Grandson merely riding the rides. It shows them talking, with Silent grandpa sharing his knowledge of Disney history with his grandson and being hip enough to connect with him and gain his admiration. A rich relationship. A strong bond.

This is excellent messaging to this generation of passionate grandparents and great grandparents.

Globus & Cosmos

One of my Denver clients is a travel company called Group Voyagers, one of the world's largest providers of escorted group tours.

As the executive director of sales and marketing (he went on to became the CEO) told me when we first met, the escorted group tour industry had enjoyed a profitable run with the G.I. Generation; it understood that generation's preferences regarding group travel. But now, he said in the mid-2000s, the Silents had become the new target, with the Boomers right behind them. (Not only that, but these were also the immediate post-terrorist-attack years). And he sensed accurately that Silents and Boomers will be very different group tour travelers than G.I.s. So here's what we did together:

I trained Group Voyagers' sixteen-person marketing team in Generational Marketing Strategy at its Denver offices.

The moment I finished, the executive director stood and asked each member of the team what they thought of Generational Strategy, and they all said they wanted to use it. The executive director turned to me and asked, "What's our next step?"

I asked him if his company had focus-grouped the Silents. "No," he answered. So we did.

I designed a generation-specific research study, moderated Silent focus groups in multiple states to discover their hot buttons, and then presented the Final Report to Group Voyagers.

Group Voyagers then incorporated the findings into its product development, marketing, and advertising. It revised the layout and copy in its catalogues and introduced generationally strategized marketing elements to enhance bottom-line sales.

Soon after the research project, the executive director emailed me: "Your generational research study for us has been very helpful in directing our planners and marketing people. We will incorporate the findings not only in the creation of tours, but also in how we talk about travel experiences in brochures and ad copy. Thank you!"

And about six months later, he emailed again: "Your work with us continues to shape what we do here. Business is finally picking up..."

Wendy's

Wendy's primary target demo had always been age 18 to 49. But like Del Webb, an early embracer of generational research, Wendy's detected a shift and launched an advertising campaign that targeted the Silent Generation Core Value of closeness to grand-kids. And one TV spot stretches Wendy's target demo well beyond 18 to 49 to include Silents. Here's the creative:

Teenage granddaughter, wearing braces on her teeth, walks into the house with a carryout bag of Wendy's food. White-haired Silent grandmother awaits her. They sit down together at the kitchen table:

Silent Grandma: "So where ya been?"
Teen Granddaughter: "Out."
"Where'd ya go?"
"Wendy's."
"Wha'd ya get?"
"Junior Bacon Cheeseburger, fries, and Coke."
"Your grandfather and I love that Junior Bacon Cheeseburger. Two strips of bacon, right?"
"Mm-hmm."

"We get a side salad; used to be 99 cents."

"It's still 99 cents."

(Announcer inserts "sell" message).

Grandma (twinkle in her eye): "Does that nice blond boy still work there?"

Granddaughter: "No, Gram, not anymore."

"Too bad. He was *hot*."

"GRANDMA!!!!"

Silent Generation grandmother is so hip and "with it" she can actually cause her teen granddaughter to blush. Excellent Silent messaging by Wendy's.

Energizer Batteries
Grandpa's In-Your-Face Victory Dance

Energizer Batteries demonstrated a similar advertising strategy in a holiday campaign. At holiday time, wouldn't you think Energizer would target the *young parents* of the young children who are going to get all of those battery-powered toys and games as gifts?

Not this time. Energizer seized upon Silent Core Values of wanting to (1) think and act young and (2) connect with their grandkids.

The TV spot shows a Silent grandfather and his pudgy pre-teen grandson, sitting across from each other in overstuffed living room chairs, each one furiously working his hand-held, battery-powered Bormoto console as they compete against each other in a video game.

White-haired and bespectacled Silent grandfather missed the technology revolution, so grandson keeps beating him, game after game, telling Gramps, "I win, you lose. I win again, you lose. This is getting ugly." And Grandpa is becoming progressively frazzled and discouraged.

But suddenly, the grandson's console—which does not use Energizer batteries—begins to slow down. Grandpa, with Energizers that are outlasting his grandson's Brand X batteries, begins to catch up, and he finally wins a game! He shouts, "Yeah!!!", leaps out of his chair, stands over his seated grandson, raises his arms to the sky and yells "Yeah!" again, and then does a wild, in-your-face victory dance as his grandson slumps in the chair and rolls his eyes in frustration. Grandpa taunts him: "How do ya like Granddad? How do ya like him now?!!!"

Silent grandfather is so physically vigorous, so youthful, that he can jump from his chair, dance, and rejoice.

Generational Core Values—the Silents' desire to be youthful and vital, and the desire to bond with grandchildren—become advertising hot buttons.

Sony Camcorders

As with Energizer, this was a holiday advertising campaign for Sony camcorders. It captured another unique Core Value of the Silent Generation: a passion to live life fully, take a risk or two, and "squeeze life for all of its satisfactions," which many Silents feel they didn't do during their childhood of don't-rock-the-boat conformity.

Once again, during the holiday gift-buying season, wouldn't you assume that Sony Camcorders would advertise to young parents who want to videotape their kids' childhoods?

This sixty-second TV spot begins by showing a white-haired, modern-thinking Silent male jogging through a field in an early morning workout, then drinking a protein milkshake for breakfast, then working out at the gym, then packing his Sony Camcorder in his suitcase, checking the weather in Moscow online, hugging his Gen X daughter and son and saying goodbye, flying to Moscow, entering a space-center facility heavily guarded by stern-looking Russian guards, and then blasting off in a Soviet spaceship with his camcorder, and joyously taping his own floating back-flip inside the ship in anti-gravity outer space. There's no dialogue during this spot, only music playing under the video.

The on-screen text at the end of the commercial is perfect messaging to a generational Core Value of *it's now our time:*

"When your kids ask where the money went...show them the tape."

Public Television And Doo Wop

Silents have rightly felt overlooked and under-appreciated because they're sandwiched between two wave-making generations: the save-the-world, nation-building G.I.s; and, the save-the-world, social-activist Boomers. Even *their generation's war*—the Korean Conflict—has always been overshadowed by World War II and Vietnam.

Here's what happened:

In the late '90s, public television stations aired a single, two-hour music concert that showcases a style of music that is indigenous to the formative years of the Silents: the '40s and '50s and very early '60s.

This made strategic sense.   Silents now stretched in age from their early 50s to early 70s, thus occupying the demographic "sweet spot" that public TV targets for call-in donations during its "pledge drives", which occur about four times a year.

PBS stations aired this concert during one such pledge campaign. The concert was called, simply, *Doo Wop.*

I learned later from T. J. Lubinsky, the energetic creator and executive producer of *Doo Wop,* that the previous best pledge-generating first-run program in public television history had raised about $12.5 million.

Doo Wop, in its first run, raised *twice* that: $26 million!

So stations aired the same show again a few months later, and Lubinsky told me the total reached some $50 million. And it has continued and grown into additional music shows that have raised a *fortune* in pledges for public television. All because the mass medium of television decided, for once, to *acknowledge* and *celebrate* the lives—through the music unique to their youth—of an overlooked and under-appreciated generation.

And Silents responded by reaching for their phones and check books and pledging record-shattering donations.

Again, these are just a few examples of the many industries that are cashing in on the wealthy, free-spending, non-brand-loyal Silent Generation. There are many others. Silents spend on a long list of categories. They've worked diligently in their careers and feel they've now *earned the right* to reward themselves.

They embrace digital technology, especially to stay in touch with their children and grandchildren.

Not only that, but a number of them also harbor that vague sense of having lived conforming lives that were, as one Silent wrote, "safe, apolitical, and boring, but now it's our turn!" They have a pent-up desire to grab life for all they can, and many possess the spending power to act on that urge.

Silents are a charitable generation. Unscrupulous hustlers target them, and their money, so they've become wary. But they do give.

They can recall the sturdiness of the American family during their own childhood era, and they've witnessed its deterioration over the past several decades. So they welcome the opportunity to re-strengthen the family unit by being a positive presence in the lives of their adult kids and grandkids. Because so many of their own children are time-stressed and/or divorced or single parents, a noteworthy number of Silents are involved in the *primary* care of those grandkids and, as such, are involved in the purchases of products and services associated with such care.

When I was presenting this information at a Midwest business conference in Indianapolis and showed the Walt Disney World commercial showing Silent grandfather and grandson vacationing together without the boys' parents, a Silent grandfather in the audience smiled and raised his hand.

"Amazing," he said. "At this very moment, my wife and our grandchildren are at Disney World together, giving our busy Gen X children a chance to have some time to themselves."

Aging In Place

Yes, some Silents want to retire to a warm climate. But for most, their current home is where their heart is. So they wish to "age in place", remaining in the same house or at least the same area.

The marketplace opportunity? Smart-home technology that helps them to age in place safely and comfortably, especially those who live alone. *Help is only one button-push away.*

Programmable thermostats and lights. Anti-scald devices on showers. And as gerontologist Ken Dychtwald told *USA Today*: "There may be homes that can be reshaped and remodeled to accommodate visitors or guests. Imagine walls moving and desks disappearing and trundle beds coming out when the grandkids come. The good news is that all of these breakthroughs are on the drawing board or already available, but they're waiting for the market to take more full advantage of them."

Or Not Aging In Place

But if forced into a nursing home by infirmity, Silents will benefit from this kind of sensitivity and strategy, as described in a *USA Today* story:

David Dillard, president of D2 Architects in Dallas, wanted his younger architects to "get it" when they designed senior housing. So he created a new protocol: the employees did sleepovers in senior housing and were told to "spend 24 hours under the conditions of an 85-year-old". This meant taping fingers together to get a sense of how arthritis feels, putting dew on eyeglasses or wearing another person's eyeglasses to appreciate diminished eyesight, wearing ear plugs to experience hearing loss, tying shoelaces with only one hand, eating the institution's food and drinking its beverages that taste horrible.

The company, at the time of the interview in 2014, had conducted 25 to 30 sleepovers.

The outcome? Dillard says, "The biggest benefit is when I send 27-year-olds out, they come back with a heart twice as big. They meet people and understand their plights."

But more fundamentally, D2 is now lowering window sills, designing larger windows ("they want to see the outdoors"), using more indirect light, no ramps or steps, and creating quieter rooms by way of better acoustics and staggering the doors up and down the hallways instead of placing them directly across from each other so that noise from one room won't penetrate another room as easily.

Pumping Iron

The research is now absolute: regular exercise, even *intense*, is safe and beneficial for older adults. Aerobic workouts. Strength training. Stretching and toning. Exercise fuels the brain, as well as the body. It improves quality of life.

Many Silents are probably hesitant, with their aging bodies, to join trendy gyms and fitness centers where they're surrounded by younger, trimmer X'ers and Millennials.

So, what's the marketplace opportunity for the fitness industry to serve this receptive generation's unique needs? Experts in senior personal training, home-gym providers, and outreach to this generation by fitness clubs (most of which prefer to be young and cool, which perhaps opens the door for private, *senior-only* gyms).

Silents And Dining

Restaurants, do you have slow nights? Maybe Mondays or Tuesdays? At a training seminar in Columbus, the owner of a local chain of pizza parlors said Tuesday evenings were slow at his seven stores. We brainstormed a "Silent Night" on Tuesdays, with the stores playing Silent-era music, offering Silent-trivia placemats on the tables, hanging larger posters of the fashions and autos and celebrities of their formative years, and so on, and encouraging Silents to bring their grandkids.

Tips, Tactics, Guidelines

Many of them don't know they're called the Silent Generation, and some who do know don't like the label. But when you explain the name's history, they get it and accept it.

They grew up before cold and impersonal shopping *malls* over-ran America. They remember when local shop owners and clerks were their friends and neighbors, knew their names and their families, and stood behind their products and services in a one-to-one way. So give Silents that same genuine personal service. To many Silents (and Boomers, for that matter, who also remember *pre-mall*), current-day customer service is frequently cold and often downright incompetent. This means *opportunity* for the vendor who delivers it to Silents' high standards. Develop a relationship with them. Get to know them. Talk with them. Most importantly, listen to them.

Courtesy is very important to Silents. And it's okay to be a bit more formal when communicating with this generation. Silents came of age with a strong emphasis on manners and politeness and so are receptive to it. "Please," "Thank you," "Sir," and "Ma'am" are appreciated. So are prompt and full responses to their questions. And especially with older First-Wave Silents, don't let your young sales clerk walk up to a couple and ask "How can I help you guys?" A Silent woman is not a "guy".

If your firm targets Silents, do you employ Silents? If not, WHY NOT?! It might it be a good idea to hire a Silent, or Silents, even if on a part-time or consulting basis. Or create a Silent Advisory Group that meets periodically. Or conduct Silent-specific research.

Are you planning on giving a Silent client or prospective client your business card? If so, what type size and color contrast are you using on the card? Is it Silent-friendly, or has your younger graphic artist, with excellent eyesight, decided to express his or her creative side with a clever design that is also a small-type, low-color-contrast, difficult-to-read card? Is your artist trying to create a work of art that looks good in her portfolio but is a piece of crap as a reader-friendly business card? I've seen this mistake many times.

Is your Point of Purchase and Point of Sale signage Silent-friendly? When it comes to shelf signage at many supermarkets, the answer is no. Too tiny. Same with the type-size on product packaging.

Use multigenerational images and audio in your advertising to them. Silents and their adult children. Silents and their grandkids.

Nostalgia and sentimentality work: these emotions connect Silents to their comfortable past, rather than their uncertain future as they age. Plus, Silents feel overlooked and under-appreciated, and nostalgic references from their earlier years acknowledge and validate them.

Also: use the music of their youth, from the 1940s, '50s, and early '60s. It's just about impossible to overstate the positive impact of music when used in generation-specific marketing.

Vivid memories of the Great Depression and World War II give this generation a special respect for the value of a dollar. So, bargains and discounts and coupons and premiums work. Silents grew up with green stamps, yellow stamps, and plaid stamps. They also remember receiving a free drinking glass for each fillup at the "service station". These are joyous memories. Banks, try this: pitch Silents to open a savings account for their great-grandchildren and *give them a free gift* for doing so.

Celebrate Silents' maturity, wisdom, and experience with your message.

Demonstrate how your product or service gives Silents the opportunity for first-time experiences and personal growth. But wrap these first-time experiences in security and safety, not high-risk uncertainty. Soften the idea of "new" and punch-up the idea of "enhance your life."

Don't hype. Don't lie. Prove your claim. Over the years, this generation has been pitched a gazillion versions of "new-and-improved" laundry detergents but has seldom seen their *whites get whiter.* They've been disappointed many times.

Don't rush your story, but don't dawdle either. Silents have the time, and will take the time, to read your message. They are avid consumers of the printed word.

Newspapers and magazines and direct mail work effectively with them. As with Boomers and G.I.s, there is a wonderful ritual to holding a printed publication, touching it, and physically turning the pages, more satisfying than reading digital media on a screen.

Use the Silents' current life stages to connect with them. Grandparenthood. Retirement and free time. Loss of spouse and friends. Infirmity. These life stages influence their consumer decisions on travel, moving, hobbies, volunteerism, philanthropy, and so on.

Let them interact. They want to be experiential. Nabisco introduced *Eggbeaters* by cooking more than 300,000 breakfasts in more than 1,800 senior centers nationwide; participating seniors received a recipé book and coupons. Excellent!

Silent group events can be especially effective. One obvious example is escorted group vacation tours. Don't be afraid to create generation-specific groups; done properly, they'll succeed.

And remember the MUSIC! The joyous, wholesome, melodic, romantic music of the 1930s, '40s, '50s, and early '60s. Radio stations don't serve Silents anymore. So their generation will rejoice if you surround them with their music.

With Silents, in-person experiences will always trump online experiences. Like Boomers and G.I.s, they are very much a "people generation" and prefer eye-to-eye over eye-to-screen.

Educate. Educate. Educate. Silents are hungry to learn.

Pitch the *benefits* and *features* and *smart value* of your product or service. Silents came of age when advertising focused upon *features* more than brand or emotion. To teach this to your younger staffers, go to YouTube and view a 1950s television commercial in which actress Betty Furness demonstrates the features of a Westinghouse refrigerator.

The purchase must be easy and hassle-free.

Make it memorable by keeping it simple. Age tends to diminish short-term and verbal memory. Visual images, especially photographs, are effective. Messages should be explicit and carefully paced.

Regarding the pace of your message: get a mental picture of MTV's rapid-fire Gatling-gun approach of editing together four images per second in order to hold the attention of Millennial kids, and then do the exact opposite.

Competing Noise

Be very careful about running music or natural sound under the voiceover of your radio and TV spots. Because of hearing loss, many people struggle to hear the spoken word whenever there is *competing noise.* So don't layer competing noise over your voiceover. Television shows, such as the various *NCIS* series, constantly run music under the shows' dialogue, which makes it very difficult for people with even moderate hearing loss to understand. And take note: audiologists will tell you Gen X is likely to experience widespread *premature* hearing loss because of the damage caused by the live and loud concerts they attended and the stereo headsets they wore as kids.

Silents will enjoy being celebrated by advertisers, but they otherwise don't especially want to be *isolated* in advertising. So, connect them with other generations.

Which Media Work With Silents?

* Print. Silents devour the daily newspaper and feel it is the most trustworthy source of factual coverage of daily life. Newspapers and the weekly news magazines like *TIME, Business Week, Good Housekeeping*, and others have earned the Silents' trust over the decades.

* Magazines. Weekly and monthly magazines were immensely important and influential during the Silents' formative years because television didn't yet dominate the living room. These publications were aspirational; Silent women craved the lifestyles showcased in these magazines, and the act of reading them felt elegant; these feelings can be your marketing hot buttons with them

today. Check the most recent research at any given time as to which specific titles are hot, but generally speaking, fashion and home and travel magazines that target mature women can perform quite well. And don't overlook possible advertising in AARP's periodicals.

* Direct Mail. You can tell your story thoroughly, and Silents have time to read it. And direct mail can remain in front of them on the coffee table, unlike here-and-gone radio and TV messages. So direct mail is comfortable and enables Silents to re-check the details. But eliminate the hype and don't hide the bad news (cost, interest rate, etc.) deep in the bowels of your message. Be straight-up.

* Television. Advertisers: don't overlook the possibility of underwriting local or national *public* television shows. PBS. In an ocean of unprecedented advertising clutter in *commercial* media these days, public television remains an island of nonclutter. A chance to stand out.

* Direct-Response TV (infomercials and 60- to 120-second commercials). Longer-form messages are a good fit for Silents' time availability

and their desire and need to hear and digest the entire story. Long-form also permits you to prove your claim. Make sure your toll-free phone number is on-screen for a good long time and in large type size; and then make sure your call-center personnel know how to converse with this generation, by enunciating, speaking at a not-too-fast pace, and being courteous and unrushed.

* Telemarketing. In the 1990s and 2000s, telemarketing earned such a wretched reputation for intrusion and scamming that all generations are on guard. But it has become inexpensive with robo-calling technology, and it apparently makes money because it continues. But Silents are cautious. When technology enables us to block robo-calls and other telemarketing, I believe we will see its effectiveness decline.

Silents And The Web

The percentage of Silents who are online is increasing daily.

Digital technology is no longer a youth phenomenon. The Internet and the hardware and software that accompany it are invaluable to all of our lives. And it's relatively easy to operate. So all ages are using it.

Because technology is going to be in constant flux for some years to come, you'll need to find the latest research as to how Silents are using it and which websites they most frequently visit, but most research studies to date indicate that Silents use the Internet to:

- Email or text to family and friends;
- communicate on the social-site-du-jour with grandkids, such as Snapchat, Instagram, Facebook (Millennials, by the way, have moved on from regular use of Facebook, which is *so yesterday* to their generation), and the others;
- monitor news events and weather;
- research health information;
- make purchases online from trusted merchants;
- research other topics;
- research products/services before purchasing them offline;
- research stocks and investments and conduct online banking;
- play games, but only minimally;
- conduct genealogy research;
- and, access online discussions of interest.

Silents and G.I.s view the Internet primarily as a way to keep in touch with family members and friends. Boomers view it as an electronic encyclopedia and a source of information, although they're using it more often now for entertainment (Boomers are big Facebook'ers). X'ers view the web as information *and* entertainment. Millennials view it as the air they breathe, another appendage to their bodies.

Silents might have difficulty with complex websites. So make your site straightforward, and use *text* cues to guide them through the sites.

But don't load your pages with too much text. Also, can you give them a one-click method to increase text size? Use color-coding and other techniques to make it simple to use. Reduce your site's clutter, especially your home page.

My firm's website—www.genimperative.com—offers visitors the opportunity to purchase this book and the multiple DVDs from the *America's Generations With Chuck Underwood* television series on PBS. Because the purchase must be user-friendly to all generations, my webmaster made the layout, copy, and online purchasing process as uncluttered and easy as possible, especially for the older generations who did not grow up with the Internet.

I'm also finding that some Silents are hesitant to make the purchase online with their credit card, so I also offer them the opportunity to buy my materials the old fashioned way and mail a check.

And at the end of each of our PBS shows, a phone number is shown on the screen that viewers may call to get more information about the DVDs and book. And I'm the one who answers the phone; it's my home number. I cannot adequately describe the relief, joy, and surprise that ALL generations of callers, but especially the Silents, express when they get me directly. I answer the phone "Hello, Chuck Underwood", and there are a couple of seconds of silence, and then they say "Oh my gosh, I never thought I'd get YOU." They exhale with relief. A real human being, not the typical telephone-purchase NIGHTMARE! In addition to asking how to buy the book and DVDs, most want to talk about the shows they just watched. And I'm grateful for their interest, so I rejoice in listening to them, sometimes for 30 to 45 minutes.

Look Inward, At Your Own Company's People And Policies

Examine your own marketing/advertising/product development personnel and attitudes:

❧ Are your organization's decision makers and employees younger than Silents and therefore susceptible to stereotyping and ignorance about what makes Silents tick? Is there a good reason you don't employ Silents?

❧ Remember the current times: there is a profound shift in the American marketplace in the direction of the fifty-plus generations and demos. Do you need to erase some old tapes playing in your head?

Kevin O'Keefe, managing director of Weber Shandwick, a PR firm with clients that target Silents, told *Ad Age* magazine, "Clearly, marketers will have to reorient forty years of thinking. Marketers fall into old patterns and bad assumptions even as they realize how critical this group is."

Additional Silent Tips

They are worthy of media coverage, but they don't receive it. Cover them and win.

They are a unified generation whose members possess a strong common core or shared center. But many of them don't think of their age cohort as a generation. In this regard, they're like X'ers and unlike

G.I.s and Boomers and Millennials. So, if you'll teach them about their own generation, you'll win.

Don't patronize or offend them with your message. Silents are not brain-addled, little ol' ladies and men.

Because their generation's Core Values are rooted in the pragmatism of the Depression and war, they will respond to *rational* appeals.

Repetition of message helps.

Emotional hot buttons: nostalgia; their generation's legacy and contribution; security; independence; shared experiences with their children, grandchildren, and great-grandchildren; long and healthy lives.

Silent consumers like to work with Silent sellers and customer service personnel, not just because they're "my people" but also because they tend to be more skilled at selling to, and serving, them than younger generations.

Age 80 Is The New 60

Not just a cute phrase. It's also true. Ignore this generation's purchasing power and free spending at your own risk.

In 2015, I spoke at Arizona's annual travel-industry conference. It was a short keynote speech, not a full-blown training session, so I only had time to cover Boomers, X'ers, and Millennials. But I finished by saying this:

"We have just entered a golden era of anti-aging science, medicine, nutrition, fitness, and wellness. And many of us must erase some old tapes, playing in our heads, about what certain age markers—70, 80, and 90—actually mean today. And to help us erase those tapes, here is a member of the Silent Generation."

With that, the two big screens at the front of the hotel banquet room erupted with a high-energy concert video of mega-rocker and physically fit Silent member Tina Turner—eight months from her 70th birthday—blowing away a much younger arena audience of tens of thousands with her throbbing smash-hit, *Nutbush City Limits*. You'll probably find this concert, and that closing song, on *YouTube*. Search "Tina Turner Holland Concert".

It's a New World up there at the top of life. If businesses recognize this and make the necessary adjustments, they'll win with this generation.

CHAPTER 19

Marketing To Boomers

Tips, Tactics, And Guidelines

• • •

A LATE-2005 *BUSINESS WEEK* MAGAZINE cover shouted out the pronouncement as the leading edge of the Baby Boom Generation was about to turn 60:

"Love Those Boomers! Their new attitudes and lifestyles are a marketer's dream."

And it's still true.

Yes, another Boomer revolution—this one in the consumer marketplace—is underway. Some marketers get it and are cashing in. Some don't get it and are blowing it.

America's money is going north of age fifty at a stunning pace. According to *U.S. News & World Report* in 2014, Americans 50+ control 77% of the nation's total net worth!

But even more important, that money is *available* to marketers and advertisers because of these four well-documented truths about Boomer consumers:

1. They're not brand loyal, *famously* so;
2. They're receptive to advertising and new products and services;
3. They control disproportionate spending power in the U. S.;
4. They're free-spending.

Brand Loyalty

Boomers generally are not brand loyal; never have been, and never will be. And in the American marketplace, this puts the Boomers "in play".

If they've purchased five Toyotas in a row, it's not because of blind brand loyalty. It's because Toyota has earned them five separate times. Note to Toyota: don't get cocky; if Ford or Chevrolet or Honda comes along with a car that better suits their needs, Boomers will dump you in a New York Nanosecond.

Think about this: the parents of Boomers are the younger G.I.s and most of the Silents. As Boomer kids were coming of age, they frequently heard their parents pledge to never purchase a German or Japanese car and to remain loyal to American-made autos. This sentiment was pervasive in the aftermath of World War II, when Germany and Japan had been the enemies who killed our fellow Americans. (Millennials, would you buy a car today that was manufactured by, and with the profits going to, Al-Qaeda or the Taliban or ISIS?)

So, what was the first major purchase by the Baby Boom Generation, in the early 1960s?

The German-made Volkswagen Beetle.

And with that consumer decision, this generation was announcing that all bets are off. The Beetle best suited their unique generational values: it was less expensive and more reliable and fuel-efficient than many American-made cars, and its advertising was loaded with self-deprecating humor about its lovable ugliness and anti-snob attitude, which also appealed to this generation. And its cheap price left Boomers with more money to spend being experiential with their lives: travel; skiing; scuba-diving; rafting; hobbies.

Disproportionate Spending Power

As famed New York advertising guru Jerry Della Femina once reportedly said, marketers are in business to do three things:

1. *Follow the money.*
2. *Follow the money.*
3. *Follow the money.*

Boomers control a disproportionate amount of this country's wealth because of their massive population and career hard work.

In addition, they continue to receive the largest transfer of wealth in human history, as their parents—the first Americans to financially benefit from Social Security and entitlement programs like Medicare and Medicaid, and who enjoyed a steadily growing U. S. economy through most of their work years—pass away and bequeath their estates to their Boomer children.

Free-Spending And Receptive To Advertising

Boomers remain free spenders. As a classic Schlitz beer commercial from the mid-1960s said, "You only go around once in life, so you grab for all the gusto you can." Boomers agree.

And so Boomers *spend*, and this includes giving to charity.

And they are receptive to advertising and new products.

And all of these truths change just about everything.

With prior generations who prided themselves on their brand loyalty, marketers had come to embrace the axiom that, once those people reached about age 50, no amount of advertising could persuade them to switch brands or even try a new product. And so advertisers had given up on age 50+, and this decision made 18 to 49 the demographic they coveted.

But a Roper/ASW research study, conducted for AARP, announced the "new normal" back in 2001, when Boomers were aged 37 to 55:

"Americans 45-plus, contrary to conventional wisdom, are no more brand loyal than younger people in most categories. With the exception of only a few categories, the majority of 45-plus Americans are not loyal to any one brand."

In fact, this study found that age 45+ Americans, in certain product categories, were even *less loyal than younger consumers.*

In the late 1990s and early 2000s, as generational strategy was first emerging on a grand scale, a few national marketers created generationally strategized ad campaigns, instead of traditional demographic or age-based advertising. And lo and behold, these campaigns worked; sales increased. Cadillac. The Gap. Walt Disney World. And a few others.

And with that, my telephone was ringing off the hook with calls from marketers, ad agencies, commercial media outlets such as newspapers and radio and TV stations, all of them clamoring for training in Generational Marketing, Advertising, and Communications Strategy. And for several years they utilized it, and it consistently worked very effectively for them.

But then, the tsunami known as New Media rammed our country and our world. And suddenly, all of these marketers had to shift their training time and training budgets to understanding this astonishing revolution. And generational strategy was back-burner'ed.

But those marketers never forgot how powerful and successful this strategy can be. And now today, they are returning to it and requesting the training and consulting.

But many of the best case studies in generational marketplace strategy continue to be the ones from the decade of the 2000s.

It Cuts Through The Clutter

Generationally strategized messaging consistently cuts through all of the clutter floating around out there in the marketplace.

Examples:

Walt Disney World

Let's say you're on the marketing and advertising team at Walt Disney World in Orlando, Florida. In another year, the one-hundred-year anniversary of the birth of founder Walt Disney will occur. You want to seize the moment. You want to lure visitors to the park for a yearlong celebration of Mr. Disney.

You decide to go after Baby Boomers, even though their children are now long beyond the age that the park targets. So, why do you go after Boomers?

1. Follow the money.
2. Follow the money.
3. Follow the money.

And Boomers possess that lopsided percentage of this country's wealth.

You want to create a thirty-second TV spot that homes in on Boomers. How do you do it? How can you get this generation's attention with a 30-second television spot about Disney World?

Well, the research documents that Boomers' formative years molded such Core Values as:

1. forever young;
2. free spirited, exuberant, boisterous—jeez, if you blink your eyes, those wacky Boomers will take over the whole doggoned event;
3. they don't mind being center stage—Boomers have been in the spotlight all their lives;
4. and, they're competitive, they like to win, they like to be #1, they like to finish "first"...

Eureka! Boomers were Disney's *first generation!*

The TV commercial opens with a wide-angle shot of an elementary-school spelling bee in a hushed auditorium. With an audience of Baby Boomers watching and listening in perfect stillness, the PA announcer somberly instructs the pigtailed elementary-school girl standing nervously on stage to "Spell microphone."

She slowly and carefully begins to spell microphone. "M-I-C" —

Suddenly from the audience, a gray-haired Boomer interrupts, jumping out of his seat, turning to the other audience members, and continuing the spelling, but now of a different word: "K-E-Y!"

All Boomers in the audience instantly stand, twirl, and raucously finish their childhood anthem:

"M-O-U-S-E! Mickey Mouse! Donald Duck! Forever let us hold our banner high! High! High! High!"

To the astonishment and bewilderment of the wide-eyed young girl and a scholarly young boy seated in the audience, the Boomers are now out of control, including the Boomer judge and emcee, dancing with each other, grinning and laughing, eleven years old all over again, taking over the event as they finish the song at the top of their lungs.

The spot then cuts to outdoor camera shots at Walt Disney World, showing two Boomer women dancing with Disney characters (*Goofy!*) with a large crowd of park visitors encircling them, as the off-camera announcer begins the sales pitch asking them to come to the park:

"You were Disney's first generation. Come be a kid again."

I include this spot in my seminars, and audiences love it. Boomers laugh and applaud: *Yep, that's us.* After a seminar for a couple hundred supervisors at Beaumont Hospitals in Detroit, one participant wrote this evaluation of the seminar:

"Very, very interesting, and the Disney commercial blew the Baby Boomers at our table off our chairs."

This is powerful, generation-specific "creative" from the folks at Disney World. And within the first few seconds of this spot, Boomer viewers know it is meant for them. It *cuts through the clutter.*

The Great Boomer Love Affair With Cars

"Detroit Rediscovers Boomers" shouted the headline in an AARP national publication. From 2009 to 2014, the percentage of new-car buyers over age 55 jumped from 33% to 42%, according to car-market research firm Edmunds.com.

For generations, car buying declined when Americans entered their golden years.

But Boomers being Boomers, they are turning conventional habits inside-out. They're buying more pickups, utility vehicles, compact sedans, and funky compacts once designed for teens and young adults. Said Toyota advertising manager Bob Zeinstra, "This generation really sees autos not only as providing freedom but as an expression of their personality and who they are. Cars are not just a utilitarian machine. They are a part of who they are."

According to a recent study by the University of Michigan's Transportation Research Institute, 55- to 64-year-old Boomers replaced the 35- to 44-year-old Gen X demo as most likely to purchase a new car. Boomers' passion for the automobile, and their purchasing power, have lots of miles ahead of them. And the study suggests that the auto industry should spend less on marketing to Millennials and more on the Boomers, especially given that Boomers will remain in the workforce and continue the daily commute into later years than ever before.

Why this generation's romance with the automobile? As with everything generational, it goes back to their formative years. Boomers were kids (1) during the golden age of the American car, and (2) when the construction of the interstate highway system made long-distance driving safer and easier, and (3) when exploring America was celebrated in weekly TV shows like *Route 66*.

Generational Event Marketing
Boston Pops Orchestra
Baby Boomer Bash Concert Series

The Boston Pops Orchestra created a summer tour with a generation-specific concert it took to seven cities east of the Mississippi River.

It was called the *Baby Boomer Bash Concert Series*.

I called the Pops' PR director afterwards, and he said attendance was record-breaking and free media coverage was sizable. The Boomers came to hear The Pops play the music of the Beatles, Carole King,

Elvis, and Simon and Garfunkel, and to sing along (Boomers prefer to participate, not simply spectate) with music they had heard on the Saturday morning TV cartoon shows of their childhood days.

A quick point for those of you in public relations:

The legitimate *print* media—daily newspapers, the national news magazines, and others—have demonstrated a very enthusiastic interest in writing generationally angled news stories, especially newspapers. When the Pops announced its *Baby Boomer Bash* series, the Cincinnati Enquirer wrote two pages in its lifestyle section on this generationally strategized event.

So if you're looking for free media, identify legitimate generational angles for your PR thrust and incorporate them into your news releases. This is especially true today, as print media also pursue the young-adult Millennials. Gen X? *Incredibly* overlooked and ignored by the nation's news media. X'ers, you have every right to grab the news media by their throats and shout in their faces, "Hey! We're here!"

Morgan Stanley

With one of its print ads, Morgan Stanley connects very effectively with Boomer Core Values of assertiveness, willingness to take control, devotion to their parents, and that Boomer optimism.

The photo in the ad is a cozy living room, showing two well-worn leather chairs, a table and lamp, and a few books on a shelf, clearly at the home of the Boomers' parents. No people are shown, just the furniture. The copy reads:

"Mom, Dad, have a seat. There's something we've got to talk about. Should you sell your house and buy a smaller place? Live with us? Or travel forever and ever and ever? Don't worry. We'll figure it all out."

Boomers—aggressive, assertive, protective of their parents, and eternally optimistic—are often involved in decisions about Mom and Dad. Industries such as assisted-living and retirement communities, healthcare, financial services, and others that target G.I.s and Silents are now marketing directly to their assertive Boomer kids, especially with direct mail.

Taylor Guitars

The guitar industry enjoyed a nice uptick in sales when Boomers—relentlessly experiential and always eager to learn something new—started to become empty nesters and had the time and money to develop a new hobby. And bunches of them apparently want to be rock-and-rollers!

Taylor-brand guitars created a national-award-winning print ad. The photo shows a balding Boomer guy wearing a tank-top T-shirt as he stands outdoors *in snow* and strums his guitar. The copy reads:

"You're right. You're probably too late to get into the Rock and Roll Hall of Fame. But you're never too late to give the world another cover version of *Smoke on the Water.*"

And this brings us to a critical point about messaging to Boomers:

Never Say Never

The ad copy does not say "you're too old"; it doesn't even say "you're too late". It says you're *probably* too late to get into the Rock and Roll Hall of Fame. And this choice of words speaks to that unsinkable Boomer optimism:

Oh, okay, probably too late, you say? Well that's all I need to hear. I've still got a chance! I'm goin' for the Hall of Fame!!

When messaging to Boomers, never say never; there's always hope!

Finding The New Outer Limit For The Aging Body

Boomer Core Values of *forever young* and *squeeze life for all of its satisfactions* explain why their generation will continually establish new outer limits for the endurance of the human body at each age marker.

Boomers are hiking up mountains and skiing down them. Skydiving from the heavens and scuba diving to the depths. Zumba. Boxing. Weights. Running. Swimming. Vitamins. Health foods. Label reading. *Push it to the max!*

Some Boomers are realizing a lifelong fantasy by purchasing their first Harley Davidson motorcycles, thinking they still have the muscles to control them, and promptly crashing them.

But they are always seeking the outer limit of what they can achieve, and they are willing to pay the price to find that limit.

To orthopedic surgeons, Boomers have become a *Joint Replacement Jackpot.*

When this generation was first bringing this live-life-to-the-fullest Core Value into adulthood in the 1970s, a market opportunity became very obvious. And the rapid construction of fitness clubs became a coast to coast phenomenon.

Rule of thumb when marketing to this generation:

Never say never to a Boomer.

The 7 Dirty Words You Can Never Say To A Boomer

Speaking of never: when dealing with Boomers, marketers must never, never, never refer to this generation in the following terms; not now, and not when they're 138:

1. **Senior Citizen**—*a noble label for Mom and Dad, but not us.*
2. **Retirement/Retiree**—*we will never retire.*
3. **Aging**—*Ohmygod, nooooooooooooooooooooooooo!*
4. **Golden Years**—*again, a label for our parents.*
5. **Silver Years**—*ditto; in fact, a good rule of thumb is...no references to* any *precious metals.*
6. **Prime Time**—*every day of our lives* has been prime time! *Don't get* cute.
7. **Mature**—*Never! I'm a Mouseketeer for life!*

After I presented these "never" terms to a national transportation conference at Skamania Lodge, nestled along the Columbia River Gorge in Stevenson, Washington, one audience member returned to work and emailed a summary of the entire conference to her colleagues working for the City of Seattle, saying, "What I especially liked were Chuck Underwood's *seven dirty words* when marketing to Boomers." I hadn't thought of them that way, but *The Seven Dirty Words*, as Boomers remember, is the title of the well-known routine by stand-up comedian George Carlin and his *Seven Words You Can Never Say on Television.*

And within a few weeks, *Arizona Republic* reporter Susan Felt had written a story about *The Seven Dirty Words You Can Never Say To Boomers*, and other newspapers around the country reprinted it, which is a reminder to you PR professionals that these kinds of generational tidbits are embraced by print media.

AARP And Generational Media Strategy

The nice folks at the American Association of Retired Persons (AARP) surely must have begun drooling out of both corners of their mouths in 1996. The leading edge of the massive Boomer Generation was now reaching AARP membership age: 50. *Hallelujah!! Here comes the Boomer tidal wave; we're gonna be flush with members and cash!*

Boomers avoided AARP like the plague.

You want me to join an organization called the American Association of RETIRED PERSONS?! Are you kidding?! You want to mail me your monthly magazine called "Modern Maturity"? I'd be mortified if my neighbors saw the mailman putting that thing in my mailbox!

Clearly, dramatic change was required for this important advocacy organization. So it officially changed its name to simply its acronym *AARP*, which minimizes the nasty phrase "Retired Persons" that Boomers disdain.

AARP took the additional and significant step of launching a completely separate magazine, just for Boomers. Instead of *Modern Maturity*, AARP titled its Boomer version—what else?—*My Generation*. Different editorial content, specific to Boomers. Boomer-targeted advertising, graphics, everything. But later, it unified its multiple titles under the single name *AARP The Magazine;* the organization had simply built too much brand equity in that acronym over the years to dilute it with multiple titles.

And with these generationally strategized changes, AARP membership by Boomers inched upward, and this was during an era when the rest of the magazine and membership industry was struggling with declining circulation, ad revenues, and member counts.

AARP and Boomers, in principle, *should* be a powerhouse marriage. Both are social-change advocates. Both feel they can take on government and other major institutions, when necessary, and *win*. This should be a beautiful collaboration of clout, empowerment, and engagement waiting to happen *if* AARP makes effective use of generational strategy to connect with Boomers.

By the way, as younger Gen X'ers now enter their fifties, AARP will face a very difficult challenge. X'ers, as a generation, simply have not been "joiners", thus far. And their Core Values are different from any prior generation. So generational strategy with X'ers will be imperative for AARP, and it still might not be enough.

Cadillac

In the early '80s, Cadillac sales were sluggish. The oldest Boomers were just reaching luxury car age but weren't buying Cadillacs, which to them represented the snobbery, pompous display of wealth, and class status that First-Wave Boomers railed against. Even worse: to their generation, Cadillac also meant *old people.*

So Boomers turned to Japanese and German luxury cars, whose sales soared. And Cadillac suffered through two decades of what, by the early 2000s, the *Wall Street Journal* politely described as "lagging sales".

But then in 2002, Cadillac sales shot up a striking 16%, its biggest gain in some twenty years.

Cadillac did it with Boomer-strategized *product design*—its CTS model—and an advertising campaign that was a bold departure from the way Cadillac had always presented its product.

With its design of the CTS, Cadillac nostalgically returned Boomers to the muscle-car era that had been such a prominent and fond part of their formative years in the '60s and early '70s. And instead of accentuating wealth and power and country club snobbery, its TV commercials now focused upon engine power and speed and *"young"*. One TV spot shows the CTS screaming down a dusty old country road with pounding rock-and-roll music by Led Zeppelin. *Cadillac and Zep? Wow!*

This generationally savvy campaign was a huge success. And the *Boomer-strategized* CTS goes down in history as "the car that saved Cadillac".

"This is not your father's Oldsmobile."

In the late 1980s, luxury brand Oldsmobile suffered from the same malaise as Cadillac. Boomers perceived these brands as *my father's car.* So Oldsmobile mounted a full frontal attack with an advertising campaign anchored by a blunt, cut-through-the-clutter tag-line that left no doubt the ad was meant for Boomers. The memorable tagline was:

"This is not your father's Oldsmobile."

So Boomers certainly noticed the ads, took a look at the 1988 Oldsmobile, maybe even test-drove it, and made their decision:

The hell it isn't.

And Oldsmobile tanked.

The lesson? Sometimes, you have to change more than your slogan.

This campaign slogan is so memorable to Boomers that, all these decades later, there is a line of women's blue jeans meant for Boomers that plays off that Oldsmobile tag line: "Not Your Daughter's Jeans".

Gap: A Successful Multigenerational Campaign

In 2003, men's apparel sales in the United States were down 2% from the year before, and women's apparel sales were down 4%. But the Gap was up 6%. A *Wall Street Journal* report credited the robust year to the chain's merchandise—of course—and its *multi-generational advertising campaign.*

A two-page magazine spread shows two models wearing Gap's hooded sweatshirts, "hoodies". On the right is young model Bridget Hall, the typical teenage-looking, very skinny, lots-of-attitude model we've seen forever in women's apparel ads. On the left is *57-year-old* model Lauren Hutton. 57!

Women's apparel has historically been one of the more age-discriminatory categories in all of advertising. But Gap launched a massive campaign using a variety of multigenerational on-camera talent in its print and television campaigns. In one TV spot, it used guitarists Willie Nelson to appeal to Boomers and Ryan Adams to appeal to X'ers. And it worked. Its slogan for this campaign?

"The Gap. For Every Generation."

I showed the Bridget Hall/Lauren Hutton ad to a focus group of ten Gen X women, then in their twenties and thirties, and asked them which of the two images would be more persuasive in getting them to buy the "hoodie. Although much closer in age to Bridget Hall, they nonetheless voted in favor of 57-year-old Lauren Hutton. What surprised me was their vote:

10-0.

I asked them, "Why?" One X'er replied, "She (Hutton) is beautiful and sexy, and she looks so comfortable in her own skin." Another added, "I love that she's smiling and actually flashing that gap in her front teeth. You go, girl!"

I pushed it. "Yeah, but Lauren Hutton is so much older than you. You're much closer in age to the younger model." They shook their heads, one of them saying about the younger image, "She's trying too hard. I don't identify with her."

I pushed it further. "Yeah, but this one (I pointed to Hutton) is almost *sixty years* old!" At that moment, they just shrugged. But a few moments later, one of the women, twenty-eight years old, said, "Do you know what sixty years old means to women my age? Tina Turner."

Capital One: Generational Credit Cards

The corporations that comprise the financial services industry are locked in brutal competition to land Boomer clients and get their hands on all of that Boomer money.

One of them, Capital One, created a direct-mail piece, offering what it called its *Generations MasterCard.* Members could receive their plastic card with any one of nine Boomer-nostalgic images imprinted on the front: a big-finned Cadillac from the late '50s, when Boomers were still too young to drive; the yellow, have-a-nice-day "smiley face" that was seen everywhere in the '60s and '70s; the international peace symbol, also everywhere during the Vietnam War protests; a ticket stub from the legendary Woodstock music festival; the silver spinning disco ball from the '70s; and others.

This is straightforward generational marketing. If you're a Boomer, it would be just about impossible to *not* look at each of those nine images and know *this ad is meant for me.*

Fidelity Investments

In another advertising campaign targeting Boomers, Fidelity Investments created print ads and TV spots that show a montage of nostalgic images of Boomers throughout their youth, accompanied by copy that matches the images. One such ad shows a Boomer woman's birth photo and a collage of photos from her childhood, teen and college years, young adult, and current-day photo. The copy reads:

"This is Carol. She's been called a hippie, preppy, yuppie, protester, Democrat, Republican, mom, CFO, CEO, cancer patient, cancer survivor, fundraiser, spokesperson, caregiver, journalist, and soon-to-be world traveler. Reaching retirement is no small achievement. We'll help you make the most of it."

Ameriprise

And Ameriprise goes unabashedly for Boomers in its campaign, repeatedly inserting the word "generation" in its copy and voiceover:

"Think the generation who lived through all this (as we see footage of fashion, protest, celebrities, and other images from the '60s and '70s) is going to go out...(camera shot of an empty rocking chair on a front porch)...like *this?* NO WAY!"

The spot goes on to acknowledge that Boomers are "reinventing what retirement means" as it shows shots of energetic Boomers conducting business, traveling, and making a difference.

And Ameriprise uses a beloved song from 1966 in this campaign: Spencer Davis Group's *Gimme Some Lovin'*.

Pop Music: The Music Or Just The Lyrics

Oh my goodness, Boomers and their music.

Pop music is probably the most generation-specific of all mass media. TV, radio, the Web, and print tend to cut across multiple generations. But music is specific to a generation's youth.

So, if you want to target a generation and can afford to license the rights to use a hit song from their youth, the music can deliver instant recognition to the viewer or radio listener: *this message is meant for me.*

But if you can't afford or obtain the licensing, then perhaps you can write copy that simply includes a well-known line from a song's lyrics. An example:

Hosted by the *Quad-City Times* newspaper in Davenport, Iowa, I conducted a half-day training session in Generational Strategy for about eighty of its local advertisers. Two weeks later, I returned to Davenport to meet privately with individual advertisers and their respective newspaper account reps to discuss their own utilization of this strategy.

One homebuilder was developing a new community of upscale custom-built homes called Fieldstone Pointe. He advertised in the Sunday-edition Home section of the newspaper, which was packed with display ads by all of the local builders. The ads looked the same: small rectangular ads in which each builder crammed as much typed copy as possible. The page was a boring blur of identically sized rectangles.

This builder wanted to target two generations with separate ads: Boomers and X'ers. To make his ads stand out from the clutter, we sharply reduced the copy to create more white space. And then we put two call-out headers atop each ad, and we used lyrics from pop music of each generation's youth as the call-out. To suggest the wonderful quality of life in this upscale residential community, the Boomer-ad call-out used the title of a popular Beatles song: *Here Comes The Sun.* And the X'er ad used slightly revised lyrics from a well-known U2 song from the late 1980s:

I Still Hadn't Found What I Was Looking For (Until I Found Fieldstone Pointe).

Generational Strategy, in order to cut through the clutter.

And sure enough, these new ads did pop from the page, while the competitors' ads looked the same.

At any age, Boomers will be receptive to advertising and marketing messages, and to new products and services. They have blown to smithereens the obsolete but long-held notion that people aged fifty-plus cannot be influenced by advertising because they're too "set in their ways".

Cut The Crap

Although receptive to advertising, Boomers are also streetwise and can smell hype a mile away. So communicate your product's benefits in an honest, fact-based manner. Cut the crap.

Marketers: be careful. Because the hard-working and career-driven Boomers are now in mid- to late-career and even retirement, don't fall into the trap of pitching your products and services to them with this kind of messaging: "You've worked hard, you've *earned* it, you *deserve* it, *reward* yourself."

This works with Silents. But with Boomers, I advise you to avoid such language. In a recent Boomer focus group, I was surprised at the group's response when I asked, "Are you the *most pressured* generation?"

No!, they passionately answered. "Pressure?", asked one. "Try the Great Depression, try World War II. Whatever pressure we Boomers feel is *nothing* compared to what our parents and grandparents experienced." The others in the group agreed.

Boomers will probably never feel fully *entitled* to reward themselves. They'll never feel like they've done enough. They will always measure their achievement against that of their parents' generation. And they will always feel, accurately so, that they've had it comparatively easy. If you want to sell "entitlement" and "earned the right" and "go ahead, reward yourself," sell it to the Silents. With Boomers, this kind of messaging will probably miss the target.

Boomers are ethics-driven. Your product and your company must be "right." Socially responsible. And even cause-active.

Many Boomers ARE time-crunched. Many face extended eldercare with their parents and/or extended childcare with their adult kids or grandkids, in addition to working feverishly in their careers. So, as consumers, they seek *fast* and *convenient* and *no-hassle* and *reliable,* and they're willing to pay extra for it, if they must.

Note to direct-mail marketers: if you want to get Boomers (and X'ers, who are also time-starved) to read the 5th sentence of your direct-mail piece, you must earn them with your first four sentences. The moment your copy becomes irrelevant, you lose them. And many of you don't seem to get that. You're wasting their time by burying the important facts later in the piece, and that's a deal breaker.

Yes, Boomers have a distinct "First Wave" and "Second Wave" to their generation. But they share enough common values that they are a single generation:

* Strong sense of right and wrong.
* Confident and assertive.
* Demanding.
* Optimistic.
* Exceptional work ethic.
* Team players. "We" focused, instead of "me" focused.
* Loving reverence of their elders.
* Personal guilt over their divorces and parenting. One newspaper headline reporting on Boomers' sense of their own inadequacy as parents reads, "My Mom Was a Better Mom." They regret that their time-poor lives have prevented them from being the parents their own mothers and fathers were, and are, to them. They're now trying to be very involved grandparents, and this creates opportunities for marketers.

The *Arizona Republic* newspaper called me for a story addressing this question: do forever-young Boomers mind being called *grandmother* and *grandfather?* Well, this might give you an insight about this generation. The story quotes Boomer actress Goldie Hawn, who said this:

when she first became a grandmother, and in order to make the title more *glamorous,* she taught her grandchild to call her *Glamma* instead of *Gramma.* And I told the reporter that Boomers won't mind being called "Grandma" and "Grandpa" as long as marketers do not conjure up the stereotypical rocking-chair image of grandparenthood.

* Boomers want to make the smartest possible purchase. They do their homework before making the bigger purchases, but they also want knowledgeable salespeople on the sales floor to help them eye-to-eye. Want to drive away Boomer business? Fail to train your salespeople to know every possible detail about your product and your competitors' products.

They are in the midst of several major life passages, all of which create marketplace opportunities:

* Most are in, or near to, their peak earning years.

* Some are retiring from their current job, but few will retire completely and do nothing. Boomers remain contribution-driven. Even if they retire from one career, they will seek other pursuits that will keep them productive.

❧ Most are empty nesters or soon will be.

❧ Many of them are single, often by choice. This is a more substantial percentage of their generation's population than many marketers appreciate and understand. This creates new marketplace opportunities that target singles age 50+.

❧ Boomers have been ambushed in their careers by layoffs and offshoring. And no generation lost more retirement savings to The Great Recession of 2008 and 2009, so some are in big trouble with their finances, especially as many of them also try to help their own adult children. This dilemma is now a major focus for them and thus a major opportunity for marketers.

❧ Boomer women, an especially lucrative market, are rewriting the book about living, working, and spending at their age.

❧ Boomers are the forever-young generation because the America of their formative years imbued them with hope and love and optimism. And modern medicine is giving them unprecedented opportunities to maintain their physical wellness. And this opens up countless market-place opportunities.

But They ARE Aging, And Therein Lies An Opportunity

The *Wall Street Journal* assembled some vivid examples of how companies are adjusting their products, retail stores, and advertising as aging Boomers move into their target demo:

Kimberly Clark And *Depend* Diapers

Kimberly Clark expects 45 million Boomers to need incontinence products. *Ouch!* And so, with Boomer Core Values in mind, its adult diaper *Depend*:

* is no longer called a diaper; instead, *underwear*;
* now comes in both men's and women's styles, and in fashionable prints;
* and, is now packaged similar to regular underwear.

For crying out loud, now it's the Boomers' poop tonnage that's changing the American marketplace. Can't this generation do *anything* in moderation?

Stores Retailing

Sherwin-Williams paint stores, with empty-nest Boomers now ready to update their houses, have added more lighting and seating and serve coffee. And less fine print on their display ads.

CVS pharmacies: more carpeting to reduce slipping; the top shelves are now at 60 inches instead of 72; curbs have been eliminated from store entrances, where possible; and where not possible, the curbs have been painted yellow. They're gearing up for the Boomer tidal wave and anticipate the increased revenues that will pay for these refurbishments. Their stores no longer sell cigarettes, which conflict with their mission to be wellness destinations. (As of the writing of this book, Walgreen's and Rite Aid still sell cigarettes).

Walgreen's is adapting its seven thousand stores to be more Boomer-friendly: magnifying glasses are placed in aisles that stock products with lots of fine print on the packaging; reading glasses are more stylish; easier-to-open packages; and, more linear feet of shelf space for vitamins for the wellness-oriented Boomers.

And at some financial-services offices: coffee is now offered to Boomer clients in cups with handles for less-steady hands, instead of Styrofoam; lamps are used instead of harsh overhead lighting; and background noise, even music, is being blocked wherever conversation will occur.

Yes, most of these changes will benefit all generations of customers. But it's the Boomer tsunami that is prompting them.

And this is very similar to the makeover that many hotel chains are undergoing to appeal to Millennials and their technology addictions: the change is triggered by one generation's preferences but will benefit all generations.

Emerald Nuts

Because snack-nuts are a popular health-food, and because Boomers are embracing wellness, Emerald Nuts now come in cans that have indented sides to make them easier to grip. And the twist-off cap now requires a shorter rotation to open.

Boomers And The News

Boomers love *meaningful* detail and despise *meaningless* detail. So arrange your print collaterals for speedy and easy consumption. The newspaper *USA Today* became a success in the 1980s with this strategy.

However, the *Wall Street Journal* has reformatted its print edition and is now writing *longer* stories with *more* depth for those topics that require it. In our increasingly shallow and superficial nation of information mini-blasts, will this work? Stay tuned.

Boomers are empowered and engaged, so they devour the daily newspaper, National Public Radio, the weekly news magazines, and the nightly *network* news.

They understand and recognize good journalism. They grew up with larger-than-life pillars of integrity like CBS' anchor Walter Cronkite, "The Most Trusted Man In America", the NBC News anchor team of Huntley and Brinkley, and local newspaper reporters who were superstars in their communities. It was the *integrity*—the *ideal*—of journalism that inspired some Boomers to pursue careers in this field.

All these years later, they still embrace print journalism and still watch network newscasts. But they think *local* TV news is, as one Boomer focus-group participant described it, "a joke":

Local TV News In America

Good evening and welcome to TV 4's Live-Local-And-Late-Breaking Eyewitness News At Six! Our lead story is traffic accident # 1. Our second story is traffic accident # 2. Our third story is house fire #1. Our fourth story is crime # 1. Our fifth story is video footage from a PR firm trying to promote its client's product.

And Boomer news hounds cry out, *Where's the relevance? Where's the importance to my life? Where's the watchdog reporting? Where's the INTEGRITY?*

To Boomers (and X'ers and Millennials), local TV news is phony, shallow, inaccurate, slow-paced, irrelevant to their lives, anchored by "bubble-headed bleach blondes" instead of journalists; and thus, unworthy of their time.

Local TV news operations have lost their importance and relevance. In order to hold down newsroom costs and maximize profit, they report the stories that are *cheapest* and *easiest* to cover: crimes and accidents, in which police or firefighters do all of the legwork and then tell the reporter what happened. *Done!*

X'ers don't watch local TV news in percentages anywhere close to prior generations at their age. And from a widely circulated report from a television-industry research firm: (1) only one-third of adult-age Millennials claim to have a favorite TV station for news; and (2) *the more news they watch the lower their evaluation of that news station!*

I've consulted dozens of TV stations and explained this to their management teams. And as long as TV stations are owned by big publicly held corporations whose top executives live and work a thousand miles away and thus do not have to face their stations' viewers eye-to-eye in the local community, I don't see this changing. The view from generational study: most local TV newscasts will remain unimportant and irrelevant to the lives of most viewers; and they will fail to harness the power of generational strategy as it directly applies to story selection and presentation, set design, pace of the newscast, and anchor selection.

And then there are our nation's daily newspapers:

Boomers And Newspapers

More than ever, the big-city dailies are—here comes that phrase again—The Best Obtainable Version of the Truth, the only reliable and trustworthy source of comprehensive explanations of the important daily events in our hometowns, states, nation, and world. Unlike local TV news, whose *product* is considered feeble and irrelevant, the newspapers' actual *product* is more essential than ever, as Americans want and need to stay current on so many matters affecting their lives.

But where television is slick at *promoting* its product, newspapers stink at promotion and are losing readership, especially with X'ers, despite the importance and general excellence of their product.

I consult the newspaper industry, too. And I tell them, "Your product—good journalism—is essential to American life and democracy itself. But you are absolutely lousy marketers. You were so big and muscular for so many decades that you didn't HAVE to be good marketers. Now you do. And your industry must launch a massive, long-term, and generationally strategized *educational* campaign, not merely a marketing or promotional campaign, to teach Americans the unique journalistic integrity and necessity of your product."

But the newspaper industry is moving far too slowly, and it still doesn't fully grasp that:

⚘ its *problem* is generational;
⚘ its *opportunity* is generational;
⚘ and so, its *solution* is generational.

Newspaper Association of America, where are you? Where's your leadership? Where's the nationwide, long-term, generationally strategized, educational campaign that will *teach* instead of lamely *pitch?*

From the perspective of generational study, you're blowing it.

Diminished Eyesight, Diminished Hearing

Are you planning to give Boomers your business card? If so, what type size and color contrast are you utilizing? Is it reader-friendly for aging eyes?

Point-of-sale signage and printed takeaways, done right, are a key convenience to a generation that considers itself time-poor. Boomers want to quickly get in and out of your store, gym, office, and auto dealership, but still having made smart purchases. Make it easy for them to be smart. Make it easy to read your signage.

Don't get so carried away with your website's creative design that you slow the download of your home page. Visually interesting, yes. But your home page should download swiftly. Save the heavy video and graphics for interior pages. Ad agencies, you have been the absolute worst at this:

Loading...Loading...Loading...Skip This Intro?

Hell, yes, skip the intro!!!

Research indicates that Boomer women tend to look more excitedly and optimistically at their future than Boomer men do. Likely reason why: women foresee a long list of adventures awaiting them when they empty-nest and leave their first careers. Boomer men, who have defined themselves so thoroughly by their careers, see approaching retirement as an unclear and perhaps unsettling passage.

The message? Market your product/service to that sense of celebration in Boomer women's next passage. And help the Boomer men to feel valuable, and excited, about their future, too. A generational opportunity.

Boomers And Travel

Travel deserves a special mention: the travel industry is right-on to pursue the Boomers, who want experiential and learning vacations, not simply flopping on the beach or at the cruise ship's swimming pool. But travel, according to recent research, has not been a high priority for Boomers because of time, career, family, and financial constraints on their lives. But when they do travel, they travel quite differently from Silents and G.I.s.

One such difference is captured in a recent *Wall Street Journal* headline, "Boomers to cruise industry: less cruising!" Boomers don't want to lie on a deck chair for nine days of circling the Caribbean islands. They want to get *off* the ship and immerse themselves in the authenticity of the islands' native cultures. And they want to be physically active while on the ship and seek a rock-climbing wall, fitness center, jogging path, hobby classes. By contrast, Silents—when they were at that same age, but with different Core Values—loved the opulence and leisure and sunshine and 24-hour food onboard the ship and simply "being on a cruise". The ship itself was the lure for their generation; for Boomers, the ship is a conveyance, transportation, a water taxi to an exotic locale.

Double-check your own staffers: are they all younger than Boomers? If so, they might not accurately relate to Boomer consumer attitudes and might be guilty of stereotyping and *guessing* what Boomers want. It's a new world. Hire a Boomer. Or three.

Boomers don't possess "generation envy." They like being Boomers, and they like their current life stage.

They're not desperate to be nineteen again. They're comfortable in their own skin.

Here are a couple of right-on taglines in Boomer-female advertising, which acknowledge this generation's unique Core Values and contentment at their current age:

* Clairol: "A Beauty All Your Own."
* Victoria's Secret: "At last, I'm comfortable."
* Not Your Daughter's Jeans: "Made for real women, with real curves."

A newspaper reporter called me to get the generational angle to the surge in Boomer purchases of Harley-Davidson motorcycles, and he asked this question with cynicism:

"Isn't this nothing more than a desperate attempt by an aging generation to try to fool itself into thinking it's younger than it is?"

I answered, "Boomers are not buying Harleys to try to recapture their youth. They're buying Harleys because they can't wait for this Saturday's ride in the country and next summer's vacation across America." And maybe even to the Sturgis Motorcycle Rally, where each summer a half-million bikers, mostly Boomers, overrun this South Dakota community of 7,000.

Why their generation's love of motorcycles, more so than any other generation? Easy:

America.

The magic of this country when Boomers were growing up. The open road. *Route 66. Easy Rider.* Purple mountain's majesty. Amber waves of grain. The surf, sun, and sand of the California coast. Adventures around every corner, in a land of freedom and safety and happy, wonderful people. Wind in their hair, bugs in their teeth. *My America.*

Perfect.

Not An Oldies Act

Boomers are as *future-oriented* as a generation can be. Life is not about yesterday. Yesterday was magnificent, yes. But everything with Boomers is about tomorrow and what's next and seizing the new moment. Because of their unique formative years and Core Values, life is one long banquet table, and they want to sample every dish while they're here.

Key Point: it is a delicate balance; if you try to turn the Boomers into nothing more than an oldies' act with too much nostalgia in your marketing and advertising, *you will lose.* With this generation, it is still entirely about *tomorrow.*

And yet the utilization of nostalgia as a creative element in your advertising also can effectively cut through the clutter and announce to Boomers that *this ad is meant for you.* An example:

Varilux

Presbyopia is the name of an eyesight affliction. Varilux manufactures eyeglasses designed to relieve the condition. It ran a TV campaign that presented a fictional 1960s-style protest by the *Presbyopic Six* (harkens back to the Chicago Seven of 1960s protest fame), who chant and carry signs about their "right to see" and are arrested. This ad campaign humorously captures the social activism of the Boomers by showing sit-ins and protest songs. And yet the product itself is designed to help Boomer eyesight for *tomorrow.*

Real Estate

Boomers want choices. Builders understand they must not tell Boomers what they want. Boomers will tell them. So, give them lots of options, builders. Listen, don't talk.

Many Boomers are not doing the traditional residential downsizing thing as they become empty nesters. Instead: more space for an office, home theater, home gym, in-law suite, extra bedrooms for the grandkids, and bigger bedrooms and bathrooms and hallways that one day might need to be spacious enough for grab bars and walkers and wheelchair access. No steps.

And aging Boomers living in cold-weather climates are apparently not going to gravitate to the Sun Belt like prior generations. Begun by the Silent generation, Boomers will continue the trend to stay put to be near their families. However, those who have the money might do the second-home thing or else time-share in a warm climate.

Grandparenthood

Like Silents, Boomers increasingly participate in the *primary* care of grandchildren and thus also participate in the purchasing decisions associated with it.

As grandparents, Boomers place a premium on their grandkids' safety, education, and shared experiences, and this will show up in their purchases for their grandkids.

Personal Finance

The Great Recession ravaged Boomers' financial nest eggs, and some will probably never fully recover. During the recession, Boomers: lost jobs or dropped to lower-paying ones; saw their homes' property values plummet; saw their investments lose value; and, many of them had to reach into their savings to rescue their Gen X or Millennial kids, who were also hit by the recession. And on top of all of this, anti-aging science is beginning to sharply increase longevity, so *how long am I going to live, and how can I possibly know when to quit working and if I have enough money?*

So this generation needs help from financial planners. Those planners who understand the unique Core Values and needs of this generation, and who provide the knowledge, courtesy, and Boomer-specific products, services, and guidance to get this unique generation where it wants and needs to go, will win.

Beloved Mom And Dad

Overwhelmingly, Boomers worship their parents. They know the devotion and selflessness Mom and

Dad gave to raising them. Marketers can make use of this powerful, emotional tie.

About sixty years after World War II ended, apparel retailer Land's End put iconic war image *Rosie the Riveter* on a catalogue cover. In Boomers, this image stirs powerful memories of their G.I. Generation moms and grandmas working in the factories and offices to help the war effort. These kinds of images, honoring their parents' generation, can resonate with grateful Boomer kids.

Digital Technology

Boomers initially used the Internet for hard information: purchases; job searches; research at work; travel; weather; and so on.

But they're beginning to use it more for entertainment, especially as commercial television and radio and advertisers abandon Boomers for younger generations of viewers and listeners.

Online dating sites are now pursuing single Boomers.

Boomer-relevant videos are growing in popularity on YouTube and other sites.

Boomers also use the latest social media to stay in touch with their Gen X and Millennial kids and grandkids and to track down old friends.

In my training seminars, I'll ask Millennials in the audience for a show of hands to answer this question:

One year from now, do you think your generation—not just you, personally, but your entire Millennial generation—will be using Facebook more than you use it today, or less, or about the same?

Their constant response is *less.* And most go on to say, *we've moved on from Facebook.* Boomers, however, are active users of this site, so Facebook might now be more of a Boomer destination. And Boomers will follow their kids and grandkids to the next new sites, as well.

CHAPTER 20

Marketing To X'ers

Tips, Tactics, And Guidelines

• • •

KEY POINT: GENERATIONAL MARKETING AND advertising and communication strategy is fundamental to all media, including digital platforms.

X'ers are a numerically small generation. Fewer than 59 million born.

As a generation, they grew up skeptical and often cynical of older generations and our nation's major institutions. They offer their loyalty cautiously, if at all.

They also grew up spending less time in the presence of older people than prior generations had. Most have made their peace with their divorced parents and other elders who somehow let them down, but there is still a notable emotional disconnect between X'ers and older people.

Gen X is a "me" generation: self-focused; self-reliant; independent; individualistic. Survival of the fittest. *What's in it for me?*" In 1995, ESPN created a new kind of athletic competition known as *X Games* (the "X" stands for "extreme", not "Gen X") with young-adult X'ers in mind (in that year, X'ers were aged 14 to 30) because advertisers were now targeting their generation, and so ESPN delivered a new competition that showcased them. Two years later in 1997, it added the *Winter X Games.* What's notable is that the competitions in the X Games are individual, not team. And this appeals to Gen X's Core Value of individualism. It also gives them a new event, a creation, that is *all theirs*, made just for them, which appeals to this generation that knows it is being overlooked.

They experienced "premature wealth" as a result of the heightened spending power of their dual-career-income parents, many of whom showered their kids with expensive "things" during their formative years. So X'ers grew up with pretty refined tastes. They know quality. And to the greatest extent that their incomes permit today, they demand and purchase high quality.

And, as the first generation of youth to have their own radio stations and their own TV channels, X'ers have been heavily marketed to, and advertised to, their entire lives.

From all of this come Core Values, attitudes, and perceptions such as these:

❋ They are very street-smart and advertising-savvy.

❋ They take great pride in their individuality. They see themselves as millions of diverse individuals. But more and more, they're learning that all 59 million of them DO share a common core and are very much a "generation". The strategy for marketers? Market to their common core, but don't make it obvious. And celebrate their individualism when you can; X'ers don't especially like the idea of marketers being able to slot and pigeonhole them as a single "demo".

❋ They consider themselves a non-racist generation and take pride in their acceptance and tolerance of different ethnicities and lifestyles.

❋ They insist upon a work/leisure balance. They don't want to be workaholics.

❋ They need to be convinced. They grew up in a time of one broken promise after another from the adult world.

❧ The people they feel they can trust tend to be people their own age. Think of the theme song by The Rembrandts of the TV series *Friends,* which is very much an X'er-sensibility show (*Seinfeld,* by contrast, is very much Boomer):

"So no one told you life was going to
be this way.
Your job's a joke, you're broke, your love
life's DOA.
It's like you're always stuck in second gear,
Well, it hasn't been your day, your week,
your month, or even your year.
But, I'll be there for you, when the rain
starts to pour.
I'll be there for you, like I've been there before.
I'll be there for you, 'cause you're there
for me, too."

❧ X'ers espouse few, if any, sweeping ideologies or causes. They'll do what it takes to get through their own lives as best they can. They'll focus on a much smaller "world" that they feel they can influence.

❧ What matters most to them is their own immediate environment. National and international news and events are often deemed irrelevant to their lives. *My life is all about my neighborhood, my kids' school, my job. Things I can actually see, touch, control, and witness the results of my work.*

* With a lack of positive historical events to remember from their formative years, the pop culture of their youth assumes large proportion in their lives. They like to poke fun at it, but *it's what they have,* so it's also uncommonly important to them. Celebrities, music, fashion, TV, movies, toys, and the rest from the '70s, '80s, '90s, and early 2000s can be tools for marketers to use to reach them. *Fast Times at Ridgemont High, 16 Candles, St. Elmo's Fire.* The Brat Pack. *The Simpsons.* Pong. Nintendo, Tetris, Game Box. The launch of a new broadcast television network in 1986: Fox. *Thriller.* Madonna.

* They came of age with commercial radio and television, especially MTV, cleverly force-feeding them the message that celebrities are important to their lives. Although wised up now, X'ers remain tuned in to celebrity news more than other generations. When you think X'ers, think *People* magazine and TV shows *Entertainment Tonight* and *Access Hollywood.* This was their daily diet growing up. And as most marketers know,

celebrities can cut through all of the advertising clutter that bombards our brains every day. But choose celebrity product endorsers very carefully. X'ers have been regularly disappointed by celebrities who turned out to have clay feet.

❧ Many of them do not know that the name *Generation X* is actually a badge of honor, not an insult.

Tips, Tactics, And Guidelines For Marketing To Gen X

❧ X'ers are easily bored. So give them unexpected and clever tricks and surprises in your advertising. Don't be linear with your message. Add some twists and turns, irony and mystery, and layers.

❧ In commercial media, an element of "cruelty" has succeeded with X'ers. Examples:

From its inception, television has always produced shows featuring talent competition and athletic competition. And always before, shows like Ted Mack's *Original Amateur Hour,* Ed McMahon's *Star Search,* and the others treated all contestants with respect and compassion, especially the ones who lost.

But X'er viewers drove *Survivor* and *American Idol* into the TV ratings stratosphere. The one difference between these X'er-targeted shows and prior shows of this genre? The element of "real" cruelty. *Survivor* closed each episode with one competitor being cruelly berated and tossed off the show by the others. *American Idol's* big hook? Cruelty. Especially, the verbal bludgeoning of contestants by talent judge Simon Cowell, which sometimes reduced contestants to tears. And don't forget Donald Trump's TV show, *The Apprentice*, ending with *You're Fired!* The TV ratings don't lie. X'ers watch cruelty television.

Same with radio: shock-jock Howard Stern was paid hundreds of millions because his show delivered Gen X to advertisers. His daily diet of demeaning and cruel treatment of guests, especially female guests, and callers resonated with X'er listeners.

During the question-answer session that followed my Generational Advertising Strategy seminar with South Carolina radio and TV station managers and salespeople, one Boomer asked, "Why is that? Why do X'ers respond to this kind of real cruelty on TV?" I turned to X'ers in the audience for an answer. One X'er woman explained, "Because it makes us feel better about our own lives."

❖ Give them options. X'ers demand choices. One size does not fit all with this age cohort. Example: when Gen X reached home-buying and remodeling life stage, homebuilders learned that X'ers want wide selections in floor plans, countertop materials, paints, wallpaper, and so on.

❖ Home decorating. X'ers are more likely than older generations to *mix* décor styles. According to New York research company PortiCo Research, X'ers often decorate one room at a time so it meets their exact specifications. Also, X'er men are more involved in decorating decisions than older generations of men. So embrace both the woman and man.

❖ Humor. X'ers' sense of humor has been described as one of "ironic detachment." If you ever figure out what that means, include it in your strategy.

❖ Trust. Generally speaking, they don't blindly trust the media. Don't trust government. Don't trust big business. *If it's big, I probably can't trust it.* They do not accept media information, including the news, at face value. In my training seminars, I love that X'er audience members are consistently the ones who ask, "Where do you get your information?" (If you missed it, I answer that question in an earlier chapter of this book).

* Brand. X'ers came of age with advertising that promoted brand more than product features; think Nike. So brand is important to X'ers. And some hotel chains, when they began pursuing X'ers in the decade of the 2000s, made a point to furnish their rooms with high-profile, X'er-friendly brands: everything from the TV set to the radio to the bathroom faucet to the booze in the honor bar. When older generations are targeted by marketers, advertising tends to be more *features* oriented than brand oriented. Millennials are also less brand-conscious than X'ers.

* Video games. X'er boys were the first big gamers and still make heavy use of them in adulthood. Female X'ers are gaming in increasing numbers. They're showing diminished interest in traditional casino gambling (more on casino gaming later in this section).

* To a startling degree, Gen X has been overlooked by the nation's news media, which heavily cover

Boomers and Millennials, jumping right over X'ers, primarily because X'ers don't follow the news as closely as other generations. So, wanna score with X'ers? In your messaging to them, acknowledge and celebrate their generation. This is a Grand Slam waiting to happen for the marketer that will run with it and take it *big*.

❧ X'ers like the term "retro" more than "nostalgia." Nostalgia suggests "sentimentality," and they're not as sentimental about yesteryear as other generations. Emotional pitches will probably work better with Boomers and Millennials.

When X'ers were in early adulthood, Berry Burst Cheerios used the retro 1970s pop tunes *I Think I Love You* by the Partridge Family and the 1974 B. J. Thomas song *Hooked on a Feeling*. The campaign was "a huge success," according to the marketing manager for the brand.

❧ Anti-commercial commercials have worked well with this generation. No-nonsense honesty conveys respect for X'ers' street savvy.

❧ Attitude. Attitude. Attitude. Deliver attitude. X'ers rejoice in it.

- Have some fun. And make your fun off-center, a little cockeyed. Most of the dot-com ads of the 1990s delivered this droll, odd creative approach to advertising. But a caution: despite the clever creative of their advertising, many of those dot-com businesses also went bust.

- X'ers do not prefer a lot of text. They were the first generation to come of age with the pure visuals of MTV. So they prefer colorful, moving images. Silents and Boomers will embrace text, as will the younger Second-Wave Millennials who came of age constantly reading the typed word on their laptops and mobiles and Harry Potter books.

- Make it participatory. X'ers like the control that interactivity gives to them. They're not passive users of media. They want to sample media and make their own choices and judgments.

- X'ers came of age with major institutions breaking their promises on a regular basis so they're concerned, especially with their major purchases, about the after-sale assurance, the warranty. *If I buy this house/car/refrigerator from you today and something goes wrong with it six months from now, are you gonna be there for me?*

X'ers And Autos

General Motors delivers this list of X'er hot buttons in a single thirty-second commercial for its Chevy Cavalier:

- Attitude
- Edgy
- Cynical
- Fun
- Retro
- After-Sale Warranty

We see a single car, a Cavalier, parked in a big asphalt parking lot next to a long earthen levy. No other cars or people in sight.

Inside the car, Gen X Guy is stretched out in the driver's seat, singing along with the radio to "Bye-bye, Miss American Pie, drove my Chevy to the levy..." Outside the car, clearly bored and waiting impatiently for him, Gen X Girlfriend sits on the ground staring blankly. The song ends. Satisfied Gen X Guy crawls out of the car and orders Girlfriend "Okay, let's go." She drearily gets up, joins him, and together they slowly shuffle off for a walk, as the voiceover says, "Until the very end, we'll be there", which is the after-sale assurance.

Gen X's affluent members are at luxury-car stage: BMW, Mercedes, Lexus, Audi, Cadillac, Infiniti, and the others. But these two generations still feel financially uncertain in this post-Recession U. S. economy, so some luxury brands are building lower-priced entry-level models to build generational loyalty until X'ers—and Mils—advance to their top-of-the-line models. They're also building cars that are smaller and with souped-up engines to appear younger and cooler. *Business Week* magazine describes the problem with this strategy: "The market's getting crowded, and luxury carmakers risk tarnishing their brands by courting comparisons with mainstream models."

Multigenerational Marketing

» The Gap and Old Navy are among marketers that have had success with multigenerational marketing and advertising strategies. Gen X seems to like this style. For example, a TV spot with Boomer-era pop music from the early 1970s, but with on-camera talent from Gen X.

» One of the more high-visibility, multigenerational (Boomer + Gen X) campaigns occurred during Super Bowl 2003: the various Pepsi Twist spots that aired during the game. One spot visually transformed strait-laced and squeaky-clean singers Donny and Marie Osmond into the wacky and not-so-squeaky-clean Ozzy Osbourne family.

The Cincinnati Enquirer asked a panel of mostly Gen X'ers to judge the Super Bowl commercials that year, and Pepsi Twist was easily the most highly rated, with panelist comments such as "It integrated every generation," "It was cross-generational," and "It had all the different American icons (from different generations)."

Digital Marketing And E-Commerce

When it comes to online messaging to Gen X, begin with these fundamentals:

* Speed is essential. Fast results. So, make your e-commerce sites and transaction processing swift but exciting, with a sense of discovery.

* Make your website address fun and memorable.

* With download speed in mind, keep your website's heavy graphics and video on interior pages, not your home page.

❧ Keep your pages short and visually stimulating.

❧ Give this skeptical generation of consumers your after-sale assurance by making your contact information easy to locate. Include your physical street address and phone number. Show photos of your executives. Don't hide! Many e-commerce sites are absolutely miserable at this and DO choose—especially the dishonest scam artists—to hide from their customers.

❧ Give them a feedback link. X'ers visit your site for information, but they also want to interact with it.

Gen X, Parenthood, And Family

❧ Many X'ers grew up in nontraditional (divorced or single-parent) households. But as parents themselves, they want their own children to have a sense of family and roots and normalcy, but they might not be sure how to create it, because they didn't have it as kids themselves. *Help them.* Parenting websites and blogs, for example.

❧ The ultimate Gen X TV show is *Friends.* And one of that show's primary messages is this, according to *TIME* magazine (April 19, 2004), which wrote about the show as it was producing its final original episode: "There is no normal anymore...The characters have dealt with one problem: how to replace the kind of family in which they grew up with the one they believed they were supposed to have." If you can market a product or service or provide guidance that helps X'ers to figure this out, you win.

* Gen X moms want toys that are fun *and educational*. They want their kids to play and learn at the same time.

* X'er dads want to be involved in their kids' lives. Research documents that fathers who volunteer at school can have a very positive effect on their children's academic success. So marketers, find a way to catch this Dad Wave.

* X'er parents feel they don't have as much time to spend with their children as they would like. And they know how beneficial it would be to the kids if they did spend more time with them. The primary obstacle is the parents' work schedules. If your products and services can help them save

time or create more minutes with their children, you can score big.

❧ A TV ad campaign by Dixie paper plates shows Gen X mothers playing with their children while saying to the camera that they refuse to let dishwashing crowd their time with their kids, and Dixie's disposable paper plates help them with this.

❧ X'ers will have done their homework when they enter the store or visit the website but might still need help. The quality of eye-to-eye customer service might become the make-or-break for brick-and-mortar retailers.

❧ Find the good. From 1983's *A Nation at Risk* report and thereafter, the wonderful people of Generation X have grown up hearing and seeing their generation labeled as under-achievers, slackers, and negativists. This means marketers and advertisers face a significant opportunity: celebrate the good in this generation, its positive values and skills and qualities; tell X'ers about their generation in ways they've never heard so they will celebrate themselves.

❦ Female denigration backlash. Some marketers (beers, video games, TV programs), in their attempt to reach X'er men, have denigrated Gen X women by presenting them, blatantly, as sex objects. Make no mistake, there must be something to this strategy, because some of these marketers have made a lot of money from X'er men. But in 2004, a public backlash against the beer commercials began, and now today the beers have pretty much pulled away from the female belittlement. Consider carefully before you decide whether to use the denigration of women in order to get the attention of X'er men.

Chrysler's PT Cruiser

Here's one that missed the mark but still landed gloriously on its feet: the Chrysler PT Cruiser.

As the *Wall Street Journal* wrote: "The PT Cruiser: designed for Gen X, but it was Boomers who bit."

Seems like it should've worked with X'ers; seemed to hit all of their hot buttons: the PT Cruiser, introduced in 2000, was loaded with attitude; it was edgy, fun, and magnificently retro. But to X'ers, "retro" means the 1970s and '80s and '90s, and the PT Cruiser is retro back to panel trucks and autos from the 1940s!! Oops, missed by thirty years!

But...

By about its second or third year on the market, and according to auto industry researcher R. L. Polk, the average driver profile of the PT Cruiser was a fifty-one-year-old Boomer male. The Boomers, old enough to remember the car design from their very early childhood, went wild for the PT Cruiser, which not only enhanced Chrysler revenues but also "grew Chrysler young" and helped to erase its "old people's car" image that Boomers had previously given it.

How did Chrysler respond to the success of this model? Well, among other strategies, it promptly added two options that reminded Boomers of their youth even more: flame paint jobs (popular with "street rods" in the '50s) and fake wood grain paneling on the sides (harkens back to the heyday of the station wagon, which is a major memory of Boomer childhood).

From *Old Spice* To *Red Zone*

Here's another product that missed with Gen X. The case study is spelled out in a 2004 *Business Week* magazine headline that reads:

"Extreme Makeover: How Procter & Gamble is selling once stodgy Old Spice to a whole new generation."

Old Spice deodorant: it's been around forever, it seems. In the mid-90s, Procter rebranded it *Old Spice High Endurance,* but found that the twenty-five to forty-five age demo (at that time, older Gen X and younger Boomer guys) remembered Old Spice "as a relic from Dad's (or Granddad's) era".

So P&G decided, in essence, to skip Gen X and aim instead at very young Millennial boys by handing out samples of now-rebranded *Red Zone* to fifth-grade health classes, covering some 90% of the nation's schools and beginning in 1999. According to a P&G spokesperson, by 2001 Red Zone had become the top teen deodorant brand.

Key Point: sometimes, you must skip a generation.

Cut The Hype: Nike And Sprite

The anti-commercial commercial.

X'ers take great pride in their street savvy. They've been marketed to all of their lives. They've seen every trick in the book. They can't be fooled. They don't want hype. *So don't even try.* This generation doesn't merely laugh at phony marketing messages. They aggressively *deride* them.

So, some marketers have scored with Gen X with anti-commercial commercials. No outlandish claims: *you won't get the pretty girl or the handsome guy at the party if you buy our product; you won't score the winning goal in the big game. It's just a good product.*

Nike's slogan—*Just Do It*—is quintessential Gen X messaging: *let's cut the crap. If you want to be fit, if you want a vigorous energy and lifestyle, the reality is this: there are no lazy shortcuts. Just do it.*

Fabulous slogan. And an acknowledgement of, and a salute to, X'ers' marketing savvy.

And in an attempt to create brand loyalty with young-adult X'ers in the brutal soft drink wars, Sprite enjoyed a very successful run-up in sales with an anti-commercial commercial. The TV spot cuts back and forth—from a barber boasting to a customer, to a young adult playground braggart telling his buddy—that *they* taught basketball star Kobe Bryant all he knows about the game. After lots of braggadocio, the voiceover finally jumps in with this cut-the-crap outburst:

"Who ya gonna listen to? How 'bout yourself!!?" And then we read, onscreen, the text that carries the theme of this ad campaign: "Obey your thirst."

In the mid-2000s, I was within minutes of beginning a training program for the Massachusetts Broadcasters Association in Generational Marketplace Strategy. Talking to two X'er women who worked in radio, I asked them, "What would you say is your generation's favorite music?"

They instantly listed three rock groups from the '60s rather than their own generation's music era of the '70s, '80s, and '90s:

"Beatles. Rolling Stones. Led Zeppelin."

"Why?", I asked.

"Because their music is real."

X'ers came of age just as music was becoming calculated and corporate and processed. They recognized and wanted *real*. And so they embraced the anger and rage of rap and grunge music in the late '80s and '90s, as well as the authenticity of the '60s.

DeGreve Oil Change

Gen X's formative years' experience helps to explain a print ad that the *Quad-City Times* newspaper created for one of its clients, DeGreve Oil Change, a chain of seven oil-and-lube shops in the greater Davenport, Iowa, market.

Owner John DeGreve had attended my half-day training program on Generational Marketing and Advertising Strategy, sponsored by the *Times*. A week later, interested in learning more, Mr. DeGreve, along with the newspaper's account rep and graphic artist, sat down with me for a one-hour brainstorming session in the *Times'* conference room.

According to Mr. DeGreve and his industry's own research, G.I. and Silent and Boomer men are very consistent at changing the oil in their vehicles on a regular schedule. X'er guys are not. Why? How?

We concluded this: G.I., Silent, and Boomer boys had come of age when most of their dads changed their own car oil in the garage or driveway. Not always an easy task; kind of an "event". So it was a memorable ritual. Young boys hung around Dad to watch and learn, and help Dad a little. They also heard Dad preach, "When you learn to drive and someday own your own car, remember: you change the oil regularly!" The preaching stuck. And so in adulthood, they, too, change the oil regularly.

But: (1) X'er boys came of age with dual-career, time-starved parents who often didn't have the time to change the oil themselves but did have the money to drive the car to the quick-change oil-and-lube shops, which were just then emerging. Also, (2) because of the high divorce rate, many Gen X boys simply weren't around Dad much to learn *guy stuff*. And, (3) X'er boys have a generation of parents who didn't want to be as "preachy" as their own parents had been with them. So the ritual of the oil change and Dad's preaching were diluted during Gen X's youth.

So in our DeGreve Oil Change brainstorming session, I joked, "You know, it's almost as if fathers need to have *two talks* with their coming-of-age sons. One talk is the birds-and-bees discussion about sex. And the other talk is *you change the oil regularly!*"

The print ad, which we conceived in about fifteen minutes, shows a Boomer father standing outdoors in front of the family car with his arm around his now-adult Gen X son, smiling as he looks at him and says, "Son, it's time we had *the talk.* If you don't keep it properly lubricated, it won't last very long." And, at the bottom of the ad, the copy reads "Things my father never told me."

When an X'er guy noticed that ad in the newspaper, he could see instantly that it was meant for him.

Marketing To Gen X Women

So, how do marketers use formative-years experiences and Core Values to go after those strong, assertive, confident, and competent Gen X women? With TV commercials like one for Soft & Dri deodorant, which shows an X'er woman kickboxing. Or a fabric softener spot showing an X'er woman practicing karate.

Best Buy

Or the electronics retail chain Best Buy producing a fantasy concept for a TV spot promoting its big-screen TV sets. The commercial shows a Gen X married couple in street clothes but wearing ice skates and competing in a professional ice hockey game.

The husband, skating furiously down the ice, controls the puck. Just as he gets slammed to the boards by an opponent, he yells "Honey!" and passes the puck cross-ice to his athletic, Title IX Gen X wife, who superhumanly leaps over a fallen opponent while maintaining control of the puck and then wins the game with a long slap shot as time expires. Husband and wife then skate to the edge of the ice, where magically they're now standing inside a Best Buy store, looking at a big-screen TV set.

This spot makes several points. First, Gen X women no longer leave the big electronics purchasing decisions to their husbands; it's no longer a "man's" job. Second, the athletic, confident Title IX Gen X woman has the athletic skills and confidence to score the winning goal in a hockey game in which all other competitors are men. And third, it shows the "new" American husband: the Gen X hubby who trusts his wife's physical skills and consumer wisdom and views her as an equal.

Secret Deodorant

A Secret deodorant television commercial also celebrates the athletic, independent, assertive, Title IX Gen X female while poking lighthearted fun at the poor, emasculated Gen X guy who tried to make the passage from boyhood to manhood during the era of the Surging Female.

The gender roles are completely reversed in this spot. As the spot begins, we see a car with a flat tire parked alongside a busy roadway. A second car pulls up behind it; stepping out of it and striding confidently toward the broken-down auto is slender and athletic Gen X wife in a form-fitting dress and heels. Coming out of Car # 1 to meet her is her frazzled, sloppily dressed, and slightly effeminate Gen X husband, who is exasperated and confused, portraying the traditional stereotype of the helpless *female* as he says:

"Thank god you came! Look, I know you had that thing tonight, but I didn't know what else to do. I mean, cars were whizzing by, and I think my cell's almost dead, and I —"

Title IX wife calmly holds up her hand to stop his nervous blather and quietly asks, "Where's the spare?" Gen X husband looks at her blankly and asks, "The spare *what?*"

She swiftly changes the tire, brushes the dirt from her hands, smiles, and says "Okay, all set!" As she walks back to her own car, her emasculated husband stares blankly down at the newly mounted tire on his car and mutters, "Good, I'll take it from here."

The tagline at the end of the spot?

"Secret: strong enough for a woman."

Years earlier, the tagline for a different generation of women had been, "Secret: Strong enough for a man, but gentle enough for a woman." But not now. Not with these confident and assertive Title IX women.

New generation. New Core Values. New message.

Lowe's And Home Depot

The nation's two largest home-improvement chains, Lowe's and Home Depot, launched competitive marketing campaigns in pursuit of X'er and Boomer women, who, according to both companies' research, are willing to tackle the *big* home-improvement jobs around the house. In many cases, these two confident generations of women *want* to take on these projects. In other cases, living on their own as divorcees or singles, they *must*.

So both Lowe's and Home Depot made changes, such as renovating their stores and redesigning their websites and catalogues to be more female friendly. One of these chains found that its aisles were too narrow, that female shoppers were experiencing what the research described as "butt brush": as they squeezed past each other sideways in the narrow aisles, women's butts brushed against each other. So aisles were widened.

They also began offering periodic do-it-yourself training workshops in their stores. After attending my seminar in Oregon, an audience member who works for one of these chains said his store's Saturday morning workshops were attracting about 80% female DIY wannabes.

Generational strategy can help guide store planning and design: layout and space planning; lighting; fixturing; color palette; signage; merchandising; and more.

All of this generational marketing—the Secret deodorant flat tire commercial, Best Buy's hockey spot, the Lowe's and Home Depot strategies, and many other case studies—is the inevitable by-product of Gen X's unique formative years' experiences with girl-friendly education, Title IX legislation, boys' discouragement, and the women's movement.

Key Point: if we understand a generation's unique formative years, we can then make sense of the unique generational Core Values that will guide that generation's consumer decision-making for life. Armed with this very powerful knowledge, we can then "message" to those Core Values in the marketplace.

Marketing To Gen X Men

How about messaging to Gen X men?

A TV commercial by Hummer vehicles shows two X'er guys at a supermarket, nodding to each other as they place their groceries on conveyor belts at adjacent checkout counters. One guy is buying a package of tofu (*effeminate* is the implied message), while the other guy is buying big slabs of red-meat ribs (the message is *macho*). They look at each other's groceries on the conveyor belt. Tofu Guy is embarrassed. Red-Meat Guy gives Tofu Guy a quick nod of sympathy. Then, emasculated Tofu Guy notices a cover photograph of a Hummer on the store's magazine rack. He swiftly leaves the supermarket, drives to the Hummer dealership, buys one, and as he drives away in his macho-mobile, the on-screen copy says it all for Gen X males:

"Restore Your Manhood."

Here's how other corners of the American marketplace responded to what some marketers perceived to be, whether they're right or wrong, Gen X men's formative years' frustration with all of that *female dominance.*

Commercial television and radio (as distinguished from public television and public radio) responded to this perceived frustration by delivering *female-denigrating* programming: *Jerry Springer, The Man Show, Howard Stern,* and others, which generally target X'er men and have consistently presented Gen X women as little more than sexual slabs of meat, often without much brainpower and whose reason for being on Earth is to satisfy the most primitive male needs.

Beer commercials. Coors used big-breasted females jumping on a trampoline: the notorious *Coors Twins* advertising campaign.

Miller Beer: "Another Round Of Raunch"

Miller Beer launched its infamous "catfight" series of commercials showing two voluptuous young females arguing at an outdoor café over whether Miller Beer "tastes great" or is "less filling", tearing off each other's blouses, falling into a fountain, screaming and yelling at each other, but then in the end tantalizing male viewers by saying "let's make out".

A commentary in *Ad Age* magazine headlined "Another round of raunch", describes the ad campaign this way: "Miller Brewing Co. will take raunchy marketing to a new extreme in the coming months..."

Gaming

And the video-game industry is under similar attack. A hot seller over the years has been "GTA": *Grand Theft Auto*. In one early version, the game awards points to players who have sex with a prostitute in a car, then push her out of the car and onto the ground, and kick and shoot her to death.

The CBS television show *60 Minutes* produced a segment on *Grand Theft Auto*. Its investigative team discreetly hid a camera in a large department store's video game department during the holiday season and videotaped mothers grabbing *Grand Theft Auto* from the shelves, taking it to the checkout counter, and paying for it. *60 Minutes* intercepted those mothers as they were leaving the store. The conversations went something like this:

(60 Minutes): "Hi, what did you just buy?"
(American mother): "Oh, a video game for my son."
"How old is he?"
"Nine (or thirteen, or eleven)."
"Which game did you buy?"
"Grand Theft Auto."
"Have you seen it?"
"No, it was just on my son's Christmas list, so I bought it."
"Wanna come over to our table and take a quick look?"
"Sure."

One by one, these mothers watched in horror at what they had just purchased for their sons. Some marched right back to the checkout counter to return it.

And the gaming industry's battering of females continues to this day as it now targets Millennial males. During the 2014 holiday shopping season (when Mils were aged 18 to 33), a *Business Week* magazine profile of the gaming industry was headlined this way:

"What Do Video Games Have Against Women?"

Gen X boys, and now Millennial boys, did not explicitly request female-denigrating products and advertising messages during their formative years. The adult world simply did its homework and responded by creating products and marketing to resonate with generational Core Values. And often, it worked.

And so, female denigration and violence became a prominent part of the formative years and early adulthood of these two generations of males.

Casino Gambling And Gen X

Many state travel-and-tourism industries call their annual conventions the "Governor's Conference". In late 2013, I presented a keynote speech, followed by two breakout sessions, at the Nevada Governors Conference. After that, a corporation that owns multiple casinos around the country brought me to Lake Tahoe to train its executives in Generational Marketing Strategy. At both events, the focus was on Gen X and Millennials. And in 2014, a similar presentation at the annual Maryland Tourism Summit (Maryland then had four casinos).

The problem? It is likely X'ers and Mils will not embrace casino gaming (the industry now prefers to call it gaming rather than gambling) as older generations have done. So in Las Vegas, Reno-Tahoe, Atlantic City, and states that have opened casinos in recent years, the generational challenge is this:

How do we reinvent ourselves to lure X'ers and Mils?

For a brief period in the 2000s, Las Vegas had tried to remake its image into a family-friendly vacation destination, a marketing ploy that now ranks right up there in history with Coca Cola's *New Coke* marketing disaster of 1985 and Ford Motor Company's big *ker-plunk* with its Edsel model in 1958, '59, and '60.

In the latter half of the 2010s, casinos around the country are closing or reporting sharply reduced revenues. Atlantic City has been especially hard-hit. In other states, revenues that initially soared because of the newness of casino gaming there are now declining or leveling off.

Gen X'ers and Millennials simply are not showing an appetite for risking their precious few vacation dollars on games of chance they know are statistically rigged against them. A report on this generational disruption of Las Vegas' gaming marketplace in *TIME* magazine is headlined "Sin City Meets Low Rollers".

In response, some casinos are trying a new "club music" strategy: spectacular nightclub designs with pounding, pulsing music, played by deejays who are the new superstars *du jour* of Las Vegas.

Casinos are also going younger in their more traditional theaters. With much fanfare, Planet Hollywood brought in Gen X and Millennial entertainer Britney Spears in 2013 to go along with a long list of Boomer-focused performers who have fared well.

And because Millennials are proving to be "foodies" who love new tastes and recipes and cuisines, Las Vegas is punching up its dining options, especially with new and international foods.

Sin City is very savvy and tenacious. It has adapted to change before. And generational dynamics are forcing it to do so again.

But as of the writing of this book, it remains to be seen how gambling meccas will fare with these two generations that, right now, aren't demonstrating nearly as much interest in traditional gambling as older generations did at the same age.

As I work with this industry, it's my job to get the casino, hotel, entertainment, and restaurant managers and marketers into the heads of X'ers and Mils so they can create innovative pathways to these two unique generations.

CHAPTER 21

Marketing To Mils

Tips, Tactics, And Guidelines

• • •

THROUGH THE REMAINDER OF THE 2010s and probably beyond, America and the rest of the planet will remain in the grip of the Technology Revolution. This means marketers will continue the trial-and-error to find out what works and what doesn't. They'll get some things right, they'll get some things wrong. Investors will make fortunes by guessing right and lose fortunes by guessing wrong.

We've all been forced to race from personal computers to Internet to email to laptops to cell phones to social media to smart phones to apps.

Here's the good news about this bewildering journey through the Tech Convulsion:

No matter the platform, Generational Marketing Strategy will succeed if executed properly.

Again, here is the entire premise of generational marketing:

1. Identify the generation you wish to target.
2. Identify its members' current life stage(s): young adulthood; career start; marriage; parenthood; career advance; empty nest; grandparenthood; retirement or career-next; infirmity; loss of spouse.
3. Select one or more generational Core Values to home-in on.
4. Design your product and your marketing message to resonate with those Core Values.

Don't try to complicate it. This is it. It WILL work for you if you do it right.

Now, to Millennial marketing:

Remember, we don't become a member of a generation until we finish our high school years. Until then, the only cohort we belong to is an *age* cohort. The first 17 or 18 years of life are our Pre-Generation Years.

So if you're targeting school-age kids, do not use *generational* strategy. Instead, use *age-specific* strategy. Do not ask yourself, "How do we market to

16-year-old *Millennials?"* Instead, ask, "How do we market to16-year-olds?"

Marketers should keep in mind the following broad brushstrokes as they create products and services and advertising messages meant for this generation:

* They became a bigger generation than Gen X during the year 2015, but to be bigger than Boomers their generation must not end before 2020 and must deliver about 4,000,000 births per year. Stay tuned.

* They have delayed adulthood, but their older members are now settling in with employers, marrying, bearing children, and cautiously buying automobiles and houses. They're entering the Spending Years.

* Mils are all about technology, all about communications.

* They like to do things in groups; they are a "we" generation like Boomers, not a "me" generation like X'ers.

❋ As a marketer, you won't be able to command this generation's *undivided* attention. They are constantly switch-tasking (remember, the term "multi-tasking" is a myth; the human brain cannot literally multi-task).

❋ TV is important to them, but it's been accurately described as just one instrument in an orchestra of media constantly playing to them.

❋ Millennials care less about *brands* than X'ers do.

❋ They believe they *make* brands by discovering them. So make your brand discoverable, and don't force-feed it to them with heavy-handed "buy this" messaging.

❋ They take multiculturalism for granted. Millennials are America's most ethnically diverse generation. They are tolerant of ethnic differences, as well as divorced households and LGBTQ lifestyles, but traditional values and parental approval are still important to them.

❋ They take globalism for granted but also possess a strong sense of nation and patriotism because they experienced such childhood events as 9/11, Hurricane Katrina, and the war against terrorism.

* Those same events have molded a list of additional lifelong Core Values: giving; an appreciation of true heroism; team play; selflessness; social activism; a sense that there's more to this world than just "me"; and, an interest in their own faith and spirituality (but not a defined commitment to a specific traditional religion).

* They possess a strong commitment to community service, in part because (1) schools began to emphasize it more during their classroom passage and (2) it looks good on a college or job application. As a result, they prefer to do business with companies that are good corporate citizens and philanthropic.

* They are a nurtured generation. Their Helicopter Parents convinced them they are the center of the universe. Message to them with this in mind; celebrate them, pat them on the back, cheer them on.

* Their parents' advice and opinions matter. Want to sell to Millennials, especially the younger

ones? Sell to Mom and Dad, too. A U. S. Army recruitment campaign does this, messaging directly to the parents.

* And, they are hearing the same *you're a special generation that has come along at a special time* message that Boomers heard. Millennials are sensing the great expectations by others for their generation. Marketers can harness this vibe to connect with their generation.

* Where they go, you go. They live online. They buy online. But they also like the in-person energy that a brick-and-mortar store can deliver.

* Their first instinct is to trust people, more so than Gen X and more like Boomers. This has created marketplace opportunities and abuses, especially online where abusers can remain anonymous and undetected.

* They are not entirely tech robots. Mils are social animals. They like the human touch.

* Peer-to-peer recommendations, reviews, and approval are important. So win over their friends, too.

❧ Millennials, despite being the Tech Generation, are not entirely averse to reading hard-copy print publications. When they were in college, campus newspapers thrived. And the younger Mils remember the thrill of each new Harry Potter book and perhaps even stood outside their local bookstores at midnight, in costume, waiting to buy the next one.

❧ Multimedia messages are probably essential, in order to find Millennials and reinforce your message to them.

❧ Grandparents. Millennials generally have a very positive view of their grandparents and older people. They look up to them and welcome their wisdom. Multigenerational marketing and advertising messages should work well with this generation.

A *USA Today* headline, with a photo showing a grandmother and granddaughter texting each other, shouts out this close relationship: "OMG! My Grandparents R My BFF!" The story also pokes lighthearted fun at the tech and jargon gap that nonetheless exists between their two generations, by presenting three make-believe chats between a Mil and her grandmother and grandfather:

Grandma (finishing their live online chat): *Love you and have a great day – Fax us back!*
Me: *Fax you back?*
Grandma: *wow U-R fast!*

And:

Grandma: *Hey honey!*
Me: *uh hi g-ma.*
Grandma: *What's 'G-ma'?"*

And:

Grandpa: *I love you!*
Me: *I love you too! You're the best!*
Grandpa: *At what?*

* Like Gen X, this is a gender-bending generation. The males will pursue traditionally female activities and careers, and females will pursue what was traditionally male.

* Viral marketing—"buzz" marketing—is huge. So exploit it fully.

* Millennials are confident, even a little cocky. (Ring a bell, Boomers?) So don't talk down to them.

- Logo. Millennials have grown up with logos and brands *everywhere*: stadium names; school soft drink vending machines; apparel; websites; etc. But this generation might bring logo excess to a halt, or at least slow it down. The *New York Times,* in a story about the American Apparel retail T-shirt chain that targets Millennials, wrote the following about its apparel: "Perhaps most important to younger consumers who have grown suspicious of corporate branding, there is not a logo in sight." Adds Alex Wipperfurth of marketing firm Plan B in San Francisco, "People are sick of being walking advertisements for clothing. By stripping brands of logos...you are saying you are more about quality than image."

- Faith and religion. Take into account Millennials' strong interest in spirituality. But a Pew research study also documents that Millennials' grasp of traditional religion is *remarkably superficial.* So they're not experts. And they're still searching for a faith, spirituality, and/or religion that feels right for their Core Values.

- Don't call them Gen Y!! Or Echo Boomers!! Truly, these are irritants. Newspapers and magazines still don't get it and use Gen Y, often because that label is shorter than *Millennials* and fits into headline space more easily; just use "Mils".

Campbell's Soup And Millennial Moms

I had the pleasure to work with the Campbell Soup Company, which wanted to understand Millennials' food consumption and the generational Core Values that guide their consumer decisions. Campbell has enjoyed a very long history of success with prior generations, with its traditional canned soups served at family sit-down-together meals. But now, Millennials—and older generations, too—are eating (1) smaller meals, (2) more snack meals per day, (3) seeking unique recipes and tastes, and (4) eating/sipping while on the move.

The response by Campbell? A new brand: "Go" soups. Different packaging. International flavors, such as "Thai" and "Moroccan", "Creamy Red Pepper with Smoked Gouda", and others. With their own hip and cool "Go" website.

And now, Campbell's is pursuing Millennial *moms*, with fresh-packaged kids' snacks from its Bolthouse Farms brand.

The Automotive Challenge With Millennials

As Millennials began to turn age 16 in 1998, auto-makers began to drool: here comes a large generation, and their hard-working, dual-career parents have the money to buy *new* cars for them, rather than used ones.

But Mils showed less enthusiasm than prior generations for getting their drivers' licenses. Their best friends and weekend buddies—Mom and Dad—gladly did the driving to the restaurants and malls and movie theaters. *Who needs a license? Who needs a car?*

According to a University of Michigan Transportation Research study: In 1983, 92% of Boomers aged 20 to 24 had drivers' licenses. In 2011, only 79% of Millennials that age had their licenses. And there's also this:

John Morel, a market researcher for Honda, told *Business Week* magazine in 2013: "One of the dirty little secrets of the auto industry is all these [young-adult-oriented] cars are positioned in advertising and public relations as something a 25-year-old will buy. But your propensity to buy a car at 25 is roughly a quarter of what it is at age 65. By definition, very few cars sell in high volume to twentysomethings."

Not only that, but the social cause that is most front-and-center with this generation is the environment. And gas-powered cars pollute.

So automakers increased their focus on electric and hybrid cars and are still trying to invent THE magic bullet: a more powerful battery that will hold its charge much, much longer than current technology permits; such a battery is the Holy Grail of the industry. In 2015, pricey car maker Tesla Motors announced its plans, with partner Panasonic, to build a $5 billion battery "gigafactory" outside Reno, Nevada; it is to be the world's largest such plant and is designed to employ some 6,500 workers.

Finally, Mils have been restless job-hoppers in early adulthood, and their income stability took an additional hit with The Great Recession. And so car loans, like house mortgages, have represented a burden and long-term financial commitment they might not be able to meet.

So automakers designed funky and less expensive models to target young Millennials: Toyota Scion; Honda Element; Nissan Cube; Kia Soul; Chevy Sonic; Ford Fiesta; Fiat 500; and others. *Young, young, young!*

They marketed the cars in unique ways: Toyota representatives drove Scions to inner-city playgrounds and offered free test drives to the guys playing basketball. And it avoided advertising in media where the Scion might be seen by "older people", because the Scion would lose its "cool factor" if Mils saw their parents' generation driving it.

What happened with this cat-and-mouse game? As the *Wall Street Journal* wrote in 2013, "senior citizens are making Swiss cheese of those efforts."

The story's sub-heading said it all: "Aging Boomers Are Prime Buyers for Small Vehicles That Auto Makers Figured Would Woo Hipsters." When asked by the reporter why he purchased a Kia Soul, Boomer grandfather Brian Thulson answered, "My grandchildren love the pulsing speakers (whose lights pulse to the music's beat)." What he didn't need to add is that his own forever-younger Boomer mindset likes them, too.

But now today, as older Mils get settled in their careers and start their families, they are embracing the traditional passions for the freedom and independence that car ownership provides. And married Mils, leaving behind their generation's groundbreaking Extended Adolescence, are likely to gravitate from downtown rental units to suburban houses, thus increasing their reliance upon autos.

And as this happens, their generation is showing a special preference for compact SUVs and light trucks, whose cargo areas can accommodate their bicycles, sports gear, kids, and active lifestyles.

And yes, to state the very obvious, carmakers are installing the latest technologies in their cars to lure Mils and X'ers. Boomers and Silents welcome some, but not all, of these tech packages and often resent the high-priced "bundling" and the inability to reject the features they don't want.

The Two-Wheeled Variety

Iconic motorcycle manufacturer Harley Davidson is also facing a generational challenge. Boomers have always embraced motorcycles and the Harley brand. Gen X hasn't been a motorcycle generation. So Harley must somehow move Millennials from lying on the couch with their mobiles and video games and onto the road. Harley CEO Matt Levatich, an X'er, sees hope in the future: "People are going to want to actually live for real, and I think we have a product that has a great fit with that outlet." For Millennial consumer values, this means lower-priced Harleys and non-polluting electric batteries instead of gas-powered Hogs. And wider, deeper passenger seats for greater comfort.

And as Millennials show a clear preference for working in bigger cities and renting apartments near downtown, the motorcycle is being marketed as the perfect cost-effective and easier-to-store vehicle for the shorter daily commute.

Millennials, Banks, And Loans

After finishing a luncheon keynote speech to 1,300 people who sit on the Boards of Directors of American corporations, I welcomed questions, and here was the first one, by a Gen X man:

"If we in the mortgage lending industry lower our interest rates, will Millennials finally start to buy houses?"

My answer was a list:

"Here's the steep hill you mortgage lenders are trying to climb: Millennials face unprecedented college debt and unprecedented credit-card debt; their generation's unemployment rate during the recent Great Recession was twice the overall national rate; many remain unemployed or underemployed; they're postponing serious career commitment, marriage, and parenthood; they're not even buying cars because the loan burden scares them; and besides that, their generation views you guys in the mortgage industry as the creeps whose greed and corruption crashed our economy, ruined their grandparents' retirement nest eggs, got their parents laid off, and staggered their own generation just as it was pouring into adulthood and the workforce. Will a lower interest rate lure them to a long-term mortgage? What would you guess?"

He nodded, smiled, and sat down.

But with the oldest Mils now advancing through their thirties, this large generation will soon give the traditional housing industry a nice upward bump.

The Opportunity For Community Banks, But...

Millennials' disgust with the big Wall Street banks, whose executive corruption and greed filled the front pages with scandals for longer than a decade, opens the door for smaller and usually more ethical "community banks" to score with this generation. But those banks are now facing a problem: Mils want to do their banking online with their mobiles; they don't necessarily want to walk into a bricks-and-mortar bank to conduct their financial business.

And so the Independent Community Bankers of America is conducting Millennial strategy to

understand the Tech Generation, its spirit of entrepreneurship (and hence, the banks' opportunity to
provide small-business start-up loans), its preferences
for the ways Mils communicate with banks, and the
kind of bricks-and-mortar environment and consumer experience that will lure them into the building.

Such industries as healthcare and automotive were
among the first to train their personnel in Generational
Strategies. Industries like insurance and banking and
real estate have been very late-comers. Bankers now understand: they must train their people in Generational
Marketplace Strategy. They cannot afford to miss with
Millennials.

What are banks doing? With less foot traffic, many
are closing branches and reducing staff. They're in a
precarious position because four out of five adult generations still walk through the door, and banks want
them to do so because they can sell their financial
products more easily once they're under the roof.

One experiment: Capital One Financial in Boston
is expanding its café format, with no tellers, offering
gourmet coffee and free Wi-Fi, but with employees
guiding visitors to its website to get answers about the
bank's services, and offering so-called "Appy Hours",

which are alcohol-free gatherings that promote the smartphone apps of local businesses.

Bank of America will reportedly convert some nine-thousand tellers to "relationship bankers" who, like Capital One employees, nudge customers in the direction of online banking. Ditto with other banks.

The idea is to evolve bank branches into sales centers and slash labor costs. But Robert Meara, a senior banking analyst at consulting firm Celent, told the *Wall Street Journal*, "Most banks don't have a clear vision of where to take the branch."

And so banking becomes still one more industry being turned inside-out by the Technology Revolution and trying to determine its future.

Millennial Moms And Dads

This generation grew up receiving customized, on-demand products and marketing messages.

In the pressure cooker of parenthood, they will continue to seek out the opinions of other Millennial parents and friends. This over-guided generation of kids has grown up to be less independent and self-reliant than other generations (especially X'ers), so if you want to win them over, then win over their friends and contemporaries. They want affirmation from others that they're making good decisions.

Online efforts by marketers, as of the writing of this book, remain hit-and-mostly-miss. The Internet is still in its Wild West years: no one can figure it out and tame it; anything goes, and most of it goes awry. Instead of ready-aim-fire, it's ready-fire-aim.

Maria Bailey, CEO of mom-marketing firm BSM in Florida, wrote this about the use of Facebook, Twitter, Pinterest, Instagram, Snap Chat, and the other destinations of the moment:

"Herein lies the problem. There are thousands of brands using those same tools to get the attention of Millennial Moms. Unfortunately, the analytics aren't there yet, and the required manpower required to individually monitor a SnapChat account with thousands of followers is costly and time prohibitive. Marketers who are still spending thousands on gaining "Likes" on their Facebook page are wasting their money."

Bottom line: this generation seeks a relationship with marketers based upon transparency, reliability, and customized and personalized service. Remember, Millennials have been only *partially* robotized by technology; the kids who came of age with hovering parents and educators still desire a real, human connection.

They also want Mom Marketers to not simply push their product but to also help them with their entire lives by offering lots of advice about how to handle their current life stage issues: young adulthood; career; personal finance; car buying; house buying; marriage; and especially, with their new frontier of parenting.

As mentioned earlier, I presented Generational Marketplace Strategy to a Las Vegas audience of about three hundred marketers at the annual Nevada Tourism Governors Conference. I asked a question of the roughly one hundred Millennials in the audience:

"Will your generation be spending more time, less time, or the same amount of time on Facebook next year as you did this year?"

Their show of hands, just as I've experienced with other Millennial audiences, was emphatic: *less time.*

I followed up with the brutal, bottom-line question: "Yes or no. Has your Millennial generation moved on from Facebook?"

Yes. Overwhelmingly.

Facebook, it seems, has become a destination for empty-nest Boomers, their grandkids, and some Gen X parents who use it only to monitor their children's use of it.

Millennials came of age as the Internet was arriving and offering limitless destinations. Just as Boomers grew up eager to explore the geography of the United States, so it is that Millennials treat social media sites like a family vacation: they constantly seek *what's next* and *what's new.* Facebook? *Yesterday's news* to this generation.

Loyalty Marketing

Because brand loyalty began a long steady death-spiral as Boomers—and then X'ers, and Millennials—entered adulthood, the marketplace understandably is doing all it can to create loyalty programs that will work with these generations.

Some, like airline frequent flyer programs, have been very successful. Others have failed. What a majority of marketers agree on is this: loyalty-program participants are the most profitable customers; and, investments by companies in loyalty programs are essential.

The Chief Marketing Officer Council published the results of a study with these findings:

* A loyalty program must deliver true added value and substance, and too many programs don't;
* It must provide personalized attention to the participant;
* It must not spam participants with junk email and mail;
* And, the rewards must be easily redeemable, without hassle.

If marketers follow these guidelines, their loyalty programs stand a chance with all generations.

Millennial Guys And Apparel

The newspaper in Richmond, Virginia called me for a story on men's fashion: "What's going on with Gen X men wearing the color pink?"

X'er boys had come of age as fashion barriers were falling. Apparel, facials, hair coloring and highlighting, manicures, pedicures. What had previously been the province of females was now crossing to the other gender, too.

Boomers started it, X'ers continue it, and Millennial guys are now carrying this heightened focus upon appearance and grooming to the next plateau.

The impact? Men's Wearhouse is trying to become more fashion-forward, going more upscale with its clothing lines, getting into custom and tailored clothing instead of just off-the-rack. As CEO Doug Ewert told one reporter, "Custom clothing is new to us, but it's a big growth opportunity. [Millennials] see dressing as a way to express themselves differently than the Baby Boomers' generation did, and custom clothing is just a part of that. They like not looking like everybody else. But we've got to stay relevant for the Baby Boomer customer, as well."

And so, multigenerational marketing strategy will be critical to this re-working of Men's Wearhouse.

By the way, the apparel industry is working under a higher-powered public microscope than some other industries. Idealistic Boomers and Millennials are very keen on avoiding purchases that come from sweat-shop manufacturers that treat their workers poorly. Awareness of this dirty secret in the apparel industry increased when a Bangladesh factory that makes clothes for major retailers collapsed in 2013, killing 1,127 employees.

In part because of Bangladesh, some Millennials want to "stay local" by supporting those companies that make apparel here in the States. But foreign-made goods are usually cheaper, and so Mils are torn. In 1960, 95% of apparel sold in the U. S. was made here. Today, it's less than 5%, according to the advocacy group Save the Garment Center.

Generationally Strategized Architecture

In the decade of the 2000s, a boom occurred in college campus construction. New dorms, student centers, recreation facilities. Generational Strategy guided much of the design and architecture: *what does the Millennial Generation college student want and need in physical facilities?*

Millennials are group-focused. And so:

Ohio University re-designed its primary campus library to accommodate Millennials' inclination towards groups. And it lightened up on the *hush-hush* of the traditional library environment in order to permit more conversation. Also, a coffee bar and relaxation of food-and-drink-in-the-library policies. The strategy worked. The library is thriving.

Steelcase, one of the nation's more prominent companies in office design and furnishings, conducts generationally designed research to determine what Boomer and X'er and Millennial employees prefer and need in the workplace of the future. They gave me a tour of their headquarters building, which included mockups of futuristic offices and meeting rooms as they examined such generationally influenced decisions as:

❋ open spaces or traditional enclosed offices?

❋ walled cubicles, and if so, how high?

❋ What about the design and placement of the company's conference rooms and common spaces?

❋ And what about the ergonomic needs of the generations regarding noise suppression (according to an audiologist client of mine, an estimated 20 to 30 million Americans have significantly impaired hearing, and X'ers and

Millennials—from too many loud concerts and too much childhood use of headsets that inject the audio right into your ear from pointblank range—will probably suffer hearing loss at an earlier age and in bigger numbers than prior generations)?

❧ Cubicle and desk and chair design (Millennials are America's most obese generation of young adults ever; how does this alter office space and furniture design?)?

❧ and so on.

Steelcase executives showed me a prototype for a "meeting space" in this era of overweight Millennials (and all Americans) and their desire to trim down: 4 treadmill machines, physically connected and facing each other in a tight circle, where 4 people can meet, talk face-to-face, and take notes while walking or running.

Creating the Right Organizational Culture

· · ·

CHAPTER 22

Creating the Right Organizational Culture

The Proper Culture Is Essential Or You Will Lose Employees To Your Rivals

• • •

THE BASICS:

1. Train all executive, Human Resource, and supervisory personnel in Generational Workforce Management Strategy. It can be as short as a half-day session. If you don't get full buy-in from the c-suites right from the start, it will be very difficult to create such a culture.

2. When they buy in fully, then train all employees in Generational Workforce Diversity; slightly different from the "strategy" training for management. Again, a half-day session.

   Steelcase, the manufacturer of office furnishings in Grand Rapids, Michigan, brought together all four hundred employees. We squeezed it into a shortened two-hour session, which is acceptable if not exactly ideal.

The Veterans Healthcare Administration's administrative center in Denver did it differently: they assembled their 600 employees in two groups of 300 each; I trained one group in the morning and the other in the afternoon. In advance, a few employees were assigned the task of creating generation-specific posters, with images and text that "told the story" of each generation. They had lots of fun with this, and it stirred good conversation throughout the organization.

Then, depending upon your type of business:

3. Conduct generational workforce research, internally, to understand your employees better. I conducted such a study for a large retailer that, at the time, employed more than 200,000 people. The goal: learn how to retain Boomers and how to recruit and retain Mils. The project included this: I briefed one employee, a dynamic Millennial woman, on how to conduct a focus-group session, and the company then flew her around the country to meet with groups of Millennial employees and learn more about

their needs. Five major management and retention ideas emerged from these sessions.

4. Train all marketing personnel in Generational
   Marketplace Strategy, which can and should influence each step of the process: consumer and
   market research; product development; marketing, advertising, and promotion; selling; and,
   customer service (which, in the healthcare sector, includes patient care).

5. When everyone is trained in these generational disciplines, ask a generational consultant to
   conduct an "audit" of your entire organization.
   What, generationally, are you doing right and
   wrong? What changes are needed to create a
   comprehensive, nimble, and permanent culture
   of generational diversity and strategy?

   Such changes might include:

   A. stratifying your employee satisfaction surveys
      along generational lines to learn how the or-
      ganization is doing with each generation;

   B. ongoing generational dialogue and com-
      munications; generation-specific employee

focus groups, affinity groups, and advisory committees;

C. revised company policies; compensation/ benefit plans tailored as much as possible for each generation's unique needs;

D. and, other changes that will achieve the absolute ideal in generational sensitivity and strategy and thus maximize employee harmony and productivity and customer satisfaction.

One of my clients is a state Public Employees Retirement System that serves Silent retirees but only employs three Silents in its 700-member workforce! Solution? Assemble an Advisory Committee comprised of Silent customers, host periodic meetings with them, listen to them, and share their thoughts, suggestions, complaints, and compliments with the organization's workforce.

And to maintain this culture of generational diversity and strategy:

6. videotape the training and show it to all new hires;

7. bring back your generational consultant for additional training, as needed; and,

8. to remain "current" as generational dynamics advance and evolve through the years, receive an ongoing feed of generational information and advice from your consultant.

CHAPTER 23

Industry-Specific Applications Of Generational Strategies

In addition to the "Big Two"—Workplace and Marketplace—here are other applications of Generational Strategy...

• • •

Manners, Civility, Courtesy

• • •

WANNA MAKE A LOT OF money? Develop a training workshop in Generational Manners, Civility, and Courtesy and offer it to American business, government, education, and religion.

Five living generations. G.I.s, Silents, and Boomers came of age during more courteous and polite times than X'ers and Millennials.

When X'ers passed through their formative years, one of the first major casualties of their time-starved family units was the decrease in common courtesy, civility towards others, and manners. It started in our own homes and then spread outward.

When Millennials came of age, the mass media—desperately trying to attract Mils' attention on radio and TV—became more coarse and vulgar. The outcome? When Millennials entered the workforce, their employers were regularly shocked when Mils used cuss words and cruel comments, especially when in front of clients, that were inappropriate in a business setting. Not only that, but Millennials also have very different beliefs than all other generations as to when it is okay to use their mobiles when in the presence of others.

For these reasons, brief training programs—a couple of hours—for employees in Generational Courtesy will pay major dividends by helping each generation to understand its different exposure to courtesy and manners.

Generational Higher-Education Strategy

• • •

I RECEIVED A PHONE CALL from the Executive Vice President for Research, Education & Board Services at ACCT, the Association of Community College Trustees.

She was sitting at home in Washington, D. C. on a Sunday afternoon and watching TV, came across one of my *AMERICA'S GENERATIONS* television shows on PBS, called me the next day to discuss my work and invite me to give the opening keynote speech a few months later to an audience of nearly two-thousand college presidents and board trustees at ACCT's national conference in Chicago. And when I did, the timing was right and the dam broke. College presidents followed up after the conference with requests for training on their individual campuses, stretching from Passaic CC in New Jersey to Edmonds CC in Seattle.

Community colleges, whose relevance and importance has become even more urgent in the current U. S. economy, and which serve multiple generations of students, are ready to create permanent and comprehensive cultures of generational diversity and strategy throughout their campuses.

And so began our work together: at individual colleges; at statewide community-college conferences; and, a return engagement with ACCT at its national Leadership Conference one year after the Chicago event.

Here are the Generational Strategies that community colleges are using to create that permanent culture of generational strategy:

A. Generational Student Recruitment Strategy;
B. Multi-generational classroom management;
C. Generational content in more subjects and course materials; professors tell me this is currently a major shortcoming of college textbooks;
D. Employee recruitment, onboarding, management, retention;
E. Alumni relations;
F. Fundraising, development, and grant-seeking;

G. Legislative Relations, campaign strategy, and advocacy;

H. Marketplace: Marketing, Advertising, Events, Branding, Image;

I. Relations with local businesses;

J. And, Generational Leadership And Governance Strategy for use by presidents and trustees.

Generational Research Strategy

. . .

BUSINESS RESEARCH HAD HISTORICALLY BEEN based upon demographic guidelines: age; gender; income; education level; and so on. But when generational study finally and fully emerged in the decade of the 2000s, it added another permanent filter to each step of the process:

* the *upfront design* of research studies, which takes into account known generational Core Values when designing the study and preparing the qualitative discussion guide and quantitative questionnaire;

* the actual *execution* of the study, especially by using focus-group moderators fully trained in generational study and strategy and able to identify generational revelations and deeper-probe opportunities that the untrained will miss;

* and, an *additional chapter* in the study's Final Report that compares and contrasts the study's findings with the greater body of valid generational research.

Generational Newspaper Strategy

. . .

NEWSPAPERS, YOU POSSESS THREE UNRIVALLED advantages over all other news organizations:

1. You are the Best Obtainable Version of the Truth;
2. Your coverage of your local communities is the most comprehensive.
3. For Americans, you are the pathway to Advanced Citizenship.

You do an adequate job of promoting # 2. You're absolutely horrible at promoting # 1 and # 3.

I trained a number of newspapers and their local advertisers in seminars around the country in the early 2000s. It was working: my newspaper clients were reporting instant increases in ad revenues, and the advertisers were happy with their Return On Investment. And I was training editors and reporters in Generational Editorial Strategy.

Then, New Media slammed the industry, reader-ship and revenues plummeted, layoffs ensued, and newspapers were forced to direct their training bud-gets to understanding websites and social media and, later, mobiles and apps.

Newspapers have always delivered a magnificent product. But they have always stunk as marketers. For their entire history, until New Media arrived, they had virtually no competition and advertisers and readers considered them an essential component of their daily lives.

But the New Media tsunami has overshadowed the larger dilemma:

Newspapers, your biggest problem is not New Media; it's generational.

Gen X'ers started it: after a childhood in which the adult world was regularly lying and cheating, X'ers en-tered adulthood with little interest in the daily news of government and business, which are the core of a news-paper's main section. They still read the sports and ce-lebrity stories, but little else. So many papers moved a special celebrity section to page 2 of the main section. But X'ers remained more of a drop-out generation than the others. And today, because advertisers covet Gen X, which is in its peak buying years, their ad dollars have gone elsewhere, primarily online, in pursuit of this generation.

Millennials, who live and buy online, are more plugged in to the news than X'ers because of their generational Core Values of empowerment and engagement. But newspapers haven't explained their differential advantage to this generation.

All generations will respond to The Best Obtainable Version of the Truth. But newspapers, you are now beyond a mere *marketing* campaign. It's too late. Instead, you must launch an extensive and expensive EDUCATION campaign to teach multiple generations about the principles of journalism that you adhere to more faithfully than all other news sources. This is your opening.

But I don't see a single paper in this country seizing it. Again, lousy marketers.

I have also found that too many of your editors are too defensive, myopic, or arrogant to accept outside help to make sure their editorial content is as relevant to each generation of viewers as it must be.

Too bad: the integrity of newspaper journalism is so necessary these days.

Generational Patient Care Strategy

. . .

IT'S SIMPLE: EACH GENERATION HAD distinct formative years' experiences with illness, disease, infirmity, and the care they received. And so today in adulthood, they possess distinct preferences, needs, and expectations regarding the care they receive from healthcare practitioners.

So physicians, nurses, social workers, administrative personnel, and all other professional caregivers must understand these generational differences in order to build productive relationships with each patient, gain the patient's full support and buy-in of the treatment, and achieve the best possible outcome.

My firm's largest training client-category is healthcare. And I train healthcare clinicians in Generational Patient Care Strategy and...

Generational Behavioral Health Care Strategy

• • •

EACH GENERATION IS LIKELY TO possess (1) unique vulnerabilities to certain behavioral problems, (2) unique responses to treatment and care, and (3) unique attitudes regarding the relationship they develop with their counselor, the mental-health clinician. Generational Core Values explain these generation-by-generation differences.

During the decade of the 2000s, my largest single client was the V.A. Hospitals system. They told me the military veterans they serve, of all ages, were struggling more and more with behavioral problems: addiction; suicide; sexual abuse; domestic violence; stress; obesity; and, others. And I heard the same when I worked with active-duty troops in the U. S. Army, Air Force, and Navy.

I began to sense that generational influences might partially explain what was going on.

And in 2011, while working with the Navy's Fleet and Family Service Centers personnel at its Capodachino and Sigonella installations in Italy, a Navy psychologist said her team had been using information from my 2007 book in their counseling of sailors and their families and were enjoying a roughly 50% improvement in their outcomes. *Wow.*

And she encouraged me to create a one-day training workshop in Generational Behavioral Health Care Strategy. So I did.

This training helps mental-health clinicians—psychiatrists, psychologists, social workers, physicians, nurses, and others—to understand and successfully deal with the likely influences of generational Core Values upon each generation's vulnerability to certain behavioral problems and their likely unique generational response to treatment and care.

I first presented this program to clinicians at V.A. hospitals and clinics located in the Sacramento–San Francisco area. The training took place in an auditorium on Travis Air Force Base. Their written evaluations were especially enthusiastic, as have been the evaluations by subsequent trainees around the country.

These evaluations from the Cleveland-area V.A. hospitals are typical:

Bottom Line: Can Generational Strategy Help You In:

Initial Client Interview?	Yes 100%	No____
Evaluation/Diagnosis?	Yes 100%	No____
Treatment Planning/Design?	Yes 100%	No____
Treatment Execution?	Yes 100%	No____
Building good relationships?	Yes 100%	No____
Effecting better outcomes?	Yes 100%	No____

And after I trained an open-admission audience, hosted by Alexian Brothers Behavioral Health Hospital in Chicago, I received this email two days later from a domestic-abuse case officer working for a local police department (he asked to remain anonymous because of client- privacy considerations):

"I immediately used information from your seminar in counseling a (Boomer) couple whose young adult (Millennial) son had been violent with them. I informed them of the generational differences between themselves and their son. This information has helped the parents to be more empathetic, to let go of their parenting role, and allow the son to be fully responsible for his life. They are then able to transition into being friends with their child."

So, this training program has thankfully hit a Grand Slam with every group of clinicians who participated. Their evaluations are stunningly enthusiastic. And I'd love to put this tool to work for clinicians on a much wider basis. But when I've contacted the American Psychology Association, American Psychiatry Association, U. S. Army, the central office of the Veterans Healthcare Administration, and others to alert them to this training and show them the formal written evaluations of the training *by their own contemporaries*—their peers—around the country, they all say, *not interested*. Very disappointing, especially because it helps patients and it helps clinicians.

It works.

Labor Shortages In Manual Labor

• • •

HERE'S WHAT HAPPENED: GEN X, as a generation, has avoided careers in manufacturing, construction, and other manual-labor sectors. Longer hours. Too dirty. Too dangerous. Too unglamorous. Not high-tech enough.

And when The Great Recession hit in 2008, these sectors were especially hard-hit and layoffs were rampant, and so the younger Millennials also looked elsewhere for their careers.

Two generations. Not interested.

So: how to find workers? How to overcome the skills gap and train employees properly? How to create a fresh new image?

The answer: Generational Workforce Strategy and Generational Marketing Strategy for the manual-labor industries.

Construction has shown a strong interest in this strategy. Manufacturing has not.

Generational Economic Development And Community Planning Strategy

. . .

THE TRAINING OF LOCAL, REGIONAL, and state economic-development and community-planning personnel focuses upon this: how to use generational strategy to create an entire community that will accommodate the needs and preferences of each generation of citizens. The training and strategy focus upon:

* business recruitment and retention;
* employment opportunities;
* government services;
* education, both K–12 and higher education offerings;
* local transportation/mobility, including bus, rail, and bicycle lanes;
* healthcare;
* residential housing, amenities, and use of space;
* lifestyle;
* parks and recreation;
* leisure and entertainment;

❖ religion;

❖ and, all other components that are central to a thriving community and to the specific generations it wishes to lure and keep.

This particular generational strategy began to emerge in the 2000s when Gen X'ers were gravitating to certain cities around the country and avoiding others. And the towns and cities they were abandoning wondered what must be done to attract and retain them; they especially focused their efforts upon young professionals.

Today, as X'ers now settle in, the focus has shifted to Millennials. But the strategy has grown and now asks a much bigger question:

How can our community appeal to, and succeed with, ALL generations? What do Millennials want and need from their communities during their young adulthood? What do X'ers seek as parents and in their careers? What about empty-nest and soon-to-retire Boomers? And what are the needs and preferences of our Silents and G.I.s?

Boomers grew up in suburbs, stayed there to raise their Gen X and Millennials kids, but now as empty-nesters are migrating in noteworthy numbers into the cities, where dining, arts, college classrooms, and career-next opportunities are located. Others are staying put and keeping their large houses for grand-child visits, home offices, and home gyms.

A noteworthy number of Millennials are also rent-ing in downtown districts. But the unanswered ques-tion with their generation is this: when Millennials depart their Extended Adolescence, get married and have kids, will they head to the 'burbs?

Financial experts predict that Mils will probably (1) go suburban, (2) buy inexpensive, fix-up starter homes, and (3) be pretty enthusiastic do-it-yourself homeowners. They're likely to buy modest-sized hous-es; anything to reduce the burden of the mortgage. Long-term debt requires long-term income security and stability, and most Mils have not experienced that.

Many X'ers' memories of their suburban childhood are painful: divorced parents; isolation; unhappiness. So they, too, kind of like the idea of living a differ-ent adulthood by heading into town. For their kids in an urban environment, safety, bike trails, and quick access to work and leisure destinations are adding to an uptick in city populations after several decades of flight to the suburbs and the additional ring outside the suburbs called exurbs.

The challenge and opportunity for local communities is generational:

Generational Economic Development And Community Planning Strategy.

Generational Political Strategy:
Legislative Relations, Campaigns, And Advocacy

• • •

YOU'RE A CANDIDATE FOR ELECTED office: City Council, County Commission, Governor, Congress, President of the United States.

Or you're a campaign strategist for a ballot-issue campaign.

A speechwriter. Fundraiser. Lobbyist.

In other words, you are in business to *persuade* other human beings to see things your way. This means you are in the *marketplace.*

And this puts you squarely in the business of Generational Political Strategy, which is entirely about persuasion.

Here's what a political strategist in Ohio—Chip Gerhardt, then Vice President/Government Affairs for KMK Consulting in Cincinnati—kindly emailed to an ad agency after the agency had hosted my training seminar (nonpartisan, and open to all) on Generational Campaign and Government Relations Strategy:

"The theories that Chuck Underwood espouses have significant application to the political process. In the future, I believe generational considerations will transcend traditional demographic information in importance. Politicians and political campaigns alike would benefit greatly from this information and Chuck's insights. I understand now how each of us is a product of our times— the impressions made on us at the time in our life when we are most receptive. Those that share the same time of receptivity are vulnerable to the same messages and have the same basic values imprinted on them."

Anecdote: in one recent election year, there were four local ballot issues in the state of Ohio asking taxpayers to approve public funding for local museums and other arts-related projects. I consulted the ad agency that was marketing one of the campaigns. That year, three of the four ballot issues went down in defeat. Ours was the only one that passed.

Generational Fundraising And Development Strategy

• • •

OUR GIVING TO CHARITY INCREASES with age. And the channels through which we give differ among generations: in-person, by mail, online.

Oh, how the Internet—and now, mobiles—have complicated the field of fundraising! It has also made it easier for crooks—scammers—to sucker innocent people because they can do so with untraceable anonymity.

All generations participate at high rates in "Checkout Donation", such as when checking out at the supermarket. And most of us are first alerted to specific charities by way of mainstream media, mail, word of mouth, peer-to-peer contacts, and job/school.

Giving that is linked to religiously affiliated organizations remains pervasive. According to 2013 research by the Indiana University Lilly Family School of Philanthropy, 73% of household giving in the U. S. goes to faith-based charities; not only to religious congregations but also to nonprofits with religious ties, such as the Salvation Army.

And each generation possesses unique Core Values regarding its:

* interest, or lack of it, in philanthropic causes and "giving";
* sense of community and willingness to help others;
* and, personal financial security and capacity to give.

And so, Generational Strategy must be a permanent filter in the brains of fundraising professionals, through which they pass the planning and execution of their work.

This training program explains how to use an understanding of generational Core Values and hot buttons to plan short-term and long-term fundraising strategies, maximize donations, establish trusting relationships with donors and prospective donors, and most importantly...

close the sale.

The big picture:

G.I.s and Silents used to loyally donate to local charities like Community Chest and United Way. They remember when those charities sent representatives door-to-door to collect donations once a year, and they gladly gave. Then, fundraising moved from eye-to-eye contact to direct mail, and still they gave. Then, the scammers began to move in, especially targeting the elderly, and now these two generations are hesitant and not as trusting as they could afford to be in the past.

Boomers: generous; lots of money; strong sense of "community" and helping the less fortunate; if pitched properly, they'll give, but they want a say in how their dollars are used; they're demanding givers and will hold charities accountable for their spending; also, they are a gold mine for charitable volunteerism as they empty-nest and retire.

Another philanthropic phenomenon is occurring with Boomers: as the workaholic generation now sells their businesses or retire with significant nest eggs, they're creating family foundations. So, too, are the wealthy people of all generations who scored big with the Tech Revolution.

Gen X: feeling financially uncertain; in the midst of their big spending years with marriages, kids, homes, furniture, cars, educations, and so on; weakened sense of "community" and "nation" and "giving" as a result of their formative years; instead, a self-reliant *I'll-take-care-of-me and you-take-care-of-you* Core Value; and for the most part, too busy to give of their time and volunteer, unless it's to help their kids' schools; this generation will require careful and generation-specific messaging, and they might increase their charity—time and money—as they empty-nest.

Millennials: it will be a while before they recover from the effects of The Great Recession, settle down in their careers, and start to save money; but at some point, they're likely to become a philanthropic generation; in the meantime, and if recruited in the right manner, they will give in another way: they'll volunteer their time to worthy causes and good deeds.

Generational Selling And
Customer Service Strategy

. . .

IF I'M TRYING TO SELL a widget to a Boomer, I'm going to pitch my product differently than when pitching it to an X'er. Or a Silent. Or a Millennial. Or a G.I.

If I'm in a business where a close and trusting relationship with my clients is critical, I'm going to build a different relationship with an X'er client than with a Boomer.

I'm going to communicate differently with each generation: warm and conversational with some; no-nonsense and to the point with others; in-person and phone with some; email or texting with others; different choice of words; different areas of emphasis.

Different generations. And so, different expectations, preferences, and needs regarding the products and services I sell to them, the manner in which I sell them, and the customer service I provide.

And technology has exacerbated this generational divide: emails and texts can sound blunt and harsh if not tempered with the right choice of words. Also, how many of us have emailed three questions to a customer or sales rep and received a reply with answers to just two of them? How many times has a question or comment been misinterpreted in a digital exchange?

Solution: we all must develop, through training and practice, a *Generational Gearbox* that enables each of us to shift gears swiftly and accurately when selling and serving the generations.

And yes, Generational Selling Strategy works with Business-To-Business selling, not just Business-To-Consumer, because in both instances the person making the decision to buy or not buy *belongs to a generation and is bringing unique generational Core Values to her or his final decision.*

Silents and Boomers, and before them the G.I.s, have been excellent at customer service, where the prevailing generational Core Values are:

1. *I'm here to help you, and I'll stay with you until you're fully satisfied;*
2. *You're the customer, so you're # 1 and I'm # 2;*
3. *Please, Thank You, May I, Yes Ma'am, No Sir.*

This changed with Gen X'ers. During their child-hood, and beyond their control, common courtesy and good customer service took a massive hit. Right in their own living rooms, time-starved families no longer had as much time to be nice to each other. Retailing shifted from locally owned stores where the owner was your neighbor and friend and the person on the sales floor serving you to the impersonal "national chain" corporations, whose owners were two-thousand miles away and NOT your friend and neighbor.

And now today, X'ers are a disproportionately small percentage of sales employees. Their attitude is often:

* *I want to be as efficient as possible and take each customer from point A to point Z as fast as possible;*
* *The act of buying is sometimes a serpentine "journey", but I want it to be a straight line;*
* *I don't want to schmooze with customers, I want to process them.*

When the Tech Revolution hit us in the 2000s, electronics retail chain Best Buy hired X'ers to work its sales floor, because Boomers and Silents didn't know technology as well, and Millennials were still in school. Best Buy promptly developed a reputation for poor customer service. X'er sales associates came across as cold, indifferent, and more eager to complete the transaction than patiently and thoroughly serve the customer's needs.

The same occurred with home-center chains Home Depot and Lowe's. But walk into either store today and you'll find a lot of Silents and Boomers working the floor.

Millennials are proving to be pretty good at customer service. More outgoing than X'ers and inclined to smile and be friendly, they tend to give off a good vibe with customers.

But if you do seek no-nonsense efficiency and fast processing in customer service, as many telemarketing call-center companies do, then X'ers might be your preference.

Gen X'ers, wonderful people who want to be the best they can be, will benefit enormously from training that is NOT simply "customer service" training but instead is "Gen X Customer Service" training, which helps them to understand the unique influences on their own generation's upbringing and how those influences show up in their customer-service performance today.

With Silents and Boomers, the need is similar, but in a different skill: these two generations need more than simply technology training; they need training that is customized just for them when learning the company's newest hardware or software; training that is notably different from that for X'ers and Mils.

With technology putting the world's information at our fingertips and empowering us as consumers, customer service is undergoing a sea change. The *Wall Street Journal* announced it with a two-page story headlined in all caps, "THE CUSTOMER AS A GOD."

The sub-heading: "Businesses today tend to herd customers as if they were cattle, but a revolution in personal empowerment is under way—and buying will never be the same again."

Among the consistently low-ranked industries when it comes to customer service: technology and telecommunications; cable TV; airlines; and health insurance providers.

Scoring more highly: supermarkets; fast food; and, financial services.

In the decade of the 2000s, many U. S. telemarketing call centers offshored their customer-contact jobs because foreign employees were cheaper. It hasn't worked. Too many American customers struggle to understand the foreign accents (Indian, Mexican, Filipino, and others), especially when using cell phones with their diminished audio clarity; and when the conversation departs from the foreign employee's written script, he/she often has difficulty conversing with the American on the other end of the line.

The result: a sharply lower percentage of what the industry labels "first-contact resolution", meaning it often takes a second or third call by the customer to resolve the issue.

Other measurements document that American phone reps score much more highly than offshore reps in terms of courteousness, ease of understanding, interest in helping, knowledge, effectiveness, and overall satisfaction with American customers. And so, better first-contact resolution.

And so it has now become economically wise to bring contact-center jobs back to America.

Americans are still treated horribly by the marketplace: dirty companies have learned how to dodge the government's Do Not Call Registry and invade our privacy with unwanted robocalls. Similarly, unethical online firms and individuals bombard us with unsolicited and unwanted emails, and the tech giants still haven't invented an effective way to block them. Airlines make coach-class seats too small and too close together for reasonable comfort. Cable TV providers Comcast and Time Warner Cable...well, you know. In 2015, Time Warner Cable actually was ranked worst AND second-worst in the American Customer Satisfaction Index! Its cable service ranked second worst and its Internet service ranked worst. Time Warner Cable, what are your bonehead executives *thinking?*

Technology has enabled many companies to hide from their customers by shifting their customer service methods to anonymous, digital, and too often impersonal communication.

By contrast, brick-and-mortar retailers cannot hide. Employees at department stores, hardware stores, restaurants, and banks must go eye-to-eye with dissatisfied customers, and it's no accident that these personal-instead-of-impersonal sectors provide better customer service. So some companies do get it and understand that excellent and personal customer service can be a tiebreaker in their favor.

If Time Warner Cable rated lowest, which company ranked highest in the most recent American Customer Satisfaction Index survey?

Amazon.

Generational Faith-Based Strategy

• • •

I RECEIVED THIS EMAIL FROM an Episcopal priest in Cincinnati:

"I would like to pursue the possibility of having you share some of your Generational Study with the clergy of our diocese...at our annual Clergy Day."

Here's why I was thrilled to receive that invitation:

Previously, I had conducted training sessions for clients in the business of faith-based publishing, fundraising, assisted living, and other religious "businesses": Zondervan Publishing (bibles, Christian books and gifts); two different Christian fundraising organizations; a Lutheran organization that operates assisted-living centers; Jewish Community Centers of North America; YMCA Development Officers; and others.

In addition, individual audience members at business seminars and speeches had frequently approached me afterwards and asked if I ever work with clergy and local houses of worship. I had not.

But this Clergy Day presentation would be my first opportunity to present Generational Faith-Based Strategy to the men and women who stand on the *front line* of American religion: the ones who are charged with growing and sustaining membership and participation and belief in their messages of faith in this era when all of that is declining. One priest told me that religion in the U. S. and other nations is facing a once-every-500-years epoch, a time of noteworthy and historical shift in religious values, beliefs, and practices. He told his fellow clergy, "If we keep going in the direction we're going, I don't know if we'll have a job ten years from now."

Convinced that there is a significant generational influence upon religion, I presented Generational Strategy to 105 priests, in a half-day session.

After I finished, I looked at them, and asked, "You tell me, can Generational Strategy make a difference in American religion?"

Their answers, thankfully, were a resounding *YES.* The priests completed their written evaluations of the session with comments like these:

* *Transformational. Game-changer.*
* *It was outstanding! The information was so power-ful and clear, thus easy to carry home and give to the parish.*
* *Outstanding. New thinking applied to the challenges the Church faces.*

Side-bar: I hardly ever get sick. But I arrived for this seminar during a bitter-cold Midwest January with an especially vicious virus that, according to my doctor, hadn't been identified and was raging through the region, and for which there was no med-icine. Five minutes into my presentation, I became suddenly dizzy. I had enough strength to hastily tell them I needed to sit down. I made it to a chair next to the podium. I sat for about a minute with my head down, they brought me a sugary caffein-ated soft drink that I sipped. My head cleared, and I returned to the podium and went full-speed for the entire 3-hour program. Afterwards, one priest asked, "Did you look around while you were seated at the chair?" I said, "No, I was dizzy so my head was down" and she said with a chuckle, "You were in the right place; you were surrounded by 105 priests saying a quick prayer for you." Seems to have worked!

Here is the generational divide in religion: G.I.s and Silents tend to embrace traditional religions and services. But Boomers long ago began a journey to find a religion, faith, or spirituality that suited their generational Core Values better than those religions, and X'ers and Millennials are following that same path.

And so those younger generations either don't attend regular religious services or hop from one religion to another searching for a true home.

We're finding Gen X parents don't profess a strong affiliation to a specific religion and will not ask their children to do so, but they do want them to be *exposed* to religion and objectively taught it so they can make an informed decision.

And don't overlook the bitter aftertaste from World War II:

16,000,000 G.I.s returned from the war, with some of them saying "No God that I worship would ever have allowed this horror to happen." What they witnessed

in combat, what they had done to other human beings, stripped them of their belief in an all-knowing,
all-loving, all-powerful God. Their Silent and Boomer
kids recognized this, and it shaped their own religious
attitudes, which they have now relayed to their own
Gen X and Millennial children.

Generational Membership
And Volunteer Strategy

• • •

MEMBERSHIP ORGANIZATIONS IN AMERICA ARE struggling to recruit and retain members.

Labor unions. Local civic clubs like Rotary, Kiwanis, Lions, Optimists, Sertoma, American Legion, Veterans of Foreign Wars, and others. Business and professional trade associations around the country. Chambers of Commerce. Alumni associations. Religions. And on and on and on.

The primary reason why: Gen X.

Gen X is not a strong generation of "joiners". From their unique childhood passage, they are self-reliant, individualistic, skeptical of "organizations", and not the same enthusiastic social animals as other generations.

Millennials, on the other hand, possess ideal Core Values for "joining". But membership organizations are still learning what they must do to find and appeal to this very unique generation.

So the leaders of membership organizations must understand generational dynamics and undergo the training to develop the generational gearbox that will enable them to shift gears smoothly and swiftly when dealing with one generation to the next.

This is especially true of labor unions. At a time when America's workforce is taking such a pounding from the executive suites, unions should be gaining clout instead of losing it. And Millennials seem to be pro-little-guy and should thus be pro-union. Generational Strategy should be a big part of unions' recruitment and retention efforts, but I'm not seeing it.

Generational Leadership And Governance Strategy

. . .

WHITE SILENT MEN GUIDED AMERICA in the 1990s and 2000s, when their generation's Core Values dominated the decision-making positions in American business, government, religion, and education.

Their reign ended roughly in 2010 when the youngest of them reached the traditional retirement age of 65 and Boomers began their turn at the top.

In 2014, the National Association of Corporate Directors requested two presentations to its members, who are now overwhelmingly Boomer, to explain the three massive applications of generational strategy by executives and the boards of directors who govern them.

In Beverly Hills, California, I presented (1) Generational Marketplace Strategy and (2) Generational Workforce Strategy.

In Washington, D. C. a couple of weeks later, I presented The Generational Disruption of Leadership and Governance, which alerts directors to the reality that the Boomer Leadership Era—essentially the 2010s and 2020s—should bring dramatic transformation to the c-suites and boardrooms in the areas that are currently at the top of their priority list:

* Executive Ethics
* Treatment of U. S. Workers
* Investor Activism
* Pay Ratios
* Say-On-Pay
* Transparency
* Political Spending
* Social Matters
* Sustainability
* Board Composition
* Board Culture
* Risk
* Communications
* Boldness/Vision
* Board Harmony

I quickly mentioned this entire list of issues. But the thrust of my speech focused upon the generational influence upon executive ethics.

When I received NACD's audience evaluations of this keynote, it was clear the majority of the 1,300 directors in the audience were most interested in that one topic: ethics at the top of America, and how the Boomer Era will hopefully clean up the mess.

Because NACD's local chapters in Chicago, Atlanta, New Jersey, Dallas–Fort Worth, Southern California, and Washington, D. C. soon after asked me to come to their cities and give the exact same speech to their members...

and because other chapters wanted to do so but didn't have the money to bring me in...

and because executive ethics and treatment of U. S. employees are the single most important issues in American life at this time...

here, for your review and critique, is:

CHAPTER 24

The Speech

The Modest Goal: Save A Nation

• • •

WHAT FOLLOWS IS THE VERBATIM script of a keynote speech I began to present a few years ago after a decade of researching it.

It explains the leadership and governance calamity of the 1990s and 2000s that was created by a now-retired Silent Generation, and it calls to action—to clean up the mess and save this nation—the generation that has now taken over and will lead America through the 2020s, the Boomers…

Thank you, and hello to you all. It's a pleasure to be here.

In the 1980s, about a half dozen of us here on plan-et Earth, and we did not know each other at the time, accidentally stumbled upon the notion that "genera-tion" meant something far more important than any-one recognized.

We would learn, years later, that this thought had been lightly tinkered with in the '60s and '70s but nothing significant had emerged from it. As a field of study, it didn't exist.

So we started with a very blank canvas and created it, with each of us adding pieces to the puzzle.

And now today, training in generational strategies has become essential to achieving success in the mar-ketplace, with a workforce, and in leadership and the governance of that leadership, because we now under-stand the powerful influence of generational Core Values on Americans' minute-by-minute, month-by-month, lifelong decision-making.

Most of my clients request management training in Generational Workforce Strategy and Generational Marketplace Strategy.

And generational dynamics directly affect each step of the human resource and marketplace process.

And at a typical Board Retreat, we train Board Directors and senior leadership to understand how generational differences directly impact discussion, planning, and final decision-making on these and other issues.

The entire premise of generational study is based upon 3 now heavily researched and universally accepted truths:

Truth #1:

Between the time we're born and the time we leave the full-time classroom and get fully into adulthood—late teens to early 20s—you and I will form most of the Core Values and beliefs that we'll embrace our entire lives.

Yes, we'll evolve, we'll change. But those Core Values will remain largely intact.

And they will be burned into us by the times that we witness as we come of age, and by the teachings we absorb from older generations of parents, educators, religious leaders, and others.

And the age group that shares the same formative years' times and teachings will, by and large, share the same Core Values.

And by sharing the same Core Values, we become a generation.

And any time in American life that either the times or teachings, or both, change in a significant way and a widespread way, it means young kids coming of age during those different times and teachings will form different Core Values and become our next generation.

Truth #2:

And this is why generational study has become such a hot topic...

Life in America, in the past century, has changed so often. And when it has changed, it seems to have changed so sharply into new directions.

And we are now living 30 years longer today than we did a century ago. So for the first time in U. S. history, our life expectancy has room for 5 living generations, each of whose formative years were very different from all other generations and each of whose Core Values, as a result, are very different.

Truth #3:

Those unique Core Values that each generation molds during its unique formative years will now exert astonishing influence over that generation's career decisions and performance, consumer choices, lifestyle preferences, personal relationships, and personal behavior.

Here is the starting point of generational study. Say hello to America's 5 living generations. (Give names, birth years, and current ages).

And here is the topic I've been asked to share with you today:

The Generational Leadership of the United States of America.

The first part of this is easy to understand:

GENERATIONAL LEADERSHIP ERAS:

1. Each generation leads for about 2 decades.
2. Generational values guide USA's direction.

3. Some generations good, some bad.
4. Era begins at age 65.

Each generation takes its turn at the top of America.

Its members begin their careers down at Entry Level, and those with skill and good luck advance as they pass through their 20s, 30s, 40s, 50s, and 60s.

And then for about two decades, their generation fills the overwhelming majority of leadership positions in business, government, education, religion, all of our other major institutions and all of our minor ones on every block of every city in every state.

And while they lead...

while their one generation so thoroughly dominates our nation's decision-making positions...

they methodically install their generation's unique Core Values not just throughout their individual organizations but also *throughout all of American life.*

And those unique generational Core Values, we now know, move America in a direction that is always significantly different from the direction of the prior generation's leadership era, which was guided by a different set of Core Values.

So while, individually, they lead their individual organizations, *collectively* they are creating a much greater outcome:

they are dictating the direction of their nation.

And then their generation retires and hands off that leadership baton to the next generation, whose different Core Values once again push America in a new direction.

Some generations come of age, beyond their control, absorbing times and teachings that mold in them the Core Values and skills considered essential for good leadership...

while other generations pass through THEIR formative years absorbing very different times and teachings...

again, beyond their control...

that set them up for poor leadership.

And we've also learned this from generational study:

Any one generation's leadership era BEGINS when the oldest members of that generation reach retirement age, roughly age 65, and the rest of their generation trails downward in age through their early 60s, 50s, and late 40s.

And here is where we're headed with this program:

America has just endured one of the worst generational leadership eras in its history, but now stands at the front door—POSSIBLY—of one of its most magnificent generational leadership and governance eras, as a new generation takes its turn at the top.

And the transformation our nation is *probably* about to undergo is explained almost entirely by the fact that the outgoing generation, because of its formative years' times and teachings—over which it had no control—was never meant to lead...

and the incoming generation, because of very different formative years' times and teachings over which it had no control, was never meant to follow.

Here is what happened to American leadership with the outgoing generation…

and what should happen to America with the generation that is just getting started.

And as we begin, please remember this:

Yes, everyone is an individual, and we should never use Generational Study to unfairly stereotype anyone.

But when used properly, this stuff will serve as a trustworthy and valuable lighthouse that guides us in our interactions with other people.

SILENT GENERATION
Born 1927 Through 1945
46,582,000 Born
Formative years: Early 1930s To Early '60s

The Silent Generation.

An especially tiny generation of fewer than 47 million. And that fact will be important in a few minutes.

The white men of this generation have enjoyed the smoothest career passage in American history.

Silent generation women have experienced and influenced the before-and-after of the modern Women's Movement.

And Silent minorities have experienced and influenced the before-and-after of the modern Civil Rights Movement.

The Silents' unique formative years are essentially the 1930s, '40s, '50s, and into the very early '60s; an era marked forever by its extreme conformity; to some of them a suffocating conformity:

a *don't rock the boat, do as you're told, children should be seen and not heard* era.

"The corporation came first."
David Halberstam, *The Fifties*

David Halberstam, in his acclaimed book *The Fifties,* writes the following words about the corporate culture of General Motors in the 1950s. And back then, GM was THE yardstick by which most other corporations measured their own culture and performance.

Here's the environment those young Silent men step into as they enter adulthood from the end of World War II to the early sixties:

"The men who ran the corporation were square and proud of it. Loyalty among employees was more important than individual brilliance. Team players were valued more highly than mavericks. The corporation came first. The individual was always subordinated to the greater good of the company."

"The individual must trust the organization."
Ray Kroc

Also in the 1950s, Ray Kroc, a member of the G.I. Generation, in a famous memo he sent to the McDonald brothers as he was revolutionizing the restaurant industry, wrote this:

"We have found out that we cannot trust some people who are nonconformists. We will make conformists out of them in a hurry. The organization cannot trust the individual. The individual must trust the organization."

In this environment, the message from an older generation of bosses to these young white Silent men is very clear: "Our country is really rolling right now, so:

* Conform to the organization's way of doing things;

❀ don't rock the boat;

❀ be absolutely loyal;

❀ ANYTHING FOR THE COMPANY;

❀ and if you do all of this, you will one day be entitled to reward. Your loyalty to the organization
will be matched by the organization's loyalty to
you."

Well: after 16 years of seeing their parents and
grandparents endure depression, high unemployment,
and war, this message from the boss understandably
sounds delicious!

So the young Silent man does all of that. He DOES
work hard. He IS loyal. He does it the company way.
That is…

he "follows".

And he patiently awaits the reward to which he will
be entitled.

THESE ARE THE TIMES AND TEACHINGS
IMPOSED UPON THIS GENERATION.

And because the American economy is soaring just as his generation begins its career passage...

and because Silent females and Silent minorities are blatantly and systemically prohibited from competing against him for the better jobs and career paths...

and because this is an uncommonly tiny generation entering adulthood just as the demand for workers is sky-high...

he receives that remarkably smooth career passage.

Raging Materialism

The Silents also come of age and begin their work years during a famously materialistic era in America: the so-called American High of 1946 to 1962.

After the Depression and War and "doing without" so many things, suddenly the war ends and the economy takes off like a bottle rocket.

Americans have stable jobs and they have cash, and so they splurge on their own pent-up demand for "stuff".

And this is also an exceptional era of invention, with a blizzard of new products to buy: from television sets to transistor radios to stereo record players to Tupperware! And oh yes, during this era, cars, cars, cars.

And as the cream-of-the-crop of these Silent men climb so smoothly up the ladder during these times, and as they joyously receive financial opportunities and live lifestyles their parents never had the opportunity to experience because of the Depression and War...

they come to judge themselves, and each other, by the square footage of their office...

by how near their office is to the boss's office...

by the cars they drive; corporate executives drive Cadillacs and doctors drive Buicks...

by the neighborhoods in which they live...

the furnishings inside the house...

the restaurants they frequent...

the vacations they take.

This generation of executives measures its success by its material wealth.

THESE ARE THE TIMES IMPOSED UPON THIS GENERATION.

Brilliant At The Helping Professions

In their careers, Silents have distinguished themselves in the so-called helping professions. They have given America a bumper crop of skilled educators, doctors and nurses, salespeople, religious leaders, and professional-service practitioners: architects, engineers, accountants, attorneys.

Helping, facilitating, serving is their generation's brilliance.

However, and here comes the sensitive part:

those powerful generational Core Values of "anything for the company" and "I'm entitled to reward" and "I am judged by my material wealth" go a long way in explaining...

The Great American Corporate Meltdown

...what the *Wall Street Journal,* decades later, will describe as The Great American Corporate Meltdown but which is more accurately described as The Great American Leadership And Governance Meltdown.

Those white Silent men begin to dominate the c-suites in the early '90s as the last of the G.I.s retire. They begin their generation's leadership and governance era.

Arthur Levitt

And according to Arthur Levitt, chairman of the Securities and Exchange Commission during most of the '90s, this is precisely when the corruptive mindset, the culture of greed and entitlement, begins.

Enron And WorldCom

As Mr. Levitt said in an interview on national television in 2002 just as the Enron and WorldCom and many other executive scandals were first surfacing, "Anyone who believes this executive corruption is merely a few bad apples is sadly mistaken."

Our nation has had, Mr. Levitt calculated in 2002, ten to fifteen years of a widespread unethical culture coming out of American leadership, where the prevailing generational Core Values among those leaders were "anything for the corporation" and "I'm entitled to this wealth", and where the prevailing core value among Silent board directors charged with governing those executives is "don't rock the boat".

And during this time, it's not just corporate America.

Religion, Government, Sport, Everywhere!

It's also religion (Jim Bakker, Jimmy Swaggart), government (local, state, and national officials), and sport (Pete Rose).

Everywhere!

Coast to coast, and across many industry sectors, we Americans see white Silent male leaders taking their turn at the top and constantly falling in disgrace.

Example: there have been more Silent members of Congress formally reprimanded for unethical behavior than any other generation in U. S. history.

Why?

What's causing this epidemic?

In this one generation of overwhelmingly good people and honorable people, how is it that those white Silent men who rise to power so badly mishandle their generation's leadership era?

And why will their leadership era, during which the American middle class is ravaged, later be described as Teeter-Totter Leadership:

an era when executives perched on one end of that teeter-totter go soaring upwards in wealth and security while their U. S. workers on the other end go crashing downward?

Answer

Well, throughout their formative years of do-as-you're-told and don't-rock-the-boat, and then their early and mid-careers of *conformity* while working under their older bosses, the career opportunity for Silents is NEVER to lead. America has a generation of exceptional leaders just ahead of them:

The Greatest Generation
Tom Brokaw's book

The legendary generation that Tom Brokaw will later immortalize in his book *The Greatest Generation*.

So the career opening for Silents is not to lead but instead to follow: to take the big bold visions of their G.I. leaders and make them happen. To facilitate. To execute. To help.

It's a vital assignment and they become excellent at it.

Korean Conflict: 1950–1953

There is one other major event that damages the Silents' preparation for their leadership era. It is their generation's war, Korea.

Just 8 years earlier, World War II for the G.I. Generation had been an epic and heroic triumph.

In sharp contrast, Korea—fought primarily by Silent troops—is not a victory. It is a stalemate, a political tie, defined by the 38th parallel that divides Korea into two countries.

And I will now defer to a white Silent male, a physician living in Florida, to explain the impact of that war on his generation.

He emailed me after watching the first PBS television show in our *AMERICA'S GENERATIONS* series, which was devoted entirely to the life story of the Silents.

Our generation's war, he wrote, "significantly slowed the normal course of social development, especially for the boys, far more than would be apparent to anyone who didn't experience it.

"But more important, it left us with the knowledge that we had lost OUR war; that our generation was somehow lacking in the 'stuff' which characterized the American 'get 'er done' spirit. Basically, we were losers! That any success we might have would be more a result of good luck than to our own abilities. Perhaps that accounts for our [generation's] mantra of just putting our heads down and getting on with whatever needs doing."

AND THESE ARE THE TIMES AND TEACHINGS IMPOSED UPON THIS GENERATION, BEYOND ITS CONTROL.

The leadership and governance crisis of the 1990s and 2000s will always rest squarely in the lap of the generation that was taking its turn at the top and dictating the leadership culture and behavior according to its unique generational Core Values.

Martin Luther King, Jr., Phil Donahue, Gloria Steinem, Ralph Nader, And Many Others

And no one is more disappointed with this generational legacy than the many members of the Silent Generation who join these and other well-known Silents who are famous for the leadership, ethics, courage, and compassion they demonstrated in their careers.

And now, in the last few years, the leadership baton has been fully passed to the next generation. And we now recognize that it takes a number of years for the new generation to fully disentangle from the culture of the prior generation.

So when we close in on the end of the 2010s, we should begin to see clearly if the next generation is going to continue the leadership culture of the Silent era or alter it.

BOOMERS
Born 1946 Through 1964
79,907,844 Born
Formative years: 1950s Through Early '80s

The children of the legendary American Baby Boom have the good luck to come of age during a wondrous era when America, it seems, is getting so much right.

Their formative years have been described as A Golden Age For Kids:

* Our families are strong, neighborhoods are safe, jobs and incomes for most dads are stable, schools are excellent, our nation's best and brightest are curing polio and landing men on the moon.

* Individually, we Americans are taking on our own worst personal prejudices, especially against minorities and females, and we are making historic progress against them.

* At the same time, we are generously and compassionately helping other nations.

- And to the entire world, OUR leaders and OUR citizens are demonstrating that we stand for the highest principles.

Boomers come of age just as the Core Values of the G.I. Generation are guiding America. And what Boomer kids see every day from the G.I.s are Core Values of humility, hard work, teamwork, ethical behavior, and compassionate leadership; a powerful core value of "we're all in this together so let's TRULY take care of each other."

The Core Values Of The G.I. Leadership Era

Here's where those G.I. leadership values come from:

During The Great Depression, everyone is hurting. So when one household has one pork chop left over after dinner, they put it on a plate and carry that pork chop to their next door neighbor who might be hurting a little more than them.

We're in this together!

And then in World War II: two young G.I. soldiers, digging a tiny foxhole in Europe, crawling into it, and in the life-or-death firefight with the enemy that now begins, truly knowing they MUST have each other's back and so they DO have each other's back.

Or three G.I.s entering a dark cave on a Pacific Island, knowing the enemy is somewhere inside waiting to kill them in the next few seconds, and knowing they MUST have each other's back and so they DO have each other's back.

And one of the men in that foxhole or that cave will go on to become the president of a major corporation.

And the guy right beside him will go on to become his janitor down in the basement.

And long after the war, in which 16 million G.I. men fought, when given the chance to receive a bigger year-end bonus if only he'll lay off a bunch of employees including that janitor in the basement, what decision did that G.I. executive make?

And we all know the answer:

We're in this together. I HAVE your back.

Foxhole leadership. *We're in this together.*

Not TEETER-TOTTER leadership: *you employees go down so that I can go up.*

And this is the G.I. leadership culture—the Foxhole Leadership values, the times and the teachings—that young Boomer kids witness and absorb as they pass through their formative years.

During the G.I.s' leadership era:

* Boomer children don't hear of executives sending thousands of their parents' jobs overseas and then receiving a year-end bonus from the Board of Directors for doing so;

* They don't hear of G.I. Generation corporate raiders who buy into a corporation and then force the executives to lay off 30 thousand U. S. employees so they'll get a greater return on their investment;

* Boomers don't hear of G.I. executives making hundreds of times more than their average employee.

In my earlier career as a sports play-by-play announcer, I was interviewing then University of Wisconsin head football coach Dave McClain. I knew he had previously been an assistant coach at Ohio State, working under the legendary Woody Hayes, who had won 5 national championships and 13 Big Ten titles in his 28 years with the Buckeyes.

McClain is a member of the Silent Generation. Hayes is a G.I. who commanded a Navy force during World War II in both the Pacific and Atlantic theaters.

I asked Coach McClain, "Of the many things Coach Hayes taught you about leadership, what stands out?"

And he didn't hesitate. With an affectionate smile on his face, he said, "Back then, we had 95 players on our college teams. 85 of them were terrific athletes on full scholarships. The other ten were 'walk-on' players: guys who had played high school ball but were not good enough to receive a scholarship. But they loved the game and wanted to be part of our programs. So these were the 'scrubs' who got the tar knocked out of them every day in practice by their bigger and stronger teammates but gave us the extra bodies we needed to have full practice sessions. Woody preached one thing: 'You treat your 95th player the exact same way you treat your #1 player.' And I never forgot that."

Woody Hayes. Classic G.I. Generation Core Values:

We're all in this together.

Foxhole leadership.

It's no accident that Coach Hayes' 1973 book is entitled *You Win With People.*

"We need idealistic children"
Dr. Benjamin Spock

Thanks in no small part to these 4 words written in a book authored by pediatrician Dr. Benjamin Spock in 1946, the first year of the Baby Boom, their elders are teaching and preaching to Boomer kids a core value of idealism:

Don't accept "almost right" in your life. Demand "absolutely right": from yourself and your world.

They also absorb another core value from their elders: a no-nonsense message from a no-nonsense generation of Moms and Dads about what is right in life and what is wrong, what is good, what is bad, what you do and what you don't do.

As Boomer kids come of age, there ain't much negotiating with their parents about right and wrong.

Core Values:
Optimism. Patriotism. Empowerment.
Engagement. Social Activism. Ethics. Help The
Less Fortunate.

And in this environment, in these unique times and unique teachings, Boomers form lifelong Core Values of optimism, patriotism, empowerment, engagement, social activism, ethics, and a passionate commitment to help the less fortunate:

a strong belief, like the G.I. Generation, that "We're all in this together so let's take care of each other".

The Consciousness Movement

And in the '60s and '70s, guided by those Core Values— and yes, by their own flawed sense of immortality— young Boomers unleash their passion, their masses, and their idealism on no fewer than eight major cultural revolutions, any one of them big enough to define their generation forever, but there are eight of them flying around at once.

The Boomers propel forward the:

1. Civil Rights Movement
2. Women's Movement

3. Ecology Movement
4. War Protest Movement
5. Sexual Revolution
6. Drug Revolution
7. Religion Revolution
8. Youth Empowerment Movement

Big dreams. Big victories. And yes, Boomers will tell you they also make big mistakes.

But in all cases from THIS generation?

Bold. Decisive. Willing to take risks. Willing to fail. Willing to stand up and sacrifice for the less fortunate. Willing to be accountable for their actions.

Fearless.

Unique Core Values molded by unique times and teachings.

Adulthood

In adulthood, this generation struggles horribly with marriage, taking the divorce rate over the moon. And this has very negative impact on their Gen X kids. They also struggle with their own parenting, as the only models of marriage and family they had never known change profoundly for a long list of reasons.

But if they struggle in their personal lives, Boomers become, are today, and will be tomorrow The Golden Generation in the American workplace. Boomers always have and always will define themselves by their work and by their contribution to something bigger than themselves.

The End Of The White Male Leadership Frat Party

And thanks to the women's movement and civil rights movement of a half century ago, Boomers become the first American generation to take its turn at the top with significant numbers of females and minorities adding their unique sensibilities and skills to leadership and to the governance of that leadership.

The entire history of American leadership and governance being a fraternity of white men comes to an end with the retirement of the Silents.

With the arrival of the Boomer Era, American leadership and governance—for the first time in our nation's history—become multi-gender and multi-ethnic.

"The Country Is Starved For Integrity"

May 21, 2002.

Coleen Rowley, Boomer mother of four, primary breadwinner in the family, and only 2½ years from retirement from what everyone agrees is an excellent career, nonetheless makes the very personal decision to risk all of that by alerting the United States Congress that her employer, the FBI, deliberately obstructed investigations that might've helped to uncover the attacks of 9-11 before they occurred.

When asked why she was willing to risk everything, her reply was classic idealistic, ethics-driven, empowered and engaged Boomer:

"It was the right thing to do," she said. "The country is starved for integrity."

Same response from Boomer Sherron Watkins. Risked it all to reveal the executive corruption at Enron.

Same response from Boomer Cynthia Cooper. She exposed the executive corruption at WorldCom, saying "I'm not a hero; I'm just doing my job."

And these three women grace the cover of *TIME* magazine's 2002 year-end edition as its PERSONS OF THE YEAR.

Three Boomers, risking everything in order to do the right thing.

Three Boomers, making decisions according to the Core Values burned into them during their generation's unique formative years.

As an Associated Press reporter wrote in her story about Colleen Rowley, "When you're called to stand, you stand...even when your legs are shaking."

And to this day, Boomers continue to stand.

The Female Factor

Here are just a few of the contributions Boomer females are expected to make to their generation's leadership era. And these women *should* be joined in these contributions by their generation's men...who share the same Core Values:

1. A more clench-fisted commitment to executive ethics;

2. The influence and benefit of emotional considerations, not simply business intelligence;

3. Long-term strategic thinking, not just the current quarter-by-quarter short-term mindset;

4. Risk-taking that will also be weighed by social benefit, not just monetary profit;

5. Less complacency towards executives' decisions;

6. A greater willingness to "ask the dumb question", such as "why are we doing it this way?" and to demand an honest answer;

7. And, a heightened "people orientation" towards employees and customers and the community instead of a focus only upon share price and executive compensation and anything for the company.

America's Future Leaders: Gen X And Millennials

In this short presentation, time doesn't permit a fair presentation of Gen X and Millennials.

So here is an unfair one: unfair, because although it's the most accurate information available, I don't have the time to explain the "why" behind it.

Gen X
Born 1965 Through 1981
58,541,842 Born
Formative Years: 1970s To Early 2000s

The oldest X'ers are now in their 50s, so they are giving us a pretty good track record about their leadership strengths and shortcomings. They're in middle and senior management and hold some c-suites.

But a key point: like prior generations at this age, most of them have spent their entire careers working under leaders from other generations, so we haven't yet seen their generation's true leadership intentions and behavior. So we shouldn't judge them as leaders yet.

With that qualifier, here is what X'er leaders around the country tell me about their generation:

Our strength will probably be in Idea Leadership. We will deliver many new products, services, workplace processes and efficiencies. Creativity and entrepreneurialism are our strengths.

But we are also self-focused with strong generational Core Values of "survival of the fittest" and "I'll take care of me, you take care of you"...

and our generation feels a sense of financial uncertainty...

And if we don't confront it, our generation's leaders will be vulnerable to financial greed and thus to corruption, and possibly to dispassionate treatment of employees.

The good news for Gen X leaders:

The study of generational leadership, which is now in place, can help X'ers maximize their leadership strengths and minimize their leadership weaknesses BEFORE THEY TAKE THEIR TURN AT THE TOP if they will simply undergo training in Generational Leadership that is truly customized for their generation, not just "generic leadership training".

Boomers are receiving this training as their leadership era is underway. Silents never received it. Our field of study wasn't in place when they led America.

Millennials
Born 1982 Through 1998 (And Still Coming)
66,106,894 Born As Of Jan., 2016
Formative Years: 1980s To Early 2000s So Far

Millennials will lead America during roughly the 2050s and 2060s.

From their unique formative years and unique Core Values:

❋ they will probably lead compassionately;

❋ they will take good care of employees and customers and people. Excellent people leadership;

❋ they will struggle with accountability and the pressure of decision-making;

❋ Mils will probably usher-in an era of one corporation having multiple CEOs who share the decision-making; and,

❋ they will be team players and team decision-makers;

That's the early forecast for Millennial leadership.

But today, here's what Boomer leaders need to understand about Millennials and X'ers, and I'm guessing some of you already know this:

Many of the best and brightest of these two generations are avoiding corporate America in their career choices.

50 THINGS ABOUT MILLENNIALS THAT MAKE CORPORATE AMERICA SH*T ITS PANTS
www.elitedaily.com

This is a commentary posted on a Millennial-oriented news website called elitedaily.com and sent to me by a university professor who underwent our training program in Generational Workforce Strategy.

I'm quoting from this piece because I hear the same sentiment in city after city when I go eye-to-eye with Millennials and X'ers and yes, with Boomers and Silents.

With my genuine apology for the cuss word you're about to hear, this story is headlined:

"50 Things About Millennials That Make Corporate America Shit Its Pants."

And sure enough, this story lists 50 reasons why their generation is sickened by the executive culture, governance culture, and ruthless investor culture they've witnessed thus far in their lives.

One paragraph at the end of this piece summarizes the Millennials' Core Values about corporate America and explains why corporate America is now positioned to receive not the best and most honorable and most talented of this generation but instead the ones who are willing to embrace the greed and corruption and ruthless treatment of employees that is the only executive culture they have ever seen.

Here's the quote:

"Sorry, corporate America. We're just not interested. We gave you a shot, tried you out, and decided you weren't for us. We saw how you treated our parents, grandparents, and the Bottom Percents and realized you aren't that good of a guy."

And this is the attitude towards "leaders" by Millennials and X'ers and Boomers that Boomer leaders are inheriting as they take their turn at the top.

History Calls SOME Generations To Greatness

History called the G.I. Generation to greatness twice:

1. First, in World War II;

2. and then afterwards, in building this nation and lifting the entire world.

And most agree the G.I.s DID deliver true greatness.

As it turns out, history NEVER called the Silent Generation to greatness. The "times" simply didn't demand it.

Boomers: history will have called your generation to greatness twice in your lives.

The first time occurred in your young adulthood. And your generation delivered greatness by pushing forward civil rights, women's rights, the environmental movement, and yes, by forcing your government to more closely examine its decision-making when it comes to the matter of war.

Remarkably, you delivered this greatness back then despite holding no positions of power, possessing no financial clout, and facing a thick granite wall of resistance from the older people who did have the power and did have the money.

You Boomers achieved all of this on the strength of a single asset, and it was *all that you had*: your generation's unique and powerful Core Values, burned into you during your generation's unique formative years' times and teachings.

But now today, Boomers, and for a brief time only...

you have it all.

Your generation now holds the positions of power.

Your generation now possesses the wealth.

And because you are inheriting a leadership culture that the overwhelming majority of Americans believe is the ethical equivalent and compassionate equivalent of a Toxic Waste Dump...

your generation is being called to greatness a second time.

And a final time.

History is quite genuinely calling you to save a nation that is an absolute mess at the top.

David Brinkley

In the 1990s, respected network-television newsman David Brinkley concluded one of his weekly Sunday morning news shows *This Week With David Brinkley* with a commentary that ended with a question for all us to ponder back then and still today, more than two decades later:

"When is the last time America solved a major problem?"

Boomers: this is what you've inherited. A nation whose leadership can't solve major problems.

And because your generation's formative years, beyond your control, have prepared you perfectly for ethical and compassionate and decisive and brilliant leadership...

your generation must bear the pressure of having no excuse for failure.

There actually IS an explanation for the disappointing leadership of the Silent Generation. It's their formative years' times and teachings and early adulthood that were so different from yours.

You have no excuse.

Yes: some very wealthy and powerful people in your generation are dirty and ruthless.

But the generational leadership of America...

the direction that America takes...

is entirely about which side—the good side or the dirty side—wins the tug of war and pushes America in ITS direction:

either up, or down, or sideways.

The Bottom 85%

It seems that, although they've taken such a beating the past quarter-century, there is nothing wrong with the American masses: that is, the Bottom 85% who are living their lives in such insecurity and uncertainty and at the mercy of corporate bosses who are often at the mercy of corporate raiders.

* The Bottom Percents are still willing to give their employers more than an honest day's work.

* They are willing to pay their fair share of taxes.

* They are willing to volunteer in their communities and support their local schools.

* They are willing to stand for the right things in life...

if only the people above them, the ones who hold the power, will have their back and give them a fair shot at stability instead of selling them down the river...

and if only those leaders will behave ethically and compassionately.

Bobby Knight
Rabbits And Elephants

A number of years ago, *Sports Illustrated* magazine wrote an in-depth profile of legendary Indiana University basketball coach Bobby Knight.

Three NCAA championships. 11 Big Ten titles. His players behaved and graduated. Knight's program was clean.

In talking about the keys to leadership and greatness, Knight wanted to make the point that a great leader needs to see the big picture and not get distracted by the unimportant stuff. He said it this way:

"When you're hunting elephants, it's the rabbits that'll kill you."

Well, here is the unmistakable perspective from generational study of the Boomer Leadership Era, now that we clearly understand that individuals at the top don't merely lead their own organizations but also—as part of a generational leadership era—collectively determine the direction of the United States:

Your Rabbits

Profit	Harmony
Competition	Sustainability
Investor Activism	Communications
Board Composition	Pay Ratios
Board Culture	Say-On-Pay
Risk	Political Spending

For Boomer board directors and executives and investors, these kinds of everyday issues are your RABBITS.

Your Elephants

1. Executive Ethics
2. Treatment of U. S. Workers

And these are your ELEPHANTS: the only two issues that are will define *forever* the Boomers' leadership of their beloved America.

If you Boomers handle your two elephants successfully...

if you give America the integrity and the loyalty of Foxhole Leadership instead of ruthless and greedy Teeter-Totter Leadership...

you will live up to your promise.

And you will pull off one final Boomer revolution in your generation's final important act ever.

If you don't handle your two elephants successfully, your generation's leadership era will go down in history as a colossal failure, no matter how your individual corporations do, because...

YOU HAVE NO EXCUSE.

And because the field of generational study is now in place, yours will be the first generational leadership era ever to be chronicled and captured as it occurs and when it has ended.

So Boomers, it's your America.

One time only. One chance to fulfill the promise and live up to the special opportunity your generation was given long ago.

And Silents and X'ers and Millennials and yes, the G.I.s, stand ready to help you.

And their generations, and your own, want desperately for you to demonstrate the skill, the guts, the human compassion, and absolute integrity to pull off this miracle and save our nation...

which is an absolute mess.

And so as you Boomers inherit such troubled waters, it seems the song lyrics, from decades ago, from your old buddies Simon and Garfunkel, are calling you to action:

"Your time has come to shine
All your dreams are on their way."

Can you do it, Boomers?

WILL you do it?

Here's hoping.

Here's hoping....

About The Author

• • •

CHUCK UNDERWOOD IS ONE OF the pioneers who developed and popularized the field of generational study. His original principles are a permanent part of this discipline.

As the founder/principal of consulting firm The Generational Imperative, Inc., he consults and trains American business, government, education, religion, and other institutions on Generational Marketplace Strategies, Generational Workforce Strategies, and other niche applications of generational study.

He has also pioneered breakthrough training programs in Generational Behavioral Healthcare Strategy and Generational Leadership Strategy.

In addition to authoring this book and its 2007 first edition, he is the host of the public-television series *America's Generations With Chuck Underwood*, the first presentation of America's living generations in the history of national television.

He is formally trained in qualitative research methodology and conducts primary generational research for his clients and his own firm.

He spent his earlier career years in the mass media of radio and television, first as an award-winning broadcast journalist and national sports play-by-play announcer, and then as a creator and producer of original programming. He has hosted and produced shows that have aired nationally and internationally.

Written Evaluations Of Chuck's Seminars And Keynotes

• • •

⸎ **Quite possibly the greatest presentation I have ever experienced.**
Orlando—V.A. Hospitals Leadership Development Institute

⸎ **I was in the audience at Chuck's presentation at the national convention last weekend. I must say, I was blown away, as was everyone else who heard him.**
Washington, D. C.—National Association of Corporate Directors annual conference

⸎ **Truly a World-Class presenter.**
Spokane—Washington State Association of Community Colleges

⸎ **Outstanding; the best I've heard—ever.**
Washington, D. C.—U. S. Army/Better Opportunities for Single Soldiers

- **Best session I've ever attended at ANY conference—awesome! Captivating!**
  Chicago—Council for the Advancement and Support of Higher Education

- **The best seminar I have ever attended.**
  Cincinnati—Cincinnati Enquirer

- **Mr. Underwood was, in one word, perfect.**
  Cleveland—Veterans Healthcare Administration

- **Chuck is the "best" I've heard on this topic.**
  San Diego—National Association of Consumer Shows

- **Out of all the speakers I've heard, Chuck has been the best.**
  Davenport—Quad City Times

- **I've seen several workshops like this. Chuck's is the best.**
  Seattle—Mental Health Corporations of America

- **Best speaker at any conference that I have seen to date.**
  Indianapolis—Edison Electric Institute

❋ **The most exciting, interesting, thought-provoking, and enjoyable presentation that I have experienced.**
Louisville—United States Army/Morale, Welfare, and Recreation

❋ **Best seminar ever attended.**
Louisville—Kentucky Society of CPAs

❋ **The comments from your presentations have been spectacular. One of my Commissioners called it the best presentation ever at a Governor's Conference; they've had huge speakers in the past, so that's an extraordinary compliment. So thank you for being here and wowing this audience.**
Las Vegas—Nevada Department of Tourism and Cultural Affairs

❋ **Excellent presentation—he showed me a level of marketing and the need to know who we are and to reach out to our younger market. Excellent.**
Las Vegas—Credit Union National Association

❋ **Brilliant; my first-time exposure to this material.**
Loma Linda, CA—V.A. Hospital

❧ **Better than excellent.**
Denver—Longmont Community Foundation

❧ **I've heard half a dozen speakers on similar topics, and Chuck is by far the best. The best, because his remarks were accompanied by research results and relevant historic examples that resonated with me and, I believe, the rest of the CMC audience.**
Columbus—Columbus Metropolitan Club

❧ **This is the best, most fascinating presentation I have heard in years!**
Dallas—Texas Society of CPAs

❧ **Best session I've ever attended.**
Columbus—Ohio Association of Broadcasters

❧ **Your presentation was outstanding! Everyone was talking about your seminar all day! The only disappointment they expressed was the biggest compliment of all, which was we wanted more, we wanted the full 4 hours! It doesn't get any better than that! Thank you again. Your message will be invaluable to our organization!!**
New York—Macy's, Inc.

❋ **Since I'm a GenX'er, you know I have a low tolerance for hype and filler; your presentations had none. You delivered excellent information in a fabulous presentation. Thank you!** Chicago—Institute of Internal Auditors

The Final Thought

"Our nation will become unstoppable"

• • •

1. None of us had any control over the year we were born.

2. Therefore, none of us had any control over the specific years that would become our Formative years and mold us for life.

3. So, none of us had any control over the generation to which we belong.

IF WE WILL MAKE PEACE with these three truths, we can then make peace with the differences among our generations. And we will then begin to help each other find our own unique fulfillment in life, *given the unique hand we were dealt in that nanosecond when we were born.*

When this happens, when we finally bridge the generation gaps, we will all begin to pull in the same direction.

And when that moment arrives...

our nation will become unstoppable.

And the field of generational study is now in place to get us there.

How To Purchase

Additional Copies Of This Book And The Dvds Of Chuck's Public-Television Mini-Series,
America's Generations With Chuck Underwood

• • •

EACH DVD, EACH SHOW, IS about 57 minutes in length and presents the life-story of one generation:

1. *Millennials:* *The New World*
2. *Gen X:* *59 Million Armies Of One*
3. *Boomers:* *Forever Young*
4. *Silents:* *America's Last Innocent Generation*

And it appears a fifth hourlong show will be available beginning sometime in 2016. That show will be Chuck's presentation of the final chapter of this book on The Generational Leadership Of America.

Online, you may purchase the DVDs through this website:

www.genimperative.com/17.html

To contact Chuck directly with any questions or comments:

Email: cu@genimperative.com

The DVDs, along with this book, are used by business, government, education, religion, class reunions, Saturday night parties, and family and friend gatherings.